BRITISH POLICY TOWARDS
THE AMERINDIANS

BRITISH POLICY TOWARDS THE AMERINDIANS IN BRITISH GUIANA
1803–1873

BY

MARY NOEL MENEZES, R.S.M.

OXFORD
AT THE CLARENDON PRESS
1977

Oxford University Press, Walton Street, Oxford OX2 6DP

OXFORD LONDON GLASGOW NEW YORK
TORONTO MELBOURNE WELLINGTON CAPE TOWN
IBADAN NAIROBI DAR ES SALAAM LUSAKA ADDIS ABABA
KUALA LUMPUR SINGAPORE JAKARTA HONG KONG TOKYO
DELHI BOMBAY CALCUTTA MADRAS KARACHI

British Library Cataloguing in Publication Data

Menezes, Mary Noel
    British policy towards the Amerindians in
    British Guiana, 1803–1873
    Bibl. – Index
    ISBN 0–19–821567–3
    1. Title
    323.1'19'70881   F2379
    Indians of South America – Guyana
    Local government – Guyana

*Printed in Great Britain
at the University Press, Oxford
by Vivian Ridler
Printer to the University*

To

Celine Marie

in loving gratitude

PREFACE

In 1969 at the end of a third summer's research on the Guyana-Venezuela Boundary Dispute, I had noted in the margin of my summary: 'At a future date research in detail on the relationship of the British with the Indians.' Out of this marginal comment grew the topic of this work on *British Policy towards the Amerindians in British Guiana, 1803–1873*. At the Hague Tribunal in 1899, although the British presented very convincing evidence of their jurisdiction over and protection of the Indians, no in-depth study was ever made of the history of their policy. Vincent Roth in his article, 'Amerindians and the State', briefly mentioned the early Dutch and British policy of gift-giving and hinted at the importance of missionary enterprise, but mainly discussed early twentieth-century policy. Colin Henfrey, in two concluding pages of his book, *The Gentle People* (1964), summed up the policy in general.

Early travellers and later anthropologists have written profusely on the customs, beliefs, and attitudes of the Indians, while historians writing on Guyana (very few indeed) have always been more interested in its history of sugar, slavery, and post-emancipation immigration. But just as the local government faced problems with their indentured labourers from Madeira, India, and China, they encountered difficulties in ruling over the aboriginal natives who considered themselves free people. The mass of reports and journals of the postholders, Protectors of Indians, Superintendents of Rivers and Creeks, missionaries, and travellers found in the National Archives, Guyana, the Public Record Office and the various archives of missionary societies in London, laid the foundation of this book as it showed policy in action. The letters of the Governors of British Guiana and those of the Secretaries of State, the discussions of the Combined Court, and the perplexities of the Courts of Justice regarding the customary 'law' of the Amerindians illustrated the ambiguities of a policy of expediency which characterized the relationship between the government and the Indians. My living in Guyana and, therefore, having the opportunity to spend some time among the Amerindians helped to give some perspective to the work.

The boundary problem was discussed only in so far as it related to Indian protection, as it would have been impossible to include an investigation of the vast diplomatic correspondence engaged in by Venezuela, Great Britain, and the United States. Even though much has been said of the missionary enterprise among the Indians, a great deal has been left untold, especially concerning the role of women missionaries. The terminal point selected was 1873. With Ordinance No. 9 of 1873 the office of Superintendent of Rivers and Creeks established in 1838 ceased. By that Ordinance this official, once particularly responsible for the welfare and protection of the Indians, became a Protector of Crown Lands. A brief epilogue attempts to highlight Amerindian policy between 1873 and 1973.

I am greatly indebted to the Research and Publications Committee of the University of Guyana for its generosity in making this publication possible. My deep gratitude goes to Sr. Celine Marie Kirsch, R.S.M. who spent long hours in the time-consuming task of preparing the manuscript for the printers, and to Miss Mary Grant for her invaluable criticism and enthusiastic support. Without the warm encouragement and guidance of Professors R. A. Humphreys and John Lynch, former and present Directors respectively of the Institute of Latin American Studies, University of London, this work would never have been published. Sincere thanks to the Revd. Mathias Kiemen, O.F.M., of the Academy of American Franciscan History, Washington, D.C., and to the Revd. Patrick Connors, S.J., of Kurukabaru Patamona Indian mission, Guyana, for reading and criticizing the text; to Mrs. Iris Beharry for helping to type the manuscript, and to Sr. Rosaliene Fung, R.S.M., for preparing the maps. To that multitude of helpful librarians at the University of Guyana Library, the National Archives, Guyana, the Public Record Office, and the archives of the United Society for the Propagation of the Gospel, the London Missionary Society, the Church Missionary Society, the Jesuits in Guyana and in Farm Street, London, and the Rhodes Library, Oxford, I am most grateful.

Unpublished Crown copyright material in the Public Record Office, London, has been used with the kind permission of the Controller, Her Majesty's Stationery Office. The author also wishes to thank the University of Puerto Rico Press for permission to reprint the article on 'Indian Subsidy: A System of Annual and Triennial Presents', previously published in *Caribbean Studies*, XIII, October 1973.

CONTENTS

LIST OF MAPS   xi

ABBREVIATIONS   xiii

Introduction   1

I. The Principal Tribes of Guiana—their Customs and
   Culture—their Relations with the Dutch in the Eighteenth
   Century   18

II. The Dutch and British Policy of Indian Subsidy: A System
    of Annual and Triennial Presents   44

III. The Role and Duties of the Postholders and Protectors of
     the Indians—the Advantages and Disadvantages of the
     System   73

IV. The Superintendents of Rivers and Creeks: Police of the
    Interior or Protectors of Indians?   105

V. British Legal Jurisdiction over the Indians: Conflict between
   Native Customs and British Law   128

VI. The Boundaries, the British, and the Indians   154

VII. Indian Slavery—Industrial Employment of Indians—
     Indians and the Land   179

VIII. The Role of the Missionaries in the Protection, Civilization,
      and Christianization of the Indians   208

IX. The Balance Sheet of British Policy   254

APPENDICES   269

BIBLIOGRAPHY   298

INDEX   315

LIST OF MAPS

Map showing the Location of the Indian Tribes   265

Map of the Mission of Santa Rosa   266

Map showing the Principal Mission Stations 1817–1873   267

ABBREVIATIONS

B.G.B.	*British Guiana Boundary*
B.M.	British Museum
C.M.S.A.	Church Missionary Society Archives
C.O.	Colonial Office Records
F.O.	Foreign Office Records
J.D.A.G.	Jesuit Diocesan Archives, Guyana
J.A.L.	Jesuit Archives, London
L.A.D.O.C.	Latin American Documentation Service
L.C.G.	Law Courts, Guyana
L.B.	Letter Books (in National Archives, Guyana)
L.M.S.A.	London Missionary Society Archives
M.C.C.	Minutes of the Combined Court
M.C.G.B.	Minutes of the Council of Government, Berbice
M.C.P.	Minutes of the Court of Policy
N.A.G.	National Archives, Guyana
P.R.O.	Public Record Office
U.S.P.G.A.	United Society for the Propagation of the Gospel Archives

INTRODUCTION

TRAVELLERS, from Raleigh to those of present day, extol the beauties of the Guyana territory. P. M. Netscher, an early historian, called the Wild Coast, as the whole Guyana territory was named, a 'lovely stretch of country . . . This rich and extensive tract . . .'[1] The documentation on the beauty, richness, and vastness of the territory is overwhelming indeed. Was it the intoxicating beauty that made this land a magnet to early travellers, and later to nations? Or was it merely an interest in the strange original inhabitants, the Amerindians—the tribes of Caribs, Warraus, Arawaks, and Akawois whom they first encountered? Neither was the lure. At the dawn of the sixteenth century the discovery of new lands meant gold and glory, and for the Spaniards, God as well.

About 1500 Pinzón, a Spaniard, discovered the mouth of the Amazon and travelled along the north coast of South America to the Orinoco. Somewhere along the route he heard the story of a large salt-water lake which was supposed to be located in the interior near a town, Manoa del Dorado, filled with treasures of gold and silver. There lived a monarch, *el hombre dorado*, covered in the precious golden metal. To the Spaniards gold was always a certain lure, and a series of expeditions was launched. Thousands of soldiers and natives perished in this early quest for El Dorado. Fantastic though the tale sounded, the English did not want to be outdone by the Spaniards. In 1595 Sir Walter Raleigh, a favourite courtier of Elizabeth I, set out to find the golden city to win glory for himself and gold for his Queen. For twenty-three years the vision of El Dorado obsessed Raleigh. The price he paid to make the vision a reality was a heavy one: imprisonment, the death of his son, the suicide of his best officer, Captain Keymis, and finally his own execution.

It was not in vain. He left a legacy to the world in the marvellous description of the richness and beauty of a country that would be

---

[1] P. M. Netscher, *History of the Colonies Essequebo, Demerary & Berbice. From the Dutch Establishment to the Present Day*, trans. W. E. Roth ('S Gravenhage, Martinus Nijhoff, 1888), p. 3.

a prize *par excellence*. This richness and beauty, and, above all, the possibility of untold wealth, whetted the appetites of the Spanish and the Dutch in particular. A Guyanese historian, James Rodway, pointed out with much truth that 'The real Guiana was, however, quite as interesting as the ideal'.[1] The story of the real Guiana dates back to the Dutch. By the late sixteenth century the Dutch had cruised along the whole of the Guiana coast, but because the coastland was thickly overgrown with bush, the Courida trees, they journeyed up the rivers which emptied into the Atlantic Ocean. There they found the Amerindians with whom they began to trade in *anotto* (also rendered *annatto* and *arnatto*)—the *roucou* or *oriane* dye then much in demand in Europe, oil of *maaran*, indigo, rasins, balsams, and letterwood.[2] Hatred for the Spaniards made a common bond between the Indians and the Dutch.

There are conflicting accounts of the place and time of the first Dutch settlements. In J. J. Hartsinck's early description of the region, mention is made of the first attempt at a permanent settlement in the Amazon, as well as one on the Essequibo.[3] Netscher claims that, by the time the Dutch West India Company was founded in 1621, the Dutch had already established settlement on the River Essequibo, strengthened by Fort Kyk-over-al.[4]

The founding of the Dutch West India Co. really marked the serious beginnings of trade in the region. This goal was explicitly stated in the charter. The Company was also empowered to make contracts and alliances with natives, erect forts and strongholds, and establish a military government. To maintain its exclusive control it was instructed to ward off, or, where necessary, to attack the Spanish and the Portuguese, and capture booty.[5] Meanwhile trade

[1] James Rodway, 'Guiana: The Wild and Wonderful', *Timehri*, Third Series, II (1912), 235.

[2] *British Guiana Boundary Arbitration with the United States of Venezuela. Appendix to the Case on Behalf of the Government of Her Britannic Majesty* (London, 1898), i. 242–54. Hereafter cited as *B.G.B.* In the eighteenth century the trade was extended to hammocks and horses.

[3] Jan Jacob Hartsinck, *Beschrijving van Guiana* (Amsterdam, 1770), I, 207, 210–11, trans. Walter E. Roth. MS. in University of Guyana Library, Guyana.

[4] Essequibo, also spelt Essequebo, the largest river in Guyana, rising in the Acarai Mountains in the south near the Brazilian border. It was called Isekepe and Desekebo by the early Dutch. See Netscher, pp. 5, 16, 18, 24. The editor gives an interesting footnote in Henry Kirke, *Twenty-Five Years in British Guiana* (London, 1898; reprinted in the *Guiana Edition*, No. 12, Georgetown, 1948), p. 9, on the Indian meaning of the word Dissikeeb as cooking stones. Because the Essequibo was such a large river, the Indians had to carry flat stones in their canoes to cook on during the long trips.

[5] Hartsinck, I, 212–13.

with the Indians, and the strengthening of relations with them, continued in the Essequibo. In 1627 Abraham van Pere, a merchant and Director of the West India Co., was given permission to settle sixty colonists, including women and children, in Berbice. Not long afterwards the settlement of Fort Nassau was built on the Berbice river, and trade in tobacco, letterwood, and anotto dye sustained the early life of the colonists there. Netscher was probably echoing the sentiments of the early settlers when he wrote: 'Only one thing is wanting to make this country an El Dorado, a still more profitable possession than the finest East Indian colonies and that one thing is *men, population, labour*.'[1] Two centuries later every traveller and every Governor was to repeat the same cry. Early Dutch policy for the region was outlined in the Orders and Regulations of the States General of 1633 and 1637, namely that ships were to sail from Brazil to Florida 'to offer hostility to the King of Spain, his subjects and adherents', and to carry on trade.[2] But by 1647 the West India Co. fell on hard days; her possessions in Brazil were lost, and funds dwindled. The Company was ready to dispose of the non-profitable Essequibo settlements, but the towns of Middlebury, Vlissengen, and Veere accepted the responsibility for their administration and maintenance. According to the early documents the settlements were later called Nova Zeelandia, comprising Kyk-over-al, Pomeroon, and Moruka. The Directors decided to make the settlements profitable. Trade with the Indians was not enough—the planting of sugar cane should be initiated—a momentous decision setting a saccharine stamp on the future history of the country. Already the Berbice colonists had been provided with Negroes for field work. The Dutch had discovered that, friendly though the Indians were, they refused to be enslaved, and showed a decided unwillingness to be used as field-workers. To cultivate the sugar cane, therefore, hundreds of slaves from Africa were brought into the territory.

The beginning of the sugar industry was slow. Then the Second Dutch War broke out in 1665 and both Berbice and Essequibo were attacked by the English. Berbice was able to repulse the attack, but Essequibo succumbed to Major John Scott and became briefly English in 1666. It was subsequently regained by the Commander of Berbice. By the end of the century trade picked up, and it was reported that 60,000 lb. of sugar and 20,000 lb. of letterwood had been

---

[1] Netscher, p. 5.   [2] *B.G.B.*, Appendix I, 73–4 and 75–7. Nos. 33 and 38.

shipped to Europe. By 1675, when the New West India Co. was established, the banks of the Mazaruni, Cuyuni, and Essequibo were dotted with sugar estates; the Berbice with coffee and cotton. The plantation system had been founded, but the economy was not strictly monocultural. Trade in anotto, letterwood, and other timber still continued. To promote this trade posts manned by postholders were established in the interior. Later these posts would be the rallying points for the Indians from which bush expeditions would be launched to capture the runaway slaves from neighbouring plantations. The posts then served both as trade depots and security stations.

The eighteenth century witnessed an increase in the cultivation of coffee and cotton. Reports noted the shipment of bags of coffee and bales of cotton, as well as hogsheads of sugar to Holland. A famous Dutch official who dominated the history of this period was Laurens Storm van's Gravesande, Commander of Essequibo and founder of the colony of Demerara.[1] It was at his invitation that English planters from Barbados settled on the islands of the Essequibo and later up the Demerara river. Although a loyal Dutchman, Gravesande realized that if the colony were to flourish it needed an injection of new life and funds. By 1750 Gravesande was promoted to Director-General of Essequibo and the dependent rivers. He continued to stress friendly relations with the Indians, to carry on relentless war against the bush Negroes, to curb Spanish territorial appetites, and, above all, to concentrate on the growth of Demerara. 'I doubt not', wrote Gravesande rather prophetically, 'but that this River Demerary will in a few years be as populous, if not more so than Essequebo.'[2]

While the century was taken up with French attacks, Spanish aggression, and bush expeditions and while the sugar, coffee, and cotton plantations expanded and flourished, a formal government was established. The system of government laid down by the Dutch would remain in essence the foundation of the government of Guiana

[1] The colony of Demerara was an outgrowth of the plantations along the river of that name. Demerara was supposed to have evolved from the Spanish *De Mirara*, 'as if it meant the wonderful', claimed Rodway in 'Guiana: The Wild and Wonderful', *Timehri* (1912), 235. The Amerindians called the river Cannerary or Tamerary. See Kirke, p. 9. Other explanations are that it was derived from Immenary, the Indian name for letterwood, or Demarina, the Arawak word for water-mama. *Timehri* (1911), 56. Both the river and the colony were called Demerary until 1831 when the three colonies were united and Demerara was officially used for the first time.

[2] Gravesande as quoted in Netscher, p. 55.

4

until 1928 when it became a Crown colony. In the early days of trade and settlement the captains of the trading vessels wielded authority on shore; later the Commanders who were permanent officials. By the middle of the eighteenth century a Council of Policy and a Council of Justice were set up to help Gravesande to administer the affairs of Essequibo and Demerara. Because of the constant attacks from the French, the Spanish, and the English, as well as from the bush Negroes, burgher officers were appointed, who were expected to perform military and judicial duties. Out of this body grew the famous (later infamous) College of Kiezers, not finally abolished until 1891. First elected by the burghers, these officers were later nominated by the Commander. In 1743 Gravesande established six burgher officers into the College of Kiezers (electors) for the purpose of nominating representatives of free planters on the Council, later Court of Policy.

By the 1789 Plan of Redress, the Court of Policy, the legislative body of Demerara and Essequibo, consisted of the Director-General, two colonists from Demerara, and two from Essequibo (*ex officio*). The elected members of the Court were chosen by the College of Kiezers whose seven members were elected for life by colonists having twenty-five or more slaves. The problem that always faced these government officials was one of financial control. In 1795 the governor, having left the colony, unable to reconcile his conflicting loyalties between the Prince of Orange and the Batavian Republic, the Court of Policy and the College of Kiezers met to discuss finances, and combined themselves into a Colonial Finance Department. The following year Governor Beaujon dissolved that Department and brought together three financial Representatives from each river to hold combined meetings with the Governor and the Court of Policy. They levied taxes required by the estimate prepared by the Court of Policy, but had no power to vote on items.[1] This Combined Court, as it came to be called, gained much power; through it the representatives of the planters exercised control over the finances of the colony until 1928.

By the end of the eighteenth century European affairs affected those of the colonies. The American War of Independence had involved Europe, and hence the European possessions in the Caribbean. Consequently in 1781 the colonies of Demerara, Essequibo, and Berbice fell to the British. From then on the vicissitudes of war

[1] C.O. 114/12. Minutes of the Court of Policy, 31 Mar. 1832.

caused the colonies to change hands from the English to the French, back to the Dutch, and finally to the British in 1803. Despite the insecurity between 1796 and 1803, official accounts note that the number of slaves had doubled from 30,000 to 65,000.[1] According to the map of Bouchenroder (1798–1802), in Essequibo and Demerara there were 400 estates under cultivation; in Berbice 300. As early as 1798, in the first blush of British administration, the Secretary of State had requested from the Governor of the colonies a memorandum on the state of the colony's economic affairs and civil and military establishments. Again in 1813 innumerable inquiries as to the resources of the territory were forwarded to the governor. Returns of the questionnaires showed that planters, woodcutters, and postholders all agreed that the resources of the colonies far exceeded those of the islands.[2] Governors constantly spoke of the area as His Majesty's valuable colony, obviously convincing the Colonial Office of British Guiana's value to the Crown. Lord Aberdeen, Secretary of State for War and the Colonies, assured Sir J. Carmichael Smyth that British Guiana was 'a settlement which in wealth, population, and value holds second place in the West Indian possessions of the British Crown'.[3] Robert Schomburgk (later Sir Robert), a Prussian explorer who travelled the length and breadth of British Guiana during expeditions of discovery, between 1835 and 1839 and again from 1840 to 1844, was lavish in his praise: 'No part of the dominions under the British Crown surpasses Guiana in the commdiousness [sic] of its situation for commerce, and in maritime strength, in diversity of soil and luxuriant vegetation, as conducing to national prosperity, and in the connecting the interior with the coast regions, to make these treasures available to the fullest extent.'[4] Schomburgk was extremely impressed with 'The beautiful timber which abounds in the vast forests'—the mora, green-heart, purple-heart, wallaba, and many others—all excellent for shipbuilding as well as cabinet-making.[5] The Dutch were aware

[1] 'General Population in Demerara and Essequibo on 31 October 1829', *The Royal Gazette*, 13 Feb. 1830. Out of a total population of 78,734 the slaves numbered 69,368.

[2] C.O. 111/3. Draft to the Governors of Demerara and Essequibo and the Governor of Berbice by His Grace, the Duke of Portland, Whitehall, 9 July 1798 and C.O. 111/16. Woodcutters to Colonel E. Codd, 4 Oct. 1813.

[3] C.O. 112/18. Lord Aberdeen to Sir J. C. Smyth, 2 Mar. 1835.

[4] Robert H. Schomburgk, *A Description of British Guiana* (London, 1840; reprinted 1970), p. 88.

[5] Ibid., pp. 94–6. Schomburgk claimed that seven-tenths of approximately 2,000 employed in woodcutting were Indians.

of the value of the timber resources. In 1803 when it was obvious that the forests of the Pomeroon, Waini, and Barima were being denuded through indiscriminate felling of timber by planters and other inhabitants, it was proposed that dues be paid for the privilege of cutting timber, and that exportation of timber be prohibited under penalty of confiscation and fines.[1]

It was, no doubt, because of this vast legacy of plantations and other valuable resources of the colonies that such generous terms were agreed to by the British in the Articles of Capitulation of 1803. Nevertheless the legacy inherited from the Dutch brought not only an area of land, but a bone of contention. This bone of contention was embodied in the Articles of Capitulation signed between the two nations on 18 September 1803 which stated:

> The Laws and Usages of the Colony shall remain in force and be respected, the mode of taxation now in use be adhered to, and the inhabitants shall enjoy the public exercise of their Religion in the same manner as before Capitulation; no new establishments shall be introduced without the consent of the Court of Policy, as the Legislature of the Colony. The constituted Authorities and Public Officers, whether in the Civil law or Church Establishments, as well as Members of the respective Courts (except the Governor-General), shall be continued in their respective Offices and Situations until His Majesty's pleasure shall be known.[2]

Virtually nothing was changed in the colonies of Demerara, Essequibo, and Berbice except the flag. Even the Dutch governors continued in office: Beaujon in Demerara and Essequibo, von Batenburg in Berbice. No articles were so religiously adhered to as those of 1803. Members of the Courts then, and their successors thereafter, on the grounds of these Articles would continue to fight for what they considered their unassailable privileges. Woe betide the English governors who ignored Article I of the Capitulation!

Realpolitik in British Guiana had an added dimension, as every governor realized only too well. The Chief Executive had to maintain a rapport with the local nabobs and, at the same time, appease the Colonial Office. The local government consisted of the Court of

[1] *B.G.B.* App. IV, 182. No. 681. Extract from a Proposed Charter for the Colonies of Essequibo and Demerara, submitted to the Council of American Colonies and Possessions of the Batavian Republic by G. A. W. Ruysch, 22 June 1803.

[2] C.O. 112/4 Laws of Capitulation signed between England and the Batavian Republic, 10 Sept. 1803. Article I.

Policy and the Combined Court, the latter—a union of the Court of Policy with the Financial Representatives which in 1796 Governor Beaujon had called into being. These Financial Representatives, drawn from the College of Kiezers, were mostly planters. It was not difficult, therefore, to understand where the power in the colonies lay, regardless of the fact that Parliamentary historians claimed 'The right of the Crown, as the supreme executive authority of the empire to control all legislation', to be 'self-evident and unquestionable'.[1]

It was true that the British Crown did possess power to legislate for the Colonies, a right derived from the West India Co., the Berbice Association, and the States-General and passed on to the British Crown, as Lord Goderich at the Colonial Office, forcefully informed Governor Benjamin D'Urban in 1831.[2] To the planters who packed the Courts this was a nicety of constitutional law which they chose to disregard. Major-General Hugh Lyle Carmichael had abolished the sacrosanct College of Kiezers in 1812 on the alleged grounds that the members were not British enough in their political thinking.[3] Carmichael was probably able to get away with this move (not at all applauded by the home government and later rescinded) because at that time the rivers and the coast were being blockaded by American privateers. In the following years there was too much apprehension about the restlessness and rebelliousness of the slaves, culminating in the 1823 slave revolt on the east coast, Demerara, for there to have been any open conflict between the governors and the local government. But Governor D'Urban was hardly in the colony one year when he had his first confrontation with the Court of Policy as he tried to introduce a bill proposing compulsory manumission of slaves. The planters read this as a breach of the Articles of Capitulation which had guaranteed their property. A barrage of criticism descended on the heads of the governor and the home government, but with the abolition of slavery already in the minds of the British government, the Privy Council won the case for manumission which had been strongly argued against by the planters.

The subsequent Apprenticeship period from 1833 and Governor James Carmichael Smyth's proclamations regarding the apprentices

[1] Alpheus Todd, *Parliamentary Government in the British Colonies* (London, 1894), p. 155.

[2] C.O. 112/15. Lord Goderich to Sir Benjamin D'Urban, 1 Oct. 1831.

[3] Minutes of the Combined Court, 18 Nov. 1812. N.A.G. To Carmichael, the British law and government were second only to God's!

so angered the planters that they signed a petition asking for Smyth's removal. The anger directed against Smyth was not so much because he seemed to ally himself with the apprentices, which was bad enough, but because by his proclamations he had abrogated the powers which the Court of Policy claimed rested with itself. And to the Court of Policy this was even worse. It was in this climate of strained relations that the Secretary of State suggested a compromise on taxation policy. With the abolition of slavery there was no longer a capitation tax, hence the idea was to combine the King's Chest with the Colony's Chest[1] for the use of the legislature which would, in turn, agree to vote a Civil List for seven years to ensure the smooth running of the government. Like the Articles of Capitulation, this Civil List was to become another bone of contention. For the rest of the century each successive governor found himself in the vortex of the Combined Court's refusal to grant the Civil List, if in turn, a quota for immigrants and/or a loan for immigration were not granted. James Rodway summed up the situation when he wrote: 'The Civil List has caused more trouble in the past years than any other part of the Constitution, the Colonial Councillors and Financial Representatives being under the impression that they could do what they liked with it.'[2]

In 1835 the Colonial Office commissioned Sir Lionel Smith, Governor of Trinidad, to take over the governorship of British Guiana for a period in order to calm political passions and restore economic equilibrium. Five years later Sir Henry McLeod, Governor of Trinidad, was sent as arbitrator to British Guiana to deal with another political crisis. Governor Henry Light, appointed in 1838, had begun his term of office in troubled times. Having lost their slaves, and been given, in their opinion, a mere pittance in compensation, the planters were in an ugly mood. Although cotton cultivation had decreased, the United States and the East Indies supplanting British Guiana in the market, sugar had increased and become the main product and resource of the planters. The need

[1] During the Dutch period, the Colony's Chest was composed of taxation funds imposed by the colonists on themselves for special expenditure, 'ongeld', and kept distinct from the Company's Chest. The Company's Chest—the funds of the West India Company and later of the States-General—under the British became the King's Chest. It was funded from a head tax on slaves, as well as from customs duties on exports and imports, convoy costs, and stamps. See Sir Cecil Clementi, *A Constitutional History of British Guiana* (London, 1937), pp. 38, 49, 106–7.

[2] James Rodway, 'The Constitution of British Guiana', *Timehri*, New Series, V (1891), 217.

for labour was acute, and the big issue of the day was immigration. Portuguese immigrants from the Azores and Madeira had arrived in 1834 and East Indians from Calcutta in 1838 to fill the places of the ex-slaves on the estates. To the planters every other issue became subservient to the vital need for immigrants and profits.

By 1839 crops had failed, owing to both drought and insufficient labour. In this atmosphere Governor Light introduced a bill for the renewal of the Civil List for £40,080, almost double that of the previous one. At the opening session, the Combined Court told the governor quite emphatically what its views were regarding such an increase:

> Her [B.G.'s] future wealth depends solely upon the Home Government permitting and encouraging an extensive influx of immigrants . . . any extension of the Judicial Establishment, increase in provisions for the clergy and for the educational purposes . . . that is any augmentation of the Civil List is inexpedient without immigration simultaneously insured to the Colony as affording the only means by which increased expenditure could be met and sustained.[1]

Furthermore the Combined Court laid down conditions for its voting of the Civil List, namely that Her Majesty's Government should remove all restraints on the immigration of free labourers into the colony, as well as give the Court unrestricted power to raise funds. Governor Light refused to be intimidated and abruptly adjourned the Court *sine die*. Supplies were stopped, effecting a deadlock in government. The Colonial Office sent McLeod to Guiana to bring about a compromise without, however, adopting radical measures. Acting on this advice, McLeod allowed a reduction of £1,000 on the Governor's salary, and the Civil List was passed. Simultaneously with the Civil List Ordinance McLeod introduced an Emigration Bill by which the Combined Court could apply a large surplus revenue to immigration. Why was such a compromise made? The Crown Law Officers to whom the Colonial Office had appealed for guidance in this case, pointed out that, because Article I of the 1803 Capitulation had clearly ratified the power of taxation of the local government, it could not be cavalierly transferred to the Crown, regardless of the intransigent behaviour of the Combined Court.[2] The Crown had either to compromise or

---

[1] Minutes of the Combined Court, 24 Apr. 1840. N.A.G.

[2] A. R. F. Webber, *Centenary History and Handbook of British Guiana* (British Guiana, 1931), p. 203.

impose a new constitution on Guiana. The latter the British government was certainly not prepared to do.

Although every Governor objected to such extraordinary powers held by the Combined Court, and successive Secretaries of State would re-echo Lord Stanley's view that 'the possession of so much power as has been temporarily transferred to the Combined Court tends to the usurpation by that body of every other power' and was 'pregnant with abuse',[1] any constitutional change had to be desired by the colonists and recommended by the Governor with the concurrence of the Court of Policy and the Combined Court. It was, indeed, an awkward situation, a weakness of the constitution in which the financial reins of the government were held by the plantocracy.

In 1846 an Act of Parliament introduced slave labour sugar on the market. The Honourable Peter Rose, a leading statesman in mid-nineteenth-century Guiana and a thorn in the flesh of governors, speaking for the Combined Court, insultingly denounced the Home Government as the cause of the colony's distress and ruin, and called for a 25 per cent reduction of the Civil List. With a 25 per cent reduction in wages, the labourers went on strike.[2] As the storm clouds again appeared on the political horizon, Governor Light left British Guiana. Under the interim governorship of Lt. Governor William Walker, another deadlock ensued, and Walker's successor, Henry Barkly, an ex-planter and M.P., inherited a thorny legacy. Barkly had not served his first month as governor when the clash occurred and he, like his predecessors, adjourned the Court. The Crown could hardly send another governor to supersede Barkly, but a Committee was appointed to investigate and report on the state of the colony. Despite the early controversy with the Combined Court, Barkly was, unlike Light, pro-planter, and stressed immigration as 'an urgent necessity'. Out of the 1849 Committee came a Parliamentary loan of £250,000 for immigration. The sugar barons had again won the day. Constitutional reform was certainly vitally necessary to break the monopolistic control of the Combined Court.

[1] C.O. 112/24. Lord Stanley to Governor Henry Light, 12 Oct. 1842. Governor Light constantly deplored this power of the Combined Court. When in 1842 the Court annulled a law passed by the legislature and approved by the Sovereign, he wrote: 'The extraordinary powers allowed the Combined Court subject the Executive either to the risk of a stoppage of supplies or to yield to their wishes.' Light to Stanley, 29 Dec. 1843. N.A.G.
[2] Great Britain. *Parliamentary Papers*. 'Report from the Select Committee on Ceylon and British Guiana'. *Colonies General* (Irish University Press Series, 1968), I, 163 ff.

Henry Taylor, that most astute senior clerk of the Colonial Office, saw Crown Colony government as the only safe alternative. On the one hand there was a large uneducated population of labourers, on the other a local oligarchy of planters—profit-drunk, selfish, and unconcerned about the rest of the population.[1]

The constitutional anomaly was, therefore, the fly in the ointment of government in Guiana. Immigration was the sole concern of the planters throughout the nineteenth century and into the twentieth. In the 1840s the village movement of the free Negroes was crippled by the labour-hungry planters; in the 1860s the gold industry was barely supported; interior development was myopically neglected. A. R. F. Webber observed: '. . . the Planter was like the mouse with only one hole.'[2] The Colonial Office was stacked with dispatches from Governors of British Guiana belabouring the point of constitutional impasses. Governor John Scott's criticism was pointed:

Owing to the peculiar Constitution of this Colony which in some respects partakes of the character of a Crown Colony, but in others, and especially in regard to financial matters, is more like a colony with representative Institutions the Governor does not possess the same power of regulating the preparation of the annual Estimates as in other Colonies not possessing Representative Assemblies, and a procedure has been long established which is full of anomalies.[3]

Thus with such a government packed by 'men . . . with their pockets full of money and their hard heads-full of sugar, ever dreaming of empty *hogsheads* to be filled, -shipped-consigned-and sold . . .'[4] it was not difficult to understand why the Indians were hardly subjects of interest. The humanitarian sentiments of the Anti-Slavery Society and the Aborigines Protection Society moved the plantocracy, not to tears, but to anger.

These pressure groups had moved Parliament to an awareness of the plight of native peoples. 'The idea of Trusteeship over coloured peoples,' writes Knorr, 'was a powerful phenomenon in the thirties and forties of the nineteenth century.'[5] This idea had been spearheaded by the foundation of missionary societies between 1792 and

[1] C.O. 111/290. Minute of Henry Taylor, 10 Sept. 1852 in Governor Henry Barkly to the Rt. Hon. Sir John Pakington, 8 June 1852.

[2] Webber, p. 197.

[3] Governor John Scott to Earl Kimberley, No. 123, 29 Oct. 1870. N.A.G.

[4] The Revd. Ignatius Scoles, S.J., *Sketches of African and Indian Life in British Guiana* (Demerara, 1885), pp. 76–7.

[5] Klaus E. Knorr, *British Colonial Theories, 1570–1850* (London, 1963), p. 388.

1804; the Methodist, the Baptist, the London Missionary Society, and the British and Foreign Bible Society concerned with spreading civilization and Christianity among the natives. In the various outposts of empire the land-hungry settlers clashed with these evangelists who, in turn, solicited government support. With men like Lord Glenelg, Secretary of State, and James Stephen, Under-Secretary of State for the Colonies, both officials in the Church Missionary Society,[1] there was bound to be some agitation.

In 1836 an influential group, the Aborigines Protection Society, was formed and soon afterwards a Parliamentary Committee was appointed, advocated, and chaired by Thomas Fowell Buxton. Buxton and members of the group were concerned over the continuously diminishing numbers of aboriginals wherever Europeans had set foot—in Australia, New Zealand, Africa, and North America. The terms of reference of this Select Committee on aborigines were to formulate measures to secure Justice, Protection, Civilization, and Christianization for the native peoples in British settlements. These became the four pillars of cultural imperialism—the key slogans of the humanitarians.

The evidence given before the Committee by missionaries abroad was overwhelmingly in support of the native cause. This evidence disclosed, above all, that contact with Europeans was proving fatal to the aboriginal inhabitants who were demoralized and deprived of their lands and sustenance. The contraction of European diseases was, also, devastating and led to a drastic diminution of the population. In North America the Cree Indians had decreased from 10,000 to about 300 in thirty years; the population of the Copper Indians had halved in five years.[2] The Revd. John Williams, who had worked in the South Sea Islands for eighteen years, concluded, '. . . there is a certain something in the first intercourse between the Europeans and the natives, that introduces diseases on the part of the latter'.[3] European contact was, therefore, 'a calamity and not a blessing'.[4] The only hope for these people, asserted missionaries and doctors alike, was to Christianize them. Proof was shown to the Committee that wherever Christianity was introduced, civilization invariably followed. The Revd. John Beecham stressed 'Christianity as the parent of civilization' and was 'persuaded that true civilization

[1] Ibid., p. 385.
[2] Great Britain. Parliamentary Papers. *Aborigines*. I, Report from the Select Committee on Aborigines (British Settlements) with the Minutes of Evidence, 1837, 5370, 5402–03.   [3] Ibid., 5613.   [4] Ibid.

(could not) be produced without it.'[1] The conclusion reached was an obvious one: that Europeans had no *raison d'être* among aboriginals except to christianize them. The *Report* of the Parliamentary Committee stirred up much interest in, and sentiment for, 'the cause of the aborigines', now acclaimed to be 'the cause of three-fourths of the population of the globe'.[2]

Although the climate of opinion in the government and in England in general was, more or less, humanitarian, there were varying degrees of opposition both at home and abroad. In humanitarian circles feeling ran high against the continuation of colonization. While the *Report* of the Aborigines Committee recommended a separatist policy, that is, a keeping apart of the Europeans from the natives, the West Africa Committee suggested a supervised colonization scheme to civilize the natives; S. Bannister, a proponent of cultural imperialism writing in 1838, looked forward to 'ultimate amalgamation', the resultant product of the education of the aborigines in England.[3] The missionaries, supported in their policy by the Colonial Office, became more active against the European settlers who rapaciously deprived the natives of their lands. Settler opposition was, therefore, not long in making itself felt. In 1840, to protect the Maoris against the New Zealand Association, the British government annexed New Zealand for the Crown; two years later the Treaty of Waitangi[4] was signed between the government and the Maoris. The 120,000 Maoris did not placidly accept the take-over of their lands, which, despite the Treaty, still continued. Throughout the 1840s and 1860s there were continual hostilities between the British troops and the warlike tribes. Twice Sir George Grey was sent to New Zealand to bring about peace, but on both occasions his policy 'of amalgamation and pacification' was bitterly opposed by the settlers.[5] Grey saw the amalgamation of the races as vital but at the time, impossible, owing to the bitter-

[1] Great Britain. Parliamentary Papers. *Aborigines*. I, Report from the Select Committee on Aborigines (British Settlements) with the Minutes of Evidence, 1837, 4385.

[2] William Howitt as quoted in Knorr, p. 383.

[3] Knorr, pp. 386–7.

[4] Kenneth N. Bell & W. P. Morrell (eds.), *Select Documents on British Colonial Policy, 1830–1860* (Oxford, 1928), pp. 559–63. The Treaty of Waitangi was signed between the British government and the Maori chiefs in February 1840. In this treaty the natives surrendered sovereignty over their land to the Crown in exchange for the guarantee of their land rights with the proviso that the land should be purchased only by the Crown.

[5] W. P. Morrell, *British Colonial Policy in the Mid-Victorian Age* (Oxford, 1969), p. 474.

ness over land disputes and the consequent hostilities between the natives and the settlers. First of all the confidence of the natives must be won; 'Mercy, justice, and prudence' should be the means to this end while the natives be stimulated with a desire for civilized life.[1] This was easier said than done. After New Zealand had been given representative government in 1852 it was becoming increasingly difficult to reconcile the economic policy of a local legislature which had no use for the natives, with the humanitarian policy of the Governor and the home government constantly trying to uphold native rights. The colonials proved obstreperous, wanting Imperial military help during the periodic Maori wars, yet resisting Imperial policy regarding the natives. The Maori chiefs realized that power was in the hands of the representatives of the settlers in the legislature, and their resistance was fierce and continuous.[2] The Taranaki War in 1860 and the Waikato War in 1863 proclaimed the unyielding desire of the Maoris to protect their lands. With the withdrawal of British troops from New Zealand in 1870, Britain indicated that, although she was willing to 'take up the white man's burden', pragmatic politics weakened that will.

In Africa, and especially in Natal, a large number of settlers had poured in between 1848 and 1851, demanding land. Here, too, the settlers clashed with the natives and the home government. Lt. Governor Benjamin Pine apportioned lands alternately between settlers and Zulus in the hope that such contiguity would bring about amalgamation. His Native Management Commission was, unfortunately, comprised of settlers who regarded the natives as subordinates and ciphers.[3] As in New Zealand, so too in South Africa, the local legislatures tried to control native policy. The problem was always one of territorial disputes. Land to the settlers meant profits and prestige; to the natives livelihood and freedom. To obtain land, settlers subjugated the natives and met with resistance. The Colonial Office begged the Governor in Natal to desist from such subjugation as it would prove unsuccessful and disastrous. It was emphasized that 'Her Majesty's Government were not prepared to hand over 150,000 Natives to 8,000 white Colonists'.[4]

One perpetual headache of colonial governors was the attempt to reconcile native law with British law. Here again British policy was

---

[1] Earl Grey, *The Colonial Policy of Lord John Russell's Administration* (London, 1853: reprint edn. Krauss Reprint Co., New York, 1972), II, 121–7.
[2] Morrell, p. 223.   [3] Ibid., p. 95.   [4] Ibid., p. 123.

very much 'a rule of thumb' affair. In New Zealand Sir George Grey, though propounding a strong pro-native policy, saw the need 'to convince the natives that our laws were better than their own'.[1] For this reason he established a native, armed police-force, in order to train young chiefs in British law. In Natal a Commission for demarcating reserves realized the incongruity of foisting British law on the Bantus, and 'recommended that they should remain subject to their own customs until, by degrees they could, with advantage, be made subject to British law'.[2] Native law under the authority of the Lt. Governor as Supreme Chief was maintained, and in 1849 an ordinance was passed for the administration of justice among natives. Years later the Natal system was adopted by Transvaal where a Department of Native Affairs was also established.[3] In British Guiana, governors periodically acquainted the Colonial Office with the fact that bringing the Indians to justice under British Law was a constant 'embarrassment to the government and to the Judicial Authorities'.[4]

The preoccupation of colonial governments obviously affected policy towards native peoples. In Australia, New Zealand, and Africa greed for land met with hostile native reaction and resulted in the home government recommending specific native policy. In British Guiana the Members of the Combined Court, 'mere nominees of a few wealthy merchants and proprietors or attorneys of estates',[5] were wholly concerned over keeping their estates going with a steady influx of immigrant labour. Here there was no need to grab land from the natives; the estates were all situated along the coastland and on the banks of the main rivers; the Indians kept to themselves in the vast forest hinterland. Not even when the timber industry became fully commercialized was there any hostile clash (although there was some dissatisfaction) between the local government and the Indians. Ordinance No. 6 of 1838 and subsequent ordinances regarding land grants and licences for felling timber preserved the Indians' rights of land ownership which, needless to say, unlicensed woodcutters chose to ignore. Immigration policy,

---

[1] Grey, II, 127.

[2] The Hon. H. A. Wyndham, *The Atlantic and Emancipation*. Problems of Imperial Trusteeship Series (London, 1937), p. 245.

[3] Ibid., p. 264.

[4] Governor Philip Wodehouse to the Rt. Hon. Henry Labouchere, No. 49, 19 Apr. 1856. N.A.G.

[5] Light to Lord John Russell, No. 96, 13 June 1839. N.A.G.

not native policy, caused tension between the local legislature in British Guiana and the home government. Humanitarian sentiments, so loudly proclaimed from the housetops supporting the cause of the disinherited and abused natives in other colonies, were only re-echoed when boundary problems with Brazil and Venezuela highlighted the cause of the Guiana Indians. Indeed 'it is of the nature of . . . British policy that no one can foretell what may emerge from it'.[1] Despite the principles of Justice, Protection, Civilization, and Christianization adhered to by most of British officialdom, they, as well as colonial governors, were prompted by pragmatism according to the pressures brought to bear on them by local legislatures and local circumstances. In British Guiana, because of a unique constitutional situation, the remoteness of the Indians from urban society and their reluctance for urban contact, the paucity of their numbers, and the *laissez-faire* attitude of immigrant-conscious planters, British native policy there was neither as vigorous nor controversial as it was in Africa, Australia, or New Zealand.

[1] Wyndham, pp. 74–5.

I

THE PRINCIPAL TRIBES OF GUIANA— THEIR CUSTOMS AND CULTURE— THEIR RELATIONS WITH THE DUTCH IN THE EIGHTEENTH CENTURY

THROUGHOUT their history the Amerindians of the Guyana territory have meant many things to many men. First called 'Bokken' by the Dutch[1] from which word the name Bucks was derived, with its various shades of meaning of wild, uncouth, untamed, nimble, these 'denizens of the forest' were a proud people, despite the fact that through the years the term 'Bucks' came to be used derogatorily. The Guyanese historian, H. G. Dalton, in *The History of British Guiana Comprising a General Description of the Colony*, acknowledged the Dutch origin of the word and further referred to Dr. Hostman's *Civilisation of the Negro Race in America*, which claimed that the Dutch word 'Bok' had its roots in the word 'Lokka' which signified 'Man'.[2] The Revd. W. H. Brett, a missionary among the Indians for over forty years, testified that the plural of the word 'Lokka' or 'Loko', which the Arawaks called themselves, was 'Lokono' meaning 'the people', and that it was a mark of all American tribes to consider themselves in their pride as *the* people.[3] Also, the word 'Carinya' used by the Caribs to describe themselves had exactly the same meaning. However proudly these Indians saw themselves, they were seen in very different guises by others—from that of the naked

[1] United States Commission on Boundary between Venezuela and British Guiana. Report and Accompanying Papers of the Commission appointed by the President of the United States to Investigate and Report upon the True Divisional Line between the Republic of Venezuela and British Guiana. Vol. II. *Extracts from the Dutch Archives* (Washington, 1897), 603.

[2] H. G. Dalton, *The History of British Guiana Comprising a General Description of the Colony* (London, 1855), I, 62. fn. Hostman's explanation was taken from the lengthy discussion on the eastern origin of the word 'lokka' in H. V. P. Bronkhurst, *The Origin of the Guyanian Indians ascertained; or the Aborigines of America, (especially the Guyanas) and the East Indian Coolie Immigrants compared* (Georgetown, 1881), p. 8.

[3] The Revd. W. H. Brett, *The Indian Tribes of Guiana: Their Condition and Habits* (London, 1868), pp. 97–8.

savage, children of nature, the unfortunate race, the heathen, the untutored race, people in a state of barbarism, these benighted people, the poor, neglected Indians down to *The Gentle People* of Colin Henfrey (1964), and *The Forgotten Tribes of Guyana* of W. M. Ridgwell (1972).[1] Such a variety of images projected through the poorly focused lenses of traders and travellers, the military and the missionary, the Crown and the Combined Court of the Colony, the Governors and their go-betweens—the Protectors and the Post holders—have naturally resulted in the distortion of the true image of the Amerindian.

It is not easy to get a true picture of the Amerindian—this South American Indian—because he is, and has been, from time immemorial, a rover, a wanderer through his forest home. Thus in the eyes of the Europeans, he belongs to a race of 'benighted people' who 'thoughtlessly roam from place to place taking no care for the morrow'.[2] These were the people, however, whose ancestors set foot on the Wild Coast, as the Guiana territory was called,[3] more than 12,000 years before Columbus sighted its shores in 1498, and who filtered throughout the dense forests of Guiana and occupied over 50,000 of the present 83,000 square miles of the territory. The names and numbers of their tribes or nations, as they were called, varied with every traveller's or official's report. William Hilhouse, surveyor, ex-Quartermaster-General of the Indians in the 1820s, honorary Indian chief and champion of their cause, divided the Indians within the British boundary into eight different nations:

1.	Carabice	5.	Macusi
2.	Accaway	6.	Paramuni
3.	Arawaak	7.	Attaraya
4.	Warrow	8.	Attamacka

[1] Colin Henfrey, *The Gentle People* (London, 1964). Henfrey sees the Indian today as a 'refugee from his own culture', exploited now as he had been in the past. W. M. Ridgwell, in *The Forgotten Tribes of Guyana* (London, 1972) almost forgets them himself in this book which, despite the title, dedicates only one chapter to 'The Amerindians', pp. 53–86.

[2] M.C.P., 31 May 1849. Report of the Superintendent of Rivers and Creeks of Pomeroon, W. C. F. McClintock, 31 Mar. 1849. N.A.G.

[3] Bronkurst, pp. 8–9. Although Bronkurst referred to the Dutch description of Guiana as the 'Wild Coast' meaning 'Wild Place', he claimed that the word was of Tamil or Sanskrit derivation: 'Go'—a region or coast, 'Vana'—a wood, forest, or wilderness—hence an uncultivated, open country.

and estimated their numbers at 15,000–20,000 from the northern coast to the River Rupununi in the south.[1]

In 1837 Sir Robert Schomburgk, the famous explorer and leader of the boundary expeditions in British Guiana, agreed with Hilhouse on the number of nations, but not on the names. The spelling of the nations was also slightly different, namely:

1. Caribbees or Caribisce
2. Accaway or Waccaway
3. Attoray or Attoria
4. Macusi
5. Paramuni
6. Mapeshuma or Wapeshama
7. Warrow
8. Arawaaks[2]

This differentiation in the spelling of the names of the Indian nations was marked throughout the nineteenth century, so too were the numbers of nations, indicating that all who came in contact with these people were never quite certain of the names or the numbers of the tribes or nations. For example, the Revd. J. Williams listed thirty varieties of the spelling of the Warrau nation: 'Farautes, Guarau, Guaraons, Guaraunan, Guaraúna, Guarauno, Guaraunes, Guaraounoes, Guaranu, Guaranos, Guararinis, Guaraouns, Guaraouno, Guarannes, Houaroux, Uarau, Uarao, Uarauno, Uarow, Oaraw-it, Quavaous, Varàa, Warau, Warrau, Warow, Warraw, Warrow, Warrans, Warouwen, Warrays.'[3] Again, the meaning attributed to the word Warrau was 'the people'.

In his book on British Guiana written in 1840 Schomburgk increased the number of tribes to ten,[4] and four years later having covered almost the whole territory of British Guiana, he spoke of thirteen tribes in a paper read before the Royal Geographical Society, also claiming that smallpox had caused a decrease of 1,000 in their numbers since 1840 when he had estimated their numbers at 7,000.[5] He had, since his earlier expeditions, encountered the minor tribes of the Tarumas, Woyavais, the Maopityans, the Pianaghottos, and the Drios. J. G. Stedman, a soldier-traveller in the

[1] William Hilhouse, *Indian Notices* (Demerara, 1825), p. 7.

[2] C.O. 111/150. Governor James Carmichael Smyth to Lord Glenelg, 30 Aug. 1837 with enclosure of R. Schomburgk's account of the Indians.

[3] The Revd. James Williams, 'The Warau Indians of Guiana and Vocabulary of Their Language', *Journal de la Société des Americanistes de Paris* (1929), p. 2.

[4] Robert H. Schomburgk, *A Description of British Guiana* (London, 1840), p. 49.

[5] Schomburgk, *On the Natives of Guiana* (read before the Society, 27 Nov. 1844), p. 264.

Guiana territory gave the number of tribes as five, although he accounted mainly for the tribes in the Surinam area.[1] H. V. P. Bronkurst and R. Montgomery Martin, who described the British area, agreed that the five main tribes were the Arawaks, the Akawois, the Caribs, the Warraus, and the Macusi; Bronkurst comparing the tribes to the five Hindu castes![2] Today four is the accepted number: (1) The Warraus, (2) The Arawaks, (3) The Caribs, and (4) The Wapisiana with the Arecunas, Akawois, and the Macusi as sub-tribes of the Caribs.[3]

In various writings on the Amerindian, the words 'tribe' and 'nation' are used interchangeably. In the early lists compiled for the purpose of regulating the distribution of presents to the Indians, 'nations' was the word used. Dr. Lucy Mair, the noted anthropologist, has observed that the word 'tribe' is used by so-called civilized persons to describe those whom they considered uncivilized. However, anthropologists meant it in a very different sense; 'tribes' to them connoted units of people, each in their own territories, mostly independent of each other, sometimes hostile to each other and speaking different dialects.[4] It is in this anthropological sense that the word 'tribe' will be used in discussing the Amerindians of British Guiana. Although the Caribs and their sub-tribes could understand each other, they also spoke different dialects. According to Schomburgk, 'Each *nation* has its own language, which by no means resembles the dialects of the Indians of Mexico, Columbia and Peru' nor 'those of North America'.[5]

Schomburgk had quite aptly observed in 1840 that it was 'difficult, if not impossible, to form an estimate approximating to truth of the number of aborigines within the boundaries of British Guiana'.[6] At the end of the nineteenth century the local government was still bedevilled by the impossibility of such a task. After attempting in the last two decades to take a census of the mobile population at

[1] Capt. J. G. Stedman, *Narrative of a Five Years' Expedition against the Revolted Negroes of Surinam in Guiana on the Wild Coast of South America, from the year 1772 to 1777* (London, 1796), I, 379.

[2] R. Montgomery Martin, *History of the British Colonies* (London, 1834), II, 34, and Bronkhurst, p. 11.

[3] The spelling and the number of tribes are taken from the *Handbook of British Guiana* (Demerara, 1909). This spelling will be used throughout the text for the sake of consistency.

[4] Lucy Mair, *Primitive Government*, Penguin Books (London, 1970), pp. 14–15.

[5] C.O. 111/150. Smyth to Glenelg, 30 Aug. 1837.

[6] Schomburgk, *A Description of British Guiana*, p. 49.

great expense and with great difficulty while 'productive of results of little economic value',[1] they fell back on careful estimates from previous returns. But these returns could hardly be considered accurate as the mobile Indians defied statistics.

James Rodway claimed that when the Indians were discovered in the sixteenth century in this area in South America there were 140,000 Caribs—a quarter of whom lived between the Corentyne and Essequibo Rivers, the remainder in Caribana—the North-West district and the Orinoco delta. There were four great Carib centres known as the kingdoms of Pawrooma (Pomeroon), Moruga (Moruka), Waini, and Barima.[2] The Caribs were especially noted because they were *the* force in the land. But there were other tribes: the Arawaks, the Akawois, the Warraus, and the Macusi. General Byam's Journal of 1665–7 gave the number of Carib families at 20,000 from the Waini to the Orinoco, Barima, and Amacura.[3] Major John Scott in his estimate of 1666 listed 28,000 families of Caribs up the Orinoco delta, as well as 8,000 Arawaks besides Akawois and Warraus.[4] Almost two centuries later Alexander von Humboldt estimated the number of Caribs between the Essequibo and the Rio Branco at 40,000.[5] But all such population data were merely fascinating guesses. No traveller or historian could possibly have ascertained the true number of the nomadic Indians. In the nineteenth century the estimates periodically taken seemed somewhat more reasonable, if not convincing. In 1825 Rodway and Hilhouse placed the number at 15,000–20,000—a quarter of whom received the share of presents, while 1,000 could be raised to bear arms in the service of the colony.[6] An estimated census of 1851 tabled the number of aborigines at 8,229 or 4 per cent of the population. Mr. Dalton, the Registrar-General, submitted that 10,000 more of that estimated number wandered about the interior of the colony.[7]

[1] *Results of the Decennial Census of the Population of British Guiana, 1931.* National Archives of Guyana. This 1931 census estimated the Amerindian population at 7,379 out of a total population of 310,933. See Appendix I for a more complete discussion on the Amerindian population.

[2] James Rodway, 'Indian Policy of the Dutch', *Timehri* (1896), 13.

[3] British Museum. Sloane MSS. 3662. f. 39 b.

[4] Rodway, loc. cit.

[5] Alexander von Humboldt and Aimé Bonpland, *Personal Narrative of Travels to the Equinoctial Regions of America, During the Years 1799–1804,* trans. Thomasina Ross (London, 1869), III, 77–8.

[6] Rodway, *A History of British Guiana* (Georgetown, 1894), II, 308; and Hilhouse, *Indian Notices,* p. 7.

[7] E. D. Rowland, 'Census of British Guiana, 1891', *Timehri* (1892), 56.

This total of between 18,000 and 20,000 coincided with the estimate of 20,000 given by Superintendent McClintock in 1851 which was quite likely accepted for the census by Dalton. The writer of the article on the 'Census of British Guiana, 1891' concluded his comments on the aboriginal races with the callous observation that the race was of 'little or no social value and their early extinction must be looked upon as inevitable in spite of the sentimental regret of missionaries'.[1] To such an inferior position had the Indian fallen by the end of the nineteenth century!

But even before the white man had touched the shores of Guiana four centuries before, the Caribs, the noted warriors throughout the Caribbean as well as the Guiana territory, were feared by other tribes whom they fought and enslaved. They were proud and deeply resented the intrusion of the white man. The Spaniards unwisely tried to de-militarize them by settling them in mission areas, thus restricting their prized freedom, and for their pains won the undying hostility of the Caribs. The Dutch, to whom commerce and not religion was the goal, shrewdly summed up the situation when they arrived, assured the Caribs of their freedom, and enlisted them for the purposes of trade and later for the hunting of their runaway slaves. Storm van's Gravesande, the Director-General of Essequibo, knew them as 'good allies and friends but formidable enemies'.[2] The British had their first brush with the Caribs when the Carib chief, Mahanarva, strode into the capital city and threatened an awed Court of Policy to unleash his Indians unless they were appeased by the usual presents they had been accustomed to receive from the Dutch.[3] The Colonial Government bowed to his request although two years later Governor H. L. Carmichael would object to such political blackmail.

The Caribs were not only settled along the right bank of the Orinoco which even the Spaniards considered the 'Carib frontier', but also in the Upper Essequibo in the Mazaruni, the Pomeroon, the Upper Cuyuni, the Barima, and even the Berbice Rivers. Of all the tribes they were described as 'the tallest, strongest built, and of the most warlike appearance'.[4] They had the straight, black hair,

[1] Ibid.
[2] P.R.O. 474/195. Despatch to the Director of the Zeeland Chamber of the West India Company, 21 Feb. 1768.
[3] M.C.P., 29 Oct. 1810. N.A.G.
[4] C.O. 111/69. Governor Benjamin D'Urban to Horace Twiss, 2 Feb. 1830, enclosing reports from Doctors to the Royal College of Physicians. J. G. Stedman put forward the

the muscular and clean-limbed appearance, the slanting eyes, and high cheek-bones which denoted their Asiatic origin. In general the Amerindians are of copper-colour, but the Caribs and the Akawois are of a lighter shade than the Arawaks and the Warraus.[1]

Next in importance were the Akawois—the traditional foe of the Caribs. Murder, through jealousy, many times initiated a war of attrition between them. Mainly a trading people, however, the Akawois were as nomadic as the Caribs and although their settlements were found chiefly on the Essequibo, Upper Cuyuni, Demerara, and Pomeroon, they were also scattered throughout the three colonies of Demerara, Essequibo, and Berbice, later to become one as British Guiana in 1831. Brett, who called them the 'Acowoi', pointed out that unlike the other tribes who were confined to a limited territory, they had 'an enormous range' and 'their expeditions, whether for war or traffic . . . extend far into Brazil and Venezuela'; furthermore, they were known as 'the pedlars and news-carriers of the whole eastern coast'[2]. Brett sanguinely hoped that they would also carry the news of the gospel to distant parts of the country.

The gentlest of all the tribes were the Arawaks, regarded by both the Dutch and their successors, the British, as the 'aristocracy' of the Indian tribes.[3] They were used by the Dutch and the British as 'interior police' for the capture of runaway slaves, and after Emancipation became the woodcutters on the grants. The Spanish Arawaks, who fled from Angostura in 1817 during the Bolivarian revolution, sought and gained the protection of the British government.[4] They settled on the Moruka River and became known throughout that region and the colony in general as an exemplary people, greatly superior in the scale of civilization to all other tribes,

rather interesting but dubious explanation for the difference in colour between the Indians and the Negroes, namely, 'The Americans [Indians] are of a copper colour or red, and the inhabitants of Africa called Negroes are black, viz. the one being more burnt by the sun than the other, and not because they are two distinct races of people.' Stedman, I, 380. The anthropologists and the sociologists would hardly agree with such naive reasoning.

[1] Ibid. D'Urban to Twiss.

[2] W. H. Brett's Report, 18 Aug. 1864 in *The Colonist*, 19 Nov. 1869. N.A.G. Brett also stated that the Akawois had the unsavoury and evil reputation as 'Canaimas' or night murderers.

[3] M.C.P., 26 Feb. 1849. McClintock's Report, 31 Dec. 1848. N.A.G.

[4] Holy See, Sacred Roman Congregation 'de Propaganda Fide', Acta, 1835, Vol. 198, 347 ff. Report of Fr. John Hynes, O.P.

'very industrious and expert in the use of fire-arms'.[1] Fr. John Hynes, the Vicar-General in British Guiana, visiting their settlement at the request of their Captain, Juan Aguilar, remarked on their cleanliness and the vastness of their cultivation. Settled on the slightly elevated lands of the coast, they grew crops of coffee, plantains, yams, cassava, maize, and even sugar cane. Above all, they were conscious of their superiority, not only to other tribes, but to other people in the colony.[2] Superintendent McClintock always praised the Spanish Arawaks, or Morocco [Moruka] Indians as they were called, as being more industrious and contributing more labour towards the cultivation of sugar cane than any other tribe.[3] A previous Superintendent, William Crichton, while on a visit to Moruka in 1838 was amazed at seeing well-dressed Indians living in good houses, and growing an abundance of crops, thereby he concluded 'evincing a superior degree of civilization'.[4] Their 'mild and peaceable' disposition placed them high in the esteem of the Revd. W. H. Brett.[5]

On the other hand, the Warraus, living on the low-lying coastlands between Barima and the Pomeroon and their tributaries—the 'swamp Indians'—had the unsavoury reputation among their other fellow Indians and Europeans alike, as being uncombed and unwashed, content to live in squalor. Schomburgk, among others, noted that 'the dirtiness of a Warau is proverbial among the other Indians.'[6] However, their skill as boat-builders was unsurpassed and unquestioned. Both Sir Walter Raleigh and Major John Scott called them 'the nation of shipwrights',[7] while William Hilhouse, re-echoing both, claimed that the speed, seaworthiness, cheapness and durability of their craft 'far exceed any European production'.[8] Surrounded by water as they were, it was vital for the Warraus to perfect this art; their craft, called 'corials', were pirogues large

[1] William Hilhouse, *Reconnaissance of the Post of Pomeroon with the Adjacent Indian Settlements in the Morocco Creek and its Vicinity*, November, 1825. N.A.G.

[2] Letter of W. Hilhouse, n.d., but possibly between 1833 and 1834. Jesuit Diocesan Archives, Guyana.

[3] M.C.P., 10 Jan. 1849. McClintock's Report, 30 Sept. 1848. N.A.G. A later spelling of Morocco was Moruka or Moruca.

[4] Report of W. Crichton, No. 7, 1838. N.A.G.   [5] Brett, p. 96.

[6] R. Schomburgk (ed.), *Discovery of the Large, Rich and Beautiful Empire of Guiana* (Hakluyt Society, 1848), p. 51.

[7] Sloane MSS. 3662, f. 37, B.M.

[8] Hilhouse, 'Memoir in the Warrow Land of British Guiana', *Journal of the Royal Geographic Society*, IV (1834), 328.

enough to carry comfortably as many as seventy persons. With their bows and arrows, the Warraus were also expert fishermen. McClintock spoke of their 'extraordinary skill and unerring aim'[1] which alone maintained the fishery in the Moruka, but he hastened to add that there was 'no People who appear more destitute of imagination'.[2] Yet it seems strange that such so-called unimaginative people could so cleverly make the baskets and the Ita,[3] or Siroco hammocks, those relaxing swing-'beds' of the Indians, who, when not hunting or fishing, swing all day in them, and a real delight to the white men who would like to do the same. The Revd. Ignatius Scoles aptly described the hammock: 'The hammock for the Indians is chair and table, sofa, bed, smoking saloon and all.'[4] Commenting on their laziness, Hartsinck observed that the Indians spent most of their time in a hammock, plucking hair from their faces and playing the flute.[5] Despite the description of their laziness by Hartsinck, most officials and travellers testified to the Warraus' industry: to Laurens Storm van's Gravesande, they were good workers but dishonest; to Hilhouse and the Revd. James Williams, they shirked no toil;[6] and were later known, this pariah of the tribes, as 'the hewers of wood and carriers of water'.[7]

A tall, stalwart people, who with their exotic head-dresses and nose and ear ornaments alarmed the timid Warraus, when in 1865 they arrived at Waramuri Mission from up the Caroni and Cuyuni rivers, were the Arecunas. Schomburgk described them as 'a powerful tribe' who were 'more properly the inhabitants of the Venezuelan territory',[8] because no doubt, they were the most westerly of all tribes. In feathers and red paint they were 'never before seen', according to Brett at whose mission they appeared in their 'woodskins' desiring to be taught Christianity, and just as suddenly disappearing to their far-distant homes after a few days.[9] Yet in 1862

---

[1] McClintock's Report, 30 Sept. 1848. N.A.G.   [2] Ibid.

[3] The fibre prepared from the young leaf of the Ita palm was called 'tibisiri' by the Arawaks. Williams, p. 16. McClintock claimed that the Warrau women were more vivacious than the men; maybe they were more imaginative, also, as they were the makers of the hammocks and baskets. McClintock, 30 Sept. 1848.

[4] Scoles, p. 100.

[5] Hartsinck, I, 6, 11–12. Laurens Storm van's Gravesande, *The Rise of British Guiana*, compiled from his despatches by C. A. Harris and J. A. J. Villiers (Hakluyt Society, 1911), II, 460.

[6] Williams, p. 14.

[7] M.C.P., 26 Feb. 1849; McClintock's Report, 31 Dec. 1848. N.A.G.

[8] Schomburgk, *Description* . . . , p. 50.

[9] Brett's Report, 24 Nov. 1865 in *The Colonist*, 19 Nov. 1849. N.A.G.

the Acting Superintendent of Rivers and Creeks of Essequibo, F. M. Bury, spoke of the 'Arakoonas' as the principal growers and suppliers of cotton to other Indian tribes in the Essequibo area for the making of cotton hammocks.[1] Though they traded with them in cotton balls and blow-pipes, the Macusis feared these news-carriers.

Further south of the Arecuna country lived the Macusi along the Rupununi, Ireng, and Takutu rivers in the savannah lands and between the Pakaraima and Kanuku mountain chains, together with the Wapisiana, their neighbours, and the Wai-Wais in the far south of the country where the Essequibo has its source.

Like the Arecunas, the Macusi are cotton growers but their fame rests on their skill in preparing the ourali poison.[2] This deadly poison is made from the lianas and used effectively in their blow-pipes and arrow heads by the Macusi, noted as keen huntsmen. A. S. Kok considered the Macusi 'the most numerous tribe of Guiana',[3] most probably having read Schomburgk who had estimated their number in 1840 at no fewer than 3,000.[4] Their neighbours to the near south are the Wapisianas, traders and canoe-builders who have in the past century, mostly through intermarriage, absorbed their neighbours, the Atorais, already nearly extinct in Schomburgk's time. In 1842 only thirty had survived the smallpox epidemic;[5] they had indeed reached 'the evening of their life as a people'.[6] A few remnants of the Atorai tribe are said to exist at Achiwib, an Atorai village of the past where the language is still spoken.[7] Almost at the end of the nineteenth century, Sir Everard im Thurn, Curator of the Museum in British Guiana and the earliest serious writer on Amerindian life, confessed that 'of the Wayawais, only the name is known'.[8] This tribe, living in the remote jungle in the deep south of the country bordering on Brazil, is still almost completely untouched by civilization. First seen by Schomburgk in

[1] M.C.C., 15 May 1863. Report of F. M. Bury, 31 Dec. 1862. N.A.G. See also Sir Everard im Thurn, *Among the Indians of Guiana* (London, 1883), republished (New York, 1967), p. 271.

[2] Also called 'wurali' poison by A. S. Kok, *Colonial Essays*, translated from the Dutch (London & Holland, 1864), p. 73, and curare (*strychnos toxifera*) from an alkaloid of the liana bark-curarine which paralyses the nerves. See Michael Swan, *British Guiana. The Land of Six Peoples* (London, 1957), p. 167.

[3] Kok, ibid.   [4] Schomburgk, *Description* . . . , p. 50.

[5] Schomburgk, *On the Natives of Guiana*, p. 264, and Kok, p. 73.

[6] Schomburgk as quoted in N. O. Poonai, 'Extinct Tribes and Threatened Species of the South Savannahs', *Timehri*, XLIII (1967), 78.

[7] Ibid., p. 80.   [8] Im Thurn, p. 163.

1837 and later by Barrington Brown, the geologist, in 1870, this only real primitive tribe in Guyana[1] still holds out the charm of mystery to travellers and anthropologists. Other tribes concede that they are the best makers of the cassava-graters. Among the Wai-Wai the men and women share the work in the cassava fields, but the preparation of the farine and the drink is specifically women's work;[2] like all other Amerindians, the men hunt in the cool of the morning and sensibly rest in their hammocks during the hotter part of the day.[3]

Other lesser known tribes were the Tarumas, Maopityanas, and Maiongkongs. The Tarumas were described by Schomburgk in 1840 as an athletic people[4] and by Bury, as a rarely seen, 'black Indian resembling the coolie'[5]—the name given the East Indian immigrant in the colony. The Maopityanas were given a passing reference by Schomburgk; the Maiongkongs, known as canoe-makers, numbered six at the Waramuri Mission in 1864.[6] But at the end of the century these tribes, together with the Pianoghottos, Cocoipityans, Carawayannas, Barokotos, Drios, Maipuripiyannas, Zurumatas, Dauri, Amaripas, and the Paravilanos, had disappeared from the country, been absorbed by other tribes, or become extinct.[7]

Although Schomburgk had written reams of paper to the Governor and Secretary of State about the Indians he had encountered in his expeditions throughout British Guiana, a knowledge of the customs and culture, the characteristics and beliefs of 'so extraordinary and singular a race of beings' had not been shared with the 'curious and enquiring reader'[8] in the colony. The Protectors and Postholders of the Indians in the first three decades of the century merely acquainted the local government with the routine occurrences on their posts and the distribution of allowances and rations to the Indians, but hardly studied the Indian in his natural habitat. It was a later official, a Superintendent of Rivers and Creeks, W. C.

---

[1] Yet it was this remote tribe that in May 1972 the Guyana government brought to the city to build a diplomats' lounge for the meeting of leaders of the non-aligned countries held in August 1972. Their typical, conical-roofed hut was erected in record time, giving the city-dwellers of the Co-operative Republic an example of communal co-operation. See also works of William Curtis Farabee, *The Central Caribs* (The Netherlands, 1967) and Jens Yde, *Material Culture of the Waiwai* (Copenhagen, 1965) for twentieth-century in-depth studies of the Wai-wais.

[2] Yde, p. 303. Also Farabee, pp. 153–4. [3] Farabee, p. 164.
[4] Schomburgk, *Description* . . . , p. 50. [5] Bury's Report. N.A.G.
[6] Brett's Report, 1865. N.A.G. [7] Poonai, *Timehri*, XLIII (1967), 77–9.
[8] C.O. 116/2. Editorial in *The Guiana Chronicle*, 1 Feb. 1837.

McClintock, who gave a deep insight into the lives of these people. But it was the missionaries who really stirred up an interest in the poor, docile, and inoffensive people,[1] as they called them. Schomburgk had exhibited the Indian to the British public, which led *The Royal Gazette* in British Guiana to express the hope that the specimen of that interesting race 'will influence the philanthropist to contribute towards bringing them to the state of civilization'.[2]

By and large, the public, no doubt influenced to a certain extent by the press, looked on the Indians as specimens or museum pieces, and like so many visitors to museums hardly knew what to make of the exhibits. The explorers, travellers, and missionaries who did look beneath the surface, looked with European eyes from the peak of their so-called civilization—their one goal to lead these savages into the orbit of their civilization. Even Schomburgk brushed aside discussions on their manners and customs and deemed it necessary 'to alienate them from Indian life and manners, and, from their earliest youth, to point out to them the beneficial examples afforded by the Christian religion and Civilization'.[3]

But the Indians, like any other people, can never be understood unless a long and deep look is taken at their culture. In any descriptions of the characteristics of the Indian, laziness and 'unconquerable indolence' are by-words. McClintock, who devoted more than forty years to their service, while praising them for their industry, never lost sight of their apathy. Vincent Roth, a writer on Amerindian life, described the Indian as 'neither hurried nor worried'.[4] Dr. Waddell reporting to the Royal College of Physicians showed that there was little need for the Indian to exert himself. Every means of subsistence came through hunting or fishing, while cassava was grown with minimal trouble.

The Indian considered himself perfectly free and shied away from every kind of compulsory exertion. It would be difficult, Dr. Waddell concluded, to bring about a change in his habits.[5] One of the early Governors of Guiana, J. C. Smyth, remarked on the happy, carefree life of the Indians, and felt that they were too in-

---

[1] The Revd. W. T. Veness, *Ten Years of Mission Life in British Guiana* (London, 1875), pp. 5 and 32.

[2] *The Royal Gazette*, 31 Mar. 1840. N.A.G.

[3] C.O. 111/180. Governor Henry Light to Lord Stanley, 21 Oct. 1841. Second Report of Robert H. Schomburgk, Aug. 1841.

[4] Hon. Vincent Roth, 'Amerindians and the State', *Timehri*, XXXI (1952), 9.

[5] C.O. 111/69. D'Urban to Twiss, 2 Feb. 1830. Dr. Waddell's Report.

dependent and free in their natural habitat to submit to the restricting bonds of civilized life.[1] Superficial observers of Indian life label the men lazy because they do not plant the fields, nor split the wood for the fire, nor carry the burdens. But a closer look at their daily routine would show that there is a division of labour—the men make the canoes and the houses, look after the children, and protect the women on the long treks across the forest and along the rivers from snakes and animals of prey. No one explains what are considered by Europeans the vices of the Indian better than the traveller, Charles Waterton:

> Some travellers and colonists call these Indians a lazy race. Man in general will not be active without an object. Now when the Indian has caught plenty of fish, and killed game enough to last him for a week, what need has he to range the forest? He has no idea of making pleasure grounds. Money is of no use to him, for in these wilds there are no markets for him to frequent . . . he has no taxes to pay, no highways to keep up, no poor to maintain, nor army nor navy to supply; he lies in his hammock both night and day . . . and in it he forms his bow, and makes his arrows, and repairs his fishing tackle. But as soon as he has consumed his provisions, he then rouses himself, and, like a lion scours the forest in quest of food.[2]

Obviously, climate and environmental factors influenced his habits. Almost two centuries of European rule have not fundamentally changed the Indian, although those exposed to civilization are being weaned away from their subsistence economy into commercial agriculture.

It is always a matter of conjecture why the Amerindian of the Guiana forests never reached the political, cultural, and religious sophistication of the Aztecs, the Mayas, and Incas, their Central and South American brothers. It has been partly explained by archaeologists and geographers that the Indian of the equatorial forests found the challenge of his environment unsurmountable. It would, indeed, have been difficult to erect such urban and ceremonial cities as Tikal and Chichen Itza, yet Tenochtitlán rose from 'chinampas'—floating islands on Lake Texcoco and Tiahuanaco at an elevation of over 13,000 feet. Obviously the builders of these cities had greater human resources which explained their political and cultural advances, as well as their agricultural productivity. Sherburne Cook and Lesley B. Simpson estimated the population

[1] P.R.O. 35/18. J. C. Smyth to Stanley, 5 Oct. 1833.
[2] Charles Waterton, *Wanderings in South America* (London, 1879), pp. 244–5.

of Central Mexico in 1519 at 11,000,000 and, although at the end of the sixteenth century it decreased, it was still in the millions.[1] Even the highest estimate of the Amerindians at the end of the nineteenth century never numbered more than 20,000. Their settlements varied between seventeen and seventy individuals, and life in such small tribal groups was lived at a subsistence level. Political and religious stimuli were also lacking among the Guiana Indians. There was no Quetzalcoatl—'culture hero' to guide the people in the art of living and to weld them together in religious unity, no Montezuma, no Inca. They had neither the imperial complex of the Incas nor the need for *Lebensraum* which some historians attribute to the Aztecs. But in pride they matched their distant brothers.

The Dutch never ignored this characteristic of the Indians, and very early in their relationship made treaties assuring them that they would never be enslaved, a policy which their British successors prudently followed. One English lay missionary, Mary Davson, called pride and indolence the chief characteristics of the Indians, the latter a by-product of the former, because their pride caused them to despise all drudgery as unworthy of them.[2] This pride led them to look down upon the Negro slaves whom they hunted in the pre-emancipation period. Yet the cause of this dislike was attributed more to jealousy over their females and anger over the Negroes plundering their fields.[3] Governor Murray claimed that the Negroes were in 'great awe' of the Indians, knowing them to possess fire arms and poisoned arrows;[4] McClintock maintained it was 'jealousy and not pride' which made the Caribs, that proud nation, object to their children mixing with those of other tribes on the missions. They feared that far removed from their own tribe, their females would form alliances with other tribes.[5] Yet McClintock showed that the Indian asserted himself over the Africans and the Coolies—the latter being 'naturally submissive', accepted 'the

---

[1] Sherburne F. Cook and Lesley Byrd Simpson, *The Population of Central Mexico in the Sixteenth Century* (Berkeley, 1948), p. 38. Charles Gibson computed the population in the Valley of Mexico in 1519 at 1,500,000. The Amerindians never reached the millions in any area. Charles Gibson, *The Aztecs under Spanish Rule* (London, 1964), p. 6.

[2] CW/o4/3/1. Mary F. Davson to the Revd. H. Venn, 27 June 1848. C.M.S.A.

[3] C.O. 111/20. Colonel Edward Codd to the Earl of Bathurst, 4 Sept. 1815.

[4] Ibid. Governor John Murray to Bathurst, 19 Oct. 1815.

[5] M.C.P., 28 July 1868. McClintock's Report, 30 June 1868. N.A.G.

dictates of his new master—the Indian'.[1] At the same time, McClintock noted with surprise the rather unusual course adopted by the Indians who, desiring the services of the Africans, offered them Indian women as their wives![2] As early as 1834 one of the missionaries, the Revd. John Armstrong, agreed that the Indian looked upon the Negro as a slave and himself as a freeman, but he said he had 'never discovered any ill-feeling, in either party, on that account'. Armstrong was of the opinion that the white planters, on account of fear, played upon a real or imagined antipathy between the two races[3]—an opinion that is indeed borne out by a look at population figures, namely 60,000 slaves to 2,000 whites.

The Indian, surrounded by the primeval forest, came to terms with nature. The plants of the earth, their bark, stems, leaves, seeds, and fruit provided him not only with his means of livelihood but were used to treat and cure his illnesses. Although the reports of Drs. Bell and Waddell, in reply to questions of the Royal College of Physicians, stated that the native Indians had no knowledge of disease and preferred the incantations of their medicine men to the remedies of the white man, they admitted that the native plants abounded in medicinal properties little known by them, but well known to the Indians and used by them.[4] In 1851 and 1853 two catalogues of articles from British Guiana exhibited in New York and Dublin listed remedies made from the barks, stems, fruits, and seeds of plants for the treatment of diseases, as well as antidotes for snake-bites. Such tongue-twisting names as Pacurie, Kihurema, Waracouri, Bemeticucuni, were used as decoctions in cases of what was known as Caribisce sick—a malignant ulceration of the rectum peculiar to the Indian.[5] The Indians, however, suffered from few diseases until smallpox, measles, cholera, and above all, tuberculosis were, together with the benefits of civilization, introduced by the white man and a heavy price was paid in the loss of lives. They feared the vaccination needle and many fled into the forests when the

---

[1] Ibid. The East Indian indentured labourers were called 'coolies', possibly a term derived from the Tamil, *huli* (a porter, a labourer). See Dwarka Nath, *A History of Indians in Guyana*, 2nd ed. (London, 1970), p. 10, fn. 2.

[2] Ibid.

[3] CW/014/28. John Armstrong to D. Coates, 27 Oct. 1834. C.M.S.A.

[4] C.O. 111/69. D'Urban to Twiss, 2 Feb. 1830.

[5] C.O. 111/292. British Guiana Catalogue, 15 Mar. 1851 and C.O. 111/294. Governor Barkly to Duke of Newcastle, 5 May 1853 enclosing Catalogue of Articles. Another section listed over 100 articles of Indian manufacture from arrows to Yarracoom, a cap made of Wicker work, and War Clubs.

epidemics reached their settlements—fearing equally both death and the vaccine. Their type of nutrition had not built up a resistance to such foreign diseases and they had had no time to work out cures for them.

While these diseases threw the Indian into fear and consternation, the social customs of the Indians worried the white man, especially the missionaries. All writers testified to the fondness of the Indians for their children and a lack of parental discipline. The missionaries deplored this attitude, especially when the Indian objected to leaving his children at the mission settlements.[1] Their marriage customs varied somewhat from tribe to tribe. Like the aristocratic Arawaks, the Akawois, or Waikas were monogamous, but the husbands suffered from their Amazonian wives who kept their husbands in 'perfect subjection'.[2] In general, polygamy was the order of the day and particularly widespread among the Warraus whom Fr. de Betham, a Jesuit missionary, called 'the helots of the land'.[3] He spoke of a certain celebrated Warrau chieftain, Mai-ce-wari, who had no fewer than fifteen wives, and felt that the polygamous custom stemmed from their Asiatic origin.[4] Despite the glut of wives among the Warraus and the Caribs, no jealousy was observed in the harem.[5] If a wife were beaten by her husband she quietly cooked and drank the deadly poison of the cassava root.[6] Anthropologists claim that polygamy is the hallmark of cultivators of the soil who need many hands to plant and to reap. The Caribs did not settle down to agricultural pursuits until the mid-nineteenth century,[7] but their polygamous propensity might well be explained by the spoils of war, particularly women, whom they captured during their early inter-tribal wars. The Indians were proud of their innumerable wives; the missionaries looked upon them as so many impediments to baptism. Among all Indian tribes, adultery—the theft of their wives by another—was punishable by the instant death of the offending wife. This act, in turn, set in motion the law of retribution by which the relatives of the dead woman never rested until they avenged her death. Hilhouse remarked that this custom tended greatly 'to pre-

---

[1] Brett, p. 99.

[2] M.C.P., 26 Feb. 1849. McClintock's Report, 31 Dec. 1848, N.A.G., and 'Fr. de Betham's Narrative', *Letters and Notices*, II (Apr. 1864), 75. J.A.L.

[3] Ibid.   [4] Ibid.

[5] Pere de la Borde, 'History of the Caribs', trans. G. J. A. Boschreitz, *Timehri*, V (1886), 240. See also de Betham's 'Narrative . . . .'   [6] de Betham, p. 82.

[7] M.C.P., 28 July 1868. McClintock's Report, 30 June 1868. N.A.G.

vent the increase of population'.[1] It showed, above all, that in the case of a secular offence, law and justice were personal matters.

A most interesting, but not unique custom, was connected with birth—the *couvade*. After the birth of a child, the man remained in his hammock or hut and received the care and congratulations of his friends, while his wife continued her slightly interrupted work in the cassava fields. Although this custom, illustrating a deeply shared paternity, was usually considered peculiar to the Amerindian, it was not so. It was noted among the English and Irish peasantry, the Chinese and the Brazilians, and described as 'a real physico-sympathetic connection between a man and his wife'.[2] Dr. Walter E. Roth, who spent years studying and writing about the Indians' customs, characteristics, and occupation, observed that *couvade* rested on the supposition that 'the infant's body proceeds from the mother, but the spirit . . . from the father, and that a mysterious connection binds the child's spirit to the father's for some weeks after birth.'[3] Malinowski asserts that absurd though the custom of *couvade* might seem, it is both meaningful and necessary; it not only emphasizes the father's biological relationship to the child and makes him 'painfully' aware of his offspring, but it accentuates 'the child's need of a father',[4] all very vital and basic for secure social relationships. *Couvade* was also bound up with the superstitious beliefs of the Indian. The Carib believed that if a man left his hut during the week after the birth of his child, the evil spirit which took delight in killing babies would smell the child on him, and thus endanger the young one's life.[5]

To the Amerindian, his forest world was dominated by spirits, good and evil, hence his life was governed by his beliefs in these

[1] Hilhouse, *Indian Notices*, p. 14.

[2] 'Couvade', *Timehri*, III (1884), 149. In the same article E. B. Taylor gives the derivation of the word *couvade* thus: 'French (Provincial, south) from couver to hatch as if the man hatched the young brood. At least, that is something near the way in which the word shaped itself. It is in fact the same word as our covey, French couve, a hatching or brood.' p. 150. See also im Thurn, *Among the Indians . . .*, pp. 217–19.

[3] Walter Edmund Roth, *An Introductory Study of the Arts, Crafts and Customs of the Guiana Indians*. Smithsonian Institution, Bureau of Ethnology (Washington, D.C.; Government Printing Office, 1924), pp. 695–6. Before coming to British Guiana, Dr. Roth was a Protector of Aboriginals in Australia. See also 'Couvade', *Timehri*, II (1883), 160.

[4] Bronislaw Malinowski, *Sex and Repression in Savage Society* (London, 1961), pp. 215–16.

[5] John Gillin, 'Crime and Punishment Among the Barama River Caribs of British Guiana', *American Anthropologist*, New Series, XXXVI (1934), 334.

spirits—their power to help or harm him. The Indian mind understood 'good' and 'evil' where others saw 'right' and 'wrong'. The forest trees which rose to majestic heights around him; the cool, brown streams; the creeks and rivers in which he fished and swam and paddled his own corial;[1] the rapids, cataracts, and falls which abounded with fearful life; the rocks standing sentinel; the birds and animals which were both food and foe—all this, and the lush vegetation, spoke to him of supernatural powers beyond his ken. And so he imbued them with a spirit-life. Because he could not control them, he feared them; to him there were more evil spirits than good ones—'high mountains, large rocks, Cataracts' were inhabited by them, and, as Schomburgk observed, the Indian became a 'professor of Demonology'.[2] The *piai*-man, or shaman, medicine man of North America, witch-doctor of Africa, pretended that he held great powers over the spirits, and above all could restore health to the sick, whose illness was caused by an evil spirit. Fr. de Betham, among others, described the treatment of the sick patient by the piai-man to whose hut he was brought. Here, the piai-man fumigated him with tobacco smoke while chanting and rattling his 'maracca'—a hollow calabash containing seeds or small fruits, and with a feather-topped handle. He then blew on the patient and produced some object, the evil, which he proclaimed he had extracted from him.[3]

A candidate for initiation into this art of piaism, or more correctly, craft, spends the night alone with a seasoned piai-man who shouts loudly over him, sometimes puffing tobacco smoke in his face. He is then shut up in a dark hut with nothing but a block of wood for a week and for food only a bit of cassava bread, dried fish and some water. At the end of the week he is given about a gallon of piwari—the fermented and intoxicating liquor made from cassava, which naturally sickens him. During the week also, in their nightly meetings, the piai-man instructs the initiate in the arts of

[1] These dug-outs or corials are also described as 'buck shells'. Roth claims that the island Caribs called them *couliala* of which corial is considered a corruption. (See Walter E. Roth, *An Introductory Study of the Arts, Crafts and Customs of the Guiana Indians*. Smithsonian Institution (Washington: Government Printing Office, 1924), p. 611.

[2] C.O. 111/150. J. C. Smyth to Glenelg, 30 Aug. 1837. Schomburgk's account.

[3] de Betham, 'The Piai-Man', *Letters and Notices*, II (1864), 151. McClintock states that the fangs of a snake was a precious commodity to a piai-man, who exhibited it to his gullible patients as the evil spirit of sickness which he had extracted. See W. C. F. McClintock, 'Colonial Jottings', *Timehri*, V (1886), 94.

the trade.[1] The piai-man maintained his influence over the people, even after he himself had been converted to Christianity. Fr. de Betham commented that when he preached against witchcraft, 'the old rascals', who, although they took medicines from him but still pretended 'to cure people with the rattle of their matracca and fumigations of tobacco', would look rather discomfited.[2]

The piai-man, according to the Indian, had the power to call down the 'Kanaima' or evil spirit on one.[3] Obviously then the piai-man was 'the power behind the throne' and the chiefs consulted him. The Kanaima is also a cult practised by self-made avengers of dastardly deeds, although many innocent victims fall a prey to their sorcery. No one is more feared than the kanaimas, the name adopted by the avengers themselves. Kanaimas are said to lead an austere life in preparation for their work of vengeance on their victims. A kanaima must be avoided at all costs, but as no one really knows who is or is not a kanaima, certain plants, which are said to frighten kanaimas away, are hung in the huts. While working his black magic, the kanaima makes sure that his identity will not be divulged by piercing his victim's tongue with a snake's fang.[4] The victim dies a lingering death. A self-appointed avenger of evil, the kanaima is the embodiment of the retaliatory law.

The recognition of the existence of spirits—good and evil—with the evil in the ascendancy and 'the mental attitude which men held towards these spirits', was defined by im Thurn as Animism.[5] The spirits of the forest, water, and mountains were generally referred to as Imawali or the Bush spirits.[6] These spirits were dominated by Makonaima, the Great Spirit, whom the Guyanese poet, A. J. Seymour, immortalized in his poem, 'The Legend of Kaieteur', in which Old Kaie, the Indian chief, sacrificed his life for the good of his tribe to this Spirit who:

> . . . dwelt
> In the huge mountain rock that throbbed and felt

---

[1] C.O. 111/169. D'Urban to Twiss, 2 Feb. 1830. Report of Dr. Michael McTurk.

[2] de Betham, 'Report of a Missionary Voyage up the Moruca and Wayini', *Letters and Notices*, I (1863), 199. J.A.L.

[3] The fear of the 'Kanaima' still strongly exists even among the Christian Indians as recently told me by Mr. P. Gorinsky, who has lived for years in the Rupununi. May 1972.

[4] Gillin, pp. 340–2.

[5] im Thurn, *On the Animism of the Indians of British Guiana* (London, 1882), n.p. See also im Thurn's, *Among the Indians . . .* Ch. XVII on 'Religion', pp. 341–70.

[6] Dr. Audrey Butt, 'The Birth of a Religion', *Timehri*, XXXIX (1960), 28, f.n. 23.

> The swift black waters of Potaro's race
> Pause on the lip . . .

Because most rocks are held in awe by the Indians, it is surprising that the rocks found at certain points along the Essequibo, Quitaro, Ireng, Corentyne, and Berbice rivers and on the southern slopes of the Pakaraima Mountains covered with picture writing and attributed by some to the handiwork of the Great Makonaima are not reverenced by the Indians. On the other hand, many large, unmarked rocks are never looked at by piai-men who squeeze tobacco juice in their eyes when passing them.[1] The origin of the Timehri, the Carib word for ideographic writings on the rocks, still remains a mystery, and their meaning even more inexplicable than the Mayan hieroglyphics. Schomburgk compared them to the Carib drawings on one of the Virgin Islands, while Humboldt felt that they were executed by tribes of a very ancient civilization.[2] The markings are so worn that it is difficult to conclude what instrument or tool had been used. Bronkurst, the Wesleyan missionary who continually saw analogies between the cultures of the Hindu and the Amerindian, likened them to drawings of figures he had seen on the walls of Hindu temples.[3] Among the specimens found on the rocks on the southern slope of the Pakaraima Mountains is a drawing similar in shape to the *quipu*—the Inca recording device made of different coloured strings with knots of various shapes. Farabee noted that the Wai-wais sent invitations to the Tarumas for their dances and sprees on knotted strings made out of the ita palm with knots dyed in various colours.[4] The crude drawings depict what appears to be part of the solar system, together with animals, snakes, and a head surrounded by rays which could possibly be interpreted as having some religious significance in the spirit world of long-forgotten Indian tribes.

In the Akawoi Hallelujah religion, a syncretism of the Christian religion and animism, both the prophets of the Akawoi and the Macusi had 'spirit experiences during the dreams and the spirit flights during prayer' which imbued them with special knowledge.[5] The dreams of the prophets showed that in seeking Hallelujah—inspiration from God—they encountered various spirits, Imawali,

---

[1] C. B. Brown, 'Indian Picture Writing in British Guiana', *Journal of the Anthropological Institute of Great Britain and Ireland*, II (1872), 255–6.
[2] Brett, p. 449.   [3] Bronkurst, pp. 35–6.   [4] Farabee, pp. 162–3.
[5] Butt, p. 28.

the forest spirits, as well as angels. Dr. Butt makes the parallel between a shaman's visiting the evil spirit in order to bring back the spirit of the sick man, and that of Abel, the prophet of the Akawoi Hallelujah, who, after his dream flight, said he had brought the spirit back from God 'to increase Akawoi strength'.[1] This religion, which spread from the Macusi to the Akawois after 1845 and later to the Caribs, still exists today and indicates the tremendous importance of the spirit world to the Indians of the forests. In the Akawoi Hallelujah cult the graves of their dead are ignored for, explains Dr. Butt, it is believed that the person's spirit 'is with God in heaven',[2] while Brett observed that among the Akawoi in general their dead were buried in an upright position, possibly to indicate that the spirit was still living within them.[3] Brett also had the personal experience at Waramuri Mission where there was a gathering of Arawaks, Caribs, Warraus, Akawois, and a few Maiongkongs, of the Indians' unwillingness to dig up a tumulus in which human remains were met with four or five feet from the surface.[4] When this information was forwarded to Professor Richard Owen, a distinguished naturalist in London, he refused to press for a transmission of the human remains, respecting the feelings of the Indians, 'which do betoken a kind of religious veneration for the resting-places of ancestors and some dim sense of the sanctity of sepulture'.[5] Im Thurn affirmed that the Indians, with the exception of Kenaimas, regarded burial places as sacrosanct.

The Hallelujah cult involves much singing and dancing. During Abel's dream flight he encountered the spirits (*Imawali*) and the angels (*Akono*) dancing Hallelujah.[6] This was in good Indian tradition as the Indians love to sing—really a monotonous chant—and to dance, especially when they are enjoying a *piwari* or *cassiri* feast. An interesting dance of the Caribs and Warraus is the 'mari-mari' in which a row of women linked together with their arms around waist and shoulder dance towards a similar row of men, then backwards and fan out sideways while the musicians keep time with the maraccas. The 'macquari' or funeral dance of the Arawaks represents a type of single combat to test the power and endurance of the

---

[1] Butt, p. 31. [2] Ibid., p. 33.
[3] Brett, p. 343; also im Thurn, *Among the Indians . . .* , p. 225.
[4] C.O. 111/355. Governor F. Hincks to Cardwell, 8 June 1866, transmitting a letter from Brett to Archdeacon Jones, 4 Jan. 1866.
[5] C.O. 111/361. Professor R. Owen to Sir Frederick Rogers, 12 Feb. 1866.
[6] Butt, p. 30.

pair of dancers. The Warraus are considered an extremely carefree people who enjoy themselves with song and dance,[1] whereas the Caribs tend to be more melancholic.[2] The Revd. J. Williams gives the words and translation of a Warrau song and dance, the Aruhoho, which celebrated the clearing away of the bushes in preparation for planting the cassava—the staff of life of the Indian:

> Hiatu moku-moku nevikarié
> Domu-sanuka siborori
> Kohóko nehurehure buakata Nevikarié!
> Aru-sanuka karuriani ho-ho-ho-ho-u
> Kauri waka nakaitehi orwakaiyani
> Aru-sanuka karuriani
> Háke tametakuri inarerate Wihi witu onate

Cut down the undergrowth (so as to make a good field). There is the little sparrow, the siborori. Listen carefully (so as to sing just as nicely as he does). Cut away the bushes. We are dancing, sporting with only a little cassava. Sing ho-ho-ho-ho, etc. How glad we are that the sport is fixed for today. We are sporting with only a little cassava. By this time tomorrow, everything will be quiet. The pigeon also will be making a noise.[3]

The planting of the cassava is an important part of the Indians' life, for the cassava or manioc is the staple diet of the Amerindians, like the bread of western man. The ground flour is made into cassava bread which looks like a round, huge pancake that is dried out on the roof of the hut. The juice of the cassava root squeezed out by the *matapie*, an elongated extractor made of *tibisiri*, is a deadly poison. The sickeningly sweet and intoxicating drinks of *piwari* and *cassiri* drunk in vast quantities at their sprees or feasts are made from the fermented cassava. The Mexican Indians have their *pulque*, the Incas their *chicha* for their merry-making; why should not the Guiana Indians have their *cassiri* and *piwari*? These drinks, intoxicating though they are, contain substances necessary for the Indians' health, and it has been attested that their prohibition by missionaries lowered the resistance of the Indian to disease.

On the other hand, rum, that bane of the Amerindians, condemned by officials and missionaries alike, but still supplied to the guileless Indians by unscrupulous employers, had a devastating

---

[1] Padre Joseph Cumilla, *El Orinoco Llustrado, y, Defendido, Historia Natural Civil, y Geographica de este Gran Rio, y de sus caudalosas vertientes*, I, 161, as quoted in Williams, p. 22.
[2] de la Borde, p. 238.   [3] Williams, p. 58.

effect on them. Rum drinking became the Indian 'vice' *par excellence*, and the Indians seemed to 'learn nothing so fast as the habit of swallowing rum'.[1] Hilhouse constantly deplored the lavish distribution of rum to the Indians by the early Protectors and Postholders. Indeed, rum headed the list of allowances and rations shared out to the Indians for their services. Superintendent McClintock branded this 'the authorized system of demoralization'.[2] The usually mild, stolid, and apathetic Indian under the influence of spirituous liquors, became aggressive, swore dreadfully in English, and even committed murder. It was amusing to read the press's advice to Europeans unable to hold their liquor, and that was to go 'up among the highly civilized [!] though much neglected race of people, the BUCKS, in order . . . to be taught by them how to get scientifically drunk'.[3] Most likely the press meant the drinking of *piwari* and *cassiri*, not rum. The missionaries, Bernau and Brett, complained that the rum ruined the Indian morally, while every traveller and explorer who encountered the Indian in the nineteenth century affirmed that 'excessive drinking' was the greatest vice of the Indian,[4] a vice taught him by the European.

But in European eyes the Indians possessed praiseworthy characteristics, or virtues in our language. They were extremely honest—lying or stealing were hardly ever heard of among them.[5] Sawkins, a surveyor, recounted this incident on his trip through the Guiana forests with Barrington Brown. On finding the owners of an Indian settlement absent, Brown and himself proposed to take what they wanted, leaving the value of the articles in cash, 'but the Indians of the party would not agree to it believing such a course would be a breach of that faith and custom of never touching anything belonging to another during his absence'.[6] Indeed, the Indians leave their huts, troolie-roofed and open to the four winds and go off on their hunting or fishing trips while the women work in the cassava fields

[1] C.O. 116/3, 'The Aborigines of British Guiana', *The Guiana Chronicle*, 6 Sept. 1839. Netscher claimed that 'the passion for strong drink is up to now the one thing that the Indians have willingly adopted from European civilisation.' Rum was called Kiltum or Dram by the Dutch, Killdevil by the English. See P. M. Netscher, *History of the Colonies Essequebo, Demerary & Berbice. From the Dutch Establishment to the Present Day*, trans. Walter E. Roth ('S Gravenhage Martinus Nijhoff, 1888), p. 6.
[2] M.C.P., 5 Nov. 1850. McClintock's Report, 30 Sept. 1850. N.A.G.
[3] C.O. 111/327. *The Berbice Gazette*, 20 July 1859.
[4] Rodway, *A History of British Guiana*, II, 28.
[5] CW/04/3/1. Mary Davson to Penn, 27 June 1848. C.M.S.A.
[6] M.C.P., 16 July 1869. 'Observations of Sawkins', 20 Apr. 1869. N.A.G.

all day. Their possessions, few but meaningful to them, the *matapie*, a cylindrical cassava squeezer, cassava graters, baskets, pots, hammocks, pegalls, the Indian 'trunk' made from the stems of palm, their paddles, possibly pepper-pot in the buck-pots, and cassava bread on the roof, are never disturbed.

As among most primitive cultivators of the soil, land is sacred. Although Miguel Angel Asturias and Ciro Alegría probe the mind of the Central American and the Peruvian Indian in their respective novels, *Hombres de Maiz* and *La Serpente de Oro*,[1] they express also the sentiments of the Amerindian of Guyana who does have a feeling of oneness with nature and the land. Thus he burns only enough bush needed for a clear field to plant his cassava, and in felling trees he makes a propitiatory offering to their spirits which might harm his crops.[2]

Hospitality is a hallmark of Amerindian culture. Once welcomed into the Amerindian's hut, everything he possesses is at one's service. To refuse to share his food and drink is to insult him; to eat and drink with him is to forge bonds. This custom is somewhat similar to that of the Maori's, in which a gift, including food, binds the recipient to the donor,[3] and, also, to the Brahmins', in whose society the gift of food forms such 'an irrevocable link' that 'a man does not eat with his enemy'.[4] Once a friend, the Indian is always a friend, as the early Dutch settlers realized, and he is grateful for every kindness. However, if treated discourteously, he becomes an enemy and his revengeful nature is felt. Hilhouse, who understood the Indians so well after years of close living with them, stated that 'time and unremitting kindness alone opens the door of his [the Indian's] affections', and warned the local government that 'the Executive that has once been forced to deviate from the least article of faith pledged to the Indians, has irrevocably lost all claim to their truth and confidence'.[5] How correct was Marcel Mauss in his observations of primitive people that 'Men could pledge their honour long before they could sign their names'.[6]

The Dutch, in their meeting of cultures, were well aware of this 'code of honour' among the 'naked denizens of the forests'. Through expediency—the desire to trade peacefully—they gave the Indians

---

[1] See Jean Franco, *The Modern Culture of Latin America*, Penguin Books (London, 1970), pp. 125–7.   [2] Gillin, p. 334.
[3] Marcel Mauss, *The Gift. Forms and Functions of Exchange in Archaic Societies*, trans. Ian Cunnison (London, 1970), p. 10.
[4] Ibid., p. 58.   [5] Hilhouse, *Indian Notices*, p. 129.   [6] Mauss, p. 36.

assurances of their faith in the treaties of peace and friendship which they signed with the Arawaks, Warraus, Akawois, and the Caribs. Not only political and economic, but also social bonds were forged and flourished between the Dutch and the Indians. There are innumerable references in all official records, as well as in the eye-witness accounts of travellers, of these relationships between the Dutch and the Indians. William Hilhouse observed: 'The secret attachment between the old Dutch proprietors and the Indians consisted in colonists taking Indian women for their housekeepers; and of course acquiring some knowledge of their language and becoming what may be termed "broomstick relations." '[1] Gromweagle, one of the early Dutch settlers in 1616 who was supposed to have erected the fort at Kyk-over-al, owed his success in gaining the confidence of the Indians to his marriage with a Carib.[2]

The lists of names of men, women, and children compiled by the postholders during the early period of the British administration for the purpose of estimating the number and cost of presents showed a constant recurrence of Dutch names among all Indian tribes, namely, Jan, Cornelius, Pieter, Hans, Hendrik, Cornelia, Johanna, Kaatje.[3] The Superintendent of Rivers and Creeks for Demerara, Robert King, reported to the Governor and the Court of Policy that the Indians in the Mahaica, Mahaicony, and Boeraserie creeks spoke chiefly Dutch creole.[4] So too did many Indians throughout the colony.

But even though the Dutch mingled with the Indians, closely allied in friendship for trade and protection from their runaway slaves, their culture, like that of the British afterwards, touched but never merged. For it was not cultural interest but self-interest which bound the Dutch to the Indians during the seventeenth and eighteenth centuries. In the early nineteenth century it was also self-interest which made the British aware of the 'benighted and barbarous brethren of the interior'[5] who continued to capture the

[1] Hilhouse, *Indian Notices*, p. 12.

[2] im Thurn, 'Essequibo, Berbice and Demerara under the Dutch', *Timehri*, II (1883) 60–3.

[3] Lists of Indian Chiefs, Pomeroon, 16 Mar. 1818; Return of Indians on the River Berbice, 1825. N.A.G. The British also gave their own names to the Indians, as the Indians never divulged their tribal names to outsiders. They believed that names formed an integral part of their identity and if such knowledge were shared, others would be able to wield power over them.

[4] M.C.P., 8 Jan. 1839. Report of Robert King. N.A.G.

[5] The Editorial of *The Guiana Chronicle*, 1 Feb. 1837. N.A.G.

runaway Negro slaves for the new masters of their territory. For such services the British, like the Dutch before them, paid the Indians an annual subsidy as well as triennial presents, allowances, and rations 'as a retaining fee for their fidelity and friendship'.[1]

[1] Extract from the Note Book of His Honour Charles Wray, President of the Court of Criminal and Civil Justice of the Colonies of Demarara and Essequibo. Trial of Billy William, 28 Feb. 1831. Evidence of the Protector of Indians, A. van Ryck de Groot. N.A.G.

II

THE DUTCH AND BRITISH POLICY OF INDIAN SUBSIDY: A SYSTEM OF ANNUAL AND TRIENNIAL PRESENTS

F IRST advertised by Sir Walter Raleigh in 1595 in his *Discoverie of the Large Rich and Bewtiful Empyre of Guiana*, the territory of Guiana on the northern coast of South America was a golden magnet to adventurers on the hunt for instant riches. Not finding gold, the European adventurers resigned themselves to trading with the native Indians and made sporadic attempts to settle—'fighting the climate, the jungle, and the Indians'.[1] By the late sixteenth century the Dutch had gained a foothold in Guiana and between 1613 and the Treaty of Munster 1648, the Dutch settlements stretched along the coast from the River Maroni in the east to the Barima in the west.[2]

In 1631, while the Netherlands were at war with Spain, the charter of the Dutch West India Company was granted, designating the Orinoco as the westernmost limit of the territorial and trade monopoly. Regulations issued by the States General of the United Netherlands on 16 July 1627 authorized Dutchmen 'to sail westward of that Oronoque and do all hostilities and damage to the King of Spain'.[3] It was obvious that to the Dutch the 1494 Treaty of Tordesillas meant nothing more than a 'scrap of paper'.

As early as 1599 the Dutch had settled on the Essequibo River at Fort Kyk-over-al or See-over-all and later at Cartabo on the opposite bank. The end of the seventeenth century saw three well-established settlements along the Essequibo, Pomeroon, and Moruka rivers. Because of their progress, these settlements soon

[1] Gordon Ireland, *Boundaries, Possessions and Conflicts in South America* (Massachusetts, 1938), p. 230.
[2] *Documents and Correspondence Relating to the Question of Boundary between British Guiana and Venezuela. No. 1, 1896* (London, 1896), p. 2.
[3] C.O. 884/4. *British Guiana Boundary.* Précis of Documents from the Hague Archives. West Indian 61. Sept. 1888.

attracted immigrants and promised to become some of the most flourishing plantations in America.[1] None were more aware than the Dutch of the potentialities of these settlements. In 1674 the Charter of the West India Company was renewed by the States-General—the western limit of the Company's jurisdiction still fixed at the River Orinoco. On the other side of the Orinoco were the Spaniards with whom the Indian tribes had a somewhat ambivalent relationship.

Unlike the Dutch, who were more interested in trade than proselytization, the Spaniards looked on the Indians as souls to be Christianized, civilized, and duly chastised in the process. For the dual purpose of Christianization and civilization, the Spanish missionaries who formed the vanguard of Spain's colonial ventures, insisted that the Indians be brought out of their natural habitat and made to live in the missionary settlements. Here they could be chastised for their own salvation whenever they deviated from civilized Christian behaviour. Yet Spanish reports showed that the Indians were cramped by this type of living which they felt to be a 'mode of subjection', and escaped into the interior whenever the opportunity presented itself.[2] Isolation—unwanted isolation—proved a hindrance to amicable Spanish–Indian relations.

What was the key to the rapport between the Dutch and the Indian tribes who were, for the most part, hostile to the Spaniards?[3] The Dutch exerted themselves to foster good relations with the native tribes. This policy was one of pure expediency; success in trade and containment of their Negro slaves could rest only on the friendliness of the Indians who were familiar with the terrain and very much masters in their own land. Travellers to this part of the world were struck by this difference between the Spanish and Dutch policy. Depons, writing in 1806, observed how carefully the Dutch strove to maintain alliance and friendship with the Caribs, one of the most hostile tribes. He felt that they succeeded well in this because they never imposed on the Indians the rigid and troublesome morality

[1] Ibid.
[2] F.O. 420/27B. *Translation of Spanish Documents Relating to the Boundary Dispute Between British Guiana and Venezuela: 1597–1875, 1896*, pp. 8 and 43. The Governor of Guyana, Miguel Marmión, to the Secretary of State, Don Antonio de Valdes, 22 Sept. 1789, writes of the Indians as 'a people without civilization, nor subordination, lovers of their independence and liberty, which the enemy (the Dutch) would undoubtedly offer so as to attract them to their side'.
[3] Ibid.

of the Spaniards, but made allowance for the differences in their manners and habits.[1]

Summing up the situation, the shrewd, businesslike Dutch mapped out a definite policy towards the Indians for the purpose of their internal and external security:

(1) Treaties of alliance and friendship were made with the Indian chiefs.

(2) A system of annual presents was established for services rendered by the Indians.

(3) 'Postholders' were stationed at various posts to hold the area, to foster good relations with the Indians, to attach them to the posts, and to lead them in slave-catching expeditions.[2]

In a 'terra incognita' surrounded by restless Negro slaves on one hand, and the Spanish on the other, it was vital for survival for the Dutch to secure the support of the native tribes. Rodway gave due credit to the Indians for preventing Guiana from falling into Spanish hands in this early period of its history.[3]

There are records of treaties made with the Indians as early as 1672. These were mainly treaties of friendship incorporating promises that the Indians would not be reduced to slavery.[4] At the beginning of the eighteenth century some Captains of the Schotjes (family of Arawaks whose chief was named Schot) were sent to the Netherlands to conclude Treaties of Peace with the Dutch. It was noted that they 'were well-received and sent back with presents and with clothes and handsome furnishings'.[5] Hartsinck mentioned treaties of friendship which the Dutch had made with the Arawaks and Warraus, the Akawois and the Caribs around 1769.[6] The Council of Ten at Amsterdam constantly enjoined the colonial authorities that the friendship of the Indians should at all times be

[1] François Depons, *A Voyage to the Eastern Part of Terra Firma on the Spanish Main in South America, during the Years 1801, 1802, 1803 and 1804*, III (New York, 1806), 258–9. See also James Rodway, 'The Old Boundary of Essequibo', *Timehri* (1895), 344.

[2] Im Thurn, 'Essequibo, Berbice and Demerara Under the Dutch', *Timehri*, II (1883–4), 42–3.

[3] Rodway, 'Indian Policy of the Dutch', *Timehri*, X (1896), 34–5.

[4] *Tribunal of Arbitration between Great Britain and the U.S. of Venezuela, 1899, Proceedings*, i. 200.

[5] Ibid.   [6] Hartsinck, I, 289–90.

cultivated.[1] Both the Dutch officials on the spot in Guiana and the Directors of the West India Company in the Netherlands acknowledged their reliance on the Indians, and in various proclamations and resolutions gave protection and privileges to the tribes.[2]

No Dutch official realized the importance of alliance and friendship with the Indians more than Laurens Storm van's Gravesande, Director-General of Essequibo from 1743 to 1772. During these years of his administration he did much to consolidate Dutch policy. The use of Indians for both trade and defence became the main feature of Dutch colonization in the territory. The following dispatch of 1769 to the Directors of the Company both illustrates and sums up his expedient policy:

> There is no one, Your Honours, who is more convinced how advantageous and necessary the friendship of the Indians is to this colony, because so long as we are fortunate to have them living around us we are quite safe inland, and have nothing to fear concerning the desertion of our slaves. I therefore neglect no possible opportunity of cultivating their friendship and protecting them from all ill-treatment and tyranny of the whites as far as it is expedient to do, and in this way I have made myself so beloved of them that I can now get them to do whatever I wish.[3]

This pragmatic and diplomatic policy of the Dutch reaped its reward during the 1763 Berbice Slave Rebellion, a Negro revolt against their Dutch masters. The journal of the Governor of Berbice, W. J. van Hoogenheim, is replete with references of Dutch reliance on the Indians, who acted as patrols, scouts, and couriers between Cuffy, leader of the revolt and his rebels, and the Dutch. The chiefs of the Caribs, Arawaks, and Akawois led attacks against the rebels, killing as well as capturing many.[4] This assistance given

---

[1] N. Darnell Davis, 'The Records of British Guiana', *Timehri*, II (June 1888), 348–9.
[2] Ibid.   [3] Gravesande, I, 88.
[4] *Journal of W. J. van Hoogenheim*. Kept since the Revolution of the Negro slaves in Rio Berbice begun 28 February 1763. Transcribed and translated by Barbara L. Blair (Mrs. J. D. Bangs) and read in comparison with the original Dutch by Jeremy Dupertius Bangs (Typescript, University of Guyana Library, Georgetown, Guyana, 1973), pp. 49–50, 58–90, 95–133, 155–65, 182–92, 204, 215, 232, 259. See also, 'The Story of the Slave Rebellion in Berbice 1762', Trans. from J. J. Hartsinck, *Beschrijving van Guiana* (Amsterdam, 1770), by Walter E. Roth. MS. in University of Guyana Library. Also trans. W. E. Roth in *Journal of British Guiana Museum and Zoo*, Nos. 20–7. For other accounts of the Slave Rebellion see Gravesande, II, 438; Netscher, pp. 90–120; Bolingbroke, p. 130.

to the Dutch at a critical time 'proved of the greatest importance for the quelling of the rebellion in Berbice, and at the same time rendered Essequibo and Demerary free from the extension of the rising into their area'.[1] Again in 1772 when the slaves of P. C. Hooft revolted, killing both his wife and himself and other planters, and setting fire to houses on plantations, 300 Caribs came to the rescue.[2] During both these revolts the Indians rendered invaluable service and were the chief means of crushing them. They, therefore, formed the 'resistance movement' for the Dutch against the Spaniards to the west and the Negroes within the territory.

As a reward for these services presents were liberally shared out to the Indians. After the 1772 uprising, suppressed by the Indians under Captain van der Heyden, the Indian chiefs were given 'blue drill, combs, corals, mouth organs, and looking glasses' by the colonial authorities.[3] In 1774 the Court of Policy suggested that in order to cement the bond of unity between the Dutch and the Indians, staves of office should be presented to the chiefs. First awarded in 1778, these staves became symbols of a chieftainship under the Dutch. They were prized by the Indian chiefs, and this practice was very advantageously carried on by the British in the following century.[4] In a letter dated 1783 from the Directors of the Company to the officials in the colony, stipulations were laid down to maintain the favour of the Indians, especially the Caribs. Land was to be given them so that they might be induced to remain in one place, presents were to be distributed at regular intervals, and the Captains or Owls were to be provided with silver-headed sticks of office engraved with the Arms of the Company, and with silver collars and rum among other things.[5] As the desertions among the Negroes increased, the Indians were more and more utilized in the

[1] Netscher, p. 98.

[2] *B.G.B.* IV. No. 511. 'Director-General, Essequibo to the West India Co., 29 August 1772', 105.

[3] Ibid. No. 515. 'Extract from the Register of Resolutions of the Honourable the Representative of his Highness and Directors of the Chartered West India Co. . . . held at Amsterdam, Tuesday, April 6, 1773', 108.

[4] Ibid., p. 103. Several staves of office were exhibited before the Hague Tribunal in 1899 to prove the early jurisdiction of the Dutch over the Indians. In a letter written by the Roman Catholic pastor of the Morocco Mission in 1837 to the Governor of British Guiana, Sir James Carmichael Smyth, the Revd. Hermant mentioned the dissatisfaction of the Indians of Morocco with the women of the late Captain Juan, because they had taken away the '*Batton de Capitan*' which amongst them is as the sceptre in the hands of the King'. N.A.G.

[5] Rodway, *A History of British Guiana* (Georgetown, 1894), II, 28.

bush expeditions for their capture. This development led to the adoption of a regular system of presents shared out by the postholders.[1]

Undoubtedly and irrefutably, as the records illustrate, the Indians accepted the jurisdiction of the Dutch. Thus, when the colonies were ceded to the British in 1803 and the Terms of Capitulation confirmed by the Convention in London in 1814, the Indians recognized the British as heirs to the Dutch. Very early they presented themselves to the new authorities and claimed the same privileges they had enjoyed under the Dutch. They were certainly within their rights as the Articles of Capitulation showed.[2] In 1782, when the three rivers, the Essequibo, the Demerara, and the Berbice were first captured by the British, Lieutenant Colonel Kingston wrote to his Majesty's Government, suggesting that the British follow Dutch policy regarding the Indians.[3] Even when the colonies were tossed back and forth in bewildering rotation between the French and the British, and the British and the Dutch, the policy remained unswerving. Dutch postholders continued in office for the necessary communication with, and protection of the Indians.

The first decade of the nineteenth century found the British the new masters of the Guiana territory by right of conquest, later ratified by the Treaty of London in 1814. There were many items on the agenda for administering the new colonies, and that of Indian policy did not appear to be noticed at first. From an anonymous memorial written in 1802 regarding the colonies of Essequibo and Demerara, it was noted that since the English had taken over the colonies, the Indians had retired farther inland, 'because they got no encouragement . . . received no presents, and obtained no signs of that esteem and friendship on which they prided themselves upon being held by the Dutch'.[4] These observations were supported by a letter of Colonel Hislop, Commander of Berbice, Essequibo, and Demerara to Lord Hobart, the Secretary of State, at the King's request giving information on the position and circumstances of the colonies in June 1802. Colonel Hislop enumerated the Indian tribes living in the interior but pointed out that now they rarely appeared, and from this it could be 'apprehended that this Circumstance has

[1] Id., 'Indian Policy of the Dutch', *Timehri*, X (1896) 19.
[2] C.O. 112/4. 'Laws of Capitulation signed between England and the Batavian Republic, 10th September, 1803.'
[3] C.O. 111/1. Colonel Robert Kingston to Lord George Germain, 18 July 1782.
[4] C.O. 111/4. Hague, *West India Papers*, vol. 2010.

49

arisen from dissatisfaction'.[1] It was obvious that the Indians were dissatisfied that the new rulers had failed to notice them and acknowledge their contribution to the political security of the country. As a military leader, Hislop realized the value of the Indians—their knowledge of the terrain, their skill and ability, which would prove as invaluable to the British as they had to the Dutch, especially in keeping the Negroes under control. Thus he advised the home government: 'It would be better Policy to keep these People in good humour and as their Wants are but few and of the most trivial description their attachment may be secured at a very small expense.'[2]

Undoubtedly, there was much wisdom and prudence in Hislop's advice, especially as the abolition of the slave trade was in the air, and the numbers of deserting Negroes were on the increase. Hunting the 'bush Negroes' became the sport of the day and no success was possible without the help of the most excellent of trackers, the Indians. The price had to be paid in presents and supplies to the natives who in one sense could be called the military allies of the British, as they had been to the Dutch. In 1802 9,000,000 guilders were voted for presents for the 'bucks'; in 1804 £110 were paid out of the King's Chest to one Henry Lookey for making two silver medals with chains for 'the Bucks or Indians at the Post of Morocco,[3] and in 1805 2,500 guilders were placed on the estimate for gratuities or occasional presents to the Indians.[4] The Minutes of the Court of Policy affirmed that 'the British policy was to assure the Indians of the friendly disposition of the Government and of the colony to-

[1] C.O. 111/4. Hague, *West India Papers*, vol. 2010. 'Remarks and Observations relating to the Colonies of Berbice, Demerara, and Essequibo . . .'

[2] Ibid.

[3] C.O. 111/5. Expenditure of the King's Chest since the surrender of the Colonies to H.M. Forces, 20 Sept. 1803.

The amount of guilders to the pound sterling fluctuated between 12 and 14. The prefix f to sums of money meant the number of guilders or florins; the letter s—the number of stivers. Colonial currency under the British was a mixture of Dutch guilders, British pounds, and dollars and cents. By proclamation on 8 Sept. 1825 British coins—half-crown, shilling, sixpence, one and a half penny, and farthing—became legal tender. (See the *Local Guide of British Guiana, 1832*, pp. 408–10.) The decimal system of dollars and cents was introduced by Ordinance No. 8 of 1839. It was also enacted that guilders, stivers, and pennings should no longer be considered as monies of account of British Guiana. (See the *Local Guide of British Guiana, 1843*, p. 353.) Despite this Ordinance calculations in guilders continued, and not until 1900 were the guilders and other coins abolished by Ordinance No. 8 of 1900. (See *The British Guiana Directory and Almanack* (Daily Chronicle, 1902).)

[4] C.O. 111/6. Estimate of Ordinary or Permanent Revenue and Expenditure of the Sovereign's Chest in Essequibo and Demerary.

wards them'.[1] The motives behind this friendly policy were neither altruistic nor humanitarian, but purely pragmatic and expedient.

The officials who carried out this policy and led the famous 'bush expeditions' were the Protectors and Postholders of the Indians. Outstanding among such officials was Charles Edmonstone, Protector, 'an intrepid leader of bush expeditions' who commanded fifteen such expeditions and for his services was presented with a sword and silver urn by the Governor and the Court of Policy, plus the added bonus of having his property freed from taxation.[2]

Bush expeditions were extremely important episodes in the early history of Guiana. These expeditions, undertaken by the military with strong and invaluable support by the Indians, underlined five significant points:

(1) that there was continuous resistance to the system of slavery;
(2) that the planters feared the loss of their labour and, above all, attacks on their life and property;
(3) that it was imperative to keep up friendly relations with the Indians who, with their knowledge of the terrain, were the only ones able to locate and contain the runaways;
(4) that the Negroes were by no means the helpless children they were made out to be; that the bush communities indicated that the Negroes were quite able to organize, to govern, and to provide for themselves;
(5) that the cost of these military reconnaissance and capturing expeditions placed a heavy burden on the colonies.

The records of the innumerable desertions of Negroes from the estates, sometimes in large groups, sometimes small, completely destroy the myth of apathy and lethargy among the Negroes, and the bizarre notion that, after years of subjugation they became content with their lot—content to conform. The desertions, and the establishment of bush settlements in the Guiana territory, illustrate that resistance to the slave system was chronic.

To escape the brutality of enslavement, to escape even when the treatment was not unduly harsh, forms a vast part of the history

[1] C.O. 114/6. M.C.P., 26 Oct. 1807.
[2] Waterton, p. 244. Governor H. L. Carmichael praised Edmonstone to the Colonial Secretary 'as a gentleman highly esteemed by the whole Colony, and for whom the different natives have great respect and affection, having served under him with fidelity in a very dangerous insurrection in the year 1795'. Carmichael to Earl Bathurst, 13 June 1813. N.A.G.

of the plantation society, not only in Guiana but in the West Indian islands, Brazil, and the United States, wherever slavery was entrenched. In Guiana slaves deserted and ran into the bush, hence bush Negroes; their destination was the Orinoco by various routes—the Cuyuni, Moruca-Waini, and along the Atlantic sea-coast. These deserters to the Orinoco region only served to increase the tension between the Spanish and the Dutch. The Spanish constantly refused to return the runaway slaves, claiming that they had baptized them and that baptism made them both Christian and Spanish! Not that the Negroes or the Dutch accepted such an explanation. The result of constant desertions was a loss of labour, and a loss of labour meant a loss of profits. The Director-General of Essequibo complained to the West India Co.: 'The number of our slaves there [Orinoco] now is very large . . . Those belonging to private colonists are innumerable. The numbers of the runaways increasing daily, this matter will end in the total ruin of a great many plantations, unless efficacious remedies be adopted.'[1]

If the desertions caused the planters grave concern, the bush-Negro communities made them even more fearful. Gravesande reported in 1744 that there were at least 300 bush Negroes in large encampments in the north-west area of the Essequibo.[2] Pinckard stated that by 1795 there were at least eight extensive settlements in the Demerara.[3] The stream of letters written by the Director-General to the West India Co. showed that the planters were frantic. The planters' fear of armed insurrection planned between the bush Negroes and their brethren still on the plantations was no groundless fear. In 1795 there was a strong possibility of such an occurrence. Not only for desertion, but for prevention of both desertion and attack, stringent and brutal laws were passed. The plantation owners were given *carte blanche* for the infliction of punishment. The whip was the regular instrument used both as a preventive and a cure. The punishment on capture was a horrible variety of branding, cutting off of ears, breaking at the wheel, and hanging. But despite these harsh measures the Negroes continued to run away.

[1] *B.G.B.* App. IV, 101. No. 505. Director-General of Essequibo to the West India Co., 6 Jan. 1772.
[2] *United States Commission on Boundary between Venezuela and British Guiana. Report and Accompanying Papers*, II. Gravesande to the West India Co., 1 Apr. 1744, 302.
[3] George Pinckard, *Notes on the West Indies* (London, 1806), II, 247–8.

So to capture the deserters and ferret out the bush communities the bush expeditions were organized. The military was at a disadvantage in the bush in which one could easily be lost and be captured instead of capture. Here the reliance on the Indians was total. Their familiarity with the forest, and their expertise in guerilla warfare were key advantages.

The first three decades of the nineteenth century saw the local government extremely concerned for the internal security of the colonies. This concern was fully illustrated in the monies voted by the Court of Policy in payment to the Indians for their services, as well as for rations and various supplies, especially rum liberally shared out to induce the Indians to remain at the posts. In November 1806 the Court of Policy resolved:

. . . that for the right hand of every runaway Negroe that shall be killed during the Expedition now in Contemplation, shall be paid the Sum of one hundred guilders *as a premium* out of the Colonial Chest. For every Bush negroe who shall be taken and secured alive and who shall have been less than two years in the Bush a premium of Two hundred guilders. . . . The above mentioned premiums to be divided among the Indians or negroes who are employed in the Expedition, and who Shall have taken or Shot such runaway Negroes.[1]

Although trusty Negroes were used to hunt their fellowmen on these expeditions, the Indians were preferred. As valuable presents were given to them, 'their services could be justly required'.[2]

But the Indians did not always receive the promised, much less prompt payment, neither did they hesitate to claim remuneration for their services. Governor Bentinck (1809–12) reminded the Court of Policy that it 'was indispensably necessary to give Indians promised payment for their help in scouring the woods for negroes'. The Court agreed, but like all financial bodies, were always reluctant to vote funds even for necessary and vital policies. They accepted the principle of payment, but always baulked on the practice. Many instances were brought before the Court by the Protectors who presented the claims of the Indians.[3] The reports, returns, and memorials of both Protectors and Postholders to the Governor and Court of Policy were usually requests for the annual subsidies which in some years were never received. In his memorial to the Court in 1810, the Protector, Charles Edmonstone, drew attention to the

[1] C.O. 114/7. M.C.P., 24 Nov. 1806.   [2] Ibid.
[3] Ibid., M.C.P., 20, 28, and 30 Apr. 1807.

fact that the Indians had complained to him 'that they were grieved to find that they were not treated with that consideration by the British Government that they were by the Dutch as they do not receive the *presents* they used to have from the Dutch Government'.[1]

Finally in August 1811 the Court stipulated a set annual payment to be made to the Indians employed at the Post of Morocco and all other posts as follows:

For each man:

1 piece Salempore	3 knives	4 fishhooks
3 hatchets	1 comb	1 pr. scissors
3 cutlasses	1 razor	1 tinder box
1 looking glass	2 flints	1 lb. coral

For each woman:

4 ells Salempore	1 lb. coral
1 cutlass	1 knife
1 pr. scissors	1 looking glass[2]

Governor Bentinck seemed bent on working out a systematic policy similar to that of the Dutch regarding Indian presents. Later in 1811 the Governor requested that the Protectors and Postholders present him with an accurate statement of the number of male and female Indians attached to their respective posts, including other relevant information in order to enable the Court at the next session to decide on the subject of procuring most economically the articles to be distributed annually to the Indians settled at, or attached to, the Posts.[3] Bentinck next submitted his report to the Court, giving the estimated cost for ordering the annual supply of presents for the Indians as 30,000 guilders, to which he was willing to contribute 18,000 from the funds under his immediate administration.[4] The Court agreed to insert the sum on the budget or List of Colonial Expenditures for the ensuing year, accepting the charge of 12,000 guilders for the probable amount of the Colony's share in the purchase of these presents. Under Governor Bentinck, both the Court of Policy and the Combined Court agreed on the expediency of voting money for Indian presents.

[1] M.C.P., 31 Oct. 1810. N.A.G.
[2] M.C.P., 1 Aug. 1811. N.A.G. Salempore was a blue cotton cloth made in India and exported as a slave cloth to the West Indies; it was also given to the Amerindians.
[3] M.C.P., 29 Oct. 1811, N.A.G.
[4] M.C.P., 16 Nov., 1811. N.A.G.

In a letter to H. C. Underwood, an agent in England, Bentinck sent a list of the articles required for the Indians, stating that in the present situation (constant rebelliousness of the Negroes) 'presents to the Indians are of the greatest consequence . . . the articles would satisfy them at once and keep them in good Humour'.[1] Before the year was over, however, Bentinck had been recalled and the Acting Governor Hugh Lyle Carmichael had different ideas about the system, possibly because early in his administration the warlike Caribs had appeared in Georgetown demanding the promised presents. Carmichael protested to the Colonial Office that *he* did not conceive that his powers of acting-governor gave him any *carte blanche* to give annual presents to the Indians. Above all, he feared that what the Indians received now with gratitude they might later demand as an 'unalienable right'.[2] The Under-Secretary of State for the Colonies, H. Goulbourn, immediately wrote a peremptory letter to Bentinck, then in England, asking him the nature of his promise and by what authority he had pledged the Government to an annual supply of presents to the Indians.[3] It seems incredibly odd that the Under-Secretary should be so much in the dark on this matter when the Lords in Council at Whitehall had given permission for the export of two tons of gunpowder included in Bentinck's list. Perhaps the letter had not yet reached his desk. To Goulbourn's query Bentinck gave a comprehensive reply, pointing out the practical reasons which induced him to adopt such a policy. For example, the blacks numbered 60,000 (slaves) in comparison to a white population of 2,000 dispersed along the coast. This fact made it 'absolutely indispensible for the Governor to have the Indians at his command'.[4] In this he was only following Dutch precedent. Presents had been sent by the Dutch Government in Holland and shared out in 1802 by Governor Meertens, who had been given positive orders to keep up the greatest friendship with the Indians. Under Governor Beaujon's administration, 1804–5, presents had also been given, because in the present state of the colony, the Indians were the only check upon the runaways; the only way to be assured of their help was 'to woo them with presents—independent of what the Colony allows their Protectors to purchase for them'.[5]

[1] C.O. 111/14. Governor H. W. Bentinck to H. C. Underwood, Esq., 7 Feb. 1812.
[2] C.O. 111/13. Acting Governor H. L. Carmichael to the Earl of Liverpool, 15 July 1812.
[3] C.O. 112/4. Henry Goulbourn to Bentinck, 15 Oct. 1812.
[4] C.O. 111/14. Bentinck to Goulbourn, 17 Oct. 1812.   [5] Ibid.

In conclusion, Bentinck also reminded the Colonial Office that the Indians had been the saving of the colony at two different revolts of the Negroes.[1]

Bentinck was more aware of the local situation than a Colonial Office thousands of miles removed from the scene. In East Florida his contemporary, the Spanish Governor Enrique White, had considered a 1797 Royal Order from Spain forbidding the continuation of annual presents to the Indians 'an unwise policy', which might cause the withdrawal of Indian allegiance from the Spanish and result in an expensive warfare.[2] He even jeopardized his official existence by counteracting the 1797 Ordinance (to cut off the annual presents) claiming that 'Avoiding the possibility of an Indian uprising in the province was more important than absolute obedience to a royal command'.[3] The King and Council of State accepted the *fait accompli* for its prudent wisdom. It seemed that the Colonial Office had forgotten that before the American Revolution it was an integral part of the policy of the British Crown to make annual presents to the North American Indians, a policy adopted by all colonizing powers as a method of obtaining Indian support.

Although Governor Carmichael was given permission to distribute the presents requested by his predecessor, Bentinck, the Colonial Office agreed with Carmichael's opinion that the giving of presents to the Indians placed the Government in the somewhat anomalous position of paying 'tribute' to their native subjects. Britain's unquestioned command of the seas and her successful campaigns in the Peninsular War enhanced her power and military glory. In this moment of pride, it was unthinkable that such a nation should kow-tow to the natives of a small colony in South America. The Dutch, on the other hand, had been in a position of minor strength and needed the co-operation of their Indian allies. Future policy regarding the Indians was outlined in an official communique thus: 'His Majesty's Government will not forget their services but presents received in the future were to be considered as a boon and not as a right, as a reward for their past good conduct rather than as a purchase of their future friendship.'[4] The Colonial Office advised Carmichael to scotch any hope of annual or regular presents

---

[1] C.O. 111/14. Bentinck to Goulbourn, 17 Oct. 1812.
[2] Richard K. Murdock, 'Indian Presents: To Give or not to Give', *Florida Historical Quarterly*, xxxv (1956–7), 335.
[3] Ibid.   [4] C.O. 112/4. Bathurst to Carmichael, 25 Nov. 1812.

the Indians might have, especially if there were no evidence of any treaty made with the Indians.[1] It seemed that Carmichael did enquire into the possibility of such treaties, for two months later, Charles Edmonstone informed him that, although on various occasions he called up the Indians to assist the Government, he: 'knew of no Treaty, nor agreement with the Chiefs of Indian Tribes, implying any thing of the nature of Subsidy or tribute; nor . . . was ever authorised by this Government, to make any promise of the Kind . . .'[2] Yet Edmonstone conceded that presents were made by the Dutch and expected by the Indians.

The Combined Court, ever eager to rid themselves of the financial burden of presents to the Indians, agreed at their meeting on 19 November 1812 gradually to decrease the expenditure under the heading 'Indian Establishments', and curtailed the sum for the ensuing year to 20,000 guilders. In the Estimate of Supplies for November 1812–November 1813, occasional expenses for the Indians, general expenses, and the sum for purchasing presents in Europe were listed at 144,000 guilders.[3] This drastic curtailment of funds was explained by Mr. King, a Financial Representative at the following session of the Court, not as a restriction of Indian expenses to a specific sum, but as a move gradually to reduce such expenditure.[4] Ambiguous as Mr. King's statement was, the meaning was clear. The Court felt that such large sums could be put to better purpose. Yet they were aware that it was necessary to maintain a good understanding with the Indians, and in July 1813 a Committee was formed to work out 'a systematic plan for the future government of the Indian establishment, as well as the expenses . . .'[5] No report was forthcoming in the following year. Governor John Murray again brought the attention of the Court to a project for the better government of the Indian establishments, but because of the lateness of the hour discussion 'on such a momentous subject was deferred to the following day'.[6] On the following day and throughout the following weeks no such 'momentous subject' was discussed. The only mention of Indian affairs on the following day, 17 February 1814, was the sum of 25,000 guilders for presents placed on the Estimates for 1814.[7]

[1] Ibid.   [2] C.O. 111/15. Edmonstone to Carmichael, 18 Jan. 1813.
[3] M.C.C., 19 Nov. 1812. N.A.G.   [4] M.C.C., 20 Nov. 1812. N.A.G.
[5] M.C.C., 30 July 1813. N.A.G.   [6] M.C.P., 16 Feb. 1814. N.A.G.
[7] M.C.P., 17 Feb. 1814. N.A.G.

But between the interregnum of Acting Governor H. L. Carmichael and Governor J. Murray, another Acting Governor, Colonel Edward Codd, was faced with a state of rebellion among the Negroes on the Essequibo Coast. Only by an immediate mobilization of the Indians and a promise of presents were the Negroes contained.[1] Codd, through the force of circumstances, changed his opinion given in an earlier communication to the Earl of Bathurst that the Indian system was entirely defective and caused a considerable expense to the Colony as the Indians were for the most part idle, and in no way contributed to the benefit of the Colony.[2] The Court of Policy, once the fear of insurrection was over, forgot their promises of rewards to the Indians and had to be reminded of their obligation by the Pomeroon Protector of Indians, Mr. G. Timmerman. In his memorial to the Court Timmerman stated that 200 Indians had been assembled at different points along the Essequibo Coast and kept there until the danger of revolt had passed, when they were dismissed with promises of rewards for their readiness and goodwill in serving the colony. These rewards had not yet arrived and the Indians had complained to him, threatening never to obey any future orders. The Indians had suffered the inconvenience of having to abandon their cultivation of yams and cassava which, on their return, they found in a state of devastation. He cautioned the Court that the consequences to the colony might be sad, indeed, if the Indians were to refuse military assistance in time of revolt.[3] The Court hedged, by ordering a minute investigation into the services performed by the Indians and what would be considered a fair remuneration for such services.[4] Timmerman spelled out these services to the Court which, it would appear, wanted to remain oblivious to them. The Indians employed to quell the expected disturbances among the Negroes numbered 230. They had been ordered from their homes for nearly five weeks; some had been unable to undertake the return journey from both fatigue and starvation which had caused the death of a few. The least remuneration given should be half a piece of salempore and some other Indian articles to the chiefs. It was but little to pay for their security and the Court was bound to admit it was only just that the Indians should

[1] Colonel Codd to W. Linau, Postholder at Morocco, 14 Nov. 1813. *Letter Book.* N.A.G. Also Codd to Major General J. Murray, Berbice, 9 Nov. 1813. Ibid.

[2] Codd to Bathurst, 6 Sept. 1813. N.A.G.

[3] M.C.P., 1 Nov. 1814. Memorial of G. Timmerman, 25 Oct. 1814. N.A.G.

[4] Ibid.

be paid by the colony for such services. Out of the Colonial Fund they voted the sum of 2,500 guilders.[1]

Throughout the 1820s and until the Emancipation of Slaves in 1833 the Indians rendered valuable military service to the colony and even though there was always the reluctance of the Court of Policy to award special payment to the Indians for such service, sums for such exigencies, apart from those listed for allowances and annual and triennial presents were noted in the Estimates of Expenditure for the United Colony of Demerara and Essequibo, as well as Berbice.[2]

In 1823 the tense situation arising out of rumours that emancipation was imminent erupted in a Slave Revolt at La Resouvenir Estate on the East Coast, Demerara on the 19 August 1823. The Indians were called to town to assist the regular troops. In order to regulate the quartering and provisioning of the assembled tribes, Governor Murray appointed Mr. William Hilhouse, a surveyor and indefatigable champion of the Indians, as Quartermaster-General. This appointment was unceremoniously cancelled by Murray's successor, Sir Benjamin D'Urban in the following year[3] possibly at the instigation of the Protectors who disliked the meddling Hilhouse intensely for his constant and vicious attacks on them and their office. Yet in view of Hilhouse's letters to D'Urban giving unwanted advice on Indian policy, D'Urban had personal reasons for his 'dropping the pilot'. On 26 July 1824 Hilhouse wrote suggesting to D'Urban that a small body of Indians be organized as a permanently armed guard for ensuring the tranquillity and subordination of the Negroes. For the sum of 10,000 guilders he offered to undertake the raising, equipping, and disciplining of a body of fifty able Indians. In the event of the inefficiency or sickness of the regular troops, he would mount Indian guards at the outposts. He, also, undiplomatically and imprudently stated his family connections with different Indian chiefs from whom he had received clubs of command over nearly 1,500 Indians. Moreover he 'had accepted title and rank of Captain from the whole Accaway nation, from the majority of Arrawaks and from all the Caribisee within the limits of the Colony'.[4]

[1] M.C.P., 3 Feb. 1815. N.A.G.
[2] See *Blue Books*, C.O. 116. P.R.O. or N.A.G.
[3] 'Memorandum for the Information of Mr. Hilhouse, 10th August 1824', *Letter Book*. N.A.G.   [4] Hilhouse to D'Urban, 26 July 1824. N.A.G.

It was bad enough to tell a Governor how he should work out military policy, but it was fatal to acquaint him with the fact of such vast power over the Indian tribes at such a critical time. The Governor and the Court of Policy were in no position to discount Hilhouse's claims as gross exaggerations. Like the King of Spain who feared the growing influence of their conquistadores over the Indians in the New World, they were indeed concerned that the power and position of Hilhouse among the warlike Caribs might well prove dangerous to the security of the colony. Indeed, in D'Urban's words, they feared that 'Mr. Hilhouse's influence would unsettle the minds of the Indians and render them dissatisfied'.[1] Hilhouse had not stopped his 'mischievous and inconvenient' meddling and had, over the Governor's head, written direct to the Colonial Office of his ideas on Indian policy. Wilmot Horton, Under-Secretary of State, coldly viewed his proposals in the light of *lèse-majesté* while dismissing them as visionary:

> The subject is one which has attracted and continues to occupy the particular attention of His Majesty's Government; but you must be aware on the slightest consideration, that the specific proposal which you make of appointing an English nobleman as Guardian and Conservator of the Indians, thereby superseding the functions of the Governor of the Colony is a proposal much too visionary to admit of serious observation.[2]

Apparently such an official snub did not stop this Las Casas of British Guiana from continuing to write letters, reports, and memorials on his favourite subject. In an 1829 Report to Sir George Murray, Secretary of State, he enclosed a General Chart of British Guiana from the Corentyne river to the Orinoco, and pointed out the weak defences of the country in the west. An army of 10,000 Spaniards could easily and speedily land on Plantation Richmond on the Essequibo Coast, and 'All the navy of England were useless against such an invasion, and all the armies of Europe against a land invasion by an army of Indians, through the Cuyuny River.'[3] His six proposals included in the report outlined a military brief for the regulation of the Indian population in the Districts of Demerara, Essequibo, and Pomeroon, as well as the proposed expenditure for the Indian military establishment which would save the colony £500. There would be a permanent militia who would act as the *Police of*

---

[1] D'Urban to Wilmot Horton, 16 May 1827. N.A.G.
[2] C.O. 112/6. Wilmot Horton to Hilhouse, 11 Aug. 1826.
[3] C.O. 111/68. Hilhouse to Sir George Murray, 23 Apr. 1829.

the Interior, called the King's Own *Bucks* or Interior Police.[1]
Neither the local government nor the home government heeded the
pleas and plans of that 'eccentric character'[2] for an Indian militia,
as it was felt that the 'Established Authorities of the Colony' were
'quite adequate to the due care and protection of the Indians, and to
conduct the Colonial relations with them . . .'[3] The Indians continued to serve side by side with the regular militia and in 1831 were
rounding up escaped Negroes from the estates on Hog Island,
Wakenaam, and Leguan—islands in the mouth of the Essequibo
river.[4]

During the clash between the Executive and Hilhouse over the
regulation of the Indians for military expediency, supplies of rations
and annual presents continued to be distributed to them both in the
United Colony of Demerara and Essequibo and the separate colony
of Berbice. A return of Indian presents in 1821 showed the numbers
of Indians in the rivers Demerara, Essequibo, and Pomeroon, and
in the Mahaicony and Boeraserie Creeks who received presents, as
well as the types and number of presents distributed among them.
Looking-glasses were the favourite item, 3,888 shared out among
1,603 women which would indicate that the men were not less vain.
The Indians were numbered under the following categories:

Male	*Female*	*Boys & Girls*	*Captains*	*Total*[5]
1,586	1,603	2,257	56	5,502

In the same year, Captain J. V. Mittelholzer, Commandant of the
Indians on the Berbice river, complained to the Council of Government of the Colony of Berbice that the 600 Indians under his command had not received presents since March 1819. This was in
abrogation of the custom of the government of that colony (Berbice)
to give annual presents consisting in salempores, powder shot, cut-
lasses, knives, razors, and other articles. Moreover the Indians, like

---

[1] Ibid. Hilhouse noted that 'Buck is the general appellative of all the Indian Tribes'.
See Appendix II.

[2] Hilhouse was called many names by the Governors and other officials to whom he
was a thorn in the flesh. Not to be outdone, Hilhouse caustically summed up their
characters in brief: 'Governor Murray was a quiet man—Governor D'Urban a high
Tory Gentleman—Governor Smyth was an arbitrary man—Governor Light is not his
own man.' C.O. 116/3. *The Guiana Chronicle*, 27 Mar. 1839.

[3] D'Urban to Wilmot Horton, 16 May 1827. N.A.G.

[4] D'Urban to Major Simson, Commander 1st Battalion, Essequibo Militia, Wakenaam, 2 July 1831. *Letter Book*. N.A.G.

[5] Return of Indian Presents, 20 Mar. 1821. N.A.G.

those in Demerara and Essequibo, threatened that if no payment were given for their services in the bush expeditions, 'they in future will not serve the colony or run the risk of losing their limbs or lives in such services'.[1] Mittelholzer suggested a regular supply of provisions such as a cask of salt fish, a puncheon of rum, a tierce of salt, and 300 lb. of sugar to be shared out among the Indians. These fixed allowances were supplied half-yearly to the Corentyne and Canje Posts. But the distribution of presents lapsed until 1825 when a Committee was formed on the advice of the Governor, then Sir Benjamin D'Urban, to request lists of the Indians from their respective postholders for the apportioning of the articles.[2] Commandant Mittelholzer submitted the Berbice Returns as follows:

Canje Creek	Corentyne River	Berbice River	Total
136	747	709	1,592

stating that, as the Indians had not received presents since 1821, they were all the more expecting extraordinary items. He urged that the thirteen Indian chiefs should be given some special gift to prove their superiority as captains, and they had 'expressed their wish that a Sword for that purpose Should be preferable of anything else'.[3]

At the end of that year, 1825, the Committee distributed the following presents among the Indians as Governor D'Urban had been unable to be present at the distribution:[4]

2 Barrels Gun Powder	695 Jews Harps
15 Bags Shot	422 Buck Knives
500 lbs. Tobacco	1000 Needles
13 Tradesmen Jackets	22 lbs. Thread
13 Tradesmen Hats	700 Combs
174 Cutlasses	105 pieces Salempores
1850 Gun Flints	190 Axes
189 Razors	13 Gross Pipes
248 Scissors	232 Beads
2600 Fish Hooks	

[1] Captain J. V. Mittelholzer to the Council of Government, Berbice, 19 Apr. 1821. N.A.G.

[2] Minutes of the Council of Government, Berbice, 7 July 1825. N.A.G.

[3] Mittelholzer to the Committee of the Honourable Council of Government, 29 July 1825. N.A.G.

[4] Minutes of the Council of Government, Berbice, 11 Jan. 1826. N.A.G. D'Urban asked the Committee to explain to the Indian chiefs that 'Urgent private affairs alone had prevented his presence', 1 Dec. 1825. *Letter Book*. N.A.G.

The Indians were never humbly grateful for the presents which they considered their right. On this occasion they rejected the militia fuses as useless and requested buck guns instead. The Committee procured the buck guns.[1] But as the expenses of the Colony mounted, the Committee recommended to the Council in 1828 that a reduction be made in the expenses for Indian presents.[2] The supplies of fish, rum, salt, and sugar continued every four months until 1834 when the Indian Department of Berbice came under the notice of the Court of Policy, as Berbice had since been united with the other colonies of Demerara and Essequibo in 1831. It was not surprising that the Court of Policy were aghast at the Third Fiscal's Report on the exorbitant sums expended on supplies for the Indians and decreed 'that all further supplies are suspended until further Orders'.[3] Even the Council in Berbice had considered the distribution of Ham, Tongues, and Biscuits among the Indians 'uncalled for'.[4] No doubt the Berbice postholders enjoyed such delicacies!

In 1830 the cost of allowances and rations to the Indians in Demerara and Essequibo had dropped to approximately £594 in comparison with £3,294 ten years before![5] Despite this decrease Lord Goderich, then Secretary of State, questioned the practical utility of such a system out of which no good accrued to the colony. The periodical distribution of presents also led to 'drunkenness and disorder'.[6] Governor D'Urban, promising to transmit a future report on Indian management, disclaimed the occurrence of any disorder during the distribution of the triennial presents. Moreover, as Bentinck had tried to impress on the Colonial Office nineteen years ago, he gave the practical reasons for such a policy—'the Presents so distributed are *very useful to the* Tribes, and a powerful link of amity with them, to which they have been long accustomed, and which . . . could not now be discontinued, without great disadvantage to the Interests of the Colony.'[7] The report which followed included individual returns from the Protectors and postholders showing the amount and cost of rations and supplies given quarterly to the Indians. The average total population composed of the four nations or tribes, namely the Arawaks, the Caribs, the Warraus, and the Akawois between the Boeraserie Creek to the

[1] Ibid., 11 Jan. 1826.   [2] M.C.G.B., 12–16 Sept. 1828. N.A.G.
[3] M.C.P., 24 June 1834. N.A.G.   [4] M.C.G.B., 9 June 1826. N.A.G.
[5] M.C.P., 30 Sept. 1830. N.A.G. and C.O. 111/34 Allowances and Rations, 1820.
[6] C.O. 112/15. Goderich to D'Urban, 19 Mar. 1831
[7] C.O. 111/117. D'Urban to Goderich, 17 Oct. 1831.

Essequibo river, numbered 5,096[1]—a decrease of 406 since 1821. This decrease, the Civil Commissary, James Hackett, attributed to the easy access the Indians had to rum on the sugar estates.[2] But Hackett did not comment on the quantity of rum still lavishly distributed by the postholders to the Indians. In the Schedule of Triennial presents issued to the Demerary and Essequibo Indians in 1830, looking glasses were still the most popular item.[3] The triennial presents cost the colony £2,400 in 1830 and, as D'Urban informed Goderich, '. . . the description of all things furnished has been carefully adapted to their [the Indian] wants, habits, and expectations'.[4] The Colonial Office threw up their hands in horror at the quantities of rum distributed to and consumed by the Indians,[5] but their objection was indeed a voice crying in the wilderness. The supplies of fish and plantain, as well as rum, continued until June 1837 when the Court of Policy notified the postholders that no issues of such supplies would 'in future, be defrayed by the Court'.[6] This order was officially spelled out in Article VI on 'Monies for Indians' in the 1838 Ordinance appointing Superintendents of the Rivers and Creeks in British Guiana in place of the past Protectors of Indians. The newly appointed superintendents were forbidden '. . . to distribute to the Indians, at the public expense, any plantains, salt fish, or spirituous liquors of any kind or description . . .'[7] neither would it 'be lawful to give rum or other spirituous liquor in payment of wages to any Indian or Indians'.[8] Needless to say, as far as the woodcutters were concerned, the latter stipulation was honoured more in the breach than in the observance.

The sums expended for allowances, rations, and presents to the Indians had always plagued both the Court of Policy and the Combined Court.[9] Now with the Damoclean sword of Emancipation hanging over their heads, this stronghold of the plantocracy was in

[1] C.O. 111/117. James Hackett to D'Urban, enclosed in D'Urban to Goderich, 26 Nov. 1831. See Appendix III. [2] Ibid.
[3] Ibid. See Excerpt from Quarterly Return from the Post, Three Friends in the Mahaicony Creek, in Appendix IV.
[4] C.O. 111/117. D'Urban to Goderich, 26 Nov. 1831.
[5] Ibid. H. Taylor's Minute, 17 Feb. 1832. [6] M.C.P., 23 June 1837. N.A.G.
[7] *Local Guide of British Guiana Containing Historical Sketch, Statistical Tables and the entire Statute Law of the Colony in force January 1, 1843* (Demerary, 1843). 'British Guiana. No. 6. 1838. An Ordinance passed by the Governor and the Court of Policy on the 16th day of February, 1838.' N.A.G. [8] Ibid.
[9] C.O. 114/11. M.C.P., 26 May 1831 and M.C.C., 8 Mar. 1831. Also M.C.P., 19 and 20 Nov. 1812. N.A.G.

a frenzied state of anxiety over the impending loss of its free labour. In its eyes every other issue dwindled into insignificance. During this period, which was felt to be one of 'commotion before stagnation', the issue of the Indian subsidy appeared even more irrelevant to the local government. Obviously the Courts had short memories of past services rendered by the Indians for which they had, of course, paid them reluctantly. The home government also had no time for the Indians and brushed aside any involvement in their affairs with a brief note: '. . . that during the progress of the abolition of slavery it will be hardly possible for Her Majesty's Government to devote their attention to the civilization of the Indians.'[1] They were even less concerned over Indian supplies.

Into this picture stepped the new governor of British Guiana, Sir James Carmichael Smyth, who not long after taking office in 1833 expressed his astonishment at the fact that the Indians had 'cost this colony within the last ten years £22,000, or at the rate of £2,000 per annum, for presents.'[2] Early in 1834 he brought the matter before the Court of Policy which asserted that it was entirely a question of policy whether the custom of giving presents to the Indians be continued or not. If they decided on continuing the policy, then it was necessary to make some definite and practical provision for that object before meeting with the Combined Court. Since the past items for 'Allowances and Rations, and Presents' tended only to perpetuate an idle, parasitic community of natives, the term was changed and the new item placed on the Annual Estimates read: 'Provision for promoting Industry amongst the Indians within this territory Demerara—25,000 guilders and in Berbice—5,000 guilders.'[3]

The Combined Court threw out that motion of the Court of Policy and amended it to the more honest one 'for the more efficient appropriation of the Indian Posts with reference to the internal security of the Colony—25,000 guilders.'[4]

Already in 1831 annual presents had been discontinued. The reaction of the Indians to this move was recorded in a letter of the Revd. J. Hynes, a Roman Catholic priest to Governor Carmichael Smyth. He described the Indians as being greatly incensed and

[1] C.O. 112/18. Stanley to J. C. Smyth; 20 Aug. 1833.
[2] 'Minute of H.E., the Lt. Governor, . . . 14 December, 1833', *Letter Book*. N.A.G.
[3] C.O. 114/14. M.C.P., 8 Mar. 1834. Also in N.A.G.
[4] M.C.C., 16 Apr. 1834. N.A.G.

expressing strong resentment over the discontinuance of the annual presents. Some of the most intelligent among them were heard to declare that if the Negroes revolted, they would assist them instead of fighting against them. Moreover, the Indians affirmed that 'the whites have done them no service; the country is theirs—they have their own laws and wish not the whites to govern them'.[1] Indeed, this was an early manifestation of the 'White man, go home' feeling. Hynes correctly gauged this reaction of the Indians to be extremely dangerous, and if the threats were acted upon, the peace and well-being of the colony would be seriously affected.[2]

Military expediency and internal security again won the day for the Indians. Hynes's letter was seriously considered, and the Governor urged the Court that it would be 'sound policy on the part of the Colonial Government particularly at this time, rather to encourage the friendly disposition of the Indians than by total neglect of them incite their resentment'.[3] 'This time' was one of great Negro unrest—a time of the apprenticeship system or the period of gradual abolition of slavery which did not end until August 1838. The Negroes were free but not freed; possibilities of rebellion were very much in the air. Earlier in March 1834 a Committee of Indian Affairs had been appointed to discuss ways and means of giving a new direction to the Indian Establishment. As this committee was soon due to report, Indian Affairs were set aside for later consideration. Whether the committee reported or not, or whether such a report rests in the limbo of documents, the Minutes of the Courts for the following years revealed no such report. The Estimate for 1835, however, noted a sum of 1,500 guilders for allowances and rations for Indians;[4] on presents it was silent. As mentioned previously 'the retaining fee for fidelity and friendship' ended in 1837. This fact was borne out by the 1841 report of Mr. J. Hadfield, Superintendent of Rivers and Creeks for Demerara, which stated that before the enactment of the No. 6 Ordinance of 1838, the Indians had been supplied with plantains, salt fish, and rum, as well as with presents of small articles such as gun powder, knives, looking glasses, beads, and combs. The periodic distribution of these articles had induced many Indians to attach themselves to the posts, but now there was no such inducement.[5]

[1] M.C.P., 11 July 1834. Letter of the Revd. John Hynes to J. C. Smyth, 10 July 1834. N.A.G.   [2] Ibid.   [3] Ibid.   [4] C.O. 114/15. M.C.P., 15 June 1835.   [5] M.C.P., 10 Mar. 1841. Hadfield's Report, 26 Oct. 1839. N.A.G.

The discontinuance of presents to the Indians had ended at a critical period in the colony's history between Emancipation 1833 and the end of Apprenticeship 1838. Both the colony and the legislature were apprehensive of the actions of the Negroes whom they felt were only one step away from barbarism. Why then did the Combined Court in 1837 break the bond with the Indians who were their 'cordon sanitaire' against the Negroes? A look into the legislative policy of 1837 might explain this cavalier attitude. In 1837 a Bill appointing Superintendents of Rivers and Creeks was introduced. The preamble to the Bill throws some light on the question:

Whereas the Rivers and Creeks of British Guiana afford great facility of communication with the interior of the Province, and unless the same be carefully watched, and the navigation thereof placed under very vigilant superintendence, they will furnish a easy means to the idle and dissolute to remove themselves beyond the control of the laws; and whereas the existing establishment of Protectors of Indians and of Postholders is inadequate to the efficient performance of those duties, which now are, and may hereafter, be required from those entrusted with the superintendence of the water communication of the interior . . .[1]

Although the Ordinance stated that the salaried Superintendents were to replace the Protectors and postholders, it would seem that to remedy a problematic situation they were really in place of the past 'police of the interior'—the Indians and enjoined to keep a vigilant eye on the Negroes. To the Court it was a more prudent policy to pay salaries to one's own officials than to hold oneself in fee to native tribes. In December 1839 a police force was established in place of the scrapped militia.

The local legislature thought they read the handwriting on the wall correctly and expected a mass exodus of freed Negroes up the rivers and remote creeks. The Honourable M. M'Turk, in supporting the Creek Bill, affirmed that it was 'well known . . . that the Rivers and Creeks were infested with Runaway Labourers and Squatters, and their depredations required to be checked'.[2] M'Turk must have imagined or feared such a situation but the imagination and the fear were more obvious than the reality. Four years later the Court admitted that the reason for the Bill had never really existed except in their own minds. Mr. Sandbach, the President of the Financial Representatives, openly stated the case:

An apprehension existed at the cessation of the Apprenticeship that the

[1] Ordinance No. 6. 1838.   [2] M.C.C., 3 May 1838. N.A.G.

newly emancipated labourers would resort to the Rivers and Creeks, there settle on waste lands, and relapse into barbarism.

With a view to prevent this, the Superintendents were appointed. Experience, however, has shown, that the inclination of the freeman is rather to settle in the neighbourhood of Towns and the cultivated parts of the Colony . . . than to retire to the wildernes. . . .[1]

Thus the Indians were put in their places, and back to those places in the wilderness they went. Superintendents, like W. C. F. McClintock, concerned for the welfare of the Indians, from time to time pleaded with the government for the crumbs which fell from the Negroes' table. Somehow the Indians never lost their old habits nor the expectations of presents.

Over twenty-five years later, McClintock now the Pomeroon Superintendent of Rivers and Creeks, was instructed by Governor Francis Hincks to prevent the Indians of his district from coming to town in the hope of obtaining presents, as he considered 'donations of that kind a waste of Public Money'.[2] Nevertheless, McClintock continued to pester the Governor for presents for his Indians, for in 1866 Mr. W. H. Ware, the Acting Government Secretary, wrote in exasperation that '. . . the Contingency Fund[3] at the disposal of His Excellency is completely exhausted and you must be aware that it has been most severely pressed on by the presents he sent at your suggestion a few months ago which was followed up by another application'.[4] Later the Governor did not ignore the Indians' predilection for presents, and when he visited the Waramuri Mission on the Moruka river, he took care to carry presents of knives, fish hooks, shot, gun powder, salempores, and shirts for the men, and scissors, looking glasses, beads, perfumery, cloth, etc., for the women. Neither did he forget the children.[5] As the Revd. W. H. Brett observed, the large numbers that assembled to greet the Governor had been lured by the hope of receiving presents.[6]

[1] M.C.C., 6 June 1842. N.A.G.

[2] A. F. Gore, Assistant Government Secretary to McClintock, 15 Mar. 1862. *Letter Book*. N.A.G.

[3] The Contingency Fund was used by the Governors for various items not voted for by the Combined Court. Financially shackled by the Court, the Governors were able to support their pet projects by this fund. It was subject to the control of the Colonial Secretary who, with a few exceptions, gave the Governors considerable leeway in its disposal.   [4] W. H. Ware to McClintock, 19 May 1866. *Letter Book*. N.A.G.

[5] The Revd. W. H. Brett, D28 *Letters and Papers*, No. 6820/1866. *United Society for the Propagation of the Gospel Archives.*   [6] Ibid.

To assure the Indians of the continued imperial interest in them, the Governors, as representatives of the Crown, paid out of their Contingency Fund sums for periodic presents for the Indians. In 1870 the bill paid to Bookers Bros. & Company for such presents totalled £107.[1] Governor Scott explained to the Earl of Kimberley in 1871 that it was still the custom to give small presents in goods 'When a Captain is appointed over an Indian tribe, or when a Head man with some of his followers visits the Governor . . .'[2] The Courts had washed their hands of financial responsibilities to the Indians, but the Governors, no doubt taking their cue from an outwardly paternalistic home government, still favoured the Indians with presents.

There was never any definite policy laid down by the Colonial Office for a relationship with the Indians. It more or less reflected the pro- and anti-humanitarian attitudes of the men at the head of the Colonial Office Department and by and large, not only 'the early Victorians', but also the later ones 'were tinged with humanitarianism and dominated by materialism'.[3] Henry Taylor's memorandum of the Indian situation in 1833 illustrated realistically the relations of both the local government and the home government *vis-à-vis* the Indians:

The only relations which I am aware of between the Colony of British Guiana and the Indians are of a very indefinite nature, and merely such as have grown out of circumstances and the interests of both parties. The Colonists rely upon the Indians for assistance in catching and bringing back runaway Negroes. . . . They also look to them as allies in the event of servile insurrection—with a view to keep up a good understanding with them, a quantity of presents are delivered to them triennially at the different posts upon the edge of the cultivated Country where they assemble to receive them . . .[4]

Even if the Colonial Office had advised the adoption of a more definite policy, they had no vital influence over the Combined Court of British Guiana. Like the Pharisees, the Combined Court were a law unto themselves, with the power to loose and bind in financial matters.[5] They alone decreed whether it was politic to give or not

[1] C.O. 111/389. Governor John Scott to the Earl of Kimberley, 22 Feb. 1872. 'Return of Civil List Contingencies for 1870.'

[2] C.O. 111/386. Scott to Kimberley, 27 Oct. 1871.

[3] John S. Galbraith, *Reluctant Empire* (Berkeley and Los Angeles, 1963), p. 276.

[4] C.O. 111/127. H. Taylor to W. Lefevre, 31 July, 1833.

[5] M.C.P., 2 Sept. 1844. N.A.G. 'The Governor and the Court of Policy constitute the

to give Indian presents. Benevolent Governors from time to time helped the Indians from personal or the Contingent Funds. Hilhouse, that prolific writer of letters, reminded the government that its present motto was 'Civilization throughout the World'.[1] The press often drew the attention of the public to the interest and rights of the 'nobel [*sic*] savage' and in the exuberance of mixed metaphors suggested that the government as 'Protectors of the Indians adorn the shield of guardianship that our own laws extend over them with the lamp of education'.[2] But the Court was hardly ever impressed. Its pre- and post-Emancipation *pourparlers* usually began and ended in jeremiads on 'the diminishing resources of the Colony'. At the same time they cloaked their agricultural interests in the new imperial clothes of moral righteousness and paternalism, but unfortunately no child was present.

Within this scissors action of cold economics and an alleged warm paternalism, where did the Indians stand? They were retreating more and more into the forests. McClintock, while rightly deploring the free use of rum 'the authorized system of demoralization' which had 'cemented the bonds of friendship with the whites, as well as annual presents . . .', showed that the Indians were now cast off because they were no longer required to maintain 'the balance of power' and contain the Negroes. The Whites were now telling them, he said: 'We no longer require your assistance, no more presents will be given, no more rations of fish, plantains, etc. issued, in a word, the negroes are free, and you can withdraw from the posts and return again to the wilds . . .'[3] And so they had. Governor Barkly testified that 'since the discontinuance of the presents distributed . . . while slavery existed . . .'[4] Indians had withdrawn into the interior.

ordinary and general Legislature of the Colony, their powers and authority do not, however, extend to the final passing of money votes, money appropriations, nor to fixing or levying taxes. The Combined Court on these last mentioned subjects, possess and exercise legislative functions, which are neither allowed to nor used by the Governor and Court of Policy as a Legislature apart from the Assembly in Combined Court with the Financial Representatives. . .'

[1] C.O. 116/3. *The Guiana Chronicle*, 11 Jan. 1839.

[2] C.O. 115/5. Editorial in *The Royal Gazette*, 6 Mar. 1841. Also C.O. 116/3. *The Guiana Chronicle*, 1 Mar. 1839, 7 Aug. 1839 and 6 Sept. 1839.

[3] M.C.P., 5 Nov. 1850. McClintock's Report, 30 Sept. 1850. N.A.G.

[4] Great Britain. Parliamentary Papers. *British Guiana*. II. Barkly to Earl Grey, 15 Aug. 1850, 154.

It is, therefore, not too strong a censure to maintain that the Indians were used solely to protect the colonies from slave uprisings, and that presents were given primarily as a matter of expediency, with no thought on the effect they had on the Indians for good or evil. It might have been ultimately more beneficial to the Indians and to the colony to have given them more practical presents such as agricultural implements, and to have guided them in their use of them. The Indians of British Guiana, like those of other parts of South and North America, as well as of the Pacific, were always captivated by gaudy, glittering, and novel gifts such as looking glasses, scissors, knives, and beads, which they considered their due from the white man in exchange for their land and their loyalty. Also, in the pre-Emancipation days in British Guiana it was hardly likely that the Court of Policy would have considered any other approach, as they needed the mobile and nimble Indians as their 'guerillas' in the bush expeditions against the runaway Negroes. It was thus late in the day when it was legislated that 'implements adapted for agricultural pursuits' were to be distributed to the Indians in place of that most destructive gift of all—rum.[1] Governor Light admitted that the Indians were used and presents 'often misapplied, too often baneful' had been given them.[2] Indeed, as all the missionaries later testified, rum had brought about the ruination and demoralization of the Indians. The Colonial Office, years before the 1838 Bill which outlawed the distribution of spirituous liquors, had advised that the distribution of rum and various articles should cease as the Indians, apart from their 'police' service, brought no 'substantial and permanent benefits' to the colony.[3] It was not until 1844 that the Court moved that $10,000 be placed on the Estimate for the purpose of establishing an experimental Indian Village in order to draw the Indians within the pale of civilization and to make them contribute to the economy of the country.[4] This experiment never went further than the legislative chamber of the Public Buildings because of the opposition of many members of the Combined Court who claimed that it was the throwing away of a vast sum of money 'upon a mere chimera', as the Indians preferred their

[1] Article VI of Ordinance No. 6 of 1838, p. 409. *Local Guide of British Guiana containing Historical Sketch, Statistical Tables and the Entire Statute Law of the Colony in Force, January 1, 1843* (Demerary, 1843). N.A.G.
[2] C.O. 114/15. Light to the Court of Policy, 1838.
[3] C.O. 111/117. H. T. Taylor's Minute, 17 Feb. 1832.
[4] M.C.C., 23 Mar. 1844. N.A.G.

carefree life in the forest to an organized agricultural one.[1] In general, only the few promoters of the scheme evinced any interest in the matter. Although the editorial of *The Royal Gazette* supporting the cause asked the timely question: 'What truth of science, what mystery of art has been carefully unfolded to him?' [the Indian],[2] the suggested experiment was swallowed up by the tidal wave of immigration.

At the end of the 1830s with no more runaway slaves to be caught and no further fear of imminent rebellion, the police and military usefulness of the Indians ended—so too, did the annual subsidies of presents, rations, and allowances. As the Hon. Vincent Roth commented, 'When their usefulness ceased, the interest of the State in them in actual practice ceased also.'[3] As in Nyasaland, Rhodesia, and South Africa, where the governments abdicated their responsibility for the natives to huge philanthropic corporations and institutions, so too, in British Guiana the local government passed on this duty to the institutions of the various Churches, especially the Anglican Church subsidized by Missionary Societies in England. Beyond tacitly accepting the fact that the Indians were somehow the responsibility of the State, and thus enacting some protective legislation periodically, both the Combined Court in British Guiana and the Colonial Office in the mother country, with clear if not correct consciences, bequeathed the Amerindians to the missionaries.

[1] C.O. 116/5. M.C.C., 27 Mar. 1844, in *The Royal Gazette*, 2 Apr. 1844.
[2] Ibid., Editorial of 4 Apr. 1844.
[3] Vincent Roth, 'Amerindians and the State', *Timehri* XXXI (1952), 11.

III

THE ROLE AND DUTIES OF THE POSTHOLDERS AND PROTECTORS OF THE INDIANS—THE ADVANTAGES AND DISADVANTAGES OF THE SYSTEM

ON assuming the government of the colonies, the British authorities carried on the system of their predecessors in dealing with the Indians, preserving as far as possible, an absolute continuity of both policy and administration. The Dutch West India Company had appointed 'uitleggers' or postholders as its officials in the interior.[1] Stations or posts had been established throughout the Dutch territory of Guiana for the purpose of checking trade between Essequibo and Spanish Guiana, for encouraging trade with the Caribs in annatto and letterwood, and above all, for serving as barriers to runaway slaves. Postholders were stationed at these posts to regulate trade and, as the word implies, to hold the posts. Throughout the seventeenth and eighteenth centuries there were references to these postholders residing at the various posts, namely Maykouny (Mahaicony), Arinda, Moruka, and Cuyuni.[2] The Cuyuni post was of vital importance both for trade and security. The horse trade with merchants of Spanish Guiana was carried on there, while the Cuyuni route was the most well-known to the runaway slaves.[3]

Foremost among the instructions to the postholders was the injunction in Article I that 'he shall not molest the Indians but rather encourage them in a friendly manner to serve the colony'.[4] The expediency and realism of the Dutch policy were patent and

[1] Netscher, p. 42.
[2] *B.G.B.*, App. III, 106–12. 'A brief Treatise concerning the Honourable Company's Trading Places', enc. in No. 396. Director-General to the West India Co., August 1764. See also Gravesande, II, 460–73. [3] Netscher, p. 42.
[4] C.O. 111/111. 'Instructions by which the Postholder of Canje shall regulate himself', ff. 123–5. Fort Nassau, 18 July 1756. See Appendix V for the text of the nine articles translated from the Dutch by D. Haufman.

explicit. The Dutch were, above all, businessmen, more interested in trade than in the hunt for gold which so obsessed their western neighbour, the Spanish. In such a vast country as Guiana they realized that without their positively cultivating the goodwill and friendship of the warlike Caribs who dominated the area, their survival would be impossible. Before one could trade one had to survive. The Dutch also found it necessary to use the Indians to protect them from any possible revolt of their runaway slaves—a danger which became extremely imminent at the end of the eighteenth century. It was already noted that presents distributed by the postholders became the bonds binding the Indians to the Dutch. The ultimate result was a permanent friendship and alliance with all the Indian tribes on the east of the Orinoco. This pragmatic and diplomatic policy of the Dutch resulted, not only in the peaceable possession of the territory, but in preventing Guiana from falling into Spanish hands.

After the British had first captured the colonies of Essequibo, Demerara, and Berbice in 1781, Lieutenant-Colonel Kingston wrote to Lord Germain, Secretary of State for the Colonies, of the importance of the role of the postholders: '. . . the Postholders have always been employed in keeping up an interest with the Indians of whom there are many nations bordering close upon the Colonies. . .'[1] The British Government evinced an interest in the system and the Duke of Portland wrote for more information on their duties. He was informed that: 'The Postholders together with their Assistants are Persons appointed on the part of the Government in such Districts of the Colony where the Communications may be best kept up with the Indians whom they are to protect.'[2] Their salary paid by the government was 300–800 guilders per annum or £21–£58. In 1799 there were three postholders and three assistants. When the colonies finally surrendered to the British fleet in 1803, the Articles of Capitulation guaranteed the continuance of all existing institutions under the previous Dutch Government.[3]

Quite early in the new administration the Court of Policy took into careful consideration the position of the postholders, and concluded that their retention would be beneficial, that they should be instructed to use their best endeavours to pacify the Indians in

[1] C.O. 111/1. *Private*. Lt.-Col. Kingston to Lord Germain, Demerary, 18 July 1782.
[2] C.O. 111/3. In answer to the sixteenth query of the Duke of Portland, 1798, f. 71.
[3] C.O. 111/1. Articles of Capitulation, 19 Sept. 1803. *Article 1*.

possible discords, to prevent illicit trade with them, and to summon the Indians when required for any purpose. To encourage intercourse with the tribes the postholder was to distribute gratuities to them periodically.[1] On 14 May 1803 the Honourable Court of Policy enacted the 18 Articles of Instructions to the Postholders of whom there were now six stationed on the Demerara, Essequibo, and Pomeroon rivers, and on the Mahaica, Mahaicony, and Boeraserie creeks.[2] Each postholder was enjoined to keep an accurate journal of occurrences at his post, which he was to transmit quarterly to the Protector of the Indians in his district—a new officer whose position will be considered later. He was to attach the Indians to the post and to endeavour to preserve peace and order among them. Trade was prohibited to him, nor was he allowed to hire the services of the Indians without the permission of the Protector.

It will be seen from these instructions, which were reissued in May 1815, and summarized in 1824 and 1826,[3] that the powers and authority of the postholder were much less general than had been the case during the Dutch administration. The postholder was now bound to conform to the orders of the Protector of the Indians for his district; if definite complaints of an injury were made to him by Indians, he merely acted as an intermediary to bring the Indian and the Protector together, having no power to deal with such complaints himself. His also was the unenviable task of being the intermediary between the whites and the Protector regarding any liaison with Indian women. He was to use his endeavours to bring the Indians and the Protector into communication when the Indians were travelling in the neighbourhood of that officer. He had no power to make any examination of a person charged with crime. He had to be present at the annual distribution of presents, and was also issued with rations and small presents for distribution to Indians.[4] When, in later years, the government discontinued the issue of such articles, the expense of providing these presents which the Indians still continued to expect, was borne by the postholder personally. Even before this discontinuance an assistant postholder, Hendrik Corneilisen, complained to the Court of Policy that he

[1] M.C.P., 23 Feb. 1803. N.A.G.

[2] M.C.P., 14 May 1803. N.A.G. Also see C.O. 111/60 from which the complete text of the Instructions are included in Appendix VI.

[3] C.O. 116/193 and 194. Duties of the Postholders. See Appendix VII.

[4] C.O. 111/60. Postholders Instructions enacted by the Honourable Court of Policy, 14 May 1803.

was being obliged to provide the Indians with rum, plantains, salt fish, tobacco, cloth, and many other things. His salary of 1500 guilders was insufficient to cope with these demands; if an increase to 2200 guilders were considered too high, he asked to be dismissed from his post as interpreter and assistant postholder 'to prevent him from severe losses to the great detriment of himself and his large family'.[1]

The duties of the postholders were, undoubtedly, onerous and called for the exercise of considerable tact and discretion. The position called for an unusual type of man, hardy to live in the wilderness, disinterested enough to placate both the Indian subjects and his white superiors, and to survive the geographical and financial rigours. The postholders should, preferably, have had some military experience for organizing and leading the bush expeditions; not the least among their duties was the responsibility for capturing runaway slaves.[2] What type of men were these postholders? Accounts of their character and the manner in which they carried out their duties are varied and contradictory according to the experience of the writers. Supposed to be deputies for, and protectors of, the Indians, the postholders were too often seen as their despoilers. In 1790 they were severely censured by Commissioners from Holland for their ill-treatment and extortion of the Indians. The Commissioners suggested that, instead of postholders being sent out from Holland as employees of the West India Co., they should be selected from among old plantation employees or other fit persons 'who know the ground and how to get along with the Indians' and who would constantly offer them 'friendship, good treatment, and prompt help in case of necessity'.[3] Richard Schomburgk, in his earliest work on British Guiana, noted that the postholders received a pittance for salary from the government, for which reason presumably they swindled and oppressed the Indians, as well as alienated them, 'which undermined the good object of their purpose'.[4] In this the postholders were the counterparts of the

[1] M.C.P., 25 Apr. 1815. N.A.G.

[2] *B.G.B.* App. III, 112–14. Instructions to the Postholder at Arinda, 14 Aug. 1764, enc. in No. 396. Director-General to the West India Co., Aug. 1764.

[3] Ibid. App. V, 81. No. 635. Report of the Commissioners, W. A. Sirtema van Grovestin and W. C. Boey, respecting the Condition of the Colony of Essequibo and Demerara presented to the Prince of Orange, 27 July 1790.

[4] Richard Schomburgk, *Travels in British Guiana, 1840–1844* (Georgetown, 1902), I, 53.

76

corregidores of Spanish America, who on small salaries and far away from centralized authority, embezzled and abused their Indian wards whom they were appointed to protect. In 1813 Codd criticized the fact that: 'All the Postholders are foreigners, and, therefore, not likely to inspire the Indians with that love for the English . . .', yet at the same time admitting that the postholders performed an excellent service by assembling the Indians to serve in bush expeditions.[1] That controversial figure of early Indian history, William Hilhouse, denounced the postholders pitilessly. As far as Hilhouse was concerned, there was no such being as a conscientious postholder; they were mainly drunkards and petty tyrants.[2] Hilhouse considered nothing but the Indians and their welfare. Reality showed, however, that the posts were anything but the dream of a travel agency of today; they were remote, rugged, and a long rough journey away from so-called civilization. The salary of the postholders was always meagre and their housing poor, almost to dilapidation. It was not unprecedented that men placed in such a position and in such surroundings would and did succumb to the anaesthetic of alcohol, and take advantage of the free labour of the Indians whom they were sent to protect. Although in the early nineteenth century humanitarianism was in vogue, it had not yet penetrated into the wilderness of the colonies.

Nevertheless, unless their reports are gross exaggerations or downright lies, the postholders did, in most cases, carry out their duties as laid down in the 1803 instructions, but not always thoroughly. The postholders were requested to keep accurate journals of occurrences at their posts, and to submit, quarterly, copies to their respective Protectors, as previously noted. Protectors complained that they did not receive these journals regularly. Colonel Codd enclosed the 1803 Instructions to the Earl of Bathurst observing that: 'Your Lordship will be surprized to learn that from no office could I collect the returns of their (Indian) numbers at the Posts which ought to have sent them quarterly.'[3]

---

[1] C.O. 111/16. Codd to the Earl of Bathurst, 6 Sept. 1813. The Indians preferred Dutch postholders. At the posts Arinda, Cuyuni, and Moruca they insisted that Dutchmen be appointed. See *B.G.B.* App. III, 161–2, and 164. Director-General, Essequibo to West India Co., 9 Feb. 1768 and 9 Apr. 1768.

[2] William Hilhouse, 'Reconnaissance of the Post of Pomeroon, etc.', Nov. 1823, and Letters of Hilhouse, *The Guiana Chronicle*, 28 Nov. 1834 and 19 Dec. 1834. Jesuit Diocesan Archives, Guyana, also N.A.G.

[3] C.O. 111/16. Codd to the Earl of Bathurst, 25 Sept. 1813.

In September 1813 Codd had issued a circular to all postholders asking for specific information on their posts—information which had been requested by His Majesty's Ministers as the introductory paragraph to the questionnaire indicated. The five questions asked for facts regarding the industry and possibility of the employment of the Indians with a view to curtailing the annual expense of the Indian posts. The returns of the men, women, and children were to be forwarded with separate totals of the males fit for military service and of the sick.[1] Codd later complained, after receiving a very poor response to his circular, that the accounts of the Indians were so badly kept that he was unable to get satisfactory information on the exact number of articles distributed to the Indians, as well as the length of time they lasted.[2] According to the records only three out of six postholders returned answers to the questionnaire—H. Linau of Pomeroon, M. Mauvielle of Mahaica and Mahaicony, and H. Bremner of Post Seba. All three agreed, in general, that because the Indians were given to a roving life and were of fickle minds it would be impossible to get them to settle down to any particular employment. Stock-raising would also prove difficult because of climatic conditions. Linau felt that the cultivation of the soil and the raising of cattle by the Indians might be realized if a specific area were allocated for their use and they were superintended by someone who would instruct them in the principles of religion and 'inspire them with some degree of awe of the power of the British Government'.[3] All the postholders hedged on Question 2 regarding the allowances and the cost to the government, and referred the answer to the Protectors to whom they submitted their journals and who were really responsible for sharing out the rations and allowances. The only numbers returned to Codd were from M. Mauvielle of Mahaica and Mahaicony Indians (679: 157 males fit for military service), and from H. Bremner of Post Seba Indians (3,000: 290 males fit for military service).[4]

Unless the journals required to be forwarded quarterly through the Protector to the Governor's office were either mislaid or

[1] Circular of Col. Codd to the postholders, 15 Sept. 1813. *Letter Book*, p. 30. N.A.G. See Appendix VIII for text of the questionnaire and returns of the Indians forwarded by M. Mauvielle and H. Bremner.

[2] C.O. 111/16. Codd to the Earl of Bathurst, 18 Nov. 1813.

[3] C.O. 111/16. Reply of H. Linau, Postholder, in answer to the Acting Governor's Circular Letter of 15 Sept. 1813, 25 Sept. 1813.

[4] C.O. 111/16. Returns of Indians from M. Mauvielle and H. Bremner, Sept. 1813.

destroyed, very few exist. The postholders, as Codd realized after his investigation, neglected to keep their books in order and thus had nothing to forward at the end of the quarter. The very few journals that have survived read like a combination of a weather report, a medical chart, and a receipt book. The weather was either fine or showery, the postholders and/or the Indians were sick, and the rations of plantains, salt-fish, and rum, were duly received from the Protector and distributed. Taken at random from among the journals is a report for the Boeraserie Indian Post for April 1833:

April 1833

6—Dispatch 2 Indians to the Protector.
8—The 2 Indians return from the Protector.
12—The Indian woman Henriette delivered of a Girl.
13—Received from Pln. Poederooy, 42 bunches plantains.
15—Received from Pln. Vergenoegen one Jug Rum and one molasses.
26—Went to the coast . . .
30—This month allowance of plantains, fish, salt, molasses and Rum have been served to the Indians.[1]

Another report from the Pomeroon Post reads:

May 1833

Sunday 12th—Weather fine, served allowance Beef, Pork, Molasses, Plantains, Salt and Tobacco.
      13th—Rain all day—Doctor visited the Post–Bucks from Morocco.
      14th—Weather fine. Doctor returned.
      16th—Weather fine—Schooner John sailed for Town.
      17th—Weather fine.
      18th—Weather fine. Received from Aberdeen 80 bunches plantains . . .[2]

A nominal list of Indians at the respective posts stating name and tribe—called Nation on the form—was sometimes submitted.[3] Requisitions for articles for distribution were sent through the Protectors, and a statement of articles received and delivered. It is therefore difficult to ascertain from these brief and terse journals of the postholders how well they actually carried out their role of

[1] Report of M. I. I. Mottet, Postholder of Boeraserie, Apr. 1833. N.A.G.
[2] Report of B. Tonge, Postholder of Pomeroon, May 1833. N.A.G.
[3] See *Nominal List of Indians on Mahaica Creek for quarter ending 30th June 1833.* N.A.G.

protection to the Indians. The journals afford mere glimpses into the routine, day-to-day life at the posts.

The letters of the postholders are more revealing; they give evidence that they looked out for themselves as well as for the Indians. Postholder H. C. Wahl of Massaruni in one of his letters to the Government Secretary requested 120 bunches of bananas for the post and '120 ditto for my private account', one cask of rum for the post and one for himself.[1] Yet he commended himself for treating his Indians well for he observed 'The Indians rather work for Wahl than for the country on account of the good payment.'[2] Obviously, he was a generous man, generous to his Indians and himself.

More detailed information on the posts and the welfare of the Indians had to be extracted from the postholders through specific questionnaires. Meagre information had been gathered by the Codd circular in September 1813. In April 1836 Henry Baird, the Assistant Government Secretary, circularized questionnaires to the postholders of Demerara, Essequibo, and Berbice requesting them to furnish the Governor, Sir James Carmichael Smyth, with the detailed information regarding the names and number of Indian tribes in the vicinity of their posts, the character and disposition of the Indians for work, the names of the posts and distances from each other, the status of the postholder and his ability to communicate with the Indians in their own language, the date of the last distribution and the number of presents, and the religious sect of any missionary instructing the Indians.[3] The only reply found among the journals and reports of the postholders in the Guyana Archives was that of the postholder of Mahaicony and Abary, John Watson. He stated that there were two tribes of Indians within fourteen hours' journey from the post—Arawaks and Warraus totalling 295; they were friendly and peaceable, but did not appear desirous of religious instruction; the Warraus occasionally hired themselves out to the woodcutters, while the Arawaks preferred to cultivate their land, hunt, and fish. He was a bachelor, had been a postholder for three years and ten months, and could converse a little with the Indians in their own language. Since he had been postholder no distribution of presents to the Indians had been

[1] H. C. Wahl to Government Secretary, 8 Mar. 1813. N.A.G.
[2] H. C. Wahl to Government Secretary, 16 Dec. 1812. N.A.G.
[3] Henry Baird, Assistant Government Secretary to the Postholders of Demerara, Essequebo, and Berbice, 6 Apr. 1836. *Letter Book*. N.A.G.

carried out—the last such distribution had taken place in 1831 by order of Sir Benjamin D'Urban. He enclosed a rough drawing of the post-house, pointing out that it was in need of repair. There were five Indian huts contiguous to the post-house and five others about 250 metres distant. There was not a single white or free coloured inhabitant nearer than the Posts of Berbice and Mahaica, neither had the Indians at his post ever been visited by any missionary.[1]

The reason for this rendering an account of their stewardship to the Governor was not difficult to discern. During the past two decades the usefulness of the office of postholder had been called into question by the Court of Policy, and had been under fire from the hot-tongued Hilhouse whose constant letters to the press vehemently attacked both the office and the officials. Although the charge of jealousy might be levelled at Hilhouse, other observers would support his allegations. Hilhouse regarded the postholders as 'the enemy within'. In his petition to the Court of Policy on 31 October 1832 he declared that the Indian posts were being deserted and this was 'attributable to the trafficking of the Postholders and others—by which only such Indian captains are appointed as are subservient to their private interests from which it results that the Indians have no confidence in these appointments...'.[2] According to Hilhouse inefficiency, irregularity, and debauchery were the trade marks of both postholders and Protectors and he recommended a speedy revision of the system before the coast tribes were completely annihilated. The Court of Policy circulated copies of Hilhouse's 'phillipic' requesting them to report on the situation. The Protectors emphatically refuted these charges laid against their respective postholders. Mr. Richard Watson declared in his report that, although the Warraus were addicted to immoderate drinking, 'excessive drinking and debauchery *is not* however, encouraged as Mr. Hilhouse asserts—on the contrary the Postholder at Mycony not only sets a good example of temperance (not using himself any spirituous wines or even malt liquor), but does all in his power to check intemperance among the Indians'.[3]

The postholders were, in this instance, supported by their Protectors. Hilhouse was no friend of the Protectors whom he had as

[1] Report of John Watson, Postholder of Mahaicony and Abary, 25 Apr. 1836. N.A.G.
[2] M.C.P., Wednesday 31 Oct. 1832. Petition of William Hilhouse. N.A.G.
[3] Richard Watson to the Court of Policy, 19 Jan. 1833. N.A.G. Watson, in disclaiming the charges, pointed out that he had been in office for sixteen years and had never heard of the post being visited by Mr. Hilhouse!

81

harshly censured, so they probably acted on Benjamin Franklin's dictum that 'those who don't hang together will hang separately'. The Court of Policy accepted their reports 'after a most careful consideration of the contents', and ruled that 'the assertions and allegations' of the Hilhouse petition had not been 'borne out'.[1] The Court had been acquainted with Hilhouse's opinion of these officials at an earlier date. Writing in 1823 his 'Reconnaissance of the Indians at Morocco', in praise of the bravery and high-mindedness of the Spanish Indians who had claimed the protection of the British Government in 1817, Hilhouse had advocated that 'no European of bad caste should be allowed to approach them, and drunken postholders should not be tolerated'.[2] Championing the establishment of a mission at Moruka and the granting of land for this purpose, he wrote several letters to the press. In his letter of 28 November 1834 to *The Guiana Chronicle*, he accused the postholders of obtaining land in Moruka by underhand means, and so violating the rights of the Indians. He spoke of the machinations and high-handedness of the present postholder, who not only instructed the Indians in drinking at the post, but 'strut as Inspector or Protector General of Indians'.[3] The postholder was far off when famine and sickness demanded succour; instead of protecting the Indians he had taken 'unfair advantages of the forlorn miserable state of this ill-used race'.[4] Both the Church and the press admired him for having the courage to expose these abuses. Not so the Governor, who although he agreed that Hilhouse's knowledge of Indian affairs was valuable, considered him a meddler and an 'unauthorised person' where the Indians were concerned.[5]

A Captain J. E. Alexander of the 42nd Highlanders, writing his memoirs of his visit in *Transatlantic Sketches*, was equally denunciatory. He classified the postholders as '. . . altogether unprincipled and worthless, shamefully neglecting or abusing the charge committed to them. Their sole aim seemed to be to enrich themselves, or to find the means of living a debauched life by inducing the Indians to cut wood for them by presents of rum, therefore de-

[1] C.O. 114/13. M.C.P., 2 Feb. 1833.
[2] Hilhouse, 'Reconnaissance of the Post of Pomeroon . . .' J.D.A.G.
[3] *The Guiana Chronicle*, 28 Nov. 1834. J.D.A.G.
[4] Ibid.
[5] P.R.O. 35/18. *British Guiana*. No. 26. J. C. Smyth to the Rt. Hon. T. Spring Rice, 17 Sept. 1834. Governor Carmichael Smyth's Papers. Vol. I. Despatch Book, Demerara, 1835-5.

moralizing the people they were intended to protect.'[1] The expenditure in presents, provisions, and salaries paid out to the postholders was over and above their merits, as they abused their office, and as a result the Indians were decreasing in numbers.[2] The Chief of the Arawaks, Santa Anna Efeerocoona, wrote to the Protector of Indians for the Pomeroon asking 'that the Postholder, as heretofore, may be prohibited from vexatiously interfering with the Indians of the Morocco Creek . . .'[3] In another of his many letters to the press Hilhouse intimated that the postholders drank themselves to death, and gave his experience of this in the following melancholy data:

Zeno	Pomeroon	*Died of gout*		
Stohl	,,	,,	,,	,,
Timmerman	,,	,,	,,	,,
Stohl, jun.	,,	,,	,,	,,
Tonge	,,	,,	,,	,,
Wahl	Massarooney	,,	,,	,,
Richardson	,,	,,	,,	,,

claiming, also, that the 'present Post-holder in Essequebo is gouty'.[4] Drunkenness was the main vice, it seemed. Hilhouse was not telling tall tales, for a report in 1839 attested that one of the postholders, a Mr. Hawker, had been in a state of drunkenness for two or three days together and while in that state had treated an Indian boy brutally. The drunkenness and the abuse had been witnessed by the managers of the Estates Welgelegen and Herstelling.[5]

But in the early 1800s when the government were very much aware of the importance of keeping the Indians on their side, the postholders served a need. They acted as arbitrators between Indian tribes and protected them from ill-treatment by other persons, as the following incidents proved. In 1807 when the Protector of Indians heard that disturbances between the Indians of Essequibo and the free coloured people had broken out, postholder Linau was

[1] Captain J. E. Alexander, *Transatlantic Sketches Comprising Visits to the most interesting scenes in North and South America, and the West Indies.* With notes on Negro Slavery and Canadian emigration (London, 1833), I, 71.

[2] Ibid., p. 75.

[3] B.G.B. *Appendix to the Case on Behalf of H.B.M.*, VI, Santa Anna Efeerocoona, Chief of the Arawaks to Peter Rose, Protector of the Indians for Pomeroon, n.d. (*c.* 1834), p. 58.

[4] C.O. 116/3. Letter of Hilhouse in *The Guiana Chronicle*, Friday 4 Oct. 1839.

[5] Report of the Superintendent of Rivers and Creeks, James Shanks, for the County of Berbice, for the Quarter ending 30 June 1839. N.A.G.

immediately dispatched to collect information about the matter and to assure the Indians of the friendliness of the Colony towards them.[1] In 1826 the warfare carried on for some time between the Caribs and the Paramona tribes of the Akawoi nations in Mazaruni was ended by the mediation of Mr. McKie and the assistant post-holder, G. P. Wischropp, who arranged for the chiefs of both parties to sign a treaty of Peace and Alliance at the residence of George Bagot, Protector of Indians, on 13 December 1826.[2]

The system of postholdership suffered from the disadvantages of a meagre salary, lack of supervision, the defects of human nature, and simple economics. The defects of human nature were aggravated by the meagre salary and the meagre salary by the ever-increasing financial embarrassments of the local government. If their salary did not allow them to be well-fed and well-housed, at least it seems they were well-dressed. The resplendent uniform of a green coat with scarlet facings and lapels, hat with scarlet plume, and a sabre with a crimson sash required to be worn by the postholders of Berbice, was obviously paid for out of government funds.[3] The postholders began to traffic in slaves, to use the Indians in their wood-cutting grants without paying them, contrary to their instructions, and to complete the demoralisation of the Indian by the liberal distribution of rum.[4] Dr. Hancock wrote that 'multitudes have been destroyed by the deleterious new rum so liberally placed at the disposal of the postholders and protectors of Indians so termed'.[5] The postholders and the Protectors alike succumbed to the

[1] Minutes of the Court of Policy, Monday 26 Oct. 1807. N.A.G. The report of Linau's describing the hostility between the free coloured people was carefully checked. The Court of Policy sent two competent persons familiar with the Indian dialect on another expedition back to the villages with Linau 'to ascertain the truth of the said Post-holder's statements and to assure the Indians of the determination of the Government to afford them every protection'. M.C.P., Monday 25 Jan. 1808. The free coloured people were stirring up trouble among the Indians and in April 1808 Postholder Wahl in the River Essequebo was appointed Adjutant to the Burgher Militia with the rank of Captain. Ibid.   [2] George Bagot to D'Urban, 13 Dec. 1826. N.A.G.

[3] Approved by Governor B. D'Urban. *Letter Book*, 14 January 1826. N.A.G.

[4] C.O. 111/180. The case brought by Mrs. Fraser against the Postholder Spencer and his wife for enslaving Indians was outlined in a letter of Governor Henry Light to Lord John Russell, 20 Aug. 1841. In this letter the Governor said that he had legislated in vain against the payment of Indians in rum but 'The Indians will not work without rum'. Cases against employers who neglected to pay wages to their Indians will be fully discussed in Chapter V and the trafficking in Indian slaves in Chapter VII.

[5] John Hancock, M.D. *Observations on the Climate, Soil and Productions of British Guiana, and on the Advantages of Emigration to and Colonizing the Interior of that Country* (London, 1840), p. 39.

temptation of using cheap labour for their own devices and their affluence. In this they were following in the footsteps of the Spanish *encomendero*, who entrusted with the responsibility of protecting the Indians, used them illegally. Like their Spanish counterparts, these officials would read the instructions, 'place them over the head', and conveniently forget them. Some officials neglected to reside at their posts which, at a meeting of the Court of Policy on 25 October 1830 the Governor deplored as being to the 'great detriment of the Public Service'.[1] The postholder of the Pomeroon, Dr. Gilbert, was reprimanded by the Governor for his frequent absence from the Post, and for his general inefficiency, and requested to give an explanation.[2] It had also been reported to the Governor that George Hawker, the postholder of Berbice, had been absent from his Post for a considerable period without leave. Hawker was written a very stern note by the Government Secretary, stating that the Governor required 'an explanation of the circumstances which lead to the irregularity', and that 'should you fail in satisfying His Excellency with good and sufficient reasons, it will become his duty to remove you from your situation'.[3]

By the 1830s the Court of Policy had already begun to get irritable over the Indian system, undoubtedly motivated by the embarrassing financial situation which loomed ahead when slavery would be abolished. The clouds of Emancipation had been gathering on the horizon. On 12 June 1833 the House of Commons had passed five memorable resolutions which set in motion the machinery for the final abolition of slavery, and on 28 August 1833 the Act was passed. Even though the slave-owners in British Guiana received £4,297,117. 10s. 6d. as compensation for their 82,915 slaves, all the money did not trickle down to the rightful owners and, when it did, it was still not enough. Many planters were faced with ruin and their resulting bitterness was turned against the Chief Executive. The Court of Policy was the stronghold of the plantocracy who were now obsessed with one idea—how, in the absence of slave labour, they could uphold the sugar industry and be assured of continued prosperity. Other items on the agenda which called for an outlay

[1] C.O. 114/11. M.C.P., Monday 25 Oct. 1830.
[2] H. E. F. Young, Government Secretary to Robert King, Superintendent of Rivers and Creeks, Essequebo, 5 May 1840, notifying him of a letter written to Dr. Gilbert on the same date. *Letter Book*.
[3] Government Secretary to G. Hawker, Postholder of Berbice, 18 Feb. 1840. *Letter Book*.

of expenditure were given short shrift. The Court directed their attention to what was now considered a withered branch of the tree politic—the Indian system and the officials within it.

Already the Combined Court had abolished the post of Assistant Postholder by not voting their salaries.[1] A drastic reduction of the allowances, rations, and presents to the Indians was next considered. The postholders were still being lax and inaccurate in submitting accounts for supplies furnished them by the Protectors. On 4 June 1834 a Committee was appointed to enquire into the expenditure of Post Seba for the past four years ending December 1833, and also into the conduct of the postholders in connection with that expenditure. The Protector was directed to order the attendance of the postholder to town where he would be required to give an account of his stewardship. He was to submit to the Committee the original journals for the years 1830–3.[2] The findings of the Committee are in the limbo of missing reports, but it can be concluded that they were not complimentary to the postholders.

A year later the Honourable Members of the Combined Court were objecting to the salaries of the postholders. Captain Warren stated that the objection was not raised 'for the purpose of depriving them of salaries . . . but with a view to bring the whole subject of the Indian Establishments under the consideration of the Court of Policy at the earliest possible period and to place them on a more efficient footing'.[3] Efficiency was not numbered among the peculiarities of the postholders. Despite the tug-of-war over the motion, the salaries of the postholders were included in the Estimate for 1835 as for previous years as follows:

In Demerara and Essequibo
  6 postholders @ f 2,200 each (£157) = f 13,200 (£942 approx.)
In Berbice
  3 postholders @ f 1,600 each (£114) = f 4,800 (£342 approx.)[4]

The question of the postholders' salaries was reopened every year. When the Berbice Estimate was discussed in the Combined Court the members were divided on the issue of the three postholders,

[1] C.O. 114/13. M.C.P., Wednesday 22 May 1833.
[2] C.O. 114/14. M.C.P., Wednesday 4 June 1834. Three months before the Governor had raised the matter of relations between the Colonial Government and the Indians in the Court of Policy and had recommended that a Committee be formed to investigate and suggest changes for the improvement of the system. C.O. 114/14. M.C.P., Monday 3 Mar. 1834.   [3] C.O. 114/15. M.C.C., Thursday 11 June 1835.   [4] Ibid.

with the result that the Court recommended to the Court of Policy 'to take early measures for revising the entire system of the Colonial Relations with the Indians generally throughout British Guiana'.[1]

Throughout March 1837 the Combined Court hotly debated the system of postholdership. On 8 March Captain Warren proposed that the whole establishment be lopped off as a decayed branch of a tree. Objections were voiced at this rather ruthless suggestion. The High Sheriff warned that the tree itself would be in danger of being uprooted if Warren's proposal were acted upon. Another member attested that the postholders living among the distant squatters on the rivers and creeks checked their lawlessness. Feeble though the check might be, 'all semblance of authority and power ought not, on that account, be taken away'.[2] Again the vote for the abolition of the office of postholder was lost. The following day it was even more strongly discussed. Mr. E. Bishop, a Financial Representative, read a paper to the Court containing his reasons for voting against the salaries of the postholders as follows:

On a matter of so serious importance as the Abolition of Postholders and Indian Establishments, towards which I yesterday most reluctantly contributed by my vote, I deem it right as an old Colonist of Essequebo, to have my Reasons recorded on the Minutes of this Court.

The Establishment dates nearly from the earliest settlement of Guiana, and proved on several occasions of most essential service and protection to this Colony. But lately has been suffered to become the means of mere private speculation, the very law prohibiting Traffic by the Post-Holders with the Indians, become a monopoly in their hands unrestrained by Protectors of Indians, some of them Members of the Honourable Court of Policy; and thus, while the Colony continues to be burthened with upwards of Twenty-five Thousand Guilders yearly, an important Establishment, which might, under proper regulations have become of most essential service, particularly now at the approaching crisis of social change in a Colony so extensively spread, has been suffered to dwindle and become useless; the Indian made dissatisfied through the arbitrary presumption of subordinates—the Planter obstructed in making the Indians useful; and the annual recommendation as far back as the year 1834 of this Combined Court, even under solemn pledges, disregarded.[3]

[1] M.C.C., Monday 28 Mar. 1836. N.A.G.
[2] Report of the Proceedings of the Combined Court on Wednesday 8 Mar. 1837. *The Guiana Chronicle*, 10 Mar. 1837. N.A.G.
[3] M.C.C., Thursday 9 Mar. 1837. N.A.G. 'the very law prohibiting Traffic by the Post-holders with the Indians' referred to by Mr. Bishop was Article 10 of the Post-holders' Instructions of 14 May 1803. See Appendix VI.

The accusations brought against the Protectors, 'some of them Members of the Honourable Court of Policy', raised a storm of protest, particularly from the High Sheriff, himself a Protector of Indians, who called upon Mr. Bishop to substantiate his charge. The next day the proceedings of the Combined Court opened with members demanding Mr. Bishop to either drop the offensive accusations or to support them by specific names. Bishop, realizing that he had pushed the matter too far to retract, stated that the Protector of Essequibo, Mr. George Bagot, had not restrained his postholder from trafficking with the Indians.[1]

This controversy undoubtedly resulted in the subsequent issuing of an Ordinance appointing Superintendents of Rivers and Creeks in lieu of the Protectors of Indians on 16 February 1838.[2] By this Ordinance all laws regulating the duties of Protectors and postholders were repealed. The office of postholder, however, was still retained. The blame for the postholders' misdemeanours was indirectly placed on the shoulders of the Protectors. The Court of Policy, despite their financial liabilities, were aware of the expediency of maintaining the office for the protection of, and liaison with, the Indians. Article XXVII of the Ordinance affirmed that it was necessary to define the duties of the postholders more accurately and explicitly, while Article XXXIII contained the new regulations to be observed. The postholders were now under the direct supervision of the Superintendents of Rivers and Creeks who possessed much more authority than their predecessors, the Protectors. The postholder was bound to reside at his post and could hire Indians to perform labour, but had to pay them punctually. It was now forbidden to pay the Indians in rum or any spirituous liquor in lieu of wages. Greater emphasis was placed on the keeping of an accurate journal of all occurrences at the post and transmitting a duplicate every quarter to the Superintendent who would check its accuracy by regular visits to the posts.[3] But with the notable exception that the postholders were ordered to ascertain that the money voted for the Indians was spent in the purchase of agricultural implements and not in plantains, salt-fish, or spirituous liquors, the regulations differed little from the previous instructions. Neither did a fresh issue of regulations under a different name give birth to a new breed of postholders.

[1] M.C.C., Thursday 10 Mar. 1837. N.A.G.
[2] M.C.P., Friday 16 Feb. 1838. Ordinance No. 6. 1838.   [3] Ibid.

When the 1839 Estimate was being discussed in the Combined Court, the item of postholders was again the bone of contention. The whole question was now bound up with the movements of the emancipated population. It was felt by one member that the number of postholders should be increased as they were a 'sort of Internal Police' and prevented people from squatting, while another contended that the Indians congregated where the postholders were and would never come to the Estates. Mr. Peter Rose, who opposed every item that called for the spending of funds not connected with the planters' interests, urged that all six of the postholders should be struck off, but Mr. Bishop disagreed, claiming that it was necessary to have someone to act for the Superintendents in their absence. Finally, an amendment of the motion for four postholders was carried.[1] A few days later the Court dropped the postholder at Canje as it was argued that there were only a few Indians at the post and, in general, 'the post-holders did more harm than good'.[2]

In the following year it was suggested that the postholders should be appointed magistrates, to which the Governor agreed, provided that they would be given the necessary authority to deal with cases.[3] In the end, eleven postholders were placed on the item and the Estimates read: 11 Post-holders @ $733\frac{1}{3}$ each = $8,063.[4] In 1841 there were seven postholders, and on 18 May 1842 a motion in the Combined Court was carried that the postholders be reduced to five from the first of October.[5] The Court, always reluctant to vote the salaries of the postholders were supported by the opinions of John Chapman, who pointed out to Lord Stanley at this time that 'one of the *errors* of the administration of this Colony seems to be that there are *too many functionaries* or public officers, for instance, there are Post-holders, Superintendents of Rivers and Creeks, and Commissaries of Taxation'.[6] He advised combining the duties of the officials, and highlighted the 'unprecedented distress of the Colony', claiming that the fraud and illegal trafficking carried on

[1] C.O. 116/3. M.C.C., Wednesday 20 Mar. 1839, in *The Guiana Chronicle*, Friday 22 Mar. 1839.
[2] C.O. 116/3. M.C.C., Tuesday 26 Mar. 1839, in *The Guiana Chronicle*, Monday 15 Apr. 1839.
[3] C.O. 116/3. M.C.P., Monday 9 Mar. 1840.
[4] C.O. 115/5. *The Royal Gazette*, Saturday 23 Jan. 1841. 'Estimate of the Amount required to be raised by Taxes in the Colony of British Guiana for the Service of the Year 1840.'
[5] C.O. 114/16. M.C.C., 18 May 1842.
[6] C.O. 111/198. John Chapman to Lord Stanley, 31 Mar. 1842.

by these functionaries prejudiced the cultivation of the Estates.[1] Obsessed as they were with the need to curtail expenses, the planter-minded Combined Court were always willing to heed such advice and proposed to merge the duties of the officials, despite the objection of Governor Light.[2] They not only incorporated the duties of the postholders with those of the Superintendents of Rivers and Creeks, but added those of the Commissaries of Taxation. The item on the Estimates for 1843 read: 'Postholders and Superintendents of Rivers and Creeks acting as Commissaries of Taxation— six in number—$10,800.'[3]

Thus from 1843 the postholders lost their identity and became submerged with that of the Superintendents of Rivers and Creeks, although all their reports were signed Postholders and Superintendents of Rivers and Creeks.[4] These reports were fuller and more detailed, but the emphasis on their duties had, undoubtedly, shifted from overseeing the Indians to overseeing the Crown lands along the rivers and creeks.

Meanwhile, what was the record of the postholders in their treatment of the Indians? One of their chief responsibilities in the past three decades was security for the fear of revolts of the runaway slaves; this fear was no myth as the population returns showed. In 1811 out of a total population of 77,031 there were 71,180 slaves![5] Thus the possibility of such revolts was the Damoclean sword hanging over the heads of the white minority. In the remote areas of the interior where the runaways took refuge, their only salvation was the Indian. Hence the recurring injunction to the postholders 'to use every exertion to attach the Indians . . . to the several Posts'.[6] Regardless of their multiple faults and failings, and even of their vices, the postholders had to be men who could win the allegiance of the Indians, enlist and lead them on the bush expeditions. Dealing with the naturally suspicious Indian who did not (and do not) easily trust the white man required some amount of leadership and aplomb. The Indians might not understand rule by either love or fear, but they understood the policy of presents. A scrutiny of the day to day life at the posts as depicted in the

[1] C.O. 111/198. John Chapman to Lord Stanley, 31 Mar. 1842.
[2] M.C.C., 30 May 1842. N.A.G.   [3] C.O. 114/16. M.C.C., 28 July, 1843.
[4] In a subsequent chapter the role of the united Office of Postholder-Superintendent of Rivers and Creeks will be examined.
[5] C.O. 111/11. Return of the Population of Demerara and Essequibo, 26 Dec. 1811.
[6] C.O. 116/194. Duties of Postholders. *Blue Book, 1826.*

journals of the postholders showed them to be, above all, distributors of presents. Indirectly and secondly, they safeguarded the Indians.

How much did they really safeguard the Indians? The balance sheet of their record was not at all in their favour; they were condemned by many travellers, their Protectors, by the Court of Policy who constantly argued that money expended on their salaries was money squandered, and even by the Indians themselves. One of the early governors, Codd, held a poor opinion of the postholders and on the whole, judged the system 'extremely defective'.[1] He looked upon missionaries gathering the Indians into larger societies and introducing pastoral life, and not postholders assembling them at posts, as the right Indian policy.[2] Even the very necessary bush expeditions carried out by the postholders had been 'ruinously expensive'.[3] In 1813 Codd had despaired of collecting information from the postholders on the numbers of Indians at their posts and the cost of maintaining these posts. In 1834 the Court of Policy experienced a similar difficulty when the conduct of the postholders came under question.[4] Although the Court were dissatisfied with these officials, they felt they served a useful purpose as an internal security force even after emancipation. The Governor recommended, and the Court agreed, that, because of the rapidly increasing population on the banks of the Essequibo and its various creeks, an incumbent postholder at Fort Island 'would be of infinite service and would not only prevent Commission of many irregularities, but would be held responsible to give information of any illegal proceedings in the neighbourhood'.[5] More and more the postholder became an overseer of Crown lands. By 1842 there was no Indian located on or near the post at Fort Island.[6] D. Falant was then the postholder at Fort Island; he was sixty-two years old, in ill-health, and unable to carry out his duties as well as visiting the Crown lands.[7]

The greatest and most articulate opponent of the postholders and the system was William Hilhouse who, by public letters to the press and private petitions to the Court of Policy and Secretaries of

[1] C.O. 319/10. Codd to the Earl of Bathurst, 6 Sept. 1813.   [2] Ibid.

[3] C.O. 111/16. Codd to the Earl of Bathurst, 16 Nov. 1813.

[4] C.O. 114/14. M.C.P., Wednesday 4 June 1834. A Committee had been appointed early in 1834 to investigate the conduct of the postholders.

[5] M.C.C., Monday 13 Mar. 1837. N.A.G. The Court was divided on the issue, but the Governor voted for the item and it was carried.

[6] M.C.P., Monday 30 May 1842. N.A.G.   [7] Ibid.

State, urged the total abolition of the Indian posts and the post-holders. He was determined to prove the postholder a villain operating within a system which he contemptuously, if incorrectly, dubbed 'a great public nuisance and Colonial disgrace', the posts being 'founded in tyranny and maintained in fraud' by the post-holders, whose 'sole recommendation to the office is prior pauperism', but who 'make large fortunes, not stickling in the means even to the traffic of human flesh'.[1]

The trafficking in slaves by the postholders was no figment of Hilhouse's imagination; it did exist. In 1839 it became a hotly debated issue in a controversial Court case that occupied columns of print in the local newspapers and called forth endless editorials and letters for and against the whole system. Mrs. S. Fraser, a resident of a grant up the Demerara river, accused both the late Protector of Indians, Mr. John Patterson, and the late postholder, Mr. John Spencer, of 'ruling with unlimited sway over every Indian in the River . . . and enslaving them'.[2] The case brought before the Supreme Court was, however, quashed on a point of law. Governor Light felt that Mrs. Fraser's accusations were too general and that not enough evidence was forthcoming. Regardless of the legal quibbles on which the case was dismissed or the probable and possible dislike and jealousy of Mrs. Fraser for Patterson and Spencer, Governor Light stressed the fact that Indian slavery was not tolerated in British Guiana. In 1841 Mrs. Fraser again renewed charges against the Spencers and Patterson.[3] As far as these accusations went there seemed to be some truth in them. Robert King, a Superintendent of Rivers and Creeks, mentioned in his report that Mr. John Spencer had a large wood-cutting establishment where he employed Indians. King noted his dissatisfaction with this arrangement and hinted at the ease with which the postholders could and did violate the laws, especially Clause 7 of the No. 6 Ordinance. He concluded his report:

The Ordinance No. 6, clause 7, states that neither Superintendent nor

[1] C.O. 116/3. *The Guiana Chronicle*, Letter of William Hilhouse to the Rt. Revd. Bishop of Barbados, 7 Sept. 1839.

[2] C.O. 111/170. Mrs. S. Fraser to Lord John Russell, 24 Dec. 1839. Also C.O. 115/4. *The Royal Gazette*, Editorials of 12 and 17 Sept. 1839, and C.O. 116/3. *The Guiana Chronicle* Editorials of 11, 13, and 16 Sept. 1839.

[3] C.O. 111/178. Light to Russell, 8 June 1841. Also see Indictments and Evidence v. Mrs. Wilhelmina Spencer, Enclosures in Despatch of 8 June 1841. No. 64 and C.O. 111/180. Light to Russell, 20 Aug. 1841 with enclosures.

Postholder, shall traffic with the Indians, but also your Reporter humbly submits whether they should not also be forbidden to have a wood-cutting establishment on their own account, since thereby they are naturally induced to attend a private duty, are more absent from their required functions, and have less time to attend to the different parts of the Rivers and Creeks, whence public duty might call them.[1]

Not only did the postholders neglect their public duties for private gain, but to augment this gain they used the Indians as slaves. They probably felt that Indian labour could legitimately be used in compensation for their paltry salaries, their shabby and mostly dilapidated dwellings, and the restrictions of life in the interior.[2] They encroached on the liberties of the Indians in other ways but, as their Instructions proved, this was within their jurisdiction. It is hard to believe that the postholder with the authority to apply to the Protector for the permission for a white or free coloured person to cohabit with an Indian woman would not take advantage of it himself—even without the Protector's sanction. The Select Committee on Aborigines in 1837 drew attention to Articles 14 and 15 of the 1803 Instructions to the Postholders as tending directly 'to sanction and encourage immorality'.[3] It would seem that the Protectors closed their eyes to the lawlessness and the peccadilloes of their subordinates, and for this they must shoulder part of the blame.

The Protectors of Indians acted as means of communication between the postholders and the departments of the Colonial Government, and it was their duty, among other things, to supervise the postholders, to enforce the 1803 Instructions, and to report any misconduct on their part.[4] If the Protectors were also guilty of misconduct, in condemning the postholders they would have condemned themselves. The British Case on the Guiana–Venezuela Boundary Dispute submitted to the Arbitration Tribunal stated that the office of the Protector of Indians was a British creation in

[1] C.O. 114/15. Report of Robert King, Superintendent of Rivers and Creeks for the County of Demerara, 1840.

[2] C.O. 114/7. M.C.P., Wednesday 27 Apr. 1808; Report of Robert King on Posts Seba, Mahaica, Mahaicony, and Boeraserie read in the Court of Policy on Wednesday 9 Jan. 1839, N.A.G.; and Journal of Postholder A. F. Baird read in the Court of Policy, Wednesday 20 Apr. 1842. N.A.G.

[3] Great Britain. *Parliamentary Papers*. 'Aborigines'. II. Report from the Select Committee on Aborigines (British Settlements) with Minutes of Evidence, Appendix and Index, 1837, 9.

[4] C.O. 111/60. 'Instructions for the Protectors of Indians', Sir B. D'Urban, King's House, 10 Aug. 1824. See Appendix IX for the text of these Instructions.

1803, while Hilhouse in 1823 claimed that it was a recent creation.[1] It was neither. Although the office was of later origin than that of the postholders, during the interregnum of the Batavian Republic when Instructions to the postholders were enacted on 15 May and issued on 18 May 1803, there were constant references to the Protector in Articles 2, 3, 6, 7, 8, 13, 14, 15, 17, and 18.[2]

The number of the Protectors fluctuated between five and six for the districts of Mahaicony, Mahaica, Demerara, Boeraserie, Essequibo, and Pomeroon.[3] They received their appointment from the Governor as follows:

TO: . . . .

His Majesty having been graciously pleased to authorize me to appoint all Officers Civil and Military in this United Colony—I, reposing special trust and confidence in your loyalty, courage and capacity, do hereby nominate, constitute, and appoint you the said . . . to be the Protector of Indians for the . . . and you are enjoined strictly to perform all the Duties of that office by affording due countenance and protection to the Indians in the District confided to your care, and enforcing among the Postholders under you an exact observance of the Instructions issued for their guidance, and by obeying all such orders and Instructions thereupon as you may receive herewith, or as I may hereafter cause to be transmitted to you.[4]

It was to the Protectors and to the postholders under them that the Colonial Government looked for information and guidance in native policy. Maybe the indifference of the government in this respect was a reflection of the indifference of the Protectors. Captain Alexander wrote that it was not the charge of corruption that could be laid at the feet of the Protectors, 'highly respectable gentlemen', but the charge of indifference.[5] In his desire to get information regarding the condition and custom of the Indian population, he had quite rightly approached one of the Protectors, but to his utter amazement he discovered 'that he knew nothing whatever about them, and seemed to care as little!'[6] This fact was hardly surprising as the Protectors, for the most part, lived in town and thus they had little

[1] Hilhouse, 'Book of Reconnaissances and Indian Miscellany, 1823', in *Tribunal of Arbitration between Great Britain and the United States of Venezuela*, VI (London, 1899), 30.

[2] 'Instructions to the Post-Holders, 14th May, 1803', in Appendix VII.

[3] D'Urban to Bathurst, 16 May 1827. N.A.G.

[4] C.O. 111/60. Letter of Appointment for the Protector of Indians.

[5] Alexander, I, 75–6.   [6] Ibid., 71.

first-hand knowledge of the Indians whom it was their duty to protect.

The office was an honorary one, and hence the Protectors had to be men of substance, mostly chosen from among merchants and planters, many of them Honourable Members of the Court of Policy.[1] The Governor claimed that they were chosen from the most respectable gentlemen in the districts close to their respective Indian residences, and although they received no salary, their responsibility was 'apparent and unquestionable'.[2] Unquestionable indeed was their responsibility.

Even though they had no magisterial authority, the Protectors acted as mediators in complaints of the Indians, and it was their duty to procure adequate redress for the complainant where mediation was useless or did not apply, by referring the facts of the case to the legal authorities.[3] In Indian vendettas, the Protector had to protect the criminal from his avengers and have him safely conveyed to town for trial.[4]

According to the 'Instructions to Protectors', their prime duty was to enforce among the postholders the 'strict and diligent observance' of the 1803 Instructions and to report immediately any breach. They were to transmit the quarterly returns of the postholders to the Governor, as well as a confidential report on the number and condition of the Indians in their respective districts. Theirs was the privilege of recommending for special favour and presents any Indian captains or others whose good conduct warranted such recognition. Suggestions for the smooth working of the system were also solicited.[5]

Although they did not supervise their postholders as diligently as they should, and remit returns as regularly as required, they exercised their authority in various ways. Mr. Knollman, Protector of Indians in Essequibo, discharged the postholder, William Anthon, for quitting his post without leave, and the assistant postholder, B. Pieterse, because he had 'rendered himself obnoxious to the Indians'.[6] The Protector was authorised both to discharge and

[1] Martin, I, 63, and Rodway, *A History of British Guiana*, II, 306.
[2] D'Urban to Bathurst, 16 May 1827. N.A.G.
[3] Extract from the Notebook of His Honour Charles Wray. N.A.G.
[4] C.O. 111/117. Bagot to D'Urban, 20 Sept. 1831, enclosed in D'Urban to Viscount Goderich, 26 Nov. 1831.
[5] 'Instructions for the Protectors of Indians', 10 Aug. 1824. Appendix IX.
[6] M.C.P., Tuesday 27 Oct. 1807. N.A.G.

engage postholders and assistant postholders, but his action had to be ratified by the Court of Policy. The Protector of Indians, Essequibo, Mr. F. I. Vandershott, in a memorial to the Court notified them that, being unable to find a suitable white person to fill the position, he had appointed a coloured man, Amon Cornelius, as postholder. Cornelius had a knowledge of the Indian languages and the confidence of the Indians. The Court, after weighing the case, resolved in this single instance to confirm the Protector's appointment, as Cornelius had suitable qualifications.[1]

On a few occasions the Protectors even defended their postholders. The postholder of Morocco was supported by his Protector in the Court of Policy for doing his duty;[2] H. C. Wahl, postholder of Essequibo, was given a very meritorious report and his salary increased by the Court of Policy on the request of the Protector.[3] The Protector himself might receive the praise of the Court for swift and judicious decisions in an emergency, as did Knollman when he dispatched his postholder to investigate the disturbances between the Indians and the free coloured people on the Essequibo river.[4]

Most of the Protector's time and energy were expended on the requisitioning and distributing of presents and allowances to the Indians. Early in 1807 Councillor Knollman, in his capacity as Protector of Indians in Essequibo, petitioned the Court of Policy to make a long overdue payment to the Morocco Indians who had been employed in a bush expedition under the late Protector, Mr. Mack. The Court then requested Knollman to take over the presents for the Indians which were left at the house of the deceased Mr. Mack, and to share out a 100 gallons of new rum every month among the Indians living near the post of Morocco, as well as a similar quantity to the Indians in the Upper Essequibo river.[5] Large sums were voted

[1] M.C.P., Tuesday 1 May 1804. N.A.G. The Court feared to set a precedent with the appointment of a coloured man which Councillors van der Velden and Kroll claimed was contrary to the Resolution of the Court on 18 May 1803. Vandershott maintained that the resolution, although inserted in the Minutes of 18 May 1803, was not taken until some time after that date, and he was not aware of it when he appointed Cornelius.

[2] M.C.P., Tuesday 1 Sept. 1807. N.A.G. A case was brought against Postholder H. Linau by John Ley Harrop of Pomeroon, who claimed that Linau had fired at his boat on entering the Pomeroon River. According to the evidence and the support of the Protector, the Court upheld the action of the postholder who was acting on the grounds of Article 8 of his Instructions.

[3] Ibid.   [4] M.C.P., Monday 26 Oct. 1807. N.A.G.

[5] M.C.P., Thursday 30 Apr. 1807. N.A.G.

to the Protector for the allowances and rations to the Indians from 1808 to 1814.[1] Early in 1816 a detailed table of the number of Indians and the cost of articles was submitted to the Governor and the Court of Policy. According to this report of the Protector of Indians for the District of Pomeroon, the number of Indians—Warraus, Arawaks, Akawois, and Caribs—was 297. The cost of articles required for distribution in this district amounted to 3,576 guilders or £256 approximately.[2]

The Protector always had to submit the list of articles to the Court of Policy and request their authorization to purchase them for the Indians.[3] For example:

Authorization to Purchase Articles for Indians as Payment

Given Mr. G. Timmerman, Protector in Essequibo for Indians at Post of Bouroem (Pomeroon)

32 pieces of Salempores	3 doz. flints
9 doz. Hatchets	3 doz. tinderboxes
10½ doz. cutlasses	3 doz. razors
10½ doz. bush knives	10 lbs. corals
5 doz. combs	Fishooks

And it was further resolved on this occasion that the annual payment to be made to the Indians employed at the Post of Morocco and at all other Posts shall hence forth be as follows, they having been paid at that rate up to the 9th April 1810, viz. for 27 men each:

1 p. Salempore	3 hatchets
3 cutlasses	3 knives
1 comb	1 pr. scissors
1 razor	1 tinderbox
2 flints	1 lb. corals
4 fishooks	1 looking glass

To 30 women each:

4 ells Salempore	1 lb. coral
1 cutlass	1 knife
1 pr. scissors	1 looking glass[4]

---

[1] Estimates for the years 1808–14 as found in the Minutes of the Court of Policy, N.A.G.

[2] Memorial of the Protector of Indians, Pomeroon, to the Governor and Court of Policy, 20 Jan. 1816. Rodway estimated the number of Indians in 1825 between 15–20,000, of whom a quarter received a share of presents. Rodway, 'Indian Policy of the Dutch', X, 13.

[3] M.C.P., Thursday 2 Aug. 1810. N.A.G.

[4] M.C.P., 1 Aug. 1811. N.A.G.

The Protectors were, also, authorized to have buildings erected for the accommodation of the Indians who called at the post and in the town.[1] The purchasing of a lot of buildings for the accommodation of the Indians in town was very carefully looked into. The Hon. A. Macrae examined personally the lots and agreed that the premises could be purchased for 6,000–7,000 guilders or £428–£500—the cost being borne equally by the Colonial Government and the King's Chest.[2]

Payment for articles, allowances, and wages was not always prompt, and the Protectors were constantly importuning the Court to expedite matters. Memorials from the Protectors abound in such appeals. G. Timmerman wrote on 27 July 1812:

Your Memorialist, as Protector of the Indians of Pomeroon and the Post of Morocco, begs leave to lay before your Excellency and the Honourable Court an account of the last three months of expenses incurred for the Indians at the said post Morocco, which your Memorialist hopes will meet with your Excellency's and the Honourable Court's approbation.

Your Memorialist further begs leave to lay before your Excellency and Honourable Court a list of articles wanted for the payment of the Indians who have now been during a full year on the Morocco station, agreeable to conditions, have left that place and have been succeeded by others that are at present with the Postholder.[3]

This appeal was held over for further consideration and was not examined by the Court until five months later. The Court was forced to admit, from the strong statements of Timmerman on the matter, that the Colony was pledged to the Indians employed at the Pomeroon Post and finally gave their permission for the payment. But the Secretary was ordered 'to inform the said gentleman that the Court trusts he will not pledge the Colony in future to such unnecessary expenses . . .'[4] The Protector of Indians for Essequibo, the Hon. William Robertson, complained that the Post Masseroeni had not been supplied with an annual allowance for nearly two years; the Mahaica Post was, also, in the same plight. He notified the Court that a body of Indians under Thomas Cathrey had been mustered to take part in an expedition which had been abandoned

[1] Memorial of Charles Edmonstone to the Court of Policy, 31 Oct. 1810. N.A.G.
[2] M.C.P., 2 May 1811. N.A.G.
[3] M.C.P., Monday 27 July 1812. N.A.G. Timmerman enclosed in his memorial a list of the articles needed for the payment of the Indians for that year.
[4] M.C.P., Wednesday 28 Oct. 1812. N.A.G.

ultimately. Nevertheless, the Indians should be remunerated for their trouble. After their usual lengthy deliberations, the Court did authorize Robertson to pay the 30 Indians at the rate of ten dollars per head and to purchase articles to that amount.[1] In 1829 George Timmerman, still Protector of Pomeroon, and George Bagot of Essequibo again submitted memorials requesting overdue payments for Indians at their respective posts.[2]

The care of the Indians included medical assistance and Protectors were expected to supply their posts with medicines. One Protector overstepped the bounds in this respect and sent in to the Court a requisition for 238 guilders for payment to a Dr. Boter for attendance and medical supplies furnished to the Indians at Post Boeraserie. For this he was severely reprimanded by the government who cautioned him 'not to employ medical attention (unless surgical assistance be required in cases of accident)'.[3] He was merely to supply the post with medicines as done by all other Protectors. This Protector was unique in his concern for the medical needs of his Indians, but any incentive to act over and above the call of duty was crushed by the Court who constantly warned their Protectors not to incur unnecessary expenses.

Other duties of the Protectors entailed the surveillance, as well as the maintenance, of the leper establishment. In 1832 Timmerman reported that it was in a deplorable state, and recommended its removal from Post Pomeroon to a mile distant where the patients would be more comfortable. The Court agreed, but continuously conscious of their coffers, inserted the proviso that 'in doing so he confine the whole expense to a sum not exceeding 700 guilders'.[4]

The Court might well have been wary of paying out funds to the Protectors because there was evidence that the Protectors were making their own profits over the transactions. In 1810 the Protector of the Indians at Mahaica, Mr. F. C. Elbers, rendered his usual account for plantains, fish, and rum delivered to the Indians at the post during 1809. The amount of 2,306 guilders, 4 stivers was queried by the Court, and Mr. Elbers was asked in future to submit vouchers respecting the prices in that quarter of articles charged to the Colony.[5] In 1833, when the Court examined the accounts sent in from three plantations for supplies furnished to the Indian posts in

[1] M.C.P., Thursday 10 Nov. 1814. N.A.G.
[2] C.O. 114/10. N.C.P., 28 Apr. 1829.   [3] C.O. 114/11. M.C.P., 27 Apr. 1831.
[4] C.O. 114/12. M.C.P., 1 May 1832.   [5] C.O. 114/6. M.C.P., 1 Feb. 1810.

the Demerara river as certified by the Protector, Mr. Brandes, they found them to be exorbitantly high. They refused to pass the accounts, and returned them for explanation.[1] As a result the Protectors were instructed to limit expenses at their posts within the specified quarterly sum, and for any extra articles were to requisition the Court.[2] Were the Indians really receiving the supplies for which the money was annually voted, or was it the old story of officials lining their pockets with the funds allocated? The Protectors might not actually have pocketed the money but they made sure that many of the supplies of provisions and, above all, of liquor were 'distributed' to themselves. One bunch of plantains here and a cask of rum there would hardly be missed and, as they received no salaries, they compensated themselves. By and large the Protectors were deemed rather useless. Rodway mentioned Charles Edmonstone and Thomas Cathrey as the only two who were noteworthy; they had suppressed Indian warfare.[3] Colonel Codd spoke of Edmonstone as being 'universally respected in the Colony and beloved by them' [the Indians], but he concluded, 'his private affairs do not admit of his taking any active measure to improve the condition of the Indians, nor does it appear to be prescribed as a duty expected of him'.[4]

From these remarks and other indications of the Protectors' lack of concern for the Indians, it almost seems that the Protectorship was a mere façade, hiding the true nature of the government's relations with the Indians. Because they were under fire, the Protectors were, therefore, extremely sensitive to criticism and censure even from their own colleagues. The accusations of the Financial Representative, Mr. Bishop, against the Protector, Mr. Bagot, for conniving with his postholder in the illegal traffic of Indians, brought down on his head the fury of the other Members of the Court. They were astounded that an Honourable Member and a Protector could be so accused.[5] This sensitivity was more marked than ever when, in 1808, Councillor and Protector Knollman had

[1] C.O. 114/13. M.C.C., 9 Mar. 1833.
[2] Ibid. The Protectors were lax in sending in accounts. In 1832 the Committee of Accounts was insistent that the Protectors should be circularized 'to take care that all demands against the Colony for and on account of Indian expenses authorized by them should be rendered quarterly'. C.O. 114/12. M.C.P., 4 Feb. 1832.
[3] Rodway, II, 306.　　　　　　　　[4] Codd to Bathurst, 6 Sept. 1813. N.A.G.
[5] M.C.C., Thursday 9 Mar. 1837. N.A.G. Also noted in C.O. 116/2. *The Guiana Chronicle*, 13 Mar. 1837.

complained bitterly of a passage in the Proclamation prohibiting the purchase of Indian slaves, which had been lately renewed by the Court. According to Knollman this passage was 'derogatory to the dignity of a Protector of Indians'.[1] The Secretary, astonished and regretful that Knollman had been offended, hastened to apologize: 'For the involuntary fault of having inadvertently so connected in that paragraph the words *Protectors of Indians* with the rest of the sense as to subject them as well as the Post-holders and other inferior officers to severe correction in case of neglect, the Secretary as composer takes every blame . . .'[2] The Court was equally anxious to soothe Knollman and accepted their share of blame, for they had all signed the publication. They begged Knollman to continue to act as Protector to which he agreed, rather condescendingly, for three months longer. The Court went so far as to order the withdrawal and a reprinting of the Proclamation 'leaving out the words Protectors of Indians, where they now stand . . .'[3] They also intimated that it was their intention that the Protectors be looked upon with respect by the public on account of the very difficult services which they rendered.[4] Yet there must have been violations of the 1793 Proclamation which moved the Court to renew it. The Protectors, as Members of the Court, were in the position of 'untouchables', and here lay another weakness of the system.

So many acrimonious accusations and counter-accusations were exchanged between the Protector of Indians, Mr. George Bagot, and Mr. William Hilhouse, that it is impossible to deduce the truth. Hilhouse had written to Governor D'Urban claiming his protection for 'the neglected Part of Your Government' and offering himself as the leader, guide, and protector of those Indians.[5] This was an indirect hint that the Protectors were not protecting. The Protectors were the Governor's appointees and, with political swiftness, the axe descended on Hilhouse's head. In less than three weeks Hilhouse was informed that:

The provisional Appointment of Quarter Master General of Indians, is therefore hereby cancelled and annulled, and as the exercise of any interference with the Indian tribes in their respective Districts to which the

[1] C.O. 114/7. M.C.P., Monday 25 Jan. 1808.
[2] Ibid. The apology also drew attention to the fact that the publication of the 1793 Proclamation was to be *verbatim*, and hence the words *Protectors of Indians* were inserted to give them recognition as there were no such officers in 1793.
[3] Ibid.   [4] Ibid.
[5] Hilhouse to D'Urban, 26 July 1824. N.A.G.

Appointment was never proposed to extend, but which Mr. Hilhouse appears to have assumed under its colour, has lately been found mischievous and inconvenient, being incompatible with, and subversive of the legitimate authorities appointed by the Government for the protection of the Indians and the regulation of intercourse with them, Mr. Hilhouse is apprised that any continuance of such interference directly, or indirectly on his part cannot be permitted, and he will be pleased to rule himself accordingly.[1]

Hilhouse's interference with the duties of the Protectors was, indeed, inconvenient to those officers, but despite the Governor's warning, Hilhouse did not 'rule himself accordingly'. Two years later Bagot wrote to Governor D'Urban that Hilhouse was detaining Indians as slaves and trespassing on Crown lands; he was apprehensive of Hilhouse's intercourse with the Indians and of 'his wild enthusiastic plans and experiments' which, 'if encouraged and persevered in', would lead 'to a total alienation of the Indians from the Colonial Government'.[2] The Governor upheld his Second Fiscal's and Protector's opinion and in a letter to Mr. Wilmot Morton, denounced Hilhouse as a mischievous individual and affirmed that 'the Established Authorities of the Colony were quite adequate to the due care and protection of the Indians, and to conduct the Colonial relations with them . . .'[3] It seemed that the Governor and Protectors did 'protest too much'. In 1839 Hilhouse was still at his game of casting stones at the Protectors. In a memorial to Governor Light which was published in *The Guiana Chronicle* he wrote: '7th. The Memorialist seeing the wretched state to which the Aborigines were reduced by the utter neglect of the Government, and the pernicious effect of the existing system of Indian Superintendence as exercised by the Protectors of that time, did resolutely and unceasingly protest against that system . . .'[4] Hilhouse

[1] Memorandum for the Information of Mr. Hilhouse, B. D'Urban, 10 Aug. 1824. N.A.G.

[2] Bagot to D'Urban, 19 Aug. 1826. N.A.G., also in C.O. 111/60.

[3] D'Urban to Wilmot Horton, 16 May 1827. N.A.G. Governor D'Urban considered the Fiscal as 'the Governor's legal adviser'. (See D'Urban to Bathurst, 19 Dec. 1824. N.A.G.) The office of the Fiscal dated back to 1772. His instructions required him 'to keep, protect and maintain with all diligence and zeal all of the company's rights, domains, jurisdictions and authorities'. M. Shahabuddeen, *The Legal System of Guyana* (Georgetown, Guyana, 1973), p. 373. The Fiscal is described as 'the supreme law officer'. Ibid., p. 374. For his duties and qualifications, see ibid., pp. 373–8.

[4] Letter of W. Hilhouse to the Editor of *The Guiana Chronicle* enclosing his memorial and another letter 'pro bono publico' in *The Guiana Chronicle*, 11 Jan. 1839.

further claimed that it was due to his persistence during three Governorships that the Protectorship had finally been abolished![1]

Were the Protectors, as Hilhouse saw them, 'petty governments over the Indians without concert and without superintendence'?[2] It would not be a travesty of truth to conclude that the Protectors were guilty of the 'crimes' of selfishness, indifference, apathy, and the disinclination and inability to promote the welfare of the Indians. The position called for self-sacrificing men who would be willing and able to bear the burdens of their rigorous office and provide essential leadership; but men of such calibre were rare, if not non-existent. The office degenerated into that of a sinecure, given to those 'highly respectable gentlemen' as a matter of prestige. The Indians were protected when it was expedient, but such protectorship was negative. Although the Protectors were responsible for recommending measures to improve the lot of the Indians and their relations with the Colonial Government, there is no record of any such recommendations except those pertaining to the punctual delivery of Indian presents. Indian affairs during the Protectorship system remained *in statu quo*. This fact made the Protectors even more sensitive to the never-ending diatribes of Hilhouse, for they brought their deficiencies into focus.

Through the years Hilhouse had argued that the Protectors were unsuited for the arduous life at the posts and in times of danger and warfare were useless. The Indians admired military prowess and leadership, and if these qualities were lacking in the Protectors they despised them and became insubordinate and unmanageable.[3] This criticism is borne out in the request of G. Timmerman to the Governor asking to be released from his post as Protector which he had held for twenty-five years on the river Pomeroon. He was now eighty years old and his duties were becoming too fatiguing to be fulfilled.[4] Active and energetic men were needed for such a position, but yet octogenarians were filling the post which was certainly not filled with an eye to Indian welfare.[5]

Hilhouse's suggestions were not so wide off the mark as they were

---

[1] Ibid.   [2] Hilhouse, 'Book of Reconnaissances . . .'.   [3] Ibid.
[4] M.C.P., Thursday 2 May 1833. 'Letter of G. Timmerman to the Governor Sir B. D'Urban and the Court of Policy', N.A.G.
[5] The post was offered to Mr. Charles Bean who turned it down on the grounds of other pressing duties, the frequent visits to Indian settlements which would be necessary and which he was unable to carry out because his residence was over a hundred miles from those settlements. M.C.P., 15 May 1833. N.A.G.

alleged to be. He was right in his assertion that personal influence over the Indians was an absolute necessity, and if this were lacking the Protectors had to pay the consequences. His recommendation to merge the influence and duties of the different Protectors under one head, and the granting to him of a salary sufficient to defray the necessary expenses demanded by his duties, was both logical and workable.[1] But Hilhouse's revolutionary ideas had made him *persona non grata* with the Governors and the majority of the Honourable Court of Policy. Whether the goad was Hilhouse or the Select Committee on Aborigines,[2] on 16 February 1838, an Ordinance was passed by Sir James Carmichael Smyth and the Court of Policy by which Article I swept away the office of Protectors and appointed in their stead Superintendents of Rivers and Creeks.[3]

[1] Hilhouse, 'Book of Reconnaissances . . .' The salary suggested by Hilhouse was 10,000 guilders or approximately £714 per annum.

[2] Galbraith claimed that 'the committee's report was of little use as a guide to policy . . . it was virtually ignored'. See John S. Galbraith, 'Myth of the "Little England" Era' in A. G. L. Shaw (ed.), *Great Britain and the Colonies, 1815–1865* (London, 1970), p. 42.

[3] Ordinance No. 6. 1838. Of the suggestions of the Select Committee on Aboriginal Tribes, the only obvious one mirrored in Article VI of the No. 6 1838 Ordinance was Suggestion III—'Sale of ardent Spirits to be prevented'. See *Report of the Parliamentary Select Committee on Aboriginal Tribes (British Settlements)*. Reprinted with Comments by the Aborigines Protection Society (London, 1837), p. 118. The Committee deplored the fact that the Instructions for both the postholders and Protectors in British Guiana contained no injunction to uplift the Indian, either socially or religiously. Ibid., p. 9. Article XXVIII of the Ordinance No. 6 does include the probability of establishing schools for the Indians where advantageous.

IV

THE SUPERINTENDENTS OF RIVERS AND CREEKS: POLICE OF THE INTERIOR OR PROTECTORS OF INDIANS?

THE growing dissatisfaction with the postholdership system caused the whole Indian Establishment to come under fire from the press, the public, and the politicians. Not only the local press voiced its disapproval of the vices of civilization being taught the aborigines, but the editor of the *Westminster Review* in London criticized the whole system of British policy toward uncivilized tribes as vicious and in need of reform.[1] Private individuals such as Captain Alexander, William Hilhouse, Dr. Hancock, and others decried the vast quantities of rum lavishly distributed by the Protectors and postholders.[2] In early 1837, Sir James Carmichael Smyth intimated that a 'New Deal' was being considered with the introduction of what was to be derogatorily called the Creek Bill.[3] When the Bill appeared in the Combined Court, the politicians hotly debated its pros and cons for months. They agreed, more or less, that abuses had crept into the past system: the Protectors and postholders had betrayed their trust and had engaged in illegal traffic with the Indians. The Indians were dissatisfied, and above all, 25,000 guilders per annum were drained from the colony. In short, expenses had to be curtailed while the Establishment had outlived its usefulness of 'most essential service and protection' to the colony.[4] For a whole year the Bill had a stormy passage through the Court. It was discussed, amended, added to, praised, and vilified. For it to have survived

---

[1] C.O. 323/319. *Westminster Review*, Jan. 1830, p. 245; *Royal Gazette*, 1 Mar. 1834. N.A.G.

[2] Captain Alexander, *Transatlantic Sketches* (London, 1833), p. 76; C.O. 116/1, Hilhouse's letter to the Editor, *The Guiana Chronicle*, 14 December 1835 on Dr. Hancock's 'Remarks on the Colonization of the Interior', 1835.

[3] C.O. 111/149. J. C. Smyth to Lord Glenelg, 8 Feb. 1837.

[4] M.C.C., 9 Mar. 1837. N.A.G.

such a barrage of words, to say nothing of the deluge of Hilhouseana, was no mean feat. In the press Hilhouse characteristically denounced this Bill appointing salaried Superintendents of Rivers and Creeks in lieu of the Protectors of Indians. Much of his criticism stemmed from wounded vanity, because a few years previously he had proposed a similar plan for the establishment of the police of the interior under the direction of a salaried 'respectable and responsible gentleman'.[1] Although the Court nominated him as a Superintendent under the new Ordinance, he objected to the negative kindness of the move and refused emphatically 'to be mixed up with a disgraceful jobbery, of this most tyranical, hypocritical, and mercenary of all Colonial Bills'.[2] Hilhouse was not alone in his criticisms and his fears for the future feasibility of the Bill. One of the members of the Court of Policy, George Warren, recorded his reasons for dissenting thus:

1. I object to the passing of this Bill because I consider that by the continuance of the office of Postholder, the amalgamation of the Indians with the agricultural population of the country will be impeded, and their advancement in civilization and instruction so far obstructed as to take from the advantages the Indians would enjoy by the encouragement of a closer connexion with the cultivated parts of the country.

2. Because I consider the powers given to Superintendents of too independent and extensive a nature.

3. Because the employment of both Superintendents and Postholders with the establishments such appointments must necessarily call for will be attended with too heavy an expense.[3]

Warren's objections to the Bill summed up those of all the objectors, conscientious and otherwise. He felt that the office of Superintendent would maintain the Indian in too dependent a position. The financial reason was never omitted. Notwithstanding such opposition the Bill was passed at that session in the Court of Policy. It still had to run the gauntlet of the Combined Court, whose members considered it defective in many respects. Innumerable amendments were made to amendments. Some members were in favour of one instead of the three Superintendents recommended, the political expression of Hilhouse's Carthaginian cry. Hilhouse claimed repeatedly that three Superintendents would involve three systems of operation—not a very valid objection since three or more indivi-

[1] C.O. 116/2. *The Guiana Chronicle*, 20 and 28 June 1837.   [2] Ibid.
[3] M.C.P., 16 Feb. 1838. N.A.G.

duals do not *ipso facto* involve three systems. Hilhouse's second argument, however, must be conceded, namely that it would be exceedingly difficult to find three just men with a knowledge of the localities and of the aborigines, as very few officials or non-officials had any idea of the vast extent of the country, to say nothing of the understanding of the various tribes which occupied those regions. Also, in terms of expenditure, the outlay for three Superintendents would obviously be more than for one with three postholders as his assistants on a smaller salary scale.[1] The Combined Court thought it would be impossible for one man to superintend the Berbice and Corentyne rivers, as well as the Canje and Abary creeks. Captain Warren spoke warmly supporting Hilhouse for the post of *the* Superintendent, not only as a matter of financial expediency, but because he attested 'no person was better qualified for the situation, either from talent and general knowledge of the Indian tribe'.[2] No member of the Court denied Hilhouse's efficiency and excellent qualifications for the post but deemed the duties beyond the capacity of one man, while the Hon. Alexander McCrae growled that places should not be made for men.[3]

In June 1838 *Government Notices* publicized the appointments of three Superintendents of Rivers and Creeks under the Ordinance No. 6. 1838:

1.	Robert King	County of Demerara.
2.	William Crichton	County of Essequibo.
3.	James Shanks	County of Berbice.[4]

They were also appointed Stipendiary Justices of the Peace as legislated in Article XII of the Ordinance. Governor Light explained to Lord Glenelg that such an added office was necessary for convenience, as the districts within their commissions as Superintendents were sometimes out of the reach of the regular Stipendiary Magistrates.[5]

What had this new Ordinance brought forth after such labour? Besides reiterating and emphasizing the duties of the postholders, paid officials were now substituted for the past unsalaried Protectors. As far as the Indians were concerned, Articles VI and VII

---

[1] C.O. 116/2. *The Guiana Chronicle*, 21 Feb. 1838.
[2] M.C.C., 4 May 1838. N.A.G.
[3] C.O. 116/2. *The Guiana Chronicle*, 14 May 1838.
[4] C.O. 115/4. Supplement to *The Royal Gazette*, 16 June 1838, and ibid., 8 January 1839.   [5] C.O. 111/162. Light to Glenelg, 4 Jan. 1839.

forbade the Superintendents to distribute 'at the public expense, any plantains, salt fish or spirituous liquors of any kind or description', or to 'trade, traffic, or barter' with them,[1] a direct move to put an end to the abuses of the Protectorship system. Strictly speaking, the Superintendents were glorified police of the interior as twenty-four of the twenty-six articles show. As the Honourable M'Turk so honestly and aptly attested, they were appointed primarily to keep an eye on the runaway labourers and squatters who were infesting the rivers and creeks.[2] Rodway observed that the results of this change 'made hardly a ripple on the waters of Indian affairs'.[3]

The passage of the Bill evoked more pen-rattling from Mr. Hilhouse. He published his memorial in *The Guiana Chronicle* condemning the Bill again, as well as criticizing the gentlemen filling the lucrative offices created by it, as having 'no influence or sympathy with the race they are appointed to govern'.[4] Further, he requested to be reinstated in his commission as 'Quarter-Master General of the Indians and the Interior'.[5] Governor Light thanked him for his advice, acknowledged his zeal and energy, but regretted his inability to grant the commission as it would 'be inconsistent . . . and repugnant to, any existing Ordinance'.[6] But a recalcitrant, unmuzzled Hilhouse appealed to the public, affirming that 'the sole object of . . . [his] Petition was to prevent the waste of public money on impracticable objects'.[7] Hilhouse was supported in these sentiments by a writer who called himself 'A Friend to the Indians and the Industrious Woodcutters', and claimed that one of the Superintendents was hated, despised, and feared by the Indians whom he over-awed by 'his mighty power and importance'.[8] On the other hand, had Hilhouse been appointed, 'The Indians and settlers up the Rivers and Creeks would have had to hail with joy, in him, a friend and protector. The Wood-cutter and Huntsman might have quitted their houses leaving their wives and daughters in safety . . .'[9] There was no evidence that even the Combined Court considered the Bill the panacea to the question of the Indians and the interior. The subsequent and many amendments made to that Bill expressed doubt and not certainty.

[1] Ordinance No. 6. 1838.
[2] M.C.C., 3 May 1838. N.A.G.
[3] Rodway, 'Indian Policy of the Dutch', p. 31.
[4] C.O. 116/3. *The Guiana Chronicle*, 11 Jan. 1839.
[5] Ibid.   [6] Ibid.   [7] Ibid., 16 Jan. 1839.
[8] Ibid., 25 Jan. 1839.   [9] Ibid.

There were early indications that the creation of a new office did not create, in turn, new and model men. Like their predecessors, the Protectors of Indians, some of them failed in their duties. About two years later J. Shanks, Superintendent of Berbice, was asked to give an account of his stewardship. Apparently he had allowed certain persons to clear the land which belonged to the Indians.[1] J. Hadfield of Demerara river was asked to resign on the grounds of an unfavourable report submitted by the Inspector General of the Police involving Hadfield's turning a blind eye to the fact that Indian slaves were kept by the postholder, W. Spencer. This case of Indian slavery highlighted a weakness of the 1838 Ordinance. An editorial in *The Guiana Chronicle* drew the obvious conclusion: '. . . that hospitality blinds the eye of the guest to the landlord's violations of the law. The Superintendent must have fed too daintily at the Post on the River, to see what the Postholder was doing.'[2] Governor Light postulated the ideal that 'constant itinerant vigilance . . . should characterise [Hadfield's] conduct as a Superintendent of Rivers and Creeks'.[3] In 1847 Richard Hancock of Mahaica was asked by the Governor to explain 'a series of grave charges . . . for misconduct in [his] official capacity . . .'[4]

But with these exceptions, the Superintendents of Rivers and Creeks were conscientious men who did their best in trying circumstances, as their elaborate and detailed reports forwarded quarterly to the Governor and the Court of Policy illustrate. They had to be men on the move, travelling constantly through their extensive districts in all kinds of weather. Governor Light in his first sanguine years 'regarded the Indians with a philosophical and almost romantic feeling'.[5] This attitude made him ever conscious of his role as the Great Protector of the Indians. In this capacity he felt it was his duty to channel the efforts of the Superintendents in the direction of the Indians. The ink had not fully dried on the Bill when the Superintendent of Essequibo was ordered 'to proceed to the Morocco, for the purposes of making an inspection into the state of things generally at that settlement, that he be required to make a *report* of the number of Indians, their habits of life, and means of

[1] Government Secretary to J. Shanks, 13 Nov. 1840. L.B.
[2] C.O. 116/3. 'The Aborigines of British Guiana', *The Guiana Chronicle*, 6 Sept. 1839.
[3] Govt. Secretary to J. Hadfield, 30 Nov. 1840. L.B.
[4] Govt. Secretary to R. Hancock, 20 Dec. 1847. Ibid.
[5] C.O. 116/3. *The Guiana Chronicle*, 6 Sept. 1839.

subsistence and such other information as would enable the Court to judge what further encouragement they might be deserving of'.[1] Crichton of Essequibo was praised by the Governor for his admirable work in redressing the wrongs perpetrated on the Indians by their employers, but when Crichton requested a travelling allowance as he had already spent 1,985 guilders of his own, the Court of Policy spent hours in involved and choleric arguments on this item.[2] The Combined Court threw out the request, and instead reluctantly raised the salary of the Essequibo Superintendent from £500 to £600 when it was logically pointed out that living up the rivers and creeks was quite a different matter from living in town.[3] In the furious row which ensued over the sum of 1,985 guilders for travelling expenses, the Hon. Alexander McRae moved that, not only travelling expenses, but the whole item of Superintendents of Rivers and Creeks should be struck off altogether. They were useless protectors of the law on the rivers as thousands of squatters were catching fish. Governor Light, like an irate parent, fussed that they were empowered as Stipendiary Magistrates to execute the law and 'if they don't do it, they must be punished or dismissed'.[4] He saw no need, however, to throw out the baby with the bath water by rejecting the whole Bill.

In the 1840s when the finances of the colony were in jeopardy and expenditures were being drastically curtailed, the Combined Court were ready and eager to abolish their reluctant creation. Early in 1840 they threatened to stop the salaries of the Superintendents. The Court in this year were desperate and would have threatened anything in the interests of their financial survival. The crops had failed and through the Governor's suggestion the home government had disallowed the Immigration Ordinance. The exports of sugar and coffee had dropped disastrously—the estates struck almost simultaneously by drought and absence of labour. The Court was thus in no mood to be patient with the Superintendents whose duties were stagnating into 'the filling up long yarns and reports of vagrants not discovered and squatters not ejected'.[5] Neither were they ready to adopt a reasonable attitude to the new Civil List of £40,080, £20,000 more than the previous year's, which

[1] C.O. 114/15. M.C.P., 16 July 1838.
[2] C.O. 116/3. M.C.P., 29 Jan. 1839, in *The Guiana Chronicle*, 4 Feb. 1839.
[3] Ibid., M.C.C., 21 Mar. 1839, in *The Guiana Chronicle*, 25 Mar. 1839.
[4] Ibid., 116/3, 26 Mar. 1839, in *The Guiana Chronicle*, 15 Apr. 1839.
[5] C.O. 116/3. *The Guiana Chronicle*, 4 Oct. 1839.

Governor Light unfortunately pressed upon them at this time. The Court held the gun of free immigration and increased privileges to the Governor's head, and when he proved fearlessly adamant they refused to pass various items on the Annual Estimate, chief among them the salaries for the Superintendents of Rivers and Creeks. Light countered this move by adjourning the Court without the Tax Ordinance being passed. This deadlock between the Executive and the Legislative bodies stopped the wheels of government. Governor McLeod of Trinidad was shipped by the home government to Guiana to bring some order out of the political confusion. When the wheels began to move again six months later, the colony had already lost thousands of dollars it could ill afford.

Again the salaries of the Superintendents came under question and Governor Light voiced his fears to Lord Russell:

> Of the Indians, it is necessary to observe that their chief protection is owing to the Superintendents of Rivers and Creeks, if these be abolished without some more effective functionary in their place, the consequences will be a series of oppression . . . I understand it is the intention of the Combined Court to abolish virtually the Office of Superintendents of Rivers and Creeks, established by Ordinance approved by Her Majesty's Government by rejecting the salary.[1]

The Colonial Office adopted, at first, a 'hands off policy', accepting the financial control of the local legislature. Against a background of ever rising costs, the Court in 1842 struck off the salaries of the Superintendents, merging their duties with those of the postholders and the commissaries of taxation. Light strongly objected and harangued the Court in no uncertain terms for providing no efficient substitute for the preservation of law and order among 'the scattered population of the Rivers and Creeks'.[2] He hoped they would not have to regret their decision. The Colonial Office stood by, only observing 'with interest the course which the Combined Court may be disposed to take in the exercise of the power which has been transferred to them for the period to which the Civil List arrangement extends . . .'[3] Not that the Court would have paid any attention to advice from that quarter since they considered the Secretary of State lacking in local knowledge and experience, and decried Light's

---

[1] C.O. 111/177. Light to Russell, 15 Mar. 1841.
[2] M.C.P., 30 May 1842. N.A.G.
[3] Ibid., Lord Stanley's Letter of 30 Mar. 1842. N.A.G.

informing him of the debate on the Estimate.[1] For the first time they came out from behind their façade of legislation for Indian protection and laid bare their real reasons of political and economic interests in framing the 1838 Creek Bill—that political bone of contention:

In striking off the Superintendents of Rivers and Creeks, we did not lose sight of the cause which originated their appointment. An apprehension existed at the cessation of the Apprenticeship, that the newly emancipated labourers would resort to the Rivers and Creeks, there settle on waste lands, and relapse into barbarism.

With a view to prevent this, the Superintendents were appointed. Experience, however, has shown that the inclination of the freeman is rather to settle in the neighbourhood of Towns and the cultivated parts of the Colony . . .[2]

Thus, as the situation no longer existed, such officials were no longer necessary. Their duties would 'now devolve upon the Commissaries of Taxation—so that the abolition of their office will only be felt as a reduction of expenditure'.[3] The Court had no intention of considering the welfare of the Amerindians and the effects of this withdrawal of protection on them.

It was evident that Governor Light again denounced the irresponsible and imprudent action of the Combined Court over the Amerindians. Without the visits of the Superintendents, he assured Lord Stanley, there would be little safety for the natives.[4] Lord Stanley was more conscious than Lord Russell, his predecessor, of maintaining a public paternal interest in Her Majesty's native subjects. Public opinion, not understanding the unique political situation in British Guiana, would make no distinction between the policy of the Colonial Office and the policy of the Guiana Combined Court. Hence the Colonial Office would be tarred with the same brush of indifferentism to the natives. Stanley acknowledged the fact that the Court was under no financial obligation for the welfare of the Indians, except where justice and humanity were concerned. Then followed the diplomatic rebuke: 'But the protection of the Aborigines in the neighbourhood of British settlements is a subject which is regarded by Her Majesty's Government and by Parliament as one of great importance. And a system of colonial Government which should lead to a permanent denial of any provision for this

[1] M.C.C., 6 June 1842. N.A.G.   [2] Ibid.   [3] Ibid.
[4] C.O. 111/191. Light to Stanley, 18 June 1842.

object would be considered in this country as standing in need of amendment.'[1]

It seemed that the admonition of the Secretary of State and the constant appeals of the Governor had their effect on the Court, which compromised by uniting the offices of the Superintendents of Rivers and Creeks, the postholders, and the Commissaries of Taxation. The Estimate of 1843 noted the item of six such officials with a total annual salary of $10,800,[2] viz.:

Berbice

No. 1—To act as Commissary of Taxation in the upper district of Berbice River . . . from Lust-tot-Rust upwards, both banks; and in the upper district of Canje, from Pln. New Forest upwards, both banks —Salary for combined duties $1,900

No. 2—To act as Commissary of Taxation on the Corentyne Coast, as far down as No. 68 Creek—Salary for combined duties. $1,700

Demerary

No. 1—To act . . . in Abary, Mahaicony, and Mahaica Creeks and Parish of St. Mary, as far as Mahaica Village—Salary for combined duties. $1,800

No. 2—To act . . . from Sand Hills and Hyde Park and Creeks—Salary for combined duties. $2,200

Essequibo

No. 1—To act . . . from Fort Island upwards, both banks— Salary for combined duties. $2,000

No. 2—To act . . . Rivers and Creeks, and Settlements, downwards—Salary for combined duties. $1,200
          _____
          $10,800

Previous reports filed by the Receiver General of Berbice had declared the office of Commissary of Taxation to be useless and expensive, costing the colony $15,000 per annum while contributing nothing to the improvement of revenue.[3] The Combined Court were only too pleased to have an excuse to freeze that office. Yet

[1] M.C.P., 7 Dec. 1842. Stanley to Light, 12 Oct. 1842. N.A.G.
[2] C.O. 114/16. M.C.C., 28 July 1843.
[3] C.O. 111/203. Reports of Receiver General of Berbice, Henry Baird, and Assistant Receiver General, M. J. Retemeyer, 3 Feb. and 5 May 1843.

Richard Schomburgk, brother of the famous traveller, Sir Robert Schomburgk, maintained that the 'severe reproof from Lord Stanley' had recalled the Combined Court to their responsibility for the Indians.[1] The editor of *The Royal Gazette* intimated a similar gratifying reason of the Combined Court, implying that the 'Court have happily evinced a disposition to comply with cheerfulness with the recommendations of the Colonial Secretary. . .'[2] Nevertheless, the editorial noted the hard-headed realism of the Court to the exigencies of the time and the practical results of their action. Economy of expenditure was always the trade mark of the Combined Court.

With the combining of three offices money had been saved, but people had been sacrificed. James Shanks, Superintendent of Rivers and Creeks, Corentyne, was notified that since the office of Superintendents had been struck off the Estimate and their duties super-added to the united functions of the postholders and commissaries of taxation, it would not be possible for him to continue in office.[3] Deprived of his office, Shanks denounced the newly appointed three-in-one official, N. J. de Wolff, as 'a notorious smuggler, and seller of Rum to the Indians . . . besides a defrauder of Revenue by cutting and selling Wood from the Crown Lands . . .'[4] In addition, Shanks pointed out, de Wolff was a foreigner. Indeed, de Wolff was a foreigner, a Dutchman, but this was not surprising; so too were many others in public office, as only thirty years before British Guiana was a Dutch colony. Dutch postholders were continued in office and later appointed as Superintendents. The tenor of Shanks's memorial was one of hurt pride and jealousy, so his accusations against de Wolff have to be taken with some reservation. There was possibly some truth in the allegations, but very few Superintendents at this period could afford to throw stones. In his protest to the Secretary of State, Shanks testified that the office of Superintendent of Rivers and Creeks was 'a necessary one as well for the protection of the interests of the Crown as that of the native Indians'.[5] He also showed in this memorial that the Combined Court, from the Secretary of State's objection to the abolition of the office, had

[1] Richard Schomburgk, *Travels in British Guiana, 1840–1844*, translated and edited by Walter E. Roth (Georgetown, 1922), I, 53.
[2] C.O. 116/4. *The Royal Gazette*, 22 Aug. 1843.
[3] H. E. F. Young, Goverment Secretary, to J. Shanks, 28 Aug. 1843. L.B.
[4] C.O. 111/203. Memorial of J. Shanks, 15 Sept. 1843.
[5] C.O. 111/207. J. Shanks to the Secretary of State, 15 Sept. 1843.

merged the three offices into one, thus continuing the vote for the salaries.[1]

Governor Light defended his motives for not reappointing Shanks. To him it seemed inappropriate to consider 'a man dismissed from an office of trust for alleged peculation . . . competent to discharge the new duties of Postholders and Superintendents of Rivers and Creeks, which made him also a Commissary of Taxation, an Assistant receiver of Public Revenue'.[2] In examining Shanks's case the Colonial Secretary criticized not only the earlier appointment of Shanks by the Acting Governor Banbury through patronage,[3] but above all the weakness of the 1838 Bill, both in principle and practice. Lord Stanley felt that 'an appearance of permanency had been given to these appointments. . .' Such an irregularity in legislation should be guarded against and Stanley recommended a repeal of the Bill.[4] Because Shanks had been returned to public office in 1838 after being dismissed from his office as Registrar in Berbice in 1834 for alleged peculation, he could reasonably complain of being passed over in favour of junior men. Despite this admission Stanley did not feel he could justifiably interfere in the case. The office, as noted in Article II of the Ordinance, rested on the Governor's favour.[5] Hence Shanks was given his *congé*, while the slandered de Wolff remained in office, his journals and reports in later years proving that he was conscientiously carrying out the duties of his office.[6]

No discussion of the men who held office as Superintendent of Rivers and Creeks, postholder, and Commissary of Taxation in Guiana would be complete without an account of the activities of W. C. F. McClintock, who added lustre to the office. Previously a postholder in the Berbice river, he was appointed Postholder and Superintendent of Rivers and Creeks of the Pomeroon District on 1 October 1840[7] after he had married a lady from the Pomeroon. This post he held until the office was finally abolished in 1873 when he was then appointed a Special Magistrate. Hence

[1] Ibid.
[2] C.O. 111/203. Light to Stanley, 2 Nov. 1843.
[3] C.O. 111/202. J. Stephens's comment on Light to Stanley, 18 Sept. 1843.
[4] C.O. 112/26. Stanley to Light, 23 Nov. 1843.
[5] H. E. F. Young to Shanks, 28 Mar. 1844. L.B.
[6] M.C.P., 4 Aug. 1847. Journal of de Wolff, 5 July 1847. M.C.P., 29 Oct. 1847. Ibid., 4 Oct. 1847. M.C.P., 10 Jan. 1849. Ibid., 30 Sept. 1848. M.C.P., 26 Feb. 1849. Ibid., 31 Dec. 1848. M.C.P., 6 Aug. and 6 Dec. 1849. Ibid., 30 June and 30 Sept. 1849. N.A.G.   [7] M.C.P., 5 Mar. 1841. N.A.G.

his insights, opinions, and suggestions on Indian policy stemmed from long experience among them. To the Indians he was literally doctor, lawyer, and Indian chief. His lengthy reports constantly emphasized his firm conviction, which through the years became almost an obsession, that the Indian could never be adequately and permanently civilized without training in industry, or in his own words—'education must be combined with industry'.[1] To him, one without the other was useless. The plan of education–cum–industry would be the only means of making the Indians economically useful to the colony. McClintock not only put his ideas to the Governor and Court of Policy on paper, but also put them into practice. As the managers of estates testified, it was mainly through McClintock's exertions that the estates on the Arabian Coast were supplied with Indian labour.[2] His reports highlighted the importance of the missions (he himself had been instrumental in helping to establish the Waramuri Mission on the Moruka river[3]), the boundary question, the characteristics of the Indians, and repeatedly denounced the rum distribution among the Indians as 'an authorized system of demoralization'.[4] McClintock had no romantic illusions about the Indians whom he described as indolent, content to pass their lives away comfortably swinging in their hammocks unless their desires and wants were stimulated by industrial training.[5]

Both the Governor and the Court of Policy credited McClintock's zeal and acknowledged his 'great experience of the Indians'[6] (although some members of the Court considered him a boaster of deeds among the Indians), but they did not embrace his multitudinous suggestions with open arms. Obviously McClintock's constant harping on the Indian welfare, coupled with his accusations that 'the Negroes of the colony . . . received all the loaves and fishes',[7] irked the Court.

Nevertheless, McClintock's reports outlined the duties of a zealous Superintendent who made regular and exhausting visits up

[1] Almost every report of McClintock read in the Court of Policy from the 1840s through 1870s held the same message. See M.C.P., 30 Oct. 1843, 23 Oct. 1846, 30 Sept. 1849; M.C.C., 27 May 1856; M.C.P., 14 July 1864 and 30 July 1875 as Special Magistrate. N.A.G.
[2] Managers' Certificates, 1845. See Chapter VIII.
[3] M.C.P., 22 Jan. 1847. McClintock's Report, 31 Dec. 1846. N.A.G.
[4] M.C.P., 5 Nov., 1850. McClintock's Report, 30 Sept. 1850. N.A.G.
[5] M.C.P., 6 Dec. 1849. McClintock's Report, 30 Sept. 1849. N.A.G.
[6] W. H. Ware, Acting Government Secretary to McClintock, 21 July 1865. L.B.
[7] McClintock's Report, 30 June 1856. N.A.G.

the rivers and creeks to the settlements of both the Indians and the woodcutters, supervised the Indians clearing the land and paaling[1] off the river dams, listened to the complaints of the Indians, shared out medicines, and supported the missionary ventures. Indeed it was an exacting programme for one man. All these jaunts and journeyings, agitations, and activities had to be recorded in quarterly, and later half-yearly, reports to the Governor and Court of Policy to show the

progress and State of any settlement on the Rivers and Creeks within the district—the number of inhabitants—whether free holders or otherwise—the state of Spiritual Superintendence and of the Schools . . . he was not to confine his observations to the above suggestions only but consider [himself] at liberty to embrace any subject that may illustrate or throw light on the general state of the settlements.[2]

Some Superintendents, however, were not always prompt in transmitting their reports; others neglected to send any.[3] Unfortunately, some destroyed the records and were severely reprimanded by the Governor who rightly considered them public property which should be preserved for their successors.[4] This lapse is borne out by the fact that the majority of reports found in the National Archives in Guyana were those regularly sent in by McClintock and a very few by his *confrères*, Hancock, King, and de Wolff, and later officials like T. Vaughan of Berbice. Yet there were six Superintendents of Rivers and Creeks until 1850 when their number was reduced to four!

In 1849 T. Fennell of Demerara wrote a memorial complaining of his financial embarrassment and reminding the Court of his onerous duties as Superintendent, postholder, and Commissary of Taxation with powers of a Stipendiary Magistrate.[5] In 1868 there was a very brief half-yearly report from T. Vaughan of Berbice mentioning that he had visited the Indian settlements and woodcutters' grants.[6] However, he was probably a very ill man then, as his death was reported the following year.

[1] i.e. supporting earth with woodwork to prevent erosion (from a word of Dutch origin).
[2] Circular to T. Fennell, A. F. Baird, R. King, R. Hancock, W. C. McClintock, N. de Wolff, Superintendents of Rivers and Creeks, 6 Apr. 1848. L.B.
[3] W. B. Wolseley, Acting Government Secretary to T. Fennell, of Demerara, 20 July 1848. L.B.   [4] A. F. Gore to A. F. Baird, 21 Mar. 1855. L.B.
[5] M.C.C., 27 July 1849. N.A.G.
[6] M.C.P., 11 Feb. 1868. N.A.G.

An important duty of the Superintendents of Rivers and Creeks was their right and obligation to recommend to the Governor fitting and able Indians as Captains, and later as Constables. This system of recognizing the chiefs of Indian tribes dated back to the Dutch period during which the chiefs exercised their authority as accredited officers under the sanction of the Dutch West India Company. They were given commissions and symbols of office such as silver collars, hats with broad silver rims, and silver-headed staves of office somewhat similar to those carried by the Inca. The British continued the practice as noted in a list of presents in 1803.[1] In 1825 J. V. Mittelholzer requested swords for the Captains as they treasured them as symbols of their authority, and in 1839 Robert King of Demerary suggested that the Court give the Indian Captains some 'honorary distinguishing mark' which would encourage them to help the Government 'since they receive no more presents'.[2] The Arawak Captain, 'John Robertson', recommended by P. A. J. Grant, Superintendent of Essequibo, as Captain and Constable was promised 'his staff . . . as soon as one can be made'.[3] The Superintendents' recommendations were always subject to the Governor's approval, but he was guided by and followed the suggestions of the Superintendents. McClintock usually elaborated on the qualifications of his nominees. In recommending Watson, an Indian, to fill the place of the deceased John Henry, Captain of the Warraus in the Moruka as well as the Arawak Cabaralli, he gave glowing qualifications.[4] McClintock looked on the Captain system as extremely important, not only because the captains kept peace and order among their own people, but through their example in embracing Christianity, civilization was progressing.[5] As rural constables over the coloured population, Superintendents in other areas reported the Indians were utter failures.[6] Written commissions for the Captains, as well as their staves of office, were forwarded through the Superintendents, although the Captains received the commissions from the Governor himself if they were in town. As Justices of the Peace, the Superintendents had the

[1] M.C.P., 27 Feb. 1803. N.A.G.
[2] M.C.P., 9 June 1839. Robert King's Report. N.A.G.
[3] Charles Austin, Acting Government Secretary to P. A. J. Grant, 16 Oct. 1866. L.B.
[4] McClintock to Walker, 1 July 1854. N.A.G.
[5] Ibid., 27 Mar. 1869.
[6] Parliamentary Papers, *British Guiana*, II, Barkly to Grey, 15 Aug. 1850, 154.

authority to swear in the Captains as Constables for any special service.[1]

In the 1850s the taking of the census in the remote areas was added to the Superintendents' duties through McClintock's zeal. Ever eager to have more knowledge of his Indians, numerical and otherwise, he stated in one of his reports that he would gladly undertake the job, provided it had the Governor's sanction.[2] Thus the Governor and the Court of Policy happily took it for granted that they would expect the same zeal from the other Superintendents and suggested to them 'the propriety of a simultaneous move'.[3] In 1851 when McClintock asked for a reimbursement of the expenses he had incurred in taking the census, the Governor reminded him that it was his idea as indicated by his offer 'shewing very clearly (he) considered it as part of . . . regular work'.[4] He had received no instructions from the executive. Yet in 1861 he was officially required to take the census on 7 April. A copy of the 1861 Census Ordinance was forwarded to him and he was cautioned to pay strict attention to its requirements, as 'Neglect on [his] part may endanger [his] official existence.'[5] C. H. Hancock of Berbice and P. A. J. Grant of Essequibo were, also, requested to take the census in their districts according to Section 13 of the Census Ordinance: '. . . with respect to the population including Aborigines residing in Rivers and Creeks and other remote parts of the Colony, not included in any particular Enumerators' Districts'.[6] This taking of a census of a mobile population was a rather impossible task. Also, the census had to be taken on one designated day. There was hardly ever enough time to muster the already suspicious Indians at the respective posts; and if the Indians had decided on a day of hunting or fishing, it was most unlikely that they would stay around to be counted.

The Superintendents acted as 'doctors', as well as census enumerators, in the remote areas. When the epidemics broke out, as they so often did, among the Indians, the Superintendents, if

[1] J. Gardiner Austin, Acting Government Secretary, to McClintock, 2 Nov. 1852. L.B. See Appendix X.

[2] M.C.P., 25 July 1845. McClintock's Report, 30 June 1845. N.A.G.

[3] J. G. Austin to R. King, Superintendent of Rivers and Creeks, Berbice, 27 Jan. 1851. (Similar letters were sent to the other Superintendents.) L.B.

[4] H. W. Austin, Assistant Government Secretary, to McClintock, 18 Aug. 1851. L.B.

[5] J. B. L. Mure, Acting Government Secretary, to McClintock, 19 Mar. 1861. L.B.

[6] J. M. Grant, Government Secretary to P. A. Grant and C. H. Hancock, 23 Jan. and 14 Feb. 1871. L.B.

unable to cope with the situation themselves, immediately appealed for medical help from Georgetown. Under the direction of McClintock, Dr. Edward Cullen vaccinated 400 Indians in settlements on the Moruka river and in the upper district of the Pomeroon river during the 1841 smallpox epidemic.[1] Requests of the Superintendents for supplies of medicine were met by the Governor out of the Contingency Fund, and even directions for the use of the medicines in the chest were forwarded.[2] In cases where doctors were not available, the Superintendents gave the vaccine themselves. The Central Board of Health, at McClintock's request, forwarded medicines, blankets, and sugar to the Indians in Anna Regina, Essequibo, during the 1857 cholera epidemic which decimated so many of the Indians.[3] The Indians were petrified and after McClintock himself became ill, they retreated into the forests, cutting down large trees to block the paths and prevent their being followed. Thus many died having eluded vaccination.

In the legal sphere the Superintendents listened to and settled complaints brought by the Indians against their employers or against another member or members of their tribe. The woodcutters often took advantage of the Indians and refused to pay them their wages. Hence the Indian's reluctance to be employed either on woodcutting grants or on estates. This aspect of the Superintendent's duties as arbitrator and peacemaker will be extensively discussed in the following chapter which will illustrate the legal jurisdiction exercised over the Indians in minor and major cases.

As ascertained from their reports, the Superintendents of Rivers and Creeks seriously accepted the responsibility for the protection of the Indians, although this responsibility was not the *prima facie* reason for their appointment, regardless of the Government Secretary's observation to Dr. Cullen that the 1838 Ordinance related 'chiefly to the protection of the Indians and the preventing of trespass on Crown Lands . . .'[4] A reversed order in that observation would have been closer to the rationale of the Ordinance. This fact

[1] M.C.P., 15 Mar. 1842. Dr. E. Cullen to Government Secretary, H. E. F. Young. 3 Mar. 1842. N.A.G. Epidemics were the perennial enemy of the Indians; in 1841 the small pox raged and again in 1854, followed by measles. In 1857 when cholera swept through the colony, it spread to the interior where the Indians died like flies.
[2] A. F. Baird, Assistant Government Secretary to McClintock, 29 Aug. 1848 and W. B. Wolseley, Government Secretary to McClintock, 26 Jan. 1854. L.B.
[3] Extract from the Minutes of the Central Board of Health, 23 Feb. 1857. L.B.
[4] H. E. F. Young to Dr. Cullen, 7 June 1841. L.B.

was again borne out in 1849 when the Estimates for 1850 came before the Court of Policy. It was recommended that the number of Superintendents be reduced from six to three—one for each of the three counties of Demerara, Essequibo, and Berbice.[1] The usual haggling over that item took place, the discussions often becoming very heated. Their usefulness was again questioned. One Member of the Court remarked that Superintendents would be seen in town almost every day; another member was not even aware of the present number of Superintendents! The Governor insisted that they were liaison officers between the local government and the people in the remote areas, and used the financial plea that they were 'very useful in preventing encroachments and squatting on Crown Lands, the revenue of which had been made over to the colony and ought to be protected by it . . .'.[2]

In 1849 the Combined Court were in one of their classically intransigent moods resulting from the strike of the previous year and the consequent evaporation of capital. They were resolutely determined to effect a 25 per cent reduction of officials which precipitated another constitutional crisis when Governor Barkly adjourned the Court on this issue. Warned by the Secretary of State, Earl Grey, that he would not sanction any reduction in the Civil List, the Court replied in no uncertain terms that it would not 'succumb to the despotic sway of the Colonial Office'.[3] It had previously launched a protest against the powers of Her Majesty's Privy Council to enact Laws for the colony.[4] The struggle over the Civil List did not end until February 1850 when the Combined Court was appeased by a grant of £250,000 from the Imperial Government for immigration.

This grant did not help to spare the office of Superintendent of Rivers and Creeks. The plantocracy of the Combined Court still felt their interests were jeopardized and they pushed for the reduction of the Superintendents from six to four for '. . . it was not in the power of the Court to keep up the establishment of the Colony at their former rate. If such distress were felt at these partial reductions—for God knew they were only partial—what would be the effect if the sugar cultivation of the colony was abandoned . . .

---

[1] C.O. 115/18, *The Royal Gazette*, 6 Feb. 1850.
[2] C.O. 111/266, M.C.P., 31 May 1849.
[3] C.O. 114/17. 26 Apr. 1849.
[4] C.O. 111/264. Barkly to Grey, 21 Feb. 1849.

what would become of them two or three years hence when the cultivation of sugar was abandoned?'[1] There was no doubt whose future concerned the Members of the Combined Court. They thus judged every item of expenditure against the backdrop of sugar and self. When, at the end of 1849 they were on the verge of reducing the number of Superintendents from six to three, the impracticality of that policy was brought to their attention by R. Hancock of Mahaica who pointed out that the Superintendent of either Demerara or Berbice would be unable to carry out a 'proper' surveillance of the Mahaica, Mahaicony, and Abary creeks or 'to adjudicate complaints and protect Indians who have never hitherto been without a Protector or Postholder for the last fifty years'.[2] Incredibly, the Court compromised and the salaries for four were voted, viz.:

1.	County of Berbice and Canje with the Corentyne	$2,000
2.	County of Demerara	$2,000
3.	County of Essequibo	$1,800
4.	Pomeroon	$1,200
		$7,000[3]

Robert King, T. Fennell, A. F. Baird, and W. C. F. McClintock were appointed to these areas respectively.[4] Hancock, who had raised the point regarding the Mahaica, Mahaicony, and Abary districts, was not included, nor were those districts provided for. There was no comparison between those latter areas and the Pomeroon, where the ever-increasing number of Indians necessitated surveillance. In 1849 McClintock had estimated the number of Indians in the Pomeroon district at 7,000.[5] Between 1840 and 1853 the numbers in the Mahaica, Mahaicony, and Abary creeks never totalled more than 500—the number in Mahaicony in 1853 being approximately 238.[6]

Nevertheless, Governor Barkly complained to Earl Grey that this reduction would 'soon prove to be as short-sighted, as it would undoubtedly be inhumane', for 'sound policy, on the contrary, suggests an increase rather than a reduction in the number of officers appointed . . . who acted both as police magistrates and

[1] C.O. 116/8. M.C.C., 25 Mar. 1850, in *The Royal Gazette*, 4 Apr. 1850.
[2] R. Hancock to William Walker, Government Secretary, 17 Jan. 1850. L.B.
[3] C.O. 114/17. M.C.C., 25 Mar. 1850 and C.O. 111/274, *B.G. Colonial Taxes*, 1850.
[4] C.O. 115/19, *Government Notice* in *The Royal Gazette*, 3 July 1850.
[5] M.C.P., 6 Dec. 1849. McClintock's Report, 30 Sept. 1849. N.A.G.
[6] Louis de Ryck, Mahaicony. Mission Report, B.G. 1, 1834–58. U.S.P.G.A.

collectors of taxes'.[1] Though his reference to the inhumane aspect of the reduction might suggest an interest in the protection of the Indians, Barkly was obviously more concerned with the bringing in of the revenue.

The item of four Superintendents of Rivers and Creeks was again challenged in 1851 and 1852,[2] but surprisingly not questioned in 1853.[3] The reason for this might have been the steady flow of immigrants from Madeira, Africa, and India, as well as the beginning of Chinese immigration, which no doubt put the plantocracy in an expansive frame of mind, but not for long. In 1855 there were again lengthy discussions on the item. Several members contended that the term postholder had no definite meaning and should be struck out, leaving the original item for the Superintendents of Rivers and Creeks. Others maintained that the whole item should be abolished. If this decision were carried, the Governor reminded the Court that it would be absolutely necessary to devise some other system for protecting the revenue. Although the Superintendents did little, they still protected the revenue![4] The editorial of *The Royal Gazette*, commenting on the Court's attitude, concluded that the office as 'at present constituted . . . is little else than a farce and a mockery'.[5] Nevertheless, the three Superintendents survived until 1856 when their number was reduced to two,[6] the Superintendent for Essequibo being struck off. At the request of the Attorney General this Superintendent was reinstated on the Estimate in 1859.[7]

In the 1860s with the timber trade rapidly becoming 'a booming industry', the Court again decided to revise the regulations for the management of Crown lands which came under the No. 6, 1838 Ordinance. The No. 14, 1857 Ordinance had empowered the sub-Registrars to act as postholders, but it had proved impracticable for them to leave their own districts and exercise any real surveillance over the revenue in the remote parts of the colony.[8] Now the *raison d'être* of the new proposed No. 14, 1861 Ordinance, which repealed the No. 6, 1838 Ordinance, was explained by the Attorney-General,

[1] C.O. 111/272. Barkly to Grey, 9 Feb. 1850.
[2] C.O. 114/18, M.C.C., 19 Mar. 1851 and M.C.C., 15 Mar. 1852.
[3] Ibid., M.C.C., 8 Mar. 1853.
[4] C.O. 116/12. M.C.C., 18 May 1855, in *The Royal Gazette*, 29 May 1855.
[5] C.O. 116/12. Editorial of *The Royal Gazette*, 31 May 1855.
[6] M.C.C., 27 May 1856. N.A.G.   [7] M.C.P., 30 Mar. 1859. N.A.G.
[8] C.O. 111/331. Enclosed in Governor Walker to the Duke of Newcastle, 6 Aug. 1861.

Lucie Smith, as a necessary move to cope with the expanding timber industry[1] and was well expressed in its title: 'An Ordinance to Make Better Provision for the Care and Superintendence of the Rivers, Creeks, Crown Lands, and Forests of the Colony.' The Office of the Superintendency now embraced not only the Rivers and Creeks, but also the immeasurably and potentially valuable forest lands.

The Ordinance legislated for a tighter control over the wood-cutters. The Superintendents were enjoined to make half-yearly or more regular visits to the settlements and grants within their districts to ascertain that the licences corresponded to the number of licencees, and thus assure the government that they were not being defrauded of revenue. Every January and July, reports from the Superintendents had to be transmitted to the Governor and Court of Policy.[2] The Indians were not ignored in the Articles of the Ordinance. Section 13 reiterated Article VII of No. 6, 1838, forbidding the Superintendents to trade, traffic, or barter with the Indians. Woodcutters who employed Indians were to keep on record a list of the names and tribes of the Indians, as well as the rate and amount of wages paid them. They were strictly forbidden 'to deliver to any Indian any spirituous liquor as an equivalent for, or in part payment of wages, or for any work or labour done or performed for him by such Indian'.[3]

This 1861 Ordinance confirmed by Her Majesty's Government in October 1861[4] continued until 1869. All future Governors recognized and realized the obvious fact that the duties of the Superintendents involved mainly the protection of 'the revenue derived from the Crown Lands and Forests',[5] and not of the Indians. Under the 1861 Ordinance the three Superintendents for Essequibo, Berbice with the Canje and Coretyne rivers, and the Pomeroon were continued with salaries of $2,400 for Essequibo and Berbice, and $1,440 for Pomeroon.[6] In 1866 McClintock was given an additional salary of $560 as long as he held office.[7] No official deserved an addendum more than McClintock who never failed to visit every part of his district and send in his reports as faithfully. Even in his 1846 report he could truthfully say that he knew

[1] C.O. 111/331. Enclosed in Governor Walker to the Duke of Newcastle, 6 Aug. 1861.
[2] Section 34 of Ordinance. [3] Section 21, III of Ordinance.
[4] C.O. 111/333. Newcastle to Walker, 14 Oct. 1861.
[5] C.O. 111/347. Governor Francis Hincks to Edward Cardwell, 5 July 1864.
[6] M.C.P., 1 Apr. 1862. N.A.G. [7] Ibid., 14 Mar. 1867. N.A.G.

personally almost every Indian in his district, Pomeroon. Ordinances were passed and amended shifting the emphasis from Indians to woodcutters, but McClintock never shifted his interest, many times to the embarrassment of the Combined Court.

The Ordinance No. 1 of 1869[1] which amended Ordinance No. 14 of 1861, was in turn amended by Ordinance No. 12 of 1871—all for the more rigid control of the Crown lands. The Superintendents were still allowed to exist and were given more jurisdiction and power as Justices of the Peace.[2] With the exception of McClintock, who still wrote about his 'poor, benighted children', the half-yearly reports of the other Superintendents spoke mainly of the timber trade, with much reference to the Portuguese traders evading the provisions of the Ordinance by carrying on illicit traffic in shingles and rum with the complicity of the Indians, 'to the prejudice and injury of licensed woodcutters'.[3] Some Superintendents were quite lax in sending in reports and explanations for their neglecting to do so were demanded by the Governor.[4]

The fact that unscrupulous traders and woodcutters used the Indians as dupes led in part to the amendment of the previous Ordinances and the enacting of No. 12 of 1871, as Governor Scott explained to Earl Kimberley:

The 1st and 2nd sections relate to the Aboriginal Indians and their privileges. Those privileges have hitherto been undefined, and their uncertainty has led to some confusion. By the regulations, which are now being prepared, all the privileges which are of any use to them will be preserved, while designing persons will not be able to make use of them as tools for the purpose of evading the law.[5]

The Colonial Office agreed that this new Ordinance was an improvement on the original one and sanctioned it.[6] Again the interest in and concern for the privileges of the Indians sprang from the desire of the local government to prevent the loss of revenue.

By 1873 even the Court realized that the veil for the frequently repealed Ordinances was wearing thin and decided to discard it

[1] C.O. 111/371. Governor James Scott to Earl Granville, 29 Jan. 1869.

[2] M.C.P., 18 Jan. 1869. N.A.G.

[3] M.C.P., 18 Feb. 1869 and 13 July 1870. N.A.G.

[4] J. M. Grant, Government Secretary to C. Cox and P. A. Grant, Superintendents, 20 July 1870. L.B.

[5] C.O. 111/386. Scott to Kimberley, 23 Aug. 1871.

[6] C.O. 111/388. Walcott to Herbert, 12 Oct. 1871.

altogether.[1] In the first reading of the newly proposed Bill which would establish a Crown Lands Department, the office of Superintendents of Rivers and Creeks was abolished.[2] The Commissaries of Taxation were reinstated. For the more effective carrying out of the provisions of the Bill, Special Magistrates were to be appointed with all the powers of Stipendiary Magistrates of the Peace. The Ordinance No. 9 of 1873 was entitled: 'An Ordinance to Make Provision for the Establishment of a Crown Lands Department, and for the Care and Superintendence of the Crown Lands, Forests, Rivers and Creeks, of the Colony.'[3] The Crown lands took precedence; the Rivers and Creeks were tagged on at the end of the title, in contrast to previous Bills.

McClintock, whose services the Court undoubtedly appreciated, was continued as a Special Magistrate for the River Pomeroon and all the rivers and creeks west of it to the limits of the colony, while M. M'Turk was appointed for the River Essequibo and its tributaries. McClintock's jurisdiction under the former Ordinances remained intact. The last communication to McClintock as a Superintendent of Rivers and Creeks was dated 11 March 1873.[4]

The 1873 Ordinance thus stripped away the last mask of the pretext of Indian protection. The preamble left no doubt about its purpose:

> Whereas it is expedient to establish a Crown Lands Department for the due record of Lands alienated, or to be alienated, whether by Grant or Licence or Occupation; for the preparation of Wood-Cutting Licences, and other grants of Crown Lands; for the survey of Crown Lands; for the collection of all moneys due, or to become due, in respect to Lands alienated, or to be alienated; and for the care and superintendence of the Crown Lands, Forests, Rivers and Creeks of the Colony . . .[5]

Crown Surveyors, Commissaries of Taxation, and Stipendiary Magistrates were to exercise the duties which their names connoted —watch-dogs of Crown lands and collectors of taxes. For the Crown these officials were to be the guardians of the Colony's 'wood, troolies, palm or other leaves, shingles, charcoal, soil, minerals, rock, stone, sand, or other substance or thing, boat, tool or imple-

[1] E. Walker, Acting Government Secretary, to P. A. Grant, 18 Feb. 1873. L.B.
[2] M C.P., 4 Mar. 1873 and 16 Apr. 1873. N.A.G.
[3] M.C.P., 14 June 1873 and 1873 *Blue Book*, N.A.G.
[4] J. Grant, Government Secretary, to McClintock, 11 Mar. 1873. L.B.
[5] No. 9, 1873. *Blue Book*, 1873. N.A.G.

ment'.[1] Although the Indians were given a nodding reference in the reiteration of previous regulations forbidding their payment in liquor and upholding their rights and privileges as defined in the 1871 Ordinance,[2] they were no longer considered worthy of attention by the Court. Individual officials like McClintock and M'Turk zealously continued to protect the Indians, but this protection was not demanded by the government as part of their duties as Special Magistrates. If records were kept after 1873 they were not preserved by the government, an indication of their complete lack of interest in the fate of the aboriginals, who not until 1881 were included in the population census.[3]

According to the previous regulations governing the duties of the Superintendents of Rivers and Creeks, these officials had been the police of the interior and the collectors of revenue. Despite the negative nature of these duties regarding the protection of Indians, lasting credit must be given to the Superintendents in general, and W. C. F. McClintock in particular, who maintained an interest in the Indians and spoke up for them even to the deaf ears of the Court.

[1] Section 33 of No. 9 Ordinance.
[2] Section 16, III and Section 53 of No. 9, 1873.
[3] *Results of the Decennial Census of the Population of British Guiana*, 3 Apr. 1881. The Preface stated that '7,656 Aborigines are included in the Census, but it is more probable that the aborigines greatly exceed that number as these people lead a wandering life . . .' N.A.G.

V

BRITISH LEGAL JURISDICTION OVER THE INDIANS: CONFLICT BETWEEN NATIVE CUSTOMS AND BRITISH LAW

In the early days of British administration the Indians continued to bring their complaints to the postholders and the Protectors of Indians, who, having no magisterial authority, acted as mediators, or failing grounds for the prosecution of a case, bought off the animosity of the Indians, although they were sometimes quite determined to fight. Later the Superintendents of Rivers and Creeks were vested with magisterial authority and exercised it in cases of civil jurisdiction.

The Indians had unquestionably recognized the protectorate of the Dutch, and the Dutch had assumed the responsibilities of a protecting power. The principal officers, the postholders, had administered this protectorate, responsible for the maintenance of order at the posts and for the prevention of ill-treatment of the Indians by both the settlers and other Indians. The Dutch had encouraged the natives to bring their complaints of murder, slavery, and ill-treatment to their courts, where they were given satisfaction. In the case of blood feuds, the Dutch West India Company either made every possible effort to reconcile the parties by bribes or threats, or failing this, allowed them to fight out their quarrels.

Among the Guyana aboriginals, as among other primitive races, there was no strict law in the modern sense—no courts, no judges, no jury, no police, no centralized authority. Custom regulated social relationships and most customs were bound up with a 'religious' meaning. The Indian lived in fear of offending a host of spirits, and the infringement of a religious law might bring down on him and his family dire punishment. For secular offences, namely homicide, poisoning, theft, and adultery, personal justice was meted out. Retribution was the order of the day. 'To obtain satisfaction from one who has committed an offence against him a man may have recourse to one or more of the following media of action: (1) poisoning, (2) sorcery, (3) violence, (4) kanaima.'[1] For if an Indian suffered death at the hands of another, this death was considered to be brought about by the evil worked on him. Hence his nearest kin was obliged to avenge his death. This obviously gave rise to a vendetta which frequently terminated in tribal war, and as Hilhouse pointed out, the rigid observance of the *lex talionis* tended greatly to prevent the increase of population.[2] The blood feuds mostly originated 'in jealousy and the revenge of connubial injuries'.[3]

To eradicate such bloodshed and to maintain law and order, the Dutch recognized the authority of the Indian chiefs and conferred on them marks of distinction and symbols of authority. Commissions were formally issued to the chiefs who in this way became accredited officers of the Dutch colony. The preservation of peace among the Indians was vital to the interests of the Dutch West India Company which needed an environment of order for both the establishment and progress of their trade.

The British found themselves in serious need of the services of the Indians as intelligence officers and security police and issued elaborate instructions to the postholders and Protectors regulating their relations with the Indians. The Indians were, above all, encouraged to bring their complaints before these officials instead of taking the law into their own hands. Instances of the exercise of jurisdiction accepted by the Indians in minor cases were numerous, but in criminal cases the acceptance of this jurisdiction was more theoretical than practical. In the light of his beliefs regarding the avenging of evil, the Indian neither understood nor felt himself bound by the British law. In his eyes such an act was a right and fitting one, and not murder. Through his experiences with the various tribes Schomburgk confirmed this aboriginal belief: 'The Principle of revenge, based upon blood for blood, life for life is implanted in their breast from the time they are able to understand their maternal language.'[4]

Neither the home government nor the local government saw eye to eye with the Indians on such a vital legal point. Neither were they completely happy with the obvious conflict which evolved between the native customs and the British law—a conflict which the British colonizers throughout the ever-growing empire never fully solved.

[1] Gillin, p. 337. [2] Hilhouse, *Indian Notices*, p. 14.
[3] Ibid. [4] C.O. 111/179. Schomburgk's Report, 1841.

In 1831, the first murder case in which Billy William, an Arawak, was indicted and tried for killing his wife, Hannah, for adultery[1] brought the local Courts face to face with two legal questions: (1) Did the Courts of Justice have legal jurisdiction over the Indians? and (2) If they had such jurisdiction, could they prosecute the Indian for violations of laws of which they had no civilized understanding?

The President of the Court of Justice, Honourable Charles Wray, argued that the Indians had never disputed the territorial rights of the British and had placed themselves under their jurisdiction. In other words, claimed Justice Wray, the Indian territorial status was that of 'a conquered nation, or, more accurately speaking, that of a nation whose lands the Dutch, our predecessors, occupied, peopled, and governed by their own laws, without any resistance from the former inhabitants'.[2] Regarding the second problem Wray's arguments were not as convincing. The evidence given at Billy William's trial by William Hilhouse, A. van Ryck de Groot, Protector of Indians, and the father of the accused, all testified that it was unwritten law among the Indians that adultery was punishable by the death of the woman. Hilhouse contended that the treaties made by the Indians with the British placed them in the position of allies and not subjects, and that therefore the Indians could not be held responsible for the violations of a law which they did not consider binding.

In his summing up, Wray countered this argument by attesting that the Indians received the benefit and protection of the laws and hence 'must be subject to the restraints and punishments which those laws adopt for the prevention and punishment of crimes'.[3] It might be justifiable homicide, he argued, to the Indian to claim the life of another Indian in the case of adultery, but if the Court accepted this Indian custom, on what grounds could they try an Indian for the murder of a white or black man or vice versa?[4] Because the Indian was still in a 'wild state of barbarianism', his peculiar customs should lead the Court, if he were found guilty, to recommend mercy and mitigation of the death sentence to His Majesty's Government.[5]

[1] Indictment Register, Aug. 1829–July 1832; Seventh Criminal Session, 1 Mar. 1831. L.C.G.

[2] Notebook of His Honour Charles Wray, President of the Court of Criminal and Civil Justice of the Colonies of Demerara and Essequibo, 28 Feb. 1831. N.A.G. See also C.O. 111/72.

[3] Ibid.   [4] Ibid.   [5] Ibid.

Billy William, speaking no English and without the slightest understanding of the legal arguments of the British courts, was found guilty and sentenced to be hanged, but because it was 'the first trial of an Indian for such an offence and his probable ignorance of our laws and Customs',[1] the Court asked that the sentence be commuted by the King.

The Colonial Secretary, Lord Goderich, concurred with President Wray in the opinion that there was 'sufficient proof both of British occupation and of the Indians claiming and enjoying the Protection of British officers in that territory'.[2] He also agreed with Governor D'Urban that Billy William, in taking his wife's life, had acted in conformity with the traditions and customs of his tribe; he, therefore, could not be held as reprehensible as a civilized Christian who had committed a similar offence. Indeed, the 'real difficulty' as Lord Goderich saw it, and a real difficulty it was, was 'to determine whether it can justly receive any punishment at all'.[3] In order to prevent a vicious cycle of 'murder' set in motion by the retaliatory law and placing the British courts in the unenviable position of trying another Indian for murder which he regarded as a necessary and praiseworthy deed, compromise in true British style was adopted. His Majesty's Government commuted the capital sentence passed on Billy William, and recommended his transportation to some part of the South American continent.

Goderich concluded his lengthy dispatch on the case by stressing that if the Indians were held responsible for the violation of British laws, they must be accorded every protection by the civil and military authorities, for 'To punish crime without establishing any system for its prevention' was 'but a very imperfect performance of the duties of good government'.[4] It was, moreover, unfair that civilized life was bringing them into touch with 'the severity of its penal sanctions' and not with its blessings. Regardless of the cost to the economy of the country, Goderich urged that immediate steps be taken to impart the benefits of religious and moral instruction to the natives as an obligation which an enlightened government owed to them.[5] Goderich was certainly aware of the travesty of justice implicit in trying to apply the common law to an indigenous people whose customs and culture differed from those of the British. But it would

---

[1] Indictment Register, 1 Mar. 1831. L.C.G.
[2] C.O. 112/15. Goderich to D'Urban, 21 July 1831.   [3] Ibid.
[4] Ibid.   [5] Ibid.

take another century before the simple truth would become obvious to law administrators dealing with other races 'that to treat other people as if they were Englishmen was at best unrealistic and at worst unjust'.[1] And even now this truth is not as simple and obvious to those who continue to insist on 'the law, the whole law, and nothing but the law'.

While the local government debated the puzzling question of where to transport the prisoner for the safety of his own life—French Guiana and other South American states naturally objected to an exiled murderer in their midst—another murder was committed on the Essequibo river above the junction of the Mazaruni. Another Arawak, Frederick, killed his mother-in-law and father-in-law when they were out in the fields, for no other reason it seemed, except that the old man, Jacobus alias Dutchman, had angered him. He had retaliated by clubbing both Jacobus and his wife, Juletta, to death.[2] Mr. George Bagot, the Second Fiscal and Protector of Indians, in reporting the murder emphasized the fact that the family of the murdered Jacobus and Juletta could have taken Frederick's life in compensation, but were satisfied on his arrest that justice would be meted out to him, and that in short, he would be hanged. Bagot proceeded to offer a number of instances in which the Indians showed 'not only their willingness but . . . their desire to have their death feuds taken up and settled by us'.[3] Five years previously, after a retaliatory feud had claimed the lives of many innocent victims, the Chiefs of the respective parties had asked him as Protector to intervene. He had agreed on condition that the chiefs sign a treaty of Peace and Alliance, as well as an agreement, to have individuals tried by the British laws. To this the chiefs had assented; hence, Bagot felt that the plea of ignorance of the course of British justice was invalid.[4] There is no evidence, however, of such a treaty, which, if negotiated, would surely have been known to the Court of Policy and a conclusive proof of their jurisdiction which was argued in the previous case.

Frederick's case again brought under discussion the *lex talionis*. Lawrence, the son of the murdered man and woman, when cross-examined at the trial, admitted that he wanted to shoot Frederick but

[1] Colin Howard, 'What Colour is the "Reasonable Man"?' *Criminal Law Review* 1961), p. 43.

[2] Indictment Register. First Criminal Session, 13 Feb. 1832. L.C.G.

[3] C.O. 111/117. Bagot to D'Urban, 20 Sept. 1831, enclosed in D'Urban to Goderich, 26 Nov. 1831.   [4] Ibid.

he had run away '. . . as he has killed . . . he must be killed'.[1] The question of jurisdiction was again raised by Mr. Arindell, Counsel for the Prisoner, but his arguments were brushed aside as that question had been settled in the previous case. The Court unanimously found Frederick guilty, showing that he did know right from wrong in his concealment of the bodies and the stick with which he had killed.[2]

Although the right of jurisdiction seemed unquestionably settled in both cases, the question of whether the Indians could be punished for the violation of laws contrary to their own tribal customs was not so easily solved. The fact that Governor D'Urban and the Court again referred the case to the Colonial Office revealed their perplexity in the matter. Lord Goderich again declared: 'The general question as to the exercise by the British Courts of a criminal jurisdiction over the Indian Tribes though it involves some difficulties, admits . . . upon the whole of little hesitation.'[3] But here certainty stopped. Goderich felt that the administration of criminal law must take into consideration the customs of the Indians, yet he hastened to add, not to the extent of 'perverting or exeeding in any degree the Letter and Spirit of the British laws'.[4]

Out of Frederick's case evolved another complication in an already complicated affair. The Chief Justice had raised the point that, although the unanimity of the Court on the verdict had been publicly declared, the unanimity of the votes as to the sentence had not. Goderich, undoubtedly the mouthpiece of his legal adviser, James Stephen,[5] brushed aside this ambiguity as a mere legal quibble as the Judges and Assessors had voted in open Court in favour of judgement, although the fact was not 'audibly announced'.[6] He advised D'Urban that if the Judges agreed on the validity of the sentence, the prisoner should be banished for life for his own safety; if on the other hand, he were discharged, he should be protected from the vengeance of the members of his own society or the result would be new homicides for adjudication before British courts.[7] In other

[1] Notes on Trial in D'Urban to Goderich, 12 Apr. 1832. N.A.G.
[2] Ibid.   [3] C.O. 112/16. Goderich to D'Urban, 17 Feb. 1832.
[4] Ibid.
[5] Stephen was appointed part-time legal adviser to the Colonial Office in 1813, an office made permanent in 1825. In 1834 he became Assistant Under Secretary and from 1836 to 1847 Permanent Under Secretary, but was more widely known as 'Mr. Over-Secretary'.
[6] C.O. 112/16. Goderich to D'Urban, 4 July 1832.   [7] Ibid.

words, the British Tribunal would find itself in the same predicament—a predicament that was not only legal and moral, but also financial. To conclude, in Frederick's case, the Judges did agree on the validity of the sentence of death which was commuted by His Majesty's Government. Both Billy William and Frederick were transported for life to Trinidad.[1]

In May 1833 an Arawak, Simon, also an assistant postholder, killed six Indians and took several female prisoners of the Paramona tribe as slaves. The First Fiscal, Mr. Charles Herbert, who seemed to have an understanding of the Indian customs, liberated him, but the Second Fiscal, Mr. George Bagot, re-imprisoned him on more conclusive evidence of his guilt[2] and transmitted him to Georgetown for trial. In a communication to Governor Carmichael Smyth, Herbert stressed the need to bring home to the Indians the fact that they came under British legal jurisdiction, and stated that the Chief Justice had requested him to direct the Protectors of Indians to inform the various tribes that they would always meet with redress whenever they applied to the government's tribunals for any wrong that was inflicted on them. He emphasized the importance of such a communication, as from the evidence given in the trial it was obvious that the Indians considered themselves avengers of their own wrongs. The Chief Justice rightly felt that 'a proper notification of our determination to interfere would prevent much bloodshed and gradually reduce them to acknowledge our authority'.[3]

It was clear that the Indians had not succumbed to the legal authority of the British and were still obeying their own retaliatory law. The Chief Judge deemed it vital that such unorthodox legal behaviour be rectified, but the Governor thought differently and opted for a non-interference policy. The advocating of the Indians' quarrels, which he considered unintelligible, would achieve nothing but great inconvenience and expense to the colony.[4] And the Members of the Court of Policy concurred in the opinion of the Governor.[5] Simon and his followers were acquitted after a three days' trial,[6] obviously because the Courts accepted the fact that the murders had resulted from a blood feud between the Paramona and

[1] C.O. 111/126. D'Urban to Goderich, 9 Mar. 1833 and D'Urban to Charles Wray, 30 Jan. 1833. N.A.G.
[2] CW/014/24. John Armstrong to D. Coates, 13 May 1833. C.M.S.A.
[3] Charles Herbert to J. C. Smyth, 2 Aug. 1833.   [4] Ibid.
[5] M.C.P., 3 Mar. 1834. N.A.G.
[6] Herbert to J. C. Smyth, 2 Aug. 1833. N.A.G.

Arawak tribes and found themselves again at a legal impasse. The Courts naturally held as an absolute value the principle of law that one should not normally kill other human beings, but when faced with the aboriginal customs regarding the killing of others as acceptable and necessary on specific occasions, they found themselves on the horns of a dilemma. Henry Taylor remarked on the Courts' perplexity in a memorandum: '. . . the Courts although they cannot clearly make out that they have any determinate jurisdiction over the Indians, are accustomed as a matter of expediency to take cognizance of any cases of a grave nature.'[1]

Expediency and realism led the Courts again to resort to the panacea of gift distribution to the Paramona tribes. The acquittal of Simon had led to an open state of hostilities between the two tribes, and to effect a reconciliation and avert bloodshed the Courts had offered gifts as peace offerings. Such language, and not legal arguments, was immediately understood by both tribes. Indeed, the Courts realized that to bring innumerable warring members of tribes to justice would have been a thankless, impossible, and expensive business.

The Governor continued to remind the officials that the Indians within the precincts of the colony were liable to the colonial laws, were always 'treated with great consideration and from obvious motives of Policy . . . ought never to be interfered with when it can be avoided'.[2] In 1839 the questions of the Courts' jurisdiction over the Indians and their liability to the laws again came under fire. When the Bill regarding the registration of craft was discussed in the Court of Policy, Governor Light proposed that the mobile Indians be exempt from the Bill.[3] His proposal raised a storm of protest. The Chief Justice, supporting the Governor, declared that the Indians were not liable to any law passed by the Court unless they settled. To the Hon. Peter Rose, the Indian who committed a murder in Georgetown was subject to the law, whereas the Chief Justice drew a fine line of distinction: if the Indian murdered a white man, yes, but if he murdered another Indian, no. Rose objected to such an argument, contending that the Indian might then commit murder with impunity. From the Chief Justice's arguments it would seem

[1] C.O. 111/127. Memorandum of H. Taylor to W. Lefevre, 31 July 1833 on Despatch of Carmichael Smyth's, 21 May 1833.

[2] H. E. F. Young, Government Secretary, to His Honour, M.A. Fowler, Sheriff, Essequibo, 25 Jan. 1837. L.B.

[3] C.O. 116/3. M.C.P., 4 Nov. 1839, in *The Guiana Chronicle*, 6 Nov. 1839.

that, because the city was not the mobile Indians' territory, the law could not be enforced against them there. Yet on the other hand, the Indian, as noted in previous murders, was held responsible for laws committed in his own territory. The conclusions of the argument in the Court of Policy showed that intransient Indians were beyond the pale of the law, but settled Indians were not. It underlined the fact that the Court of Policy was anything but unanimous on the question of jurisdiction over the Indians, or their liability to the laws. Only on banks of rivers where Indian tribes came into contact with woodcutters was there 'any attempt to subject them to the jurisdiction of the Colonial Courts and this', Taylor admitted, 'has been done only in a partial and uncertain manner'.[1]

A year later another murder case involving an Indian was brought into Court. On this occasion a colonist, John Maul, was apprehended for shooting an Indian named Bellisarius on a remote creek in the Barima river. The Superintendent of Rivers and Creeks, R. King, went up the Pomeroon to collect witnesses for the trial which took place on 25 February 1841.[2] The first indictment charging Maul with shooting with the intent to do bodily harm was thrown out by the Court. On the second indictment of assault and battery, he was acquitted on the grounds that the principal witnesses, the Indians, possessed no religious beliefs.[3]

In his opening address on 4 March 1841, Governor Light drew the attention of the Court of Policy to the quashing of criminal cases because the witnesses, Indians from the Moruka and Pomeroon rivers, were in a 'state of ignorance and barbarism' which 'deprived them of the Protection of the Law'. When brought forward as witnesses in trials, their testimony could not be taken as 'they had no idea of God, or Spirit, or future state'.[4] Lord Russell agreed that 'this state of things should not be allowed to continue, and that some Law should be made admitting the evidence of These People without an Oath.'[5] For the guidance of the Governor and the Court of Policy he enclosed the extract from a dispatch he had recently forwarded to Governor Hutt of Western Australia concerning his observations on an Act passed in that colony allowing aborigines to

---

[1] C.O. 111/180. Minute of Taylor on 'Indian Slavery up the Demerara River', 16 Oct. 1841, in Light to Russell, 20 Aug. 1841.

[2] Minutes of the Supreme Court, 24 Feb. 1841. N.A.G.   [3] Ibid.

[4] M.C.P., 4 Mar. 1841. N.A.G.

[5] Russell to Light, 11 May 1841, read in M.C.P., 8 July 1841. N.A.G. Also C.O. 112/24.

give evidence in criminal cases. The preamble read: 'To exact Oaths of Men to whom the sanctions of Religion are unknown, and who do not even recognize the elementary truths on which all religious belief must depend is a manifest absurdity.'[1] Russell admitted 'the difficulty of legislating aright for the protection of Savage Tribes living in juxtaposition with a Race of Civilized Men', but on account of certain loopholes in the Australian Act, he had to advise its disallowance.[2]

A similar titled Act as the Australian passed on 17 August 1841 by Governor Light's casting vote,[3] was disallowed by Her Majesty's Government. James Stephen wrote a lengthy memorandum on Light's enclosure of the Ordinance, giving reasons for the disallowance.[4] Thus advised, Lord Stanley, the new Colonial Secretary, incorporated these reasons in his dispatch to Light, pointing out the main loophole in the British Guiana Ordinance was the wording which implied 'that the want of an oath shall detract nothing from the force and effect of the evidence, while on the contrary the Ordinance ought to enact the admissibility of the evidence, subject however to such deduction from its weight as may be thought to attach to the fact of its being unsworn'.[5] The Colonial Office suggested a modified Ordinance. Accordingly on 13 December 1841 an amended Ordinance was passed and promulgated entitled: 'An Ordinance to permit such of the Aborigines or native Indians as may be ignorant of the nature and obligations of an oath to give information and evidence in Criminal Cases without an Oath.' The modified Ordinance reiterated the acceptance of aboriginal testimony without an oath and followed the Colonial Office's dictum quite closely in the added clause—'provided always, that the admissibility of such evidence shall be subject to such deduction from its weight as any court may deem proper to attach to the fact of such Testimony being unsworn'.[6]

[1] Extract from a Despatch of Russell to Governor Hutt, 30 Apr. 1841, read in M.C.P., 8 July 1841. N.A.G.
[2] Ibid. The Report of the Select Committee on Aborigines in 1837 had recommended that 'the suggestions made with reference to the Australian settlements' were 'with little or no variation, applicable' to British Guiana and the aborigines. In the light of these recommendations, Lord Russell felt justified in referring his observations on Australian Aboriginal policy to the Governor of British Guiana as a guide. See Parliamentary Papers. *Aborigines*, II, 87.
[3] C.O. 114/15 M.C.P., 16 and 17 May 1841.
[4] C.O. 111/179. Light to Russell, 19 Aug. 1841.
[5] Stanley to Light, 20 Oct. 1841. N.A.G.
[6] Ordinance No. 19. British Guiana. *Local Guide*, 1843, N.A.G.

And here it must be observed that although the colonial governor could veto the introduction and passing of a bill, or by his casting vote, as in this instance, push a bill through the Legislature, his power to initiate policy was shackled by the Colonial Office. On the words of Lord Grey: 'The authority of the Home Government is expressed mainly in two ways: first by the appointment of Governors, and secondly by sanctioning or disallowing the measures of the local Governments . . . It is also exercised sometimes but much more rarely by prescribing measures for their adoption.'[1]

While the Colonial Office and the Court of Policy discussed, argued, and quibbled over the Aboriginal Oath Ordinance, another murder was committed. It was alleged that a piai-man, Waihahi from Orinoco, had caused, either by his charms or by poison, the death of the family of a young Indian, Maicarawari. Maicarawari's mother, whom he loved dearly, was the last victim of the medicine man, and on him rested the obligation of avenging the deaths of the members of his family. When Maicarawari accused Waihahi of the crimes, the latter laughed and derisively warned him that he would meet a similar fate. Hence, when Waihahi came again to Moruka, Maicarawari seized his opportunity and clubbed him to death in his hammock. Schomburgk, reporting the incident to the Governor, agreed that the crime was committed within the assumed limits of the British territory, thus jurisdiction was unquestionable. He posed the question, which throughout the nineteenth century and into the twentieth has never been satisfactorily answered by either the Supreme Court in British Guiana or the Colonial Office in London, 'whether the Indian, who has no knowledge of the Christian religion, and does not acknowledge our Laws, can be punished for an act which civilized nations consider as capital crime, but which according to the manners and customs he has been brought up in, a meritorious deed?'[2] Maicarawari had presented himself to the Indian chief Cabaralli and informed him of his deed, which was certainly understandable in the light of the custom of 'blood for

[1] Earl Grey, *The Colonial Policy of Lord John Russell's Administration* (London, 1853), p. 19. An Immigration Ordinance in 1839 was disallowed by Lord John Russell who sent out a draft Ordinance, so too the 1841 Ordinance which was considered by Russell to have been unconstitutionally passed. Lord Stanley shipped back an 1843 Ordinance to be amended, and not until 1845 was it allowed on the condition that the Court of Policy vote a new Civil List. Needless to say, these 'checks and balances' infuriated the Colonists.

[2] C.O. 111/179. Schomburgk's Report, 22 June 1841, enclosed in Light to Russell, 19 July 1841.

blood, life for life'. He was brought to Georgetown and tried by a Court of Justice by laws of which he was ignorant. To Maicarawari, his act was a sacred duty to the dead; to the judges, ignorant of the feelings and customs of the Indians, it was murder. Schomburgk very forcefully declared that, because of his knowledge of the Indian, his character, customs, and manners, the young man was 'not amenable to the Courts of Law for the deed . . . committed'.[1] For want of witnesses the trial had to be quashed. It was hardly likely that the Indians would condemn Maicarawari for a deed anyone of them would be obliged to do under similar circumstances. The *Gazette* viewed the prosecution of the case as an injustice which deprived the Indian of his 'ancient hereditary right of avenging his own injuries according to the customs of the Indian tribes, until some other remedy and punishment for these injuries be first provided'.[2]

Obviously it could be maintained that Maicarawari's act was not a *crime passionel*. He knew what he had to do and waited his opportunity. Here again the difference between the civilized and the primitive man can be noted. The civilized man in a similar position would quite possibly have killed Waihahi on the spot when he arrogantly owned up to the murders. According to the law of provocation in western society, if under provocation a man loses control of his temper and commits murder, he is not held fully responsible for the killing 'if a reasonable person would have responded in the same way'.[3] The common law rule on provocation stated: 'Provocation is some act, or series of acts, done by the dead man to the accused, which would cause in any reasonable person, and actually causes in the accused, a sudden and temporary loss of self-control, rendering the accused so subject to passion as to make him or her for the

---

[1] Ibid.

[2] C.O. 115/5. Editorial in *The Gazette and General Advertiser*, 25 Nov. 1841. Almost 100 years later, Mr. J. A. Luckoo, defending the fifteen-year-old Alfred for the murder of Jonah for similar reasons, referred to the Waihahi–Maicarawari case of 1840–1 in which Maicarawari was acquitted because of his belief that he had acted in conformity with his own customs and 'code of honour'. Luckoo, in his defence of Alfred in April 1939, showed that he had acted, like Maicarawari, as an instrument of his murdered elder brother, Donis, whose spirit had reminded him of his duty to kill the evil man, Jonah, to protect the remaining members of the tribe. Again, as in the case of Maicarawari, Alfred had gone voluntarily to the police station at Kurupung and said he wanted 'to tell the white man what had happened in order that he could return home quickly'. See *The Daily Chronicle*, 27 Apr. 1939. N.A.G.

[3] Howard, p. 42.

moment not master of his mind.'[1] Hence importance was given to the cooling-off time and influenced the verdict. It seemed, therefore, that the civilized man had an edge on the aboriginal who has a low boiling-point and whose time limit of provocation extends over a longer period. No such compromise, which is 'the common law of provocation in relation to homicide',[2] was allowed him. Neither the judge nor the jury ever considered such psychological differences between races. Although the Supreme Court of Criminal Justice in the colony did appoint a competent Advocate for the defence of Indians in murder cases,[3] competent though he might be in legal matters he was totally unacquainted with the Indian character. He had never seen an Indian before, nor had he any knowledge of his customs or his feelings.

In 1848 Governor William Walker was still in the dark regarding the effectiveness of the interposition of the authorities in the domestic or clan feuds of the Indians.[4] An 1849 murder case involving an East Indian also highlighted the incompatibility of British law with an alien law. An East Indian immigrant, Anchabur Ray, had taken the life of another in accordance with oriental notions of his absolute power over the life, as well as the property, of his debtor. The sentence of death was commuted by the Governor upon the strong recommendation of the Judges of the Supreme Court on the grounds that Ray was a heathen and was ignorant of British law.[5] If such an argument of ignorance of the law was upheld in the Courts in the case of the heathen East Indian, how much more should that argument be applicable to the heathen Amerindian! But such was the roundabout of British justice. The heathen was indicted for violations of the law of which he was ignorant, and then acquitted on the same grounds. Probably the British satisfied their

[1] J. C. Smith and Brian Hogan, *Criminal Law* (London, 1969), p. 205. This rule was modified by the Homicide Act of 1957 in which 'the question whether the provocation was enough to make a reasonable man do as he did . . . [was] left to be determined by the jury.' Ibid., pp. 205–6.

[2] Howard, pp. 44–5. It was not until the 1950s in Australia when in a murder trial involving aborigines, that the law of provocation was modified in regard to the aboriginal temperament, when the Judge of the Supreme Court expressly stated 'that the degree of provocation for a white man was not necessarily the same as for an aborigine, even if this meant in practice a more lenient rule for the aborigine'.

[3] H. E. F. Young to R. Schomburgk, 26 Nov. 1841. L.B.

[4] Wolseley, Government Secretary, to Thomas Fennell, Superintendent of Rivers & Creeks, Demerara, 6 June 1848. L.B.

[5] C.O. 111/268. William Arindell, late Acting Chief Justice and Samuel Firebrace to Governor Henry Barkly, 5 Sept. 1849.

sense of justice by this method. But what stood out in sharp relief was the fact that, whenever the investigation of such murder cases necessitated great expense, the authorities invariably hedged over their prosecution. When McClintock, in his zeal to protect the Indians, asked for permission to assist in apprehending the murderer of Tamanawarie's brother, he was told that, although the Governor was anxious to protect the Indians, there would be extreme difficulty in obtaining a conviction, 'while the expense would be certain and enormous'.[1] Neither was he authorized to take steps in another murder of a Warrau Indian in the Manarie Creek because he had reported the expense entailed in holding an inquest at a place far removed from civilization.[2]

The question of finances, on many occasions, overrode the question of justice. When the Attorney-General explained to the Combined Court that the large sum under Contingent Expenses of Justice had been spent to defray the cost of bringing witnesses from the remote parts of the colony to give evidence in the Etoonie murder case, the Chief Justice feelingly proclaimed:

> The Court ought not, . . . to meddle with the Indians. They had always just the same proceedings over and over, the plea and the jurisdiction and the Court's decision, et cetera. The best mode was to let those people fight their own battles. We had nothing to do with people living 400 miles up the country; they owed no obedience, and were not subject to our laws, and were living in the interior like monkeys and baboons. They would beat one another to death with clubs, for such was the custom of their tribes.[3]

Although he agreed that the Court could not 'well pass an act to legalize outrages of that kind . . . how were they to deal with these extraordinary cases?'[4] If the Chief Justice could not see a way out of the morass, how could the Indian be expected to do so? These seemingly official comments of the Chief Justice (they were made at a meeting of the Combined Court) were immediately repudiated by Governor Walker in a letter to Superintendent R. King of Berbice, whom he ordered to disregard such remarks and continue to consider the Indians 'to be equally under the jurisdiction of the established tribunals with other of Her Majesty's subjects in this Colony'.[5]

[1] Government Secretary to McClintock, 21 Aug. 1852. L.B.
[2] J. Gardiner Austin, Acting Government Secretary to McClintock. 29 Aug. 1852. L.B.
[3] M.C.C., 6 Mar. 1854, in *The Royal Gazette*, 7 Mar. 1854. N.A.G.
[4] Ibid.   [5] Walker, Government Secretary to R. King, 30 Mar. 1854. L.B.

The press sounded as shocked as the Governor at the cold-blooded statement of the Chief Justice that the Indians should be left to slaughter each other without the intervention of the British authorities, merely to lessen the expense of justice.[1] The editorial deplored the doctrine of non-interference adopted by the Court in recent cases which excluded the Indians from the pale of legal protection. The colony owed these quiet, simple people some compensation for dispossessing them of their land; the least the government could do was to teach them habits of industry instead of washing their hands of them, legally and economically.[2]

Yet it was manifest from the Chief Justice's remarks that the recurring murders stemming from blood feuds among tribes or personal vengeance for evil, were placing the Courts in the embarrassing position of not knowing how to deal conclusively with the cases.

The massacre which took place in 1853 on the Etoonie Creek, a tributary of the Berbice river 250 miles from New Amsterdam, in which Chief Mackroo and his family were brutally murdered by Mayaroo, indicated that the Indian had certainly not accepted the British system of justice, and also that the Courts were still beating their heads against a stone wall. Lorenzo and Mackroo were rival chiefs. Deaths had occurred in Lorenzo's family and he laid the blame for these deaths on the machinations of Mackroo. From the alleged evidence, Mayaroo and his accomplices had been hired by Lorenzo to wreak vengeance on Mackroo and his family. Even as the intermediary, Mayaroo did not for a moment consider that he had committed any crime. It was all according to his cycle of justice.[3] The Courts were unable to prosecute as the principal witness 'William', who knew no English and had fled beyond the limits of the colony, while Chief Kanaimapo, whose aid had been solicited for his capture, had not exerted himself to find the fugitive,[4] although surprisingly he had helped to capture Mayaroo.[5]

The Courts again found themselves in a quandary and a vortex of their own making. Governor Walker wrote to the Duke of

[1] 'A Brief for the Indian', *The Royal Gazette*, 18 Mar. 1854. N.A.G.
[2] Ibid.
[3] C.O. 116/10. Police Magistrate's Office, 12 July 1853, in *The Royal Gazette*, 14 July 1853.
[4] H. W. Austin to R. Hancock, 26 July 1853. N.A.G. and S. H. Goodman to R. Hancock, Superintendent of Rivers and Creeks, Demerara, 10 Aug. 1853. L.B.
[5] C.O. 111/297. Walker to Newcastle, 8 Nov. 1853.

Newcastle of these legal complications arising out of the jurisdictional issue: 'The question of jurisdiction is one which I believe the Courts of Justice here have never yet been able to determine satisfactorily; partly owing to the undefined limits of our extensive territory, and partly from the migratory habits of the Indian tribes themselves and this has led to the failure of prosecutions against them for crimes.'[1] He again brought to the attention of the Colonial Secretary the barriers that constantly impeded 'the attempt to enforce the application of the Colonial Laws to the cases of aborigines'.[2] H. Taylor minuted on the Governor's dispatch his disapproval of Walker's defeatist attitude in bringing the guilty parties to justice, and strongly urged that the law officers be asked to consider legislative measures which would obviate the difficulties of jurisdiction.[3] Thirteen years earlier, on the Maicarawari case, the Colonial Office, under the legal tutelage of James Stephen, had replied that the questions on criminal jurisdiction over the Indians and their moral liability were not 'yet ripe for decision, and must therefore . . . for the present be postponed'.[4] Not only were they postponed, they were shelved and ignored. Now despite Taylor's prodding, the law officers did not venture an opinion; the questions were still unripe. A following dispatch of Walker's regarding the non-prosecution of the case, and evincing the hope that the long imprisonment of the perpetrators of the crime would duly impress the tribes, evoked no further comment from either the Colonial Secretary or the punctilious Taylor.[5]

The press was not so silent. The editor of *The Colonist* prayed, not for mercy, but for justice, and opted for 'swift and stern retribution'. He maintained: 'the savage must be brought to dread the strong arm or . . . appeal in vain to his reason, and security of life among the Indians will be at an end, if they are allowed to fancy that they . . . are out of the reach of the law', and one capital execution for the massacre would do more good 'than all the persuasions or exhortations . . .'[6] But the Portia of the press, the editor of *The Royal Gazette*, called *The Colonist*'s editor a convert to the process of civilization adopted by Spaniard for his desire to kill in the name of

[1] C.O. 111/295. Walker to Newcastle, 16 June 1853.   [2] Ibid.
[3] C.O. 111/295. H. Taylor's minute, 23 July 1853, on Walker's despatch, 16 June 1853.
[4] C.O. 111/179. J. Stephen's minute, 3 Sept. 1841, on Light's despatch, 19 July 1841.
[5] C.O. 111/297. Walker to Newcastle, 8 Nov. 1853.
[6] C.O. 116/15. *The Colonist*, 13 June 1853.

the Lord, as he felt that 'to reclaim the savage it [was] necessary and proper to hang him'. Instead, this editor with more understanding of the situation contended:

The moral obligation rests upon us to reclaim the untutored Indian, to bring him, if possible within those haunts where civilization may be found. Coax him, bribe him; we have taken possession of his heritage and we owe him this. But surely do not hang him for that revenge which, although we know, he does not, the Almighty author of us all has as a restraint on human passion reserved to himself.[1]

In his report on the Etoonie case, William Jeffrey, Justice of the Peace, concluded that it was humanly impossible to secure peace and order among remote and barbarous people, and suggested to the Governor the re-establishment of the system of Indian Captains, as well as the distribution of inexpensive presents which would go far in 'keeping alive their respect for the authorities and laws of the country'.[2]

The British had indeed followed the example of the Dutch in recognizing Indian chiefs by a formal distribution of commissions and marks of office. The aid of these Indian captains was vitally needed to furnish the necessary information on the interior and to keep the peace between the tribes after the stoppage of presents in 1838. As was noted in the foregoing chapter, the Superintendents of Rivers and Creeks recommended the appointment of Indians to the offices of captains and constables, and found them invaluable in assisting them in their duties. The commission forms[3] were even more greatly prized by the Indians than the symbols of office, for to the Indian mind a piece of paper was 'a most potent and mysterious document'.[4] Hence a captain armed with such a paper was instantly and unhesitatingly obeyed.

From the early decades of the British administration, appointments and commissions were given to Indian captains on the Demerara, Essequibo, and Pomeroon rivers. Evidence of recommendations and lists of appointments are found throughout the Letter Books from 1830 through the end of the century. The reports of McClintock reiterated the invaluable contribution of the captains in his

---

[1] C.O. 116/10. *The Royal Gazette*, 18 June 1853 and 5 July 1853.
[2] C.O. 111/295. Jeffrey to Austin, 4 July 1853.
[3] Wolseley to McClintock, 18 Sept. 1848. See Appendix XIII for Commission Form.
[4] Im Thurn, p. 212.

district, the Pomeroon, to 'the peace and order among the people entrusted to their care'.[1] It was a system that was to be pursued to the advantage of both parties. The captains acted as liaison officers between the government and their people, and were the *avant-garde* of civilization and Christianization. The Indians themselves saw the need of such a system. On the death of Captain Callistro, the oldest resident in the Moruka Creek, John Davidson petitioned the Governor for the commission in order to prevent wars among the now captainless people.[2]

As Jeffrey's request implied, no commissioned captains existed up the Berbice river, hence the need of such a system in that area to prevent bloodshed. Governor Walker acted on Jeffrey's suggestion and gave both presents and a commission to Chief Kanaimapo with the power to repress violence among his people.[3]

Although McClintock claimed that the frequent juridical visits of the Superintendents to remote districts in order 'to bring the law to every man's door' would lessen the committal of murders, and that the Indians were submitting their grievances for adjudication instead of taking the law in their own hands,[4] legal Utopia was never attained. In 1855 another atrocious murder was committed on the Berbice river by Arawaks. Again it was a 'blood for blood' expiatory murder. An Indian who had committed a previous murder and fled to Macusi country for safety, later returned with his family. His enemies, ever on the look-out, now took the lives of his two wives and children in revenge for his former crime. Although the Superintendent of the Berbice river, Mr. Brotherson, had gone up the river to bring the murderers to justice, it was doubtful whether he could do more than carry out a routine investigation of the case.[5]

That the government always found itself in an equivocal position in such instances was remarked in a memorandum of Governor Wodehouse regarding the complaint of an Atorai chief on Brazilian incursions: 'The Government is always embarrassed when it is called upon to take cognizance of such matters for we never feel warranted in applying to them our laws, of which they are wholly

[1] McClintock's Report, 1 July 1854. N.A.G.
[2] B.G.B. *Appendix to the British Case*, VI, enclosed in No. 892 'The Petition of John Davidson, an Arawak from the Moruka Creek to His Excellency Francis Hincks, 28th November, 1868.'
[3] C.O. 111/295. Walker to Newcastle, 5 July 1853.
[4] M.C.C., 14 Mar. 1854. McClintock's Report, 30 June 1853.
[5] C.O. 116/12. Editorial of *The Royal Gazette*, 25 Oct. 1855.

ignorant, and if one of them is legally tried and convicted, we are obliged to remit or commute the sentence.'[1] It was, indeed, a 'round the mulberry bush' affair, this carrying out the letter of the law and then having to revoke the sentence on grounds of ignorance of the law. The Colonial Office did not wholly agree with the observations of Wodehouse, and their mind on the matter was expressed by Taylor, who saw no reason why the 'Indians' ignorance of our laws should be any grounds of hesitation in applying them in any cases in which natural justice would go along with the application.'[2] But Taylor was not the man on the spot, neither did he have the slightest understanding of Indian customs. He argued solely on British legal grounds of the punishment fitting the crime, which ironically were the same grounds on which the Indian carried out his retaliatory measures.

With the increase of crimes of violence among the East Indians in the 1860s, the Governor issued a proclamation of warning which he likewise requested to be explained to the aboriginal tribes 'amongst whom blood feuds not infrequently occur'.[3] During this period when the boundary question loomed tensely on the political and diplomatic horizons, the Governor ordered the Superintendent of Essequibo, P. A. J. Grant, to make certain that, were Indian murders committed, they were within the boundary line claimed by the British government before pursuing and apprehending alleged murderers.[4] At this time, also, Governor Barkly visited the Pomeroon district warning the Indians against 'taking the Law, the most doubtful of things into their own hands', and 'to prefer their complaints to the Magistrate of the District'.[5] Later McClintock when reporting murders on the Barima River, was advised that it was not desirable for him 'to push too far into the country near the demarcation at present laid down for the limits of the Colony's jurisdiction'.[6] Obviously with the boundary question unsettled, legal jurisdiction which presupposed political jurisdiction had to be limited. Both McClintock and the Revd. Brett com-

[1] C.O. 111/317. Memorandum of Governor Wodehouse, 22 Jan. 1858.
[2] Ibid., Minute of H. Taylor, 25 Jan. 1858, in Wodehouse to Labouchere, 24 Nov. 1857.
[3] Proclamation of H. E. Francis Hincks, 9 Dec. 1863, issued in the *Official Gazette*, N.A.G., also Walker, Government Secretary, to McClintock, 15 Feb. 1864. N.A.G.
[4] J. M. Grant, Government Secretary, to P. A. J. Grant, 12 May and 1 June 1869.
[5] M.C.P., 9 July 1869. McClintock's Report, 30 June 1869. L.B.
[6] M.C.P., 28 Feb. 1873. McClintock's Report, 31 Dec. 1872, and E. Walker, Acting Government Secretary to McClintock, 3 Mar. 1873. L.B.

plained that this limitation consequently militated against protection of the Indians and resulted in Spanish aggression, as well as anarchy and debauchery.[1]

The whole troublesome question of legal jurisdiction over races ignorant of British law was finally discussed by the Commissioners of Enquiry in 1870. They agreed that the magistrates could not abandon their functions, but personal tact, experience, acuteness, and patience were required in magistrates dealing with cases involving different races. Apart from that observation they took no firm stand on the matter, conceding that it was 'a somewhat hopeless subject'.[2] The subject was still a hopeless one in the twentieth century when the Courts faced the same predicament in trying Indians for murders of revenge on piai-men.[3]

But the aspects of civil jurisdiction did not present a hopeless picture. The Stipendiary Magistrates and Superintendents of Rivers and Creeks travelled throughout their respective districts of Essequibo, Pomeroon, Moruka, Waini, and the Barima, settling minor cases between and among Indians, as well as between Indians and white settlers, mainly woodcutters.[4] The reports of those officials abound with references brought before them by the Indians: (1) against their employers for refusing to pay them their wages for services and goods, (2) ill-treatment by employers or by Indians themselves, (3) molestation by Negroes, (4) refusal to return their property, (5) abduction, (6) disputes between and among tribes, and (7) in rare cases, stealing. So numerous are these cases that only a few can be discussed. The settlement of these cases added even more weight to the statement of the Second Fiscal, G. Bagot, made in the early years of the British administration: 'That the Indians receive effective protection where offences are committed against them by other persons, the records of our Courts of Justice will clearly shew.'[5]

The main cases dealt with the Indians' complaints against their

---

[1] McClintock's Report, 30 June 1869; *Report of the Guiana Diocesan Society* (Demerara, 1872), 'W. H. Brett's Report of the Indian Missions at Cabacaburi and Waramuri for the Year 1871', pp. 12–13.

[2] C.O. 111/379. Report of the Commission of Enquiry into the Condition and Treatments of Immigrants in British Guiana, 26 Dec. 1869.

[3] 'The Case of Alfred', *The Daily Chronicle*, 26–8 Apr. 1939, and 'The Case of Bagit', ibid., 14–22 May 1939. N.A.G.

[4] C.O. 111/183. An Epitome of the Stipendiary Magistrates Records of Complaints for August 1841, enclosed in Light to Russell, 22 Sept. 1841.

[5] Bagot to D'Urban, 20 Sept. 1831. N.A.G.

employers for refusing to pay their wages. In 1840 Superintendent R. King noted in his journal that a Mr. Hancock had complained against the Indian, Hendrik, for refusing to work for one week, but on investigating found that Hendrik was quite willing to work out his week if Hancock would pay him all his wages, which apparently had been stopped. King 'directed Hancock to pay the man his whole wages and not to dare to stop anything'. The Indian went back to work.[1] When the Indian Dryden accused a carpenter Lynch of not paying him $16.67 for posts he had delivered to him, and a Warrau Abraham brought his complaint against John Maul who had not paid him three months' wages, both cases were settled to the satisfaction of the Indians.[2] But the Indian was not always the plaintiff. An Arawak Ian, who had refused to pay a Mr. L. Redmondt for two shirts and sundry articles, was ordered by the postholder de Wolff to work for Redmondt for one week in lieu of payment.[3] But, in general, the white employers in the remote settlements were quite prepared to fleece the Indian and hope, at times, to get away with it.

Complaints of ill-treatment, however, were rare,[4] while there were a few cases of wife-beatings arising out of jealousy when the Indian found his wife a bit too friendly with another man. The postholders and Superintendents, acting like marriage counsellors, summoned the involved parties, ordered the husbands to make up with their wives, and severely cautioned them with dire consequences if the ill-treatment continued.[5] In abduction cases the Indians were usually reminded that they were a free people and could neither enslave their own nor be enslaved.[6]

Cases of stealing were referred to the respective captains who were made responsible for stopping the depredations, thefts of cassava, plantains, and yams from the fields. The captains bore the brunt of the deed and were warned that if such cases recurred, the offenders would be sent to jail.[7] Superintendent McClintock made the

[1] M.C.P., 5 May 1840. Journal of R. King, Superintendent of Rivers and Creeks, Essequibo, 31 Mar. 1840. N.A.G.

[2] M.C.P., 20 Apr. 1842. Report of R. King, 11 Apr. 1842. N.A.G.

[3] M.C.P., 29 Oct. 1847. Journal of N. J. de Wolff, Superintendent of Upper Courantyne, 4 Oct. 1847. N.A.G.

[4] M.C.P., 20 Apr. 1842. Report of D. Falant, Postholder, Fort Island, 31 Dec. 1841. N.A.G.

[5] M.C.P., 4 Aug. 1847. Journal of de Wolff, 5 July 1847; M.C.P., 10 Jan. 1849; ibid., 30 Sept. 1848; M.C.P., 6 Dec. 1849, ibid., 30 Sept. 1849. N.A.G.

[6] M.C.P., 6 Aug. 1849. Journal of de Wolff, 30 June 1849. N.A.G.

[7] M.C.P., 10 Jan. 1849. Ibid., 30 Sept. 1848. M.C.P., 31 May 1849. Ibid., 5 Apr. 1849. N.A.G.

offenders pay for the stolen articles on the spot and threatened a more rigid law-enforcement for future thefts.[1] According to McClintock, his amicable interference in disputes among the Caribs and the Warraus averted bloodshed and led to reconciliation with each other.[2]

It would appear that Indians had the right to forward complaints direct to the Governor. McClintock reported that, on receiving instructions from the Governor to investigate a complaint made to him by an Indian Abaroony, he proceeded to Moruka to procure witnesses for the case. On the arrival of the witnesses he summoned both parties and investigated the complaint. As a result he found it necessary for Bridgewater, who had forcibly taken and illegally detained a flint-gun from the Indian Abaroony, to appear before the Inferior Criminal Court. Then the case was decided in favour of the Indian and Bridgewater was sentenced to three months' imprisonment with hard labour.[3]

The Indians were also protected against molestation by settlers when cutting timber on Crown lands.[4] They had been given the privilege of cutting wood whenever they pleased on Crown lands and encouraged to bring the timber to the posts to be sold for their benefit. Woodcutters had taken advantage of their privilege, paying the Indians in rum for the timber thus cut. Moreover, the licensed woodcutters gave the Indians articles on trust and expected them to pay them in timber cut on the Crown lands. The Superintendents of Rivers and Creeks complained of this robbery against the Crown, as well as the imposition on the Indians.[5] The Crown Surveyor took no such lenient view regarding the Indians, and felt that, with the colony suffering such considerable loss, 'the immunities and advantages hitherto tacitly conceded to them, as regards the cutting of timber on the Crown Lands for the purpose of traffic, should be withdrawn . . .'[6]

Thus it is indisputable that both criminal and civil jurisdiction

---

[1] M.C.P., 30 Oct. 1843. McClintock's Report, 30 Sept. 1843. N.A.G.

[2] Ibid.

[3] M.C.P., 20 Apr. 1843. Petition of McClintock, 24 Mar. 1843. N.A.G.

[4] M.C.P., 28 Aug. 1843. Report of Thomas Fennell, Superintendent of Rivers and Creeks, Demerara, 31 Mar. 1843. N.A.G.

[5] M.C.P., 20 Jan. 1844. R. King, Superintendent of Rivers and Creeks, Upper Berbice and Canje to Hon. H. E. F. Young, Government Secretary, 20 Dec. 1843. N.A.G.

[6] Ibid. Report of the Crown Surveyor, J. Hadfield, on the communication of R. King, 1 Jan. 1844. N.A.G.

were exercised by the British courts of law over the Indians. To a certain extent the Indians readily accepted and submitted to civil jurisdiction, because such cases involving the payment of their wages were tangible and thus understandable to them. The exercise of criminal jurisdiction over a people who held an entirely different idea of justice was not so clear-cut nor unambiguous. Although James Stephen considered 'British law, the most enlightened distillation of the best in the human intellect',[3] it was completely incomprehensible to the Amerindian intellect.

In the first place, the Indian viewed death, except in the cases of old age, snake bites, or attacks from animals (although snakes and animals were seen as embodiments of evil spirits), as due to the machinations of evil spirits. The piai-men had the power to call down the evil spirit and thus cause the death of one or more members of a family, as in the case of Maicarawari. Accordingly the nearest of kin must avenge the deaths. If he did not, other members of the family would despise him for his disobedience and cowardice. Hence the Indian found himself in a legal and moral dilemma, which needless to say, he did not even know he was in. If on one hand, he neglected to carry out the *lex talionis*, he betrayed his 'code of honour'; on the other hand, if he acted as his own judge, jury, and executioner, he violated British law and was tried for 'murder'. But it is arguable that to the Indian his deed, especially when he killed an adulterous wife, was no crime at all, although legally speaking, he had the *mens rea* which is loosely translated as a 'guilty mind'. He acted with a clear conscience, believing his act to be justifiable, and in his culture, if the term can be stretched, 'legally' right.[2] Nevertheless, in the British Courts of Justice, he was declared to have both the *mens rea*, the state of mind, and the *actus rea*, namely the conduct, relevant circumstances, and consequences of the act.[3]

The Indian, when he took the life of his wife for adultery or when he killed the piai-man in retribution for the deaths of his family, saw no moral blameworthiness in his deed. It was not difficult to prove that the Indians acted with intent in the legal sense. Ordinarily in the British system of law, motive as such is irrelevant once the *mens rea* and the *actus rea* had been performed, that is, 'a man may be lawfully convicted of a crime, whatever his motive may be, or even if

[1] Galbraith, p. 45.
[2] Smith and Hogan, p. 37.
[3] Ibid., p. 28.

he has no motive'.[1] In adapting such a system to native peoples, motive should have been taken into consideration as regards the crime itself, and not merely in the mitigation of the sentence. For would the Indian have killed had not the particular circumstances of adultery and the need for retribution, according to his lights, been present? In the case of Maicarawari, he killed for the future protection of himself and other members of his tribe, as Waihahi had threatened their lives. In the Etoonie murders, Lorenzo believed that Chief Mackroo had caused the deaths in his family.

The law of retaliation was regarded by the most primitive people throughout the world as a sacred duty, as obedience and loyalty to a dead relative, and it did seem 'irrational and illogical to condemn or punish where no law is violated, or . . . when one is conscientiously, according to his lights performing an act of obedience'.[2] The editorial of *The Guiana Chronicle* once made a strong case for the retaliatory Mosaic Law:

The exaction of *life for life* has prevailed in every country at every stage of civilization. The most sceptical and the most visionary, waver about the repeal of this portion of the code promulgated by Moses: 'Whoso sheddeth man's blood, by man shall his blood be shed' is a principle that pervades the jurisprudence of every tribe of mortals, in what shape soever it exists. All mankind, from the savage who retaliates with the unrelenting fierceness of personal revenge, to the enlightened people who cast forth the offender by common consent and according to set usage, acknowledge the accuracy. The difficulty lies in its correct application to particular cases.[3]

The rub lay in the 'correct application to particular cases'. Was it fair and just to judge an uncivilized man by the law laid down and applied by civilized men? Even in 1939 this question was posed again and again during Amerindian murder cases. Neither did anyone query the fact that the Indian was not being tried by his peers, although his peers, according to their sense of justice, would have given him short shrift.

Modern studies in criminal law stress the individualization of the punishment, showing that 'the crime is not the measure of the man'.[4] If it is so important for the judge and jury to have a knowledge of

[1] Ibid., p. 48. Also, through interviews with the Chancellor of the Courts in Guyana, Sir Edward Luckoo, and the Chief Justice, Mr. H. B. S. Bollers, May 1972.
[2] The Revd. J. Dingwall, *The Daily Chronicle*, 19 May 1939. N.A.G.
[3] C.O. 116/3. Editorial in *The Guiana Chronicle*, 24 May 1839.
[4] George W. Kirchwey, 'Criminal Law', *Encyclopedia of the Social Sciences*, IV, 518.

human nature and of the *mores* of the people in a civilized society on whom they are to pass judgement, how much more vital was an understanding of the nature of the Amerindian and his beliefs? Yet it must be conceded that, to a certain extent, the Courts of Justice in British Guiana realized this in the mitigation of the sentences.

Not only in British Guiana, but in all other colonies of the Empire, the British transplanted their system of law, together with their other institutions, and imposed them on indigenous races whose *mores* were constantly deplored, changed, or swept away, but hardly taken into consideration. The British naturally considered their law superior, and in the light of their past history, this was not surprising. In the study of comparative law, however, with its divisions of the main legal orders—tribal law, religious law, modern civil and common law, and Marxist law[1]—the superiority of British law is a moot point. In the nineteenth century the insistence on this superiority did not negate the fact that the natives of South America, Africa, and Australia also had a sense of justice, private though it might be, and quite different from the public law of the civilized man. Many taboos within primitive societies were more rigorous and binding, and fraught with severer penalties than even the laws of civilized societies. British law was seen, as was British government, in the words of Governor Carmichael, as 'the most perfect that could be framed'.[2] But both law and government exist for people, and 'the law divorced from the people to whom it applies is a mere collection of words'.[3]

Undoubtedly, there was a conflict between theoretical British law which meted out equal justice to all, and the Amerindian law of custom and personal vengeance. This conflict was never resolved during the nineteenth century and rose to the surface in 1939, evoking heated public discussion regarding the seven years' imprisonment of the Indian Bagit, who had murdered Moses, the evil man of his tribe. On the government was placed the onus and the responsibility for the Indians' ignorance of the laws of the land, while to judge from the masses of letters sent to the press, public opinion was almost unanimous in supporting the Amerindian and

[1] B. A. Wortley, *Jurisprudence* (Manchester, 1967), pp. 32–42. In British Guiana the Code of Criminal Procedure issued by Philip II in 1570 was followed as in all Dutch colonies until superseded by British Law in 1829. See R. W. Lee, *An Introduction to Roman-Dutch Law* (Oxford, 1953), p. 6, f.n. 7.

[2] M.C.C., 18 Nov. 1812. N.A.G. [3] Howard, p. 43.

his attitude towards justice. Suggestions were offered to circumvent the problem: Let the Indian be educated in British law and justice through religious and moral instruction, and let courts be held in the Amerindian settlements themselves as part of the civic education process, with 'impressive ceremonial' to awe the Indians. The suggestion that 'the State should extend its educational services to every corner of the country in which the Law operated'[1] was a move in the right direction. Viewed against the background of centuries of deep-rooted beliefs, time and the patient perseverance on the part of law officers were needed. A hundred years later the same suggestions are still being made, and the same solutions—time and perseverance —still offered.[2]

[1] *The Daily Chronicle*, 18 May 1939 and 20 May 1939.
[2] Interviews with Sir E. V. Luckoo and Mr. H. B. S. Bollers, Guyana, May 1972.

VI

THE BOUNDARIES, THE BRITISH, AND THE INDIANS

THE rights of both criminal and civil jurisdiction exercised over the Indian tribes were inextricably bound up with their protection within a considerable territorial area. And this protection which the British government felt obliged, as a humane nation, to extend to the Indians brought them into collision with both their Brazilian and Venezuelan neighbours. Throughout the nineteenth century there were continuous diplomatic debacles over the frontiers in which the desire of the Indians for British protection was used as the trump card for British territorial rights in the respective areas. Not until 1904 did arbitration proceedings settle the boundary differences between Brazil and British Guiana. A decade ago history books viewed the Hague Tribunal Award of 1899 as the finale of the British Guiana–Venezuela boundary dispute, but unfortunately in this case historians proved to be poor prophets. In 1962 the curtain rose again on the affair on the stage of the United Nations General Assembly.[1]

During the proceedings at The Hague in the 1890s evidence had been convincingly produced by the British, the result of research in the Dutch and British Guiana Archives, that the Dutch, their predecessors, had maintained effective occupation and jurisdiction over the territory claimed by Venezuela. The liaison between the Dutch and the indigenous Indians had been welded through treaties of

---

[1] Venezuela officially opened the case when, in a cablegram to the United Nations on 18 Aug. 1962, she asked that the 'Question of boundaries and the territory of British Guiana' be included in the agenda of the Seventeenth Session of the United Nations General Assembly. In 1970 the Protocol of Port-of-Spain put the case in cold storage, after a series of sessions of the Mixed Boundary Commission which had been established in 1966, an outcome of the Geneva Agreement. The Boundary Commission was given the Sisyphean task 'of seeking satisfactory solutions for the practical settlement of the controversy . . . which has arisen as the result of the Venezuelan contention that the Arbitral Award of 1899 . . . is null and void'. See 'Guyana/Venezuela Relations', *Guyana Journal*, I, No. 2 (Dec. 1968), 55.

trade and alliance, especially with the Caribs who occupied the territory between the Pomeroon and the Orinoco rivers.

Late in the sixteenth century an extract from a secret report describing the Dominions of the King of Spain in America read: 'The Dutch settlements in Guyana extend from close to the River Amazones to the Orinoco . . . the best settlement they possess in the whole of this coast is that of New Zealandia, in the River Paumeron, very near the River Orinoco, and close to the city of Santo Thomé de la Guyana, which belongs to your Majesty.'[1] In the seventeenth century Santo Thomé was a struggling city. Almost every Spanish official reported on its sparsely populated and destitute condition. On his visit to Santo Thomé, the Bishop of Puerto Rico was shocked at the poverty of its inhabitants, only forty in number, and wrote to the King of Spain in 1634 suggesting that settlement be encouraged 'first on account of the attention and care which the Dutch pay to it, who are now settled close to this great river Orinoco and in three rivers adjoining it, namely the River Berbice, Corentine and Essequibo'.[2] By then the Dutch West India Company had been established and after the Treaty of Munster, 1648, which ended the Dutch Wars, the Dutch strove to consolidate their position in the Guiana territory. In 1659 a Commission appointed by Middleburg, Flushing, and Vere in Holland noted that a large number of colonists and their families with materials necessary for colonization and cultivation had settled on the mainland coast and taken possession of the neighbourhood of the rivers Essequibo, Demerara, Pomeroon, and Corentyne, as well as the Province of Moruka.[3] Soldiers had been sent, fortifications erected, and a Commander and Director appointed to promote trade and commerce.

In 1761 the Governor of Cumaná, Don José Diguja, submitted a report and a lengthy historical description of the province of Guyana to Spain which stated in part: 'In the year 1720 the Province of Guyana was a dependency of the Government of Trinidad and no other settlement existed in it than the Presidio and the city of Santo Thomé.'[4] He noted that there were few houses, a scarcity of

[1] Great Britain, *Documents and Correspondence Relating to the Question of Boundary between British Guiana and Venezuela*, 'Bibliotheca del Rey, Madrid. Ms.' (London, 1896), I, 5.

[2] B.G.B. Archivo General de Indias, Simancas, 'Secular Audiencia of Santo Domingo' as cited in *The Counter-Case on Behalf of the Government of Her Britannic Majesty* (London, 1898), p. 10.   [3] Ibid., pp. 28–9.

[4] *Documents Relating to the Question of Boundary between Venezuela and British*

provisions, and feeble fortifications. The Dutch were trading with the Caribs and taking them away from that region to put them to work on the plantations of their own colonies at Essequibo, Berbice, Surinam, and Corentyne, which were flourishing.[1] The Director-General of Essequibo, Laurens Storm van's Gravesande (1738–72), was tireless in pushing forward the Dutch claims to the Guyana–Essequibo territory. In one of his many dispatches to the directors of the West India Company and Their High and Mightinesses in Holland he wrote: '. . . I have the honour to inform Y.Y.H.H. that we, as well as Spain, regard the River Barima as the boundary division of the two jurisdictions, the east bank being the Company's territory and the west bank Spanish.'[2]

Meanwhile the Spaniards intrigued to break the hold of the Dutch who were actively engaged in the slave trade with the Caribs on the Barima river. The Governor of Caracas, Don José Solano, fearing that they would be hemmed in by the Dutch, recommended in his report to the King that a fort be built in a strategic position to stop the Dutch from ascending the river.[3] The Caribs were more closely allying themselves with the Dutch, not only against the Spaniards, but against the bush Negroes whom they hunted down; in 1763 and 1764 they actively participated in suppressing the slave rebellions, for which service their chief received an official badge of recognition from the Dutch West India Company. The Dutch cultivated and maintained friendly relations with the Indians, giving them presents and protecting them from ill-treatment of their own traders.

While Britain was settling down to administer the Guiana territory gained from the Dutch in 1803, Venezuela was undergoing the pangs of revolution. The Napoleonic invasion of the Iberian peninsula in 1808 had violent repercussions in the Spanish colonial empire. In Venezuela Símon Bolívar and Francisco Miranda became leaders of the revolution. On 5 July 1811 Venezuela declared her independence from Spain, followed by bitter and bloody years of civil war, an earthquake, Negro revolts, counter-revolution, the defeat of Miranda, and the escape of Bolívar. In 1817 the return of Bolivar to Venezuela triggered off a series of blood baths, later dis-

Guiana. Submitted to the Boundary Commission by the Counsel of the Government of Venezuela (Washington, D.C., 1896), p. 29.
    [1] Ibid.   [2] van 's Gravesande, Dispatch of 20 Mar. 1767. II, 528.
    [3] Great Britain, *Documents and Correspondence*, I, 91–2.

claimed by Bolívar. After the massacre of their missionaries, the Spanish Arawaks fled the Orinoco region and settled on the Moruka river claiming the protection of the British government. Governor Murray reluctantly gave shelter to the fugitives at first, probably foreseeing a rash of revolutions followed by the inevitable waves of displaced persons. The military force at Pomeroon was strengthened to bolster the security of the western frontier.[1]

But in the third and fourth decades of the century it was the south-western frontier that posed the greater problem. Here from the outset the territorial squabbles involved the protection of the Indians, causing diplomatic tension between Great Britain and Brazil. In 1833 the Revd. John Armstrong of the Church Missionary Society, when visiting the Indian settlement at Pirara, found the Indians in hiding to avoid capture and enslavement by the Brazilians. Armstrong wrote to the Portuguese that he felt it 'his duty to report these things to the English Government, who, . . . will endeavour to protect these helpless subjects from being enslaved.'[2] This enslavement of the Indians inspired another missionary, Thomas Youd, even against the advice of his superior, the Revd. Bernau, to attempt to protect the Indians against Brazilian aggression and to proselytize them as well. Governor Light gave his blessing and encouragement to the Youd plan, and told him 'to assure the Indians that every possible means will be adopted for their protection and that [he] will endeavour to locate upon the Crown Lands of British Guiana as many tribes as may choose to come nearer to the civilized parts of the Colony.'[3] But the home government gave no such blessing and encouragement to Light. Protection of Indians in undetermined territory was indeed going beyond diplomatic bounds. To the Secretary of State, Normanby, it did not seem 'possible to open any negotiations with the Brazilian Government on that subject without a full report . . . relative to the southern limits of the Colony, supported by the proofs and illustrations . . . drawn from the Archives of the Colony . . .'.[4]

Meanwhile Youd had proceeded to erect schools in Pirara, which was a Macusi village of 200 inhabitants commanding an excellent position over the savannahs between the Canocan and Pararaima

[1] C.O. 111/24. *The Guiana Chronicle and Demerara Gazette*, 12 Sept. 1817.

[2] CW/014/23. J. Armstrong to the Portuguese on the Confines of British Guiana, 16 Apr. 1833. C.M.S.A.

[3] Young, Government Secretary to Youd, 8 Jan. 1837. L.B.

[4] C.O. 112/21. Normanby to Light, 12 Mar. 1839.

mountains. This was also in undetermined territory, and Schomburgk remarked that as soon as the Brazilian authorities in Pará
heard of a Protestant Mission in the area that would be 'its death
knoll'.[1] Schomburgk could not have been more correct in his deduc-
tions, but he added fuel to the fire by hoisting the British flag at the
Pirara post, after ascertaining from the oldest Indians that the
Brazilians had never extended their posts east of San Joaquim.[2]
The Brazilians came down like a wolf on the fold! Expeditions to
Pirara followed in quick succession: in 1838 a detachment of
Brazilian militia forcibly deported 'into slavery a body of Indians
on the pretext of impressment for the Brazilian navy';[3] in 1839
Lieutenant Pedro Ayres claimed possession of Pirara and ordered
the withdrawal of Youd whom he accused of indoctrinating their
subjects, the Macusis, in a false religion and the English language.[4]
In the face of military strength and distance from the city Youd had
little choice but to withdraw. The *raison d'être* the Brazilians offered
for reclaiming the Indians was a religious one, but the kidnappings
were for quite secular purposes. During his exploratory expeditions
in 1841–2, Schomburgk informed the Governor that the Brazilians
deported the Indians for national service. Later the Maiongcong
Indians, who quit their settlements on the Rio Negro, told McClintock that their 'tyrannical masters', the Brazilians, employed them
in cutting down large forest trees and preparing the land for the
planting of cassava.[5] Numbers of Wapisianas and Macusis were also
carried off to construct roads on the banks of the Rio Branco and
other tributaries of the Amazon.[6]

After Youd's forced withdrawal from Pirara, Schomburgk rushed
a report to Light tracing the Dutch claim to that territory and praising the zealous work of Youd in Christianizing and civilizing the
Indians. Thus he strongly urged the British government to take up
the cause of these Indians and bring about a settlement of the
boundaries for the mutual benefit of the Indians and the British,
for:

If the Indians who inhabit these regions are to be rendered useful

[1] C.O. 111/159. Extract from Letter of Schomburgk, Pirara, 19 June, 1838.
[2] Ibid.   [3] C.O. 111/174. Resolution of the House of Commons, 6 Mar. 1840.
[4] C.O. 111/164. Schomburgk to Light, 16 July 1839.
[5] M.C.P., 3 May 1852. McClintock's Report, 31 Mar. 1852. N.A.G.
[6] C.O. 111/320. Report of J. C. Dawson, 7 May 1858, in Walker to Stanley, 8 May
1858. One Indian told Dawson that young women were forcibly abducted to a religious
house in the neighbourhood of Fort San Joaquim.

subjects, the uncertainty of our boundary claims the particular attention of her Britannic Majesty's Government. They have frequently inquired from me where they might settle in order to come under British protection, but from the existing uncertainty, I have not been able to return them a decisive answer. Terrified by the threats of the Brazilians, and their commands not to attend the instructions of the Missionary, they wander among such haunts, as, are only known to themselves, and the Wild beasts of the forest, and the work of civilization, which began with such fine prospects, has been unfortunately checked.[1]

This plea moved Henry Taylor to scribble a query in the margin of Schomburgk's communiqué: 'Why not tell them to retire within the peopled and unquestioned limits of the Colony ?',[2] probably because he had not yet read a later paragraph in the letter showing that though the Indians feared the Brazilians, they loved their own regions more so 'that every attempt to induce them to settle on our coast region, would . . . prove abortive'.[3] To end the uncertainties of the Indians and the set-backs to their civilization, the home government should appoint a commission to determine the limits of British Guiana with the concurrence of the neighbouring countries. The local press agreed with Schomburgk that such a move was necessary to prevent Brazilian aggression upon the Indians.[4]

Meanwhile Youd became implicated in an alleged arming of Indians against the Brazilians.[5] It appeared that Avoristo, a nefarious Brazilian character, had been training the Indians who had placed themselves under Youd's protection and this had cast suspicion on Youd, especially as he had not made them disperse.[6]

As a result of the Schomburgk and Light pressure based on humanitarian grounds and cold diplomatic facts, Henry Taylor wrote lengthily to James Stephen on 11 February 1840, that after deeply considering the facts already collected, he felt that the time was ripe for negotiating the boundaries for 'Motives of humanity and the obligations which this country may be considered to have contracted towards the Aborigines, would seem to urge very strongly the duty of extending to the Indians as far as we have any right to extend it, the protection of British Territory.'[7] He now realized

[1] C.O. 111/164. Schomburgk to Light, 16 July 1839.   [2] Ibid.
[3] Ibid.   [4] C.O. 116/3. Editorial of *The Guiana Chronicle*, 29 July 1839.
[5] Young to Youd, 26 Aug. 1839. L.B.
[6] CW/o18/19c, Bernau to the Revd. W. Jawett, 10 Sept. 1839. C.M.S.A.
[7] C.O. 111/162. Taylor to Stephen, 11 Feb. 1840.

that the Indians refused every inducement to quit the territory which was rightly theirs.

Schomburgk, who had brought to England a few Indians with him, told Taylor he hoped they could return to British Guiana and their territory with the assurance of British protection against Brazilian aggression.[1] A later report of his to Vernon Smith endeavoured to prove the rights of the Dutch in the upper Essequibo region and the intermediate points between the Rio Branco inhabited by the Macusis, Atorais, Wapisianas, Tarumas, and Waiwais who specifically claimed British protection. Fifty chiefs and families of those tribes, accompanied by Youd, had come in a deputation to Governor Light to ask for help against the Brazilians.[2]

The religious overtones of the affair were seen in Stephen's minute to the Foreign Office which illustrated that diplomacy had to consider the evangelical aspect. Presuming that Youd had violated Brazilian law by converting 8,000 aborigines claimed to be Brazilian subjects, Stephen could not see how the British government could either 'support or countenance him'. Yet withdrawal of support from the Protestant missionary would be tantamount to Great Britain preventing 'the Propagation there, of what we regard, as truth'.[3] As a result of the diplomatic correspondence between the Colonial Office and the Foreign Office, the Brazilian Minister of Foreign Affairs was notified that (1) Schomburgk had been commissioned by Her Majesty's Government to survey and mark out a boundary between British Guiana and Brazil, and (2) that 'the Governor of British Guiana [had] been instructed in the meantime to resist any encroachment upon Pirara or upon the territories near the Frontier . . . hitherto occupied by Independent Indian Tribes.'[4] However, Governor Light had not recommended any military movement[5] and had even enjoined caution and prudence on Youd, advising him to impart instruction only to Indians within the recognized territorial limits.[6]

[1] C.O. 111/175. Schomburgk to Taylor, 2 July 1840.

[2] Ibid. Schomburgk to Vernon Smith, 20 Aug. 1840. See also C.O. 111/171. Light to Russell, 26 June 1840.

[3] C.O. 111/174. Minute of Stephen, 17 Nov. 1840, re Lord Leveron to Stephen, 14 Nov. 1840.

[4] Ibid. Palmerston to Ouseley, 28 Nov. 1840. O'Leary construed the 'Independent Indian Tribes' to mean those who occupied the territory between the Barima and the Moruka rivers. C.O. 111/184. Daniel F. O'Leary, Acting Vice-Consul at Caracas, to Palmerston, 14 Aug. 1841.   [5] C.O. 111/171. Light to Russell, 26 June 1840.

[6] Young to Youd, 18 Apr. 1840. L.B.

Early in 1841 W. G. Ouseley, the British Chargé d'Affaires in Rio de Janeiro, reported the continued and systematic aggressions of the Brazilians with their aim of subjugating and reducing the Indians of Guiana to slavery.[1] Ouseley then forwarded a memorandum on the actual state of the boundaries of British Guiana to the Brazilian Minister of Foreign Affairs, compiled from the Schomburgkiana transmitted to him by the Foreign Office. The main thrust of the memorandum was an accusation against the Brazilians for their ill-treatment of the Indian tribes.[2]

In the same month of April 1841, Schomburgk received his commission for the surveying and marking of the boundaries. The demarcation was but a preliminary measure, prior to negotiations between the respective governments, but one thing was certain: 'Indian tribes within the assumed limits must not be molested'.[3] Schomburgk himself took care against any molestation of the Indians by his own party by drawing up rules of conduct to be observed. Article 7 stated:

> Any person or persons in or belonging to this Expedition, who shall wilfully insult or otherwise molest any member or members of the Native Indians, on any pretense whatsoever, and who shall not at all times treat the same with mildness and forbearance, shall be mulched of his pay, or prosecuted according to Law, as the nature and degree of the offence may require or the Commander of the Expedition deem fit. . . .[4]

Schomburgk's expedition did not stop the Brazilians from impressing the Indians into slavery. Governor Light, acting on previous instructions to resist any encroachments, despatched an armed force to take possession of Pirara in December 1841. The main object of this military manœuvre was stated in the Instructions for the Officer commanding the detachment of troops to be 'for the protection of the Indians', as well as 'to assert the right of Great Britain to that portion of territory now occupied by the Brazilians. . . .'[5] The troops were also enjoined to cultivate the goodwill and friendship of the Indians. So as not to give any offence to the Indians who might object to the troops occupying their village, the troops were stationed on high ground outside the village.[6]

[1] C.O. 111/184. Ouseley to Palmerston, 11 Jan. 1841.
[2] Ibid., 17 Apr. 1841.   [3] Light to Schomburgk, 14 Apr. 1841. L.B.
[4] C.O. 111/178. Rule of Conduct drawn up by Schomburgk.
[5] C.O. 111/181. Light to Stanley, 23 Dec. 1841.
[6] Memo of Light for Colonel Bush, 30 Oct. 1841. L.B.

This expedition, the first of its kind since Gravesande's to the Cuyuni in 1766,[1] was envisaged by Light more as a protective than a punitive one, and he was anxious to avoid any flare-up of violence. He was apprehensive of the Indian response to it and in a secret communication to Youd, now at Waraputa, Light begged him to act as a goodwill ambassador 'to ensure a cordial welcome and co-operation on the part of the Indians towards H.M. Troops'.[2] This move was deplored by the Committee of the Church Missionary Society as it would deprive Waraputa of its missionary.[3] Bernau, the head of the missions in that area, disapproved of Youd's involvement with the boundary issue but realized that, in justice, the missionary could not have refused to co-operate with the government.[4]

The reoccupation of Pirara by the British detachment on 14 February 1842 was rather anti-climactic; the troops found a deserted village.[5] The presence of the troops promising protection lured the Indians back to the village, but less than four months later the romantic and philanthropically motivated expedition succumbed to the realistic arguments of finance. The Brazilians had assured the British government that they would neither carry out an armed occupation of the territory, nor interfere with the independent Indian tribes in the neighbourhood.[6] On the grounds of these assurances the home government saw no further need of maintaining troops at Pirara at great expense.[7] Governor Light viewed a hasty withdrawal in a very realistic light: it would cause the government to lose face with the Indians who would 'lose confidence in our protection'; moreover, it would support the Brazilian boast of success in driving the British from Pirara and would encourage a continuation of Indian oppression, despite the so-called good intentions of the Brazilian authorities.[8] Not satisfied in giving this prudent advice to Stanley, Light wrote again to the Secretary of State reminding him of the fatal effect a precipitate withdrawal of troops would have, not only on the minds of the Indians, but throughout the whole of the Northern States of America.[9]

[1] Webber, p. 209.   [2] C.O. 111/197. Young to Youd, 3 Nov. 1841.
[3] Ibid., C.M.S. to Stanley, 10 June 1842.
[4] CW/018/25. Bernau to D. Coates, 16 July 1842. C.M.S.A.
[5] C.O. 111/195. Light to Stanley, 18 Mar. 1842.
[6] C.O. 112/23. Stephen to Lord Canning, 26 May 1842.
[7] Ibid. Stephen to Lord Somerset, 21 June 1842. According to Schomburgk, the Pirara expedition, that 'ill-conceived project had cost the Government not less than 24,000 dollars'. Richard Schomburgk, *Travels in British Guiana, 1840–1844*, II, 109.
[8] C.O. 111/192. Light to Stanley, 13 July 1842.   [9] Ibid., 14 July 1842.

But economics was a more powerful force than public opinion and the troops were eventually withdrawn on 1 September 1842. Light again protested in vain.[1] While the Brazilian Minister of Foreign Affairs, Aureliano Souza e Oliveira Coutinho, complained of the Schomburgk landmarks at the mouths of the Mahu and Takutu rivers and accused Youd of alienating the Macusis from the Brazilian empire,[2] Light was also reporting on the continued Brazilian aggressions. He wrote to Lord Stanley that the 'Indians had fled with Mr. Youde or retired to other parts of the interior to avoid the oppressions of the Brazilians. . . . The territory is purely Indian, the Brazilians usurp the country—the Indians glad of British protection would yield to its power. . . .'[3] Schomburgk's reports which flowed continuously between Light and the Secretary of State with its constant and innumerable references to Brazilian depradations against the Indians moved Taylor again to heights of philanthropy:

The only questions which seem to make the determination of the boundary a matter of *present* importance are those connected with the protection of the Indians. But these questions seem to suggest strong motives for an early adjustment. I have scored in the margin of M. Schomburgk's last journal (amongst others) these pages which relate to the Brazilian slave hunts. If the territories in question be British, it seems to concern British honour and humanity that these barbarities should not be practiced [*sic*] within them.[4]

Schomburgk was no sooner back in Georgetown than there was a renewal of Brazilian molestation. Light wrote begging help of the missionaries whose presence he felt would prevent oppression and the dispersion of the Indians from that part of the colony.[5] He also requested the Colonial Office to issue a stern remonstrance to the Brazilians.[6] Consequent negotiations between Brazil and Great Britain led to the drawing up of a Convention of Three Articles for the settlement of the boundary, with an additional article specifically regarding the protection of the Indians and their safe passage into British territory.[7] Light somewhat reluctantly conceded the good

[1] C.O. 111/193. Light to Stanley, 9 Oct. 1842.
[2] C.O. 111/206. Hamilton Hamilton to Aberdeen, 26 Nov. 1842.
[3] C.O. 111/195. Light to Stanley, 30 Nov. 1842.
[4] C.O. 111/195. Minute of Taylor on Schomburgk's survey, 21 Dec. 1842.
[5] Young to the Bishop of Guiana, 28 Oct. 1843. L.B.
[6] C.O. 111/203. Light to Stanley, 2 Nov. 1843.
[7] C.O. 111/206. Stanley to Light, 27 Nov. 1843. For full text of Article IV, see ibid., H. M. Addington to George Hope, F.O., 22 Nov. 1843.

intentions which had prompted Article IV, but doubted whether the Brazilian government, far removed from the area, could effectively control their authorities on the south-western frontier, and in this case 'the effect of Article IV would be rendered void'.[1] The Governor was obviously quoting Schomburgk whose letter to him a few days before had expressed similar fears regarding the unsatisfactory nature of Article IV and the constant danger in which the Macusis lived.[2] With a probable determination of the boundaries becoming imminent, the inhabitants near the respective frontiers were naturally apprehensive about where the axe would fall. This fact only heightened the tension more than ever.

Broken in health, and laden with maps and botanical and zoological specimens, Schomburgk returned to England after eight years in the forests of British Guiana. Here he continued to impress the Colonial Office with the sufferings of the Indians at the hands of both the Brazilians and the Venezuelans and tried to stir them into action 'for the cause of humanity'.[3] In a memorandum on the limits of British Guiana he showed Lord Stanley that political as well as humanitarian ends could be furthered by acknowledging the Takutu and Mahu rivers as the boundary line between Brazil and British Guiana, thus enclosing Pirara for the sake of the Indians.[4] Both Schomburgk and Light had fervently championed the Indian cause, but they had both looked beyond philanthropy to economic expediency, for they saw the disputed land as being settled by future colonists and so adding to the prosperity of the colony.[5] With the exception of Superintendent McClintock, no other officials, apart from Light and Schomburgk, would ever plead so earnestly and continuously for the protection of the Indians in the future.

By 1850 the Brazilian atrocities were still being carried out and the boundary question remained *in statu quo*.[6] At this time the Church Missionary Society, desiring to return to the once promising mission at Pirara but uncertain of the diplomatic situation, asked the Colonial Office what protection their missionaries could expect in that area.[7] In less than a month the Secretary of State unequivocally

---

[1] C.O. 111/208. Light to Stanley, 9 Jan. 1844.
[2] Ibid., Schomburgk to Light, 4 Jan. 1844, enclosed in Light to Stanley, 9 Jan. 1844.
[3] C.O. 111/218. Schomburgk to Stanley, 1 Nov. 1844.
[4] Ibid., 26 Dec. 1844.
[5] Schomburgk, *A Description of British Guiana*, p. 145, and C.O. 111/204. Light to Stanley, 2 Dec. 1843.   [6] C.O. 111/276. Barkly to Grey, 20 Sept. 1850.
[7] C.O. 111/286. H. Straith, Secretary of the C.M.S., to Grey, 7 Nov. 1851.

replied that the boundary was yet undefined, and on no account could the government promise protection to the missionaries. Instead, let them encourage the Indians to withdraw into the cultivated and recognized British territory.[1] Here again, this dispatch from the Secretary of State was *à la* Taylor to the last word. Taylor could see no possibility at this time of negotiating a definition of the boundaries with the Brazilian government. Neither did he consider a definition expedient, as 'The only present object would be to make the right of this Country to protect the Indians and the Missionaries unquestionable. But an unquestionable right would involve an imperative obligation; and what the cost might be of fulfilling such an obligation may be judged from the enormous expence [*sic*] of the military expedition to Pirara a few years ago.'[2] Whatever had happened to 'British honour and humanity' which had so moved Taylor a few years ago? Was Taylor a hypocrite? Hardly so. Taylor's seeming *volte-face*, as well as his future economic arguments, must be viewed against the background of the policy of the Treasury where economic realism counted more than humanitarianism. Many a scheme proposed by the Colonial Office met its death in the Treasury. It was quite obvious that the expense of the Pirara expedition could hardly have been approved by the Lords of the Treasury, and Taylor was being prudently realistic.

A few months later Governor Barkly forwarded to London a report of Superintendent McClintock which contained a representation made to him by the Maiongcong Indians from the Rio Negro who had quit their settlements after being ill-treated by the Brazilians. McClintock pressed for an early boundary settlement to safeguard the lives of the Indians.[3] Taylor again recalled the costly Pirara affair, that *bête noire* of expeditions. A definition of boundaries would thrust upon the British government the heavy burden of Indian protection, a burden they could not afford to assume. In the words of Taylor: 'By defining the boundaries we should commit the Crown to the protection of the Indians from all foreign aggression. This protection could not be given except at an enormous cost.[4]

[1] C.O. 112/30. F. Peel to H. Straith, 27 Nov. 1851.

[2] C.O. 111/286. Minute of Taylor, 17 Nov. 1851.

[3] C.O. 111/289. McClintock's Report, 31 Mar. 1852, in Barkly to Sir John Pakington, 20 Apr. 1852. Also read in M.C.P., 3 May 1852. N.A.G.

[4] Ibid. Minute of Taylor, 27 May 1852. See also C.O. 112/32. Pakington to Barkly, 11 June 1852.

In late 1857 Brazilian outrages and slave hunts were again the subject of a dispatch by Governor Wodehouse. The Brazilians were again in their territory and John Wishrop, as a commissioned captain of the tribe, appealed to the Governor for protection.[1] The Colonial Office requested the Foreign Office to re-present the case to the Brazilian government, reminding them rather facetiously of that toothless Pirara expedition nineteen years earlier,[2] an expedition which remained to haunt Taylor in the guise of £ s.d. To Taylor the only solution was the removal of the nomadic Indians closer to recognized territory.[3] Wodehouse agreed but deemed it impracticable. The removal of one tribe into the district of another might result in feuds and bloodshed in which the government would be called upon to interfere.[4] After their past experience with such native feuds, the local government could not be blamed for shying away from such an insoluble problem.

To the British protest on 'the recurrence of such outrages',[5] Viscount de Marauguape, the Brazilian Minister of Foreign Affairs, assured Her Majesty's Legation at Rio that 'suitable orders had been transmitted to the President of Amazon in order that the vexatious seizures of the Atorai Indians, . . . may be put a stop to'.[6] But the Rupununi was a long way from Rio and there was no guarantee that the President of Amazon ever managed to get in touch with, much less curb, the slave-hunting Brazilians. Further complaints only drew from the Colonial Office the now bored explanation that the Brazilian government had been notified.[7]

But the Brazilian boundary involving the protection of Indians was not the only frontier issue causing diplomatic headaches to both the home government and the local government. As on the Brazilian frontier, so too on the Venezuelan, it all started with Schomburgk. On his return from a scientific exploration in Guiana sponsored by the Royal Geographical Society, Schomburgk wrote to Light: 'Of special importance is the determination of the Western boundary, the limits of which have never been completely settled, and it merits the greatest attention on account of the political importance of the

---

[1] C.O. 111/317. Statement of Wishrop, 12 Nov. 1857, in Walker to Labouchere, 24 Nov. 1857.
[2] Ibid. Minute of Taylor to Foreign Office, 25 Jan. 1858.
[3] Ibid., 1 Jan. 1858.   [4] Ibid. Memo of Governor Wodehouse, 22 Jan. 1858.
[5] C.O. 111/322. W. Stuart, H.M. Chargé d'Affaires to de Marauguape, 12 Aug. 1858.
[6] Ibid. Marauguape to Stuart, 2 Sept. 1858.
[7] C.O. 112/35. Sir E. B. Lytton to Wodehouse, 2 Nov. 1858.

mouth of the Orinoco.'[1] William Scruggs, legal adviser to the Venezuelan government, showed in his brief to the Boundary Commission in 1896 that 'Schomburgk's ill-advised agitation first disturbed the peace'.[2] Feeling secure in the past Dutch occupation of the Pomeroon and Barima areas, Schomburgk had foreseen no difficulties or impracticabilities in marking the limits of British Guiana on the system of natural divisions. But at that time he seemed more concerned with the Brazilian frontier and the protection of the Indians in those regions. Was there no such cause for concern on the western frontier of Guiana? Were the Venezuelans, unlike the Brazilians, living in peaceful coexistence with the neighbouring Indian tribes?

A report of Light to Normanby in 1839 proved that no such utopia existed on the western frontier. To escape enforced labour under the Venezuelan government, the Indians were taking refuge in the Barima district, confidently believing that they were within British territory.[3] Light hinted, on the basis of a report from his Superintendent of Rivers and Creeks for Essequibo, William Crichton,[4] that the absolute possession of the Waini and the Barima would be advantageous to the colony and afford protection to the aborigines who expected it of the government. The Colonial Office viewed Light's report as 'containing germs of future controversies with the South American Governments',[5] but neither Light nor any official in both the Colonial and Foreign Offices ever expected the spread of an epidemic that would last over a century.

In 1840 when the Venezuelans interfered with the property and the Indians of the Moruka Creek, Light forwarded a stern letter of protest to the Officer at Angostura.[6] By then the Colonial and Foreign Offices had given their blessing to Schomburgk to ascertain the boundaries between British Guiana and its coterminous territories with the understanding that the claims made would be presumptive and not assumptive; it was left to the respective governments to bring forward any objections whenever necessary

---

[1] C.O. 111/164. Schomburgk to Light, 16 July 1839.
[2] Venezuela. No. 4. 1896. *Further Documents relating to the Question of Boundary between Great Britain and Venezuela.* Scruggs's Brief. (London, 1896), p. 7.
[3] Light to Normanby, 15 July 1839. N.A.G.
[4] Report of W. Crichton to Light, 20 Apr. 1839, in Light to Normanby, 15 July 1839. N.A.G.
[5] C.O. 111/164. Minute of Stephen, 31 Aug. 1839, in Light to Normanby, ibid.
[6] Light to H.E. the Governor or Officer at Angostura, 23 Nov. 1840. L.B.

during the survey.[1] Schomburgk himself had already pointed out to the Colonial Office that it must expect a similar opposition from the Venezuelans as they had from the Brazilians.[2] Venezuela suggested that a treaty should precede the survey and a mixed commission mark the boundaries, but the previous instruction of the British government to O'Leary, her Acting Consul at Caracas, that 'the Governor of British Guiana [had] been instructed to resist any aggression upon the territories near the Frontier which have been hitherto occupied by Independent Tribes',[3] remained the last word at that period.

This did not prevent notes between officials in Georgetown and Caracas, and London and Georgetown from flying so thick and fast that diplomatic correspondence on the Venezuela–British Guiana boundary topped the list for its sheer volume of material. Close runners-up were Schomburgk's reports, journals, and letters. In his first report to Light, Schomburgk assured the Governor that the Warraus in the Barima district 'confessed that they had always considered themselves under British protection' and showed the sticks of office symbolizing their captaincy.[4] The Arawaks in Amacura complained that the Venezuelans had taken their people in bondage, beaten them unmercifully, and even violated their womenfolk before their eyes. Schomburgk left a document of protest with the Arawak captain, Jan, and begged Governor Light to transmit a copy to the authorities at Angostura in the hope that future atrocities against the Indians would be prevented.[5]

The Governor was so moved by the plight of the Indians that he even suggested a compromise of territory for the sake of their welfare. In March 1842 he wrote confidentially to Lord Stanley:

Yet if security be given that all the country extending between the boundary marked by Mr. Schomburgk, and the Wyana should be left to the undisturbed possession of the Aborigines the Venezuelan government binding itself to respect the rights of these unfortunate people, as well of those now existing, as of those who may retire there from the Orinoco, or elsewhere—if security be given that no fort or forts shall be constructed on the Barima either by the Venezuelans or by any other power—then

[1] F.O. to C.O., 18 Mar. 1840. N.A.G.
[2] C.O. 111/175. Schomburgk to Vernon Smith, 20 Aug. 1840.
[3] C.O. 111/184. Guillermo Smith, Secretary of Foreign Affairs to H.M.B. Consul, 28 Jan. 1841, and O'Leary to Smith, 13 Jan. 1841.
[4] Schomburgk to Light, 22 June 1841. N.A.G.
[5] Ibid.

Great Britain may yield to the national pride of the New Republic and make the Wyana—with its tributary streams—including both banks of those streams, a boundary—connecting it with the Cuyuni by such convenient line of communications as may be best found by survey.[1]

Obviously Light noted his reservations to this suggested compromise, but he was sincerely interested in the Indians and tried to influence the Colonial Office at every possible opportunity. The following month O'Leary notified Light that the Venezuelan government was only interested in 'that portion of disputed territory which is immediately washed by the Orinoco'.[2] As long as the Orinoco was hers 'Great Britain [could] then determine her own limits without the slightest opposition, even the territory between the Moroco and the Guiana (Guyana) though it may be grudged, would not be denied . . .'[3] But the landmarks erected by Schomburgk at Barima and Amacura, or more particularly the British flag placed on the posts, caused a diplomatic explosion and destroyed any remnant of goodwill that was evident in O'Leary's dispatch.[4] Light hastened to explain to the Venezuelan government that the Schomburgk marks in no way implied 'an occupation of territory, but a presumption of right'.[5] The irate feelings of their government, possibly quite unknown to them, did not prevent the Venezuelan Indians and people of the Orinoco from carrying on a brisk trade in provisions, cured fish, tobacco, and hides with the inhabitants of the Moruka and Pomeroon rivers. So many corials had entered the Moruka and Pomeroon, paying their duty in kind and money, that by the beginning of 1844 a branch office of the customs in the Pomeroon was deemed necessary to cope with the trade increase.[6] Though the respective countries glared at each other across the frontiers, the Indians traded, quite content as long as they were not molested.

While Schomburgk was involved in working out plans with the Brazilian authorities for a possible settlement of a Brazilian–British Guiana frontier,[7] the Colonial Office was immersed in the Venezuelan affair. In March 1844 Stephen advised the Foreign Office to come to an agreement, even to the point of conceding a portion of

[1] C.O. 111/195. Light to Stanley, 4 Mar. 1842 (Confidential).
[2] Ibid. O'Leary to Light, 4 Apr. 1842.
[3] Ibid.
[4] C.O. 111/197. O'Leary to Aberdeen, 17 Jan. 1842.
[5] Ibid. Enclosure in O'Leary to Aberdeen, 14 Feb. 1842.
[6] C.O. 111/208. Light to Stanley, 25 Jan. 1844.
[7] Ibid. Schomburgk to Light, 4 Jan. 1844.

the territory, with the important stipulation that such a portion should never be alienated to any foreign power. Lord Stanley insisted that regardless of any other provisos, Her Majesty's Government should make it quite clear to the Venezuelan government that they must agree to protect the Indians now residing in the district.[1] These recommendations were incorporated into the provisions of the 1844 Aberdeen line which modified the Schomburgk line, running from the mouth of the Moruka to the Acarabisi and from there on merging with the Schomburgk line thus:

All the territory lying between a line, such as here described, on the one side, and the River Amacura and the chain of Hills from which the Amacura rises on the other, Great Britain is willing to cede to Venezuela, upon the condition that the Venezuelan Government enter upon an agreement that no portion of it shall be alienated at any time to a Foreign Power, and that the Indian Tribes now residing within it shall be protected against all injury and oppression.[2]

The Indians were not forgotten. The line, an extreme concession to Venezuela, offered her almost the whole of the North West District.

Venezuela, however, ignored both the proferred hand in friendship and the land. Sir Robert Reid in his evidence before the Hague Tribunal in 1898 commented: 'There was absolutely no answer ever given to that offer at all.'[3] Señor Fortique, Minister Plenipotentiary of Venezuela, had died soon after, but Reid did not consider that sufficient reason. Grover Cleveland, President of the United States, suggested Fortique's death as a possible cause for Venezuela's silence, but also admitted that Venezuela was too distracted by internal dissension to pay any attention to boundary lines.[4] Fortique presumably wanted to accept the Aberdeen line

---

[1] C.O. 112/25. Stephen to Canning, 3 Mar. 1844.

[2] C.O. 111/216. Aberdeen to M. Fortique, 30 Mar. 1844. See also Schomburgk to Light, 18 Aug. 1841, 23 Oct. 1841, and 30 Nov. 1841, in which he gave detailed reasons for selecting Amacura as the western boundary of B.G. For a succinct account of the complex negotiations involving American intervention, see R. A. Humphreys, 'Anglo-American Rivalries and the Venezuela Crisis of 1895', in *Tradition and Revolt in Latin America* (London, 1969).

[3] B.G.B. *Proceedings*, VIII, 2376.

[4] Grover Cleveland, *The Venezuela Boundary Controversy* (Princeton, 1913), p. 16. In 1844 Venezuela, there was constant tension between the Conservative Oligarchy, fourteen years in power, and the Liberal Party founded in 1840 and then making a strong bid for power. Conspiracies and revolts had become endemic and the government had called out the military to crush them.

and not exasperate the British government while the Venezuelan government felt that it would be a compromise galling to its national dignity. Fortique, however, became involved in negotiating a treaty between Venezuela and Madrid, and as he himself stated, the acceptable time passed. According to Nuñez, 'Minister Fortique died repenting', whether on account of not accepting the Aberdeen overture, it is not quite clear.[1] Boundary negotiations reached a dead end and the territory remained undetermined.

Two years later, when blood feuds broke out among the Akawoi and Carib tribes, and the Akawoi went up the Caroni river to avenge a murder, Governor Light warned that it was impossible for the conflicting tribes to expect British protection unless they remained within the limits of the British territory. It was, indeed, the duty of the Justices of the Peace to apprehend offenders charged with murder, but not at 'inconvenient distances from the Police Force and jurisdiction of the Magistrates of British Guiana'.[2] This notice was sent to McClintock, Superintendent of Pomeroon, and it is therefore difficult, in view of the silence of the home government and the prudence of the local government regarding the boundary, to fathom McClintock's suggestion of the establishment of missions for the Warraus and the Akawois in the Barima and Waini rivers 'now as the boundary of British Guiana is defined and no likelihood of any interference by the Venezuelan Governments . . .'.[3] There was, significantly, no reply to this report of McClintock. From the continuous correspondence which existed between the Governor and McClintock as recorded in the Letter Books, McClintock could hardly have been unaware of the developments or lack of developments on the boundary issue. He was always so over-zealous for the establishment of missions that he was probably trying to force the Governor's hand for 'so desirable an object'.[4]

Early in 1849 when the new Governor Henry Barkly arrived in British Guiana, the country was engrossed in her domestic problems over immigration, labour, and the stirrings of racial antipathies. Barkly's first battle was with the Combined Court over the Civil List dispute which had resulted in a stoppage of supplies and brought the government to a standstill. For Barkly, boundary head-

---

[1] Enrique Bernardo Nuñez, *Tres Momentos en la Controversia de Limites de Guayana* (Ministerio de Relaciones Exteriores, Caracas, 1962), pp. 23–4.
[2] Young to McClintock, 3 Jan. 1846. L.B.
[3] M.C.P., 26 Feb. 1849. McClintock's Report, 31 Dec. 1848. N.A.G.
[4] Ibid.

aches paled into insignificance next to the more demanding controversies on his immediate door-step. Yet he was not insensitive to, much less unaware of, what was happening in the interior. In 1850 Taylor suggested that the 1844 Aberdeen overture should be withdrawn as it was quite useless 'to negotiate boundaries with such unsettled states as Venezuela'.[1] Barkly disagreed with Taylor—as he did in most issues[2]—and reminded the Colonial Office of the philanthropic motives which had induced it to treat with Venezuela in the past. The Indians were still being seized and illegally pressed into service by the Venezuelans to work on their farms and estates.[3] Several tribes had moved within the territory previously defined by the Schomburgk landmarks, and the population was increasing. Thus 'to surrender that Boundary would be objectionable, were it only for the disappointment which would thus be occasioned'.[4]

A disappointment for whom? Barkly seemed to be pleading for the Indians, but then he concluded his dispatch by significantly mentioning the possibility of the discovery of gold in the area and the public interest aroused in the recent findings in the Yaruary river, a tributary of the Cuyuni.[5] The possibility of a tangible 'El Dorado' now placed the boundary in a new light. The British Government withdrew the 1844 offer which had gathered dust for six years and agreed to leave the boundary *in statu quo*. But the Cuyuni area was now looked on as the promised land for gold diggers. In January 1854 Indians came to the city to complain to the Governor that their land was being intruded upon.[6] The British Vice-Consul, Kenneth Mathison, feared that Venezuela was giving grants to a New York Company to search for gold and offered what he thought was a pragmatic suggestion: 'If Her Majesty's Government could act on the principle of the United States by purchasing territory from the Indian Tribes who are the bona fide Proprietors and actual Possessors of it, the pretended claims of Venezuela would

---

[1] C.O. 111/278. Minute of Taylor, 13 May 1850.

[2] Although Taylor disagreed with Barkly's policy and considered him 'a dangerously innovating Governor . . .' he admired his astuteness and skill as an administrator. See Mona Macmillan, *Sir Henry Barkly. Mediator and Moderator, 1815–1898* (Capetown, 1970), pp. 57–8.

[3] Light had described such service as 'coerced labour at an arbitrary tariff of wages, from which the Indians seek refuge within the acknowledged limits of British Guiana'. C.O. 111/164. Light to Normanby, 15 July 1839.

[4] C.O. 111/276. Barkly to Grey, 20 Sept. 1850.

[5] Ibid.

[6] C.O. 116/12. *The Royal Gazette*, 23 Jan. 1854.

at once be set at rest.[1] Undoubtedly the Indians would have agreed to such a proposition as they constantly claimed British protection, and the British would have assured them that the settlement was primarily for their peace, welfare, and protection. But Venezuela in no way considered the Indians 'bona fide Proprietors and actual Possessors' of land they were claiming and would not have acknowledged any such purchase. Also, 'the problem of the Near East', the crisis looming ahead in the Balkans early in 1854, kept the Foreign Office much too busy to pay attention to fanciful suggestions made by a Vice-Consul in South America.

A few years later reports of gold-mines in the Upata region brought an official mission to the spot. Two members of this mission, Sir William Holmes, Provost Marshal, and W. H. Campbell, the Secretary of the Royal Agricultural and Commercial Society, echoed Mathison's advice in a private and confidential report to Governor Walker that if the disputed territory were purchased: 'there would be little difficulty as it would not be necessary to disturb the Indians—indeed they would be only too glad to make over to us their territorial rights in consideration of obtaining British Protection against the Spaniards, as they still call the Venezuelans, whom they regard as their natural enemies.'[2] Walker, in forwarding this report to Labouchere, warned that if the British did not assert their influence they would be 'forestalled by settlers from the United States who eventually may prove much more unpleasant neighbours than the Venezuelans'.[3] Walker must have done his home-work well, for years before such fears had been voiced by Schomburgk to Light.[4] However, the Holmes–Campbell suggestion and Cassandra-like prophecy of Walker were brushed aside by Taylor as 'wild notions'.[5]

The Foreign Office next commissioned Governor Philip Wodehouse, en route to resume the governorship of British Guiana, to visit Venezuela and negotiate with the government on the basis of past discussions, namely:

(1) The extent of Territory to which Great Britain should abandon her claim.

[1] C.O. 111/299. Report from K. Mathison, 11 Jan. 1854, in Walker to Newcastle, 20 Feb. 1854.
[2] C.O. 111/319. Holmes and Campbell to Walker, 22 Jan. 1858.
[3] Ibid. Walker to Labouchere, 22 Jan. 1858.
[4] Schomburgk to Light, 30 Nov. 1841. N.A.G.
[5] C.O. 111/319. Minute of Taylor on Walker to Labouchere, 22 Jan. 1858.

(2) The effect which such abandonment might have upon the Indians inhabiting the territory to be abandoned, and,

(3) The possibility of preventing any of the Territory to be abandoned from falling afterwards in the hands of any Power likely to entertain towards us any feelings of hostility.[1]

For his guidance the Foreign Office gave Wodehouse quite definite guidelines in dealing with the subject of the Indian tribes. On one hand he was to assure Venezuela that Her Majesty's government would not shirk her obligation to protect the Indians from Venezuelan ill-treatment, but on the other hand she would not jeopardize any negotiations for a successful boundary treaty on account of the Indians. In beautifully suave diplomatic language Britain outlined her practical, hard-headed policy. The Indians were to be used to further negotiations only where practicable; at any rate they were a nomadic and scanty people, and British protection of them could not be stretched to the point of going to war with Venezuela.[2] At this time Venezuela was in the throes of constitutional crises and was in no position to negotiate boundary settlements, much less go to war with Britain for land or Indians.

Out of the political upheavals in Venezuela arose the suggested annexation of Province of Guayana to British Guiana. During 1842 and 1848 the inhabitants of Ciudad Bolívar, previously Angostura, had begged Mr. Mathison, the British Vice-Consul, to hoist the British flag for their protection, and the majority seemed willing and anxious to vote for transference to the sovereignty of the British flag.[3] In 1858 Mathison wrote that, because of chronic revolution since 1836, the prospects of tranquillity and prosperity were nil, duties and taxes had increased, the Caracas government had neglected to redress grievances, and general maladministration had brought injustice in its train. 'All these continued grievances', he illustrated, 'have created in the minds of all men the desire and determination to seek the Protection of Great Britain by annexing the Province to the British Crown, or if refused to place the Province

[1] C.O. 111/322. Earl of Clarendon to Wodehouse, 22 Feb. 1858.
[2] Ibid. Wodehouse to Malmesbury, 19 Apr. 1858.
[3] C.O. 111/319. Private and Confidential. Holmes and Campbell to Walker, 22 Jan. 1858, in Walker to Labouchere, 22 Jan. 1858. The early capital of the Province of Guayana founded in 1591 was Santo Tomé, later known as Angostura and then Ciudad Bolívar. Guillermo Morón, *A History of Venezuela*. Ed. and trans. John Street (London, 1964), p. 64.

at the command of the U.S. of America.'[1] F. D. Orme, the British Chargé d'Affairs in Caracas, supported Mathison's views with added news of the current discontent in Venezuela and in particular at Ciudad Bolívar.[2] Taylor discountenanced the suggestion that if Britain refused to take up the Venezuelan burden the United States might do so, considering it imprudent and fraught with future political and diplomatic pitfalls.[3] Quite rightly, he argued that this Mathison suggestion emanated from the commercial centre, Ciudad Bolívar, and thus influenced by Europeans 'whilst a rural and remote Population and the great body of People might feel differently'.[4] The present political discontent and disillusionment which the Venezuelans now suffered might, with foreign intervention, rapidly give way to a strong national feeling. The weakness and violence of the Venezuelan character were reflected in its government which Britain would then have to rule with a strong hand. Consequently Parliament would censure such arbitrary power as a contradiction of democracy. Taylor distrusted the sentiments of the American Ministers, Eames and Turpin, in favour of the annexation, for he felt that the United States would be only too happy to use such a precedent as a pretext to annex territory in Mexico and elsewhere.[5] This 'admirable minute' of Taylor's was adopted by both the Foreign and Colonial Offices as the Gospel on the boundary issue. Deferring to the recent policy of the Colonial Office, which was 'rather to discourage than to encourage claims to territorial extension', Malmesbury informed Merivale at the Colonial Office that it was unlikely that Her Majesty's Government would 'take steps to bring about the dismemberment of the territory of a friendly Government . . .',

[1] C.O. 111/322. Mathison to F. D. Orme, 26 Aug. 1858.
[2] Ibid. Orme to Malmesbury, 12 Oct. 1858. Orme called Mathison 'an active, zealous and intelligent gentleman' well-acquainted with affairs in the Venezuelan government, but Taylor did not 'place much confidence in the summary and cursory account . . . of the grievances existing in Venezuelan Guyana . . .' which he gave. Ibid. Minute of Taylor, 29 Nov. 1858.
[3] Ibid. Minute of Taylor.   [4] Ibid.
[5] Orme had reported to Malmesbury the conversation he had with Eames as follows: 'Mr. Eames observed much to my surprise: "I expect that country (Venezuela Guiana) will soon 'drop off' and go over to you and I think it's the best thing it could do." "But," I replied somewhat incredulously, "What would you say to that?" "Nothing," he rejoined immediately. "My country has no projects in that quarter and as to the monopoly of steam navigation on the Orinoco which has been so much talked about that was a strictly private speculation in the furtherance of which my government were neither directly nor indirectly concerned or interested." ' C.O. 111/322. Orme to Malmesbury, 12 Oct. 1858.

and all things being considered, the present moment was quite un-favourable for renewing negotiations with Venezuela.[1]

By 1860s the interest in the Indians became submerged in the gold-rush. Governor Francis Hincks bombarded the Colonial Office with requests to settle the boundary with Venezuela once and for all, not for the sake of the Indians, but for the people of Guiana whom he claimed were extremely dissatisfied with the shilly-shallying of the home government. Taylor was adamant; the negotia-tions would only fail and in a caustic comment in the margin of Hincks's dispatch wrote: 'there would be still more dissatisfaction if the Colony were required to pay the expences of a military ex-pedition such as that which it became necessary to send to Pirara some years ago.'[2] Despite Hincks's tenacious stand on the issue, Taylor positively refused to extend British protection to the gold diggers who wanted to establish a British Guiana Gold Company to mine gold in the Cuyuni, and in exasperation observed that 'if the Europeans go to Cuyani to dig gold, they should begin by digging their graves.'[3] Hincks, now as strongly gold-minded as planter-minded and under the influence of the gold-digging enthusiasts, felt he owed his loyalty to them and not to the Indians. He saw no reason why the local government should be 'fettered with any obli-gations to the Aborigines', who in such a vast territory could well shift for themselves.[4]

Yet Venezuelan ill-treatment of the Indians had not stopped. To McClintock's report of continued lawless acts and abductions,[5] it was answered that the subject of boundary was a touchy one and it was anathema, according to the Foreign and Colonial Office, to bring up the subject.[6] The Court of Policy would not brave the subject for the sake of the Indians, but for gold it was a different matter. In June 1867 they submitted a memorial on the subject of the British Guiana Gold Company, praying for an urgent settlement of the boundary.[7] At the same time it was rumoured that an influential

[1] Ibid. Malmesbury to Merivale, 23 Nov. 1858, and C.O. 112/35. E. B. Lytton to Wodehouse, 29 Dec. 1858.

[2] C.O. 111/341. Minute of Taylor in Hincks to Newcastle, 16 June 1863.

[3] C.O. 111/343. Minute of Taylor embodied in a reply to a letter from Stephen from Stephen Cave, Chairman of the West India Committee, 11 June 1863.

[4] C.O. 111/365. Hincks to the Duke of Buckingham and Chandos, 9 May 1867.

[5] M.C.C., 18 May 1864. McClintock's Report, 31 Dec. 1863.

[6] W. H. Ware, Government Secretary to McClintock, 17 Jan. 1866. L.B.

[7] C.O. 111/363. Governor R. Mundy to Buckingham and Chandos, 7 June 1867. The British Guiana Gold Company was established on 12 June 1863. Enclosed in this

Venezuelan was interested in spearheading a foreign gold company in the same region in which the British Guiana Gold Company was working. Taylor suddenly executed a volte-face and declared that the time for reopening negotiations was ripe.[1] But nothing happened. The home government was too engrossed with Fenian terrorism and the Second Reform Bill, to say nothing of trying to curb the Basuto and Kaffir tribes in Africa, to attend to affairs so far away from more vital scenes of action.

While McClintock vainly looked forward to the day when the boundary question would be settled, so 'as to meet the wishes of these simple but interesting Denizens of the Forest',[2] and the Revd. W. H. Brett attested that 'The Aboriginal races . . . desire nothing more earnestly than to be subject to her [Great Britain] and under her protection as in former years',[3] a new Governor, John Scott, arrived in British Guiana, a man whom it was claimed 'conceived it his duty to maintain the *status quo* and did so successfully'.[4] After Governor Hincks's unflagging and pertinacious bombardment of the Colonial Office on behalf of the Gold Company, Scott was probably hand-picked by a harassed Colonial Office for his phlegmatic character. At least, he could be trusted to lay low and say nothing in diplomatic or domestic affairs. The only evidence of Scott's attitude to the boundary was an oblique reference in a communication to McClintock that 'we ought to exercise magisterial jurisdiction at the right bank of the Moruka beyond which is the Catholic Mission.'[5] He again voiced similar sentiments in giving permission to McClintock to build his house on the Moruka where he could keep an eye on interlopers and so protect the Indians.[6]

By the 1870s the tumult and the shouting on the cause of Indian protection and the boundaries had died down. Only one voice was now heard in the wilderness, crying for the people of the wilderness, that of McClintock's. Schomburgk's pleas in the cause of philanthropy and humanity were buried in his reports. It seemed that dispatch was also a petition of the Chairman and Directors of the Company with a full résumé of their case.

[1] C.O. 111/363. Minute of Taylor, 3 July 1867. Ibid.

[2] M.C.P., 28 July 1868. McClintock's Report, 30 June 1868. N.A.G.

[3] W. H. Brett's Report of Indian Missions at Cabacaburi and Waramuri, 26 Nov. 1869. *Guiana Diocesan Church Society*, 1869, p. 9.

[4] Webber, p. 282.

[5] E. Walker, Government Secretary to McClintock, 28 Sept. 1871.

[6] M.C.P., 22 May 1873. Comment of Scott on McClintock to J. M. Grant, Government Secretary, 29 July 1872.

the Foreign Office and the Colonial Office, so busy with events on other continents and with other natives, no 'longer recollected that the territory belonged once to those tribes from whom European nations have wrested it'.[1]

The home government, in the tortuous negotiations with Brazil and Venezuela, blew hot and cold where the Indians were concerned. Taylor's strong urging of a boundary settlement in 1840, from 'motives of humanity and obligations which this country may be considered to have contracted towards the Aborigines',[2] gave way in 1851 to a hedging on any such obligation which would burden the government with too great a cost.[3] Mesmerized by the Treasury, Taylor's axiom became 'Remember Pirara'. Practicability and economics ruled the rise and fall of the Indian question *vis-à-vis* the boundaries.

By the end of the century when Great Britain agreed to arbitrate the boundary between British Guiana and Venezuela, the Indians were officially remembered. At the Hague Arbitration Tribunal a mass of evidence was offered to prove that the Dutch, and subsequently the British, exercised jurisdiction over the Indian tribes in the basins of the Mazaruni, Essequibo, Cuyuni, Pomeroon, Moruka, Barama, Waini, Barima, and Amacura. The staves of office distributed to the Indian captains were displayed as proof of British jurisdiction over, and liaison with, the Indians. Above all British protection and sovereignty were accepted, and moreover asked for, by the Indian tribes who looked upon the neighbouring 'La Patrias', the Venezuelans, as their natural enemies.[4] In the argument of the British case Indian protection became a *cause célèbre*.

[1] Schomburgk's Report, 22 June 1841. N.A.G.
[2] C.O. 111/162. Minute of Taylor, 11 Feb. 1840.
[3] C.O. 111/286. Minute of Taylor, 17 Nov. 1851.
[4] Second Report of Schomburgk, Aug. 1841, in Venezuela. No. 5. *Further Documents relating to the Question of Boundary between British Guiana and Venezuela*. Sir R. Schomburgk's Reports (London, 1896), p. 15. Schomburgk states that the Indians called the Venezuelans by that name because they carried out their massacres during the revolution with the cry, 'Por la Patrias'.

VII

INDIAN SLAVERY—INDUSTRIAL EMPLOYMENT OF INDIANS— INDIANS AND THE LAND

BESIDES pleading the Indian cause to urge a speedy settlement of the boundaries, Schomburgk repeatedly advocated the use of Indians as a labour force. He had every confidence that, if the Indians were rationally treated and given a fair remuneration for their work, they would 'prove most useful labourers of the colony'.[1]

Schomburgk's ideas were neither novel nor unique. Every nation which gained territory by conquest or treaty used the indigenous people as a labour force. Such coercion of native labour was a historical reality. In the Spanish colonies the question of Indian labour and the treatment of the Indians constituted a social and economic problem throughout the colonial period. Despite the *cédulas*, ordinances, and decrees which poured forth from Spain on the subject, the struggle for justice was a tug-of-war between humane sentiments and practical economics. The King of Spain insisted on his *quinto* but did not wish the Indians to be enslaved; the *encomenderos* argued that no revenue would be forthcoming if the Indians were not, in one way or another, coerced into working. Las Casas, that ardent champion of the Indians, had triggered off the endless and morally weighted arguments regarding Indian freedom which boomeranged in the enslavement of the Negro. The Spanish compromise was the *encomienda* and the *doctrina* where the *encomenderos* and *doctrineros* exacted the services of the Indians and salved their consciences by giving them in exchange the blessings of Christianity. As far as the Spanish were concerned, it was an exchange in the Indians' favour; the work of the body gained the salvation of the soul.[2] Although the *Recopilación de Leyes* proves

---

[1] Second Report of Schomburgk, Aug. 1841, p. 20.

[2] C. S. Walton, *The Civil Law in Spain and Spanish America* (Washington, 1900), p. 525. So numerous were the *cédulas*, *decretos*, *resoluciones*, *ordinenamientos*, *reglamentos*

beyond doubt the concern of the Spanish crown for the welfare of their Indian subjects, there is also evidence to prove the excesses of the *encomenderos* who, far removed from King and Council of the Indies, outrageously exploited native labour.

Although the terrible accusations of Fray Bartolomé de las Casas regarding the millions of natives cruelly massacred by the Spaniards are not fully accepted today as historical fact, there was some truth in his exposé of the excessive labour and gross injustice which the Indians had to suffer.[1] Fray Toribio Motolinía, one of the 'Twelve Apostles'—the first Franciscans to Mexico, 1524—and certainly no friend of las Casas, wrote bluntly of the fear with which the Indians served their Spanish lords who exacted heavy tribute and laborious service from them. He particularly emphasized the cruelty of labour in the mines, where countless Indian slaves perished in order to satisfy Spanish greed.[2] Juan de Zumárraga, Bishop-elect of Mexico and Protector of Indians, fought a continuous battle against Nuno de Guzmán, President of the Audiencia of New Spain, who at every turn exploited the Indians.[3] Spanish records, throughout the colonial period, lay bare the manipulation of native labour and the conscientious efforts made by the King and the Council of Indies in Spain to suppress that evil.

This exploitation of native races runs like a thread throughout the history of every colonial people, but in the territory of Guiana, once ruled by the Dutch, the situation *vis-à-vis* the Indians was a different one. The question of Indian labour was naturally bound up with the question of freedom. As George Bagot pointed out, the Spanish Indians had advanced in civilization but at a price, 'confined to their respective District, or Mission, . . . the labour they performed was compulsory.'[4] From the outset the Dutch in Guiana found

enacted in Spain for the government of the colonies that a collection was ordered to be made in the reign of Philip II, but it was not until 16 May 1680, in the reign of Charles II that the *Recopilación de Leyes de los Reynos de las Indias* consisting of nine Books, 218 Titles, and 6,447 Laws was promulgated.

[1] 'The Brevíssima Relación' in Francis Augustus Mac Nutt, *Bartholomew de las Casas. His Life, His Apostolate and His Writings* (London, 1909), pp. 317 and 331.

[2] Francis Borgia Steck, *Motolinía's History of the Indians of New Spain* (Washington, D.C., 1951), pp. 90–3 and 101.

[3] Ibid., p. 13, f.n. 29. Guzmán even threatened to hang Zumárraga for his interference. See also Lesley Byrd Simpson, *The Encomienda in New Spain* (Berkeley, 1966), pp. 71–2.

[4] C.O. 111/123. Bagot to D'Urban, 4 Sept. 1832 in D'Urban to Goderich, 3 Nov. 1832.

themselves for pragmatic, economic, and strategic reasons, forced to accept the freedom of the Indians. The proud and warlike Caribs, their first contacts, even in their 'untutored minds' knew the difference between enslavement by their own people and enslavement by outsiders from across the sea. They regarded themselves as a free people. Unlike the Aztecs, the Mayas, and the Incas, gathered together in their cities, the Guiana Indians were scattered throughout a wilderness, a 'terra incognita' to the Dutch who had to rely on them as guides, messengers, spies, and allies against the neighbouring Spaniards.

Throughout the Dutch administration, instructions from the Directors of the Dutch West India Company warned 'that not the least offence should be given to the Indians'.[1] These orders were sometimes ignored by Dutch settlers who could not resist the temptation to purchase slaves, but they never attacked the Indians for the purpose of enslaving them. In 1793 an Ordinance was passed by the States-General which decreed that 'All persons were prohibited from purchasing or holding as slaves, any Indian, or the offspring of Indian women, of whatsoever tribe'.[2] On the basis of the Articles of Capitulation in 1803 by which the British agreed to maintain all prior Dutch laws and usages in the colony, this 1793 Ordinance was strictly adhered to. Like the Dutch, the British had no choice but to secure the loyal service of the Indian tribes for military and security measures against the ever-increasing numbers of runaway Negroes. They could not afford to run the risk of offending the independent Indians by coercing them for any kind of manual labour. Moreover, the Indians stood on their rights and demanded presents and subsidies for their services, a factor which irked and irritated Governor H. L. Carmichael to the point of incoherence.

In 1811 an English resident in Guiana, John Daly, accused Governor William Bentinck of keeping Indian slaves contrary to the 1793 Ordinance. The abolition of the African slave trade, said Daly, had signalled the beginning of a traffic in Indian slaves in the colony,

---

[1] Williams, pp. 423-4.
[2] *The Demerara and Essequibo Vade-Mecum* (Georgetown, 1825), p. 13. N.A.G. See also C.O. 318/72. *Separate and Private Report of the Commissioners of Legal Inquiry in the United Colony of Demerara and Essequibo and Colony of Berbice*, 28 Jan. 1828. Appendix B, which referred to the 1793 prohibition of Indian slavery by the Dutch in their colonies and compared it to the 1741 Act in Jamaica which forbade the enslavement of Indians on the Mosquito Shore by the early settlers in Honduras.

and the Governor was an offender.[1] Daly's accusation probably contained an element of truth, but Bentinck's reasons for having slaves appeared to be a matter of protection. In 1810 the Chief of the Caribs, Mahanarva, stormed into the city demanding what he should do with his slaves since Indian slavery had been abolished. When Mahanarva indicated that he had no alternative but to put them to death, Bentinck appealed to him to act humanely in exchange for a treaty of friendship and an annual subsidy.[2] The Revd. W. H. Brett mentioned in his work, *Indian Missions in Guiana*, that 'a Carib chief dashed out the brains of a slave when the governor refused to accept him as a gift'.[3] Obviously, the Indian chief was Mahanarva and the governor presumably Bentinck. After such a display of brutality, it would have been understandable for the governor to accept the gift of slaves for their protection, and explain the Indian slaves of Bentinck who of all the early governors, was extremely careful to preserve the friendship of the Indians.[4] Daly's allegations against Bentinck appeared to be more 'misrepresented' than 'unfounded'.[5]

All Bentinck's successors were on the alert against illicit traffic in Indian slaves. In 1812 Governor Carmichael ordered an investigation of such traffic in Berbice which had been reported by Mr. Charles Edmonstone, Protector of Slaves for Demerara, and Governor Gordon of Berbice was commissioned to punish the violations of the prohibitory laws against Indian slavery.[6] The Ordinance of 1793, renewed in 1807,[7] was no dead letter, as the case of the Indian woman, Joesinsky, undoubtedly proved.

In 1819 a claim was made in the Court of Justice at Demerara for the freedom of Joesinsky, her five children, and a child of her sister who had been in the possession of Mr. Robert Westley Hall, owner of Plantation Maria's Pleasure. When Joesinsky's daughter was sold to another gentleman, Joesinsky realized that they were considered

[1] C.O. 111/14. John Daly, ex J.P. for Essex, to His Majesty's Government, 20 Feb. 1811, with enclosed affidavits of Pieter Kemp, Police Officer in Demerara, and Joseph Templeman of Norwell, England.   [2] Webber, p. 130.   [3] Brett, p. 134.

[4] Ibid. See also above, p. 55, f.nn. 1–4.

[5] C.O. 112/4. Earl of Liverpool to Bentinck, 22 Feb. 1812. Bentinck was requested to furnish satisfactory proofs that such allegations were either 'misrepresented' or 'unfounded'.   [6] C.O. 114/8. M.C.P., 28 Apr. 1812.

[7] C.O. 114/6. M.C.P., 26 Oct. 1807. The Court of Policy resolved that the 1793 Ordinance against purchasing of Indian slaves be republished with the addition 'that it shall also be unlawful and criminal for any persons to take or receive Indians in pawn or as a pledge for debt due by other Indians'.

slaves and not free subjects working on the estate. Mr. N. Chapman, executor of the estate of the late Mr. Reedon, referred the case to the Court of Justice who 'deeming it to be a very important case' referred it in turn to His Majesty in Council. But the Privy Council shunted the case back to the Court of Justice.[1] While the case was being tossed back and forth between London and Demerara, the Commissioners of Legal Inquiry in the West Indies visited the colonies. To their questions regarding cases of Indian slavery, the officials replied that 'A Case was lately tried in this Court on which sentence has not yet been passed in consequence of an inquiry directed to be made as to some facts'.[2] The Berbice functionaries showed that their Court of Justice had manumitted Lubyn and Peyto on the grounds that no Indian, nor descendants of Indians, could be lawfully detained in slavery.[3]

Eventually, the Court of Justice in Demerara delivered its judgement in favour of the owner, Hall.[4] Through Chapman, Joesinsky appealed to His Majesty's Council against the decision,[5] with the strong support of the Crown Advocate, S. W. Gordon. The respondent Hall wrote to the Lords of the Treasury consenting to a reversal of judgement if he were paid the costs of the proceedings, and if no further action would be taken against him for detaining Joesinsky and her family.[6] With the case hanging fire for over ten years, Governor D'Urban understandably petitioned Viscount Goderich that it be brought to a speedy conclusion, not only because Joesinsky and her children were still enslaved, 'but because there are several other cases of a similar nature laying over for this decision by which they will also be mainly influenced, if not absolutely determined'.[7] His words seemed to have spurred the Privy Council into action; three months later, on 19 December 1831 it reversed the sentence of the Court of Justice in Demerara[8] and Joesinsky and her

[1] C.O. 111/68. N. Chapman to Sir George Murray, 30 Oct. 1829.

[2] C.O. 318/75. 'Questions asked by the Commissioners of Legal Inquiry in the West Indies'. The Commission was appointed in 1824 to inquire into the administration of justice in the colonies of St. Lucia, Demerara, Berbice, Jamaica, Bahamas, Bermuda, and settlements in the Bay of Honduras. See also C.O. 319/27.

[3] Ibid. See also C.O. 111/306. Governor Henry Beard to Murray, Berbice, 23 Oct. 1828, with enclosures from Protectors of Slaves.

[4] C.O. 111/124. Charles Bouchier to Lord Commissioners of the Treasury, 26 Nov. 1832.　　　　　　　　　　[5] C.O. 111/68. Chapman to Murray, 30 Oct. 1829.

[6] C.O. 111/118. Bouchier to Lords Commissioners of the Treasury 26 May 1831, in J. Stewart to Viscount Howick, 13 June 1831.

[7] C.O. 111/116. D'Urban to Goderich, 24 Sept. 1831.

[8] C.O. 111/124. Stewart to Howick, 24 Jan. 1832.

family were set at liberty and registered in the Fiscal's Office as free-born persons. Thus the home government fully upheld the 1793 Ordinance accepting the Indians and their descendants as free people. Consequently, the decision of the Privy Council on the Joesinsky case moved the Crown Advocate, Gordon, to proceed with claims of freedom for several Indians, their children, and grandchildren.[1]

In Berbice, cases governing the freedom of Indians from enslavement were regulated by the rules issued by Their High and Mightinesses, the States-General of the United Netherlands to the West India Company on 23 August 1636. Article LXXXVII stated: 'With regard to the Brazilians and Aborigines of the country shall be left to enjoy their liberty, and are in no manner whatsoever to be made Slaves; but shall, together with the other inhabitants, have their political and civil rights, and are to be governed conformable with their laws.'[2] As the Articles of Capitulation guaranteed the continuation of all existing laws, this 1636 Ordinance remained in force, and violators of its statutes were brought before the courts. In 1828 the case of Lubyn of Indian descent was tried before the Court of Civil Justice, Berbice. The defendant and owner of Lubyn, J. A. Dehnert, claimed that he had purchased him, among other slaves, at a vendue in 1816, and now opposed his manumission. The Courts, however, proved that Lubyn was the son of an Indian woman, Maria, and, as such, according to the 1636 regulations, was 'free from all the forms and effects of bondage or slavery'.[3] His letter of manumission entitled him 'to all those rights, privileges and advantages which, by the laws of this colony, belong to free persons of colour therein'.[4] Another Indian, Sophia, of the Akawoi tribe, was also manumitted on the evidence of Lieutenant Colonel Gallez, Protector of the Indians, who affirmed that he knew Sophia's mother to be an Indian.[5]

As the Revd. W. H. Brett so often demonstrated, 'the love of liberty is deeply implanted in the Indian bosom',[6] but this love did not prevent him from capturing members of other tribes and selling them as slaves. The Arawaks, because of their intelligence, and the

[1] C.O. 111/123. Gordon to D'Urban, 11 Dec. 1832.

[2] C.O. 111/106. Extract from the Register of the Proceedings of the Court of Civil Justice of the Colony, Berbice, 20 Aug. 1828, in Governor Henry Beard to Sir George Murray, 23 Oct. 1828.

[3] Ibid. 'The Court Fiat.'   [4] Ibid. Manumission Letter, 30 Aug. 1828.
[5] Ibid. Deputy Protector's Office, 4 July 1828.   [6] Brett, p. 236.

Caribs, their superior strength, looked down on other tribes and deduced that their superiority gave them *carte blanche* over less gifted tribes. Two interesting cases showed how the more powerful nations sold slaves to whomsoever would purchase them. In 1836 Mrs. M. H. Higgs, a widow, petitioned the Court of Policy for compensation for five slaves, descendants of Louisa, a Macusi buckeen, who had been purchased by her father-in-law in 1790. She was summoned to Georgetown by the Protector of Slaves to answer a complaint that she had been illegally holding in slavery 'certain persons named Mary, Fortune, Tiffon, Mercurius and John—they being of Indian extraction by the mother's side'.[1] Although she protested that she had brought them up from childhood more as her family than as slaves and now in her old age needed their services, she admitted that she had no defence to the Ordinance of 1793.[2] Accordingly she lost both her Indians and compensation.

But the case which rocked the country was the 'Case of Fraser against Spencer' for Indian slavery in August 1839. This case not only brought down odium on the head of the postholder, John Spencer, but exemplified Arawak enslavement of the Macusi people. Proceedings against Spencer and his Arawak wife, Wilhelmina, were initiated by Mrs. S. Fraser of the Demerara River. Previously Mr. W. D. Couchman, a woodcutter, had charged Spencer with cutting wood on Crown Lands, as well as having Indian slaves. Mr. Robert King, Superintendent of Rivers and Creeks, Demerara, investigated the case and claimed that the accusations were false,[3] and Governor Light seemed satisfied with the investigation.[4] Charges were now laid against Spencer and his wife for detaining Indian children, and the Governor seemed reluctant to take them seriously. The press appealed to him as '. . . he values his reputation, as an efficient and sincere protector of the Aborigines . . . he will set this matter forever at rest without loss of time'.[5]

By this time Hilhouse had launched a bitter attack against the whole system of the postholdership which gave postholders such power over the Indians,[6] and the press supported his polemics.[7] The

[1] M.C.P., 25 Nov. 1836. N.A.G.   [2] Ibid.
[3] Report of Robert King, 17 Apr. 1839. N.A.G.
[4] C.O. 111/166. Light to Normanby, 7 Oct. 1839.
[5] C.O. 116/3. Editorial of *The Guiana Chronicle*, 12 Aug. 1839.
[6] Ibid., Hilhouse to the Editor, 16 Aug. 1839.
[7] Ibid. Editorial, 'The Local Government and Indian Slavery,' 13 Sept. 1839.

Governor sent Hadfield, King's successor, up the river to investigate again and the press rejoiced, but Light still maintained that 'reports of slavery existing to a great degree on the River Demerara' were exaggerated.[1] The press contended that the governor was influenced by his secretary, H. E. F. Young, to cover up the malpractices, not only of Spencer, but of King and Hadfield, his superior officers who, being fed at Spencer's table, could hardly be expected to bring a case against him.[2] With the press stirring up the public in its clamour for justice, the governor next sent the Inspector General of Police, Mr. W. Crichton, to summon the Spencers 'to answer charges preferred against them to the effect that they traffick in Maucousi Indians and detain them in slavery'.[3] After a preliminary investigation Spencer was removed from the postholdership, and both his wife and himself were jailed. The Attorney-General, Henry Gloster, indicted Mrs. W. Spencer before the Supreme Court for feloniously enslaving the Macusi girl, Grace, but this case fell to the ground because of a flaw in the indictment.[4] So, too, did the case against John Spencer.

Though the Spencers were acquitted because of flaws in the first two indictments, they had to face six more connected with the same offence. While the case was in progress, *The Royal Gazette* declined to publish the evidence because of conflicting opinions and for fear of prejudicing the public mind, but commented:

The case is one of a very peculiar nature. Few indictments were ever brought before a Court of Justice, on which there was and is greater difference of opinion, . . . some would say that accusations brought against the Spencers by Mrs. Fraser have all been offspring of malice and personal enmity, arising from a clashing of interests in their respective occupations up the river; and that in such a case no credit is to be attached to her statements; others say that the Spencers are guilty of all laid to their charge, and that Mrs. Fraser has not told all the truth regarding the nefarious traffic in Indian slaves carried on in the Demerara River during many years past.[5]

As the press hinted, there was proof of Mrs. Fraser's 'malice and personal enmity' for both the Spencers and Mr. John Paterson, the

[1] C.O. 111/166. Light to Normanby, 7 Oct. 1839.

[2] C.O. 116/3. Editorial of *The Guiana Chronicle*, 11 Sept. 1839.

[3] Memorandum to Mr. Crichton, 19 Aug. 1839. Also, Young to Spencer. L.B.

[4] C.O. 111/180. Report of Henry Gloster, 18 Aug. 1841, in Light to Russell, 20 Aug. 1841.

[5] C.O. 115/4. *The Royal Gazette*, 21 Dec. 1839.

Protector of Indians, whom she also accused of ruling 'with un-limited sway over every Indian in the River' and 'enslaving them'.[1] In the evidence given, Paterson produced letters written to him by Mrs. Fraser which showed that she had been under deep obligations to him for medicines and many services since she had settled on the Demerara river.[2] Mrs. Fraser, a daughter of Governor von Batten-burg of Berbice, had fallen from her social position and found herself under obligation to the postholder and the Protector. It appeared that hell hath no fury like a woman humbled, as well as scorned. Mrs. Fraser's vindictive accusations against Paterson indicated that pride and jealousy were at the bottom of her volte-face against her previous benefactor. Indeed, those who did not live up the river could 'hardly conceive the bickerings that prevail there'.[3] 'Fair Play' in the press considered the charges against the Spencers 'maliciously trumped up by a termagant' and oratorically declaimed: 'O for a whip to lash naked through the world any rascal, who should make humanity a cloak to cover vindictiveness.'[4] Governor Light intimated to Lord Russell that Mrs. Fraser's misfortunes had caused her to war against the world;[5] the Attorney-General saw her as an officious woman,[6] and after reading the reports and dispatches from the governor on the case, Henry Taylor gleaned that she was 'a strong-minded masculine woman of a restless spirit'.[7] In general, Mrs. Fraser's denunciations of Indian slavery were supported by Hilhouse and the press, and above all by Crichton, who had been dispatched to collect witnesses for the case.

Crichton's report gave much enlightenment on Indian slavery in theory and in practice. While tracking down Meacaria and her daughter, Grace, principal witnesses for the case, he was violently abused by an Indian woman, Catteau, because he was attempting to interfere with the Macusi slaves of the Arawaks. Catteau was related to Mrs. Spencer, and Crichton discovered that there were quite a few Indians held in slavery by the relatives of Mrs. Spencer

[1] C.O. 111/120. Light to Russell, 21 Jan. 1840.
[2] C.O. 111/180. S. M. Fraser to J. Paterson, 27 Jan. 1837, 14 Aug. 1837, 21 Aug. 1837; Report of J. Paterson, 25 Nov. 1837, in which he accused Mrs. Fraser of bribing both the apprenticed labourers and the Indians with rum to work for her. In his report to Light, 27 Jan. 1840, Paterson called her 'an unprincipled and mischievous woman'. All enclosures in Light to Russell, 20 Aug. 1841.
[3] C.O. 116/3. Letter of 'Fair Play' in *The Guiana Chronicle*, 16 Sept. 1839.
[4] Ibid.   [5] C.O. 111/180. Light to Russell, 20 Aug. 1841.
[6] Ibid. Report of Gloster, 18 Aug. 1841.
[7] Minute of Taylor, 16 Oct. 1841, on Light to Russell, 20 Aug. 1841.

who were reluctant to disclose the matter to the whites for fear of 'giving offence to any member of this too powerful Buck Family'.[1] Although their owners claimed that the Macusis were at liberty to leave, they knew this was impossible. The Macusis never descended the Demerara river below the Great Falls, and no Arawak would ever take the Macusis over the Great Falls to rejoin their tribe, and so they remained slaves by necessity. The Arawaks looked upon themselves as free nations and held it their right to enslave other non-privileged nations.[2] Crichton made a practical suggestion in his report that these Macusis be returned to their own district under British protection. Taylor applauded this suggestion and noted that Governor Light had ignored it completely, 'possibly it would cost some money and that may be an objection'.[3]

The key witnesses brought down to the Supreme Court by Crichton were found to be ignorant of the knowledge of an oath. The Spencers were acquitted of the charges of enslaving Indians on the lack of reputable evidence. In dispatching the evidence and memorials pro and con in the case of the *Crown* v. *Mrs. Spencer*, Governor Light stressed the fact that Indian slavery was never tolerated in British Guiana and that the authorities did their utmost to protect Indians as the evidence clearly showed.[4] A few months later in forwarding another rash of memorials and reports on the case, Light admitted that there was slave traffic on the Demerara river, but in areas outside the bounds of law. Mrs. Fraser's allegations against the postholder and the Protector had stemmed from bitterness, for she had quarrelled with both. The Indians were warned to abandon the slave traffic, but enslaved Indians seemed resigned to their lot, contented as long as they were given their share of rum, cassava bread, and pepper-pot. Light then launched into a diatribe against the evils brought about by 'the passionate love of the Indians for ardent spirits'.[5] Light seemed to be protesting too much, reluctant to admit that an official had broken the rules. It was a case of authority upholding authority.

Despite his explanatory letter to Lord Russell enclosing the Attorney-General's defence of his actions, there had been many

[1] C.O. 111/180. Crichton's Report, 16 Oct. 1840.
[2] The Caribs, Arawaks, and Warraus were accepted as free nations by the Dutch and they obviously felt that the 1793 Ordinance referred only to them and their offspring.
[3] C.O. 111/180. Minute of Taylor, 16 Oct. 1841.
[4] C.O. 111/178. Light to Russell, 8 June 1841.
[5] C.O. 111/180. Light to Russell, 20 Aug. 1841.

flaws in the case which did not escape Taylor's eagle eye. The Attorney-General's defence of his procedure did not appear to Taylor to be 'quite satisfactory', although he conceded that his insufficient understanding of the Dutch Law might be the cause. He also questioned the Attorney-General's failure to alter the form of indictment in the second case and his explanation for not doing so.[1] Moreover, Taylor arrived at the conclusion that the evidence afforded 'the strongest presumption, if not distinctive proof that the child Grace was bought by Spencer's wife and detained by her for several years in domestic service in Spencer's house without wages and against the will of Grace's mother who made many fruitless efforts to get possession of her'.[2]

The more important question hinged on the abolition of slavery and the curbing of the traffic in slaves among the Indians themselves. In a vast territory where the three tribes, the Caribs, Arawaks, and Warraus considered themselves hereditarily superior to the other tribes and enslaved them, there was a thin line between detention and protection of slaves. In many cases it might be more humane to purchase slaves, but this would lead to the vicious circle of warfare and kidnapping. Also, the supernatural powers which certain members of the tribes possessed so terrified the Indians that they preferred slavery. Indeed, Taylor asked, 'What wise man would seek to free a people by themselves enslaved or would of inward slaves made outward free?'[3]

Lord Stanley's reply to Light incorporated most of Taylor's opinions and voiced strong objections to the purchasing of slaves by British settlers.[4] Where Taylor was inclined to be more realistic regarding the purchase of slaves, Lord Stanley declared that every effort should be made to punish the guilty parties, 'for the practice of purchasing Indian slaves must necessarily stimulate warfare and kidnapping and can hardly be justified by circumstances'.[5] He agreed with Light that the missionaries were the only answer as a check to slavery and other evils. As the Colonial Office had no means at its disposal for aiding the missionaries, he advised the governor to impress 'upon the Combined Court a sense of their responsibility for the welfare of the Indians'.[6]

It was not only improbable, but impossible, that Light could move the Combined Court to do their duty towards the Indians. He was

---

[1] Ibid. Minute of Taylor.   [2] Ibid.   [3] Ibid.
[4] C.O. 112/24. Stanley to Light, 30 Oct. 1841.   [5] Ibid.   [6] Ibid.

only then recovering from his clash with his Combined Court which had brought Sir Henry McCleod, the Governor of Trinidad to Guiana to pour oil upon troubled waters, and after a deadlock to get the government working again. The Combined Court finally passed the Tax and Civil List Ordinances for an Immigration Ordinance which brought 8,144 immigrants from the West Indies, Madeira, and Africa.[1] The cost of such immigration was high.[2] The planters, concerned about the rising cost of production, had no time to think about, nor money to expend, on the introduction of missionaries to alleviate Indian slavery. Their problems with immigrant labour were paramount.

The question now begs itself. With this pressing and vital need for a labour force, why did the planters fail to utilize indigenous labour? Several reasons can be offered for this factor which stemmed from the Indian temperament and attitude to work. In the first place, the Indians disliked steady monotonous work and refused to be tied down, as they would be on the plantations; they were 'industrious only by fits and starts'.[3] Neither were the Indians materialistic; they had no incentive to acquire material goods and their one aim was 'to get through life with as little trouble as possible'.[4] Im Thurn pointed out that this inactivity of the Indian was not due to 'blameworthy idleness' as he did exert himself to obtain the necessities of life, food, clothing, and shelter.[5]

Secondly, the Indians identified plantation labour with Negro slavery. They felt that by associating themselves with labour on the estates they would be in the position of slaves, and for years they had hunted down slaves for the Dutch and the British. Dr. John Hancock, writing to the Secretary of State for the Colonies on the labour question in British Guiana, observed: 'The Indians too ever hold plantation work in abhorence; they term it slave labour.'[6] He

---

[1] Webber, pp. 208 and 209.

[2] C.O. 116/210. The sum for Immigration Purposes listed in the *Estimate of the Amount to be raised by Taxes . . . for the year*, 1841, led the list in amount with $264,000 out of a total expenditure of $1,145,870. 46. Education required a mere $18,000.

[3] Brett, p. 230. See also C.O. 111/253. Light's Memorandum, 9 Oct. 1848. 'A gang of Indians will make a contract for three months labour with wood-cutters or others— and faithfully, if kept from rum perform their contract, but they rarely are prevailed on to prolong their service.'

[4] Ibid.   [5] Im Thurn, pp. 269–70.

[6] C.O. 111/147. Hancock to Glenelg, 12 July 1836. The same thought was expressed by W. Postlethwaite. See C.O. 111/123. Postlethwaite to D'Urban, 14 Dec. 1831, in D'Urban to Goderich, 3 Nov. 1832.

conceded, however, that with encouragement and 'under proper management' they could well become valuable labourers.[1]

Thirdly, the Indians distrusted, because of past experience, the promises of the white man. They had been so often deprived of their wages. This situation was aggravated by gangs of middlemen who hired the Indians to work on the estates and then pocketed their wages. The planters were aware of the Indians' attitude towards labour and themselves. With the furore over Indian slavery, they might also have found themselves accused of employing the Indians as slaves, already tarred as they were with the brush of Negro slavery.

The Postlethwaite project of the 1830s proved that the members of the government, no doubt influenced by the plantocracy, were unsure of a regular Indian labour force. Hence they were reluctant to place their rapidly falling profits in such unreliable hands. On the other hand immigrant labour could always be manipulated; the immigrants had to serve out their indenture and on them the planters of British Guiana placed their hopes. The Indians were too independent, a poor qualification for estate work. But William Postlethwaite, owner of four estates on the Arabian or Essequibo coast, felt differently about Indian labour. Like all estate owners, he realized that emancipation would soon be a *fait accompli* and the ensuing scarcity of labour would cause a collapse of the estates. He looked to the Orinoco for his Indian labour and asked for Governor D'Urban's approval on his novel scheme for free labour. In one of his letters to the Secretary of State in which he outlined the history of his plans, he summed up his requests thus:

1st. To be allowed and Protected for a Certain period in employing Indians on my Estates, of any class, and from any country in Amity with Great Britain.

2dly. To be assisted by Government in congregating them into a Mission, to be styled the Hibernian Mission in Community, for civilizing Indians.

3rdly. To domicile a Priest on my Lands, at a Salary from Government, but with Land from my Estate, to Superintend and form in them Religious and Industrious habits, to the end of their own *Comforts*, and *Saving to the Colony*.

4thly. If approved of by His Excellency, the Mission to be formed into

[1] Ibid.

a kind of Guerilla force for the protection of Estates from Incendiaries, and as a check to insubordination.[1]

At his own expense he planned to launch an expedition to the Orinoco to encourage the Spanish Indians to migrate to his estates where he promised to give them a home, land, employment, food, and wages in return for their labour. Postlethwaite looked on the uncivilized Indians of Guiana as burdens on the colony. The Spanish Indians were more civilized due to the influence of the Catholic missionaries, hence his intention to build a chapel and assure them of the services of a Catholic priest as the chief inducement to their leaving the Orinoco.

Governor D'Urban forwarded Postlethwaite's scheme to his Fiscal in the Essequibo, George Bagot, for his opinion. Bagot gave it short shrift; Postlethwaite's grandiose plans were both impolitic and impractical. As D'Urban's adviser, Bagot wrote to Postlethwaite that it was, above all, impolitic to induce the subjects of a foreign power to migrate to the colony and such action might have 'serious consequences'.[2] Why not, he asked, use the Spanish Indians who had already settled in Moruka? Bagot intimated that it was a cloak and dagger scheme which Postlethwaite stoutly refuted. He had no intention of inducing the Indian labourers from the Orinoco without first communicating with the Bishop of the Missions there, as well as with the governing authorities; he had also been assured of the assistance of the Revd. J. Hynes, the Superior in Guiana. Postlethwaite's arguments against using the Indians already in the territory were two-fold: (1) The bulk of Indians were uncivilized and, therefore, of no help, and (2) The Spanish Indians at Moruka, fearing that they would become slaves by working on estates, places where there were neither churches nor chapels, refused to move from their present environment.[3] Bagot still insisted that 'sanguine projectors' like Postlethwaite blinded themselves to all possible difficulties, and advised caution to D'Urban.[4] At first D'Urban had seemed keen on the venture; now influenced by Bagot, he wrote to Goderich of the 'wild project' of Postlethwaite which could lead to trouble with the Venezuelan authorities, it was 'mischievous' and 'ought to be avoided'.[5]

[1] C.O. 111/123. Postlethwaite to Goderich, 28 June 1832, in D'Urban to Goderich, 3 Nov. 1832.   [2] Ibid. Bagot to Postlethwaite, 6 Dec. 1831.
[3] Ibid. Postlethwaite to D'Urban, 14 Dec. 1831.
[4] Ibid. Bagot to D'Urban, 8 Mar. 1832.
[5] Ibid. D'Urban to Goderich, 3 Nov. 1832.

Postlethwaite had already sent his agent, Patrick Horan, to the Orinoco to assess the possibilities of bringing the Indians to his estates. Horan first gained the blessing of the Vicar Apostolic of Angostura on his mission. He next discussed the possibility of Indian emigration with the military and was assured that there would be no obstacle to emigration from the authorities, as the Indians had been 'declared by the Constitution of Colombia to be no longer in the state of minors with Guardians and Protectors over them but to be on perfect equality with all other Colombians, and consequently, as Colombians were at all times at perfect liberty first furnishing themselves with proper passports which could not be refused them to emigrate to any part of the Universe'.[1] To make sure of the correctness of that information, Horan even procured a copy of the Constitution. To gauge the Indians' feelings towards emigration, he visited the area between the rivers Caroni and Cuyuni where the great mass of population was contained in the missions of the Catalonian Capuchins. Horan estimated that the indigenous inhabitants in the missions numbered about 35,000 before the revolution, but were now reduced to 10,000. In speaking with a great number of Indians who had arrived from the missions of Upata and Capapue with tobacco for transhipment to Angostura, he discovered that they were all extremely dissatisfied with their present treatment, deprived as they were of their priests. On his proposition to emigrate to British Guiana and his lavish offers to provide them with a priest, double their present pay, and give them better rations of food and clothing, a church, school, hospital, house for their priest, and comfortable houses for themselves, 'they all with loud acclamations of joy, declared their willingness to embark . . . at any moment . . .'.[2] At another settlement a number of Indians were so anxious to accompany Horan that they came on board the ship with all their baggage, and were with difficulty persuaded to disembark. Horan discovered that although constitutionally the Indians could not be prevented from going to Guiana, the poor white and coloured Venezuelans would oppose their leaving as they depended on the Indians for support.[3]

Thus Postlethwaite found his project blocked at both ends. The

---

[1] 'Narrative of Patrick Horan, as Agent of William Postlethwaite, to the Orinoco (Angostura) to see what objections there could be to *free Labor* from thence, 17th July, 1832.' N.A.G. For Colombians, read Venezuelans.
[2] Ibid.   [3] Ibid.

Colonial Office, however, did not consider his plans brainless or improbable, and in the light of the upheavals in Venezuela, thought that the Indians would be only too glad to migrate. Nevertheless, Postlethwaite must rely on the local authorities for support, and not on the home government.[1] Postlethwaite knew that this support would never be forthcoming. Bagot had effectively poisoned D'Urban's mind against the project, partly through his fears, real or unfounded, of trouble with the Venezuelan authorities, and partly through his religious prejudices. He queried Postlethwaite's plan to provide a priest and a church: 'But is this the peculiar creed of Christianity, we as members of the Protestant Church should select to disseminate amongst them [the Indians]?'[2] And Postlethwaite, the Protestant, had countered with, 'Any religion should be tolerated . . . which is to bring to Christianization and Civilization the poor naked Indians.'[3] Postlethwaite definitely had in mind the establishment of a *doctrina* on his estates for the practical reason that Indians brought up under the Spanish mission system proved industrious. Horan's description of the mission system of the Spanish priests and its results confirmed his ideas. Horan had written of the methods of the priests thus:

They commenced by consoling the natives by the balm of Religion, pleaded their cause, resisted any violence offered them, assembled the wandering tribes into small communities called Missions or Pueblos de Doctrina which they governed with a Fatherly and fostering care . . . They by uniform and premeditated progress founded those vast monastic establishments, that singular system, so well calculated to extend the blessings of civilization and industry. The Missions seemed to be governed by a system of order and discipline, frustrating the possibility of abuse to any considerable extent.[4]

This 'singular system' did not appeal to the local government which had been asked to finance the building of the church, and a Catholic church to boot. It was both against their religion and their economics.

With a new governor in British Guiana, Sir J. C. Smyth, and new Secretary of State at the Colonial Office, Lord Stanley, Postlethwaite again presented his scheme,[5] but met with no better success.

[1] C.O. 111/130. Goderich to Postlethwaite, 6 Feb. 1833.
[2] C.O. 111/123. Bagot to D'Urban, 4 Sept. 1832.
[3] Ibid. Postlethwaite to Goderich, 28 June 1832.
[4] 'Narrative of Patrick Horan . . .' N.A.G.
[5] C.O. 111/130. Postlethwaite to Stanley, 9 Feb. 1833.

The local authorities were neither willing nor able, and the Colonial Office hedged on giving him *carte blanche* over their heads. The 'impossible dream' of Postlethwaite had become a nightmare. By 1834 Taylor concluded that Postlethwaite's failure to win the approval of the local government and his consequent bombardment of the Colonial Office indicated that there were 'some circumstances of a local or personal nature, known in the colony but unknown here, which militate against his endeavours to obtain the sanction of the Colonial authorities to his scheme'.[1] Yet there was nothing to indicate that Postlethwaite was not sincere in the goals of his project. As the owner of four estates, he was naturally concerned about their future when the labour supply came to an end, and had tried to avoid an obvious problem with his scheme for free Indian labour.

His plans were neither as bizarre nor as quixotic as Bagot had intimated, and he did succeed later in collecting a number of Indians to work at Plantation Hibernia. Governor J. C. Smyth praised this small scale operation as a 'laudable object of civilizing the Indians and accustoming them to reside in fixed habitations . . . which if successful he hoped would be followed by others'.[2] But the supply of Indians was always below the demand and Postlethwaite was forced to look elsewhere; by 1838 he was bringing out labourers from Malta.[3]

One of Bagot's main arguments against the Postlethwaite plan was his *idée fixe* that the Indians could never 'be induced to apply themselves to continuous agricultural labour' as 'every experience we have tends to prove the negative'.[4] It was true that the Spanish American Indians had attained a degree of civilization, but 'under a state of Restraint . . . and the labor they performed was compulsory'.[5] There was truth in Bagot's assertions which almost every writer on the Indians has confirmed. Hilhouse noted that the Indian 'must . . . be invited and not commanded to work', while 'his native independence was found a great obstacle to his employment'.[6] The point is

---

[1] Ibid. Draft Minute of Taylor, 17 Feb. 1834.

[2] Young to Postlethwaite, 26 May 1837. L.B.

[3] C.O. 111/160. Postlethwaite to Glenelg, 28 June 1838, and C.O. 111/170. Light to Russell, 16 Feb. 1840. Postlethwaite prevented by the Colonial Office from importing labourers from Africa, went to Malta in 1838 and brought to Guiana 120 Maltese. Despite his good faith this scheme also met with difficulties.

[4] C.O. 111/123. Bagot to D'Urban, 4 Sept. 1832.

[5] Ibid. [6] Hilhouse, *Indian Notices*, p. 65.

that if the Indians possessed land of their own they would not work for whites. Therefore, in Spanish America, the object of taking away Indian land had been not only to enlarge the *haciendas*, but also to procure a supply of dependent labour. Even McClintock, who had such great confidence in the future usefulness of the Indians as labourers, admitted their indolence which he attributed to 'the munificence of the climate'.[1] The opinions of governors varied: Carmichael felt that if the Indians were encouraged they might gradually prove beneficial to the colony, despite their disinclination 'to till the earth' for commercial purposes;[2] Murray entertained no sanguine hopes on the subject at all,[3] while Codd, an acting governor, affirmed that among the Indians, 'indolence is the ruling passion'.[4] Light, for the most part of his administration, placed every hope in the Indian becoming industrious, but became disillusioned in the end.[5]

Nevertheless, there were others who felt sure that the Indian could be made useful to the colony by cutting timber and cultivating the land to a certain extent.[6] The Indians had worked at the posts and proved excellent boatmen and guides to the Schomburgk expeditions. When he so desired, the Indian could work well. Postlethwaite's plans did not fall on completely stony ground. With the chronic scarcity of labour on the estates after emancipation, a group of managers on the Essequibo coast, in their desperation turned to the Indians, although the majority of managers on the Demerara and Berbice coasts considered the Africans, and later the East Indians and the Chinese the only worth-while agricultural labourers. With the report of twenty to twenty-five Caribs working on Plantation Anna Regina,[7] and the returns of other Indians located on various other estates on the Essequibo, Light glowed with satisfaction. If only the planters and the legislature would lend their encouragement and support, similar settlements of Indians could be made in other parts of the colony. The Colonial Office approved and applauded

---

[1] M.C.P., 6 Dec. 1849. McClintock's Report, 30 Sept. 1849. N.A.G.
[2] C.O. 111/15. Carmichael to Bathurst, 18 Jan. 1813.
[3] C.O. 319/10. Murray to Bathurst, 22 June 1813.
[4] B.G.B. *Appendix to The British Case*. VI, 'Copy of Questions and Answers put by Codd to Mynheer den Heer D. Van Sistema, 30 Aug. 1813,' 215.
[5] C.O. 111/123. Light's Memorandum on the state of the Indians, 9 Oct. 1841.
[6] Berbice. Box 1. 1813–24. Journal of John Wray. L.M.S.A.
[7] M.C.P., 20 Apr. 1842. King's Report, 11 Apr. 1842, and C.O. 111/191. Light to Stanley, 28 June 1842 with enclosure of the returns of the Indians from M. L. Fowler, Stipendiary Magistrate, 22 June 1842. See Appendix XI.

the signs of progress in that direction.[1] Indeed, the support of the plantocracy, the power in the local government, was crucial to the progress of Indian labour, but only McClintock and the managers under his influence on the Essequibo seemed to have any faith in Indian estate workers. McClintock's faith never wavered, and unquestionably it was due to his untiring efforts that the Indians turned out to work on the Essequibo estates.

Almost every report of McClintock's to the Court of Policy insisted that missionary enterprise and industry must go hand in hand, otherwise to inculcate industrious habits among the Indians would be 'as great a difficulty as in stopping the current of the River Pomeroon with a fork'.[2] Thus he begged and implored the Court of Policy to give its financial support to place the Waramuri mission, which he had helped to establish, on a firm footing.[3] If this mission were 'properly conducted thousands of Indians will flock to the Sugar Estates on the Arabian Coast to seek employment . . .'.[4] McClintock would have championed the Postlethwaite plan of fourteen years earlier for he always advocated even if he never stated it directly, an *ecomienda-doctrina* type system: 'Indians are easily lead and willing to obey and by establishing among them, on the Missions, a proper and liberal system of Industry their roving propensities would cease. This obstacle, once overcome, a more useful and better disposed class of Labourers could not be wished for . . .'[5]

The missions of Moruka and Pomeroon did, indeed, feed the Essequibo estates. One writer in the press, J. T., in refuting an attack made on the Moruka mission, attested that it was 'the only Indian Mission in the Province which adds to the labouring population of the sugar Estates and helps to increase the production of exportable staples'.[6] *The Royal Gazette* enumerated the estates on which the Indians worked: Sparta, Coffee Grove, Anna Regina, Hampton Court, and others. The 'steadiness and continuity of work' shown by the Indians was a result of the gospel. 'Religion has everywhere proceeded [*sic*] social refinement.'[7]

[1] C.O. 112/24. Stanley to Light, 11 Sept. 1842.
[2] McClintock's Report, 31 Dec. 1845, and his other reports of 2 Oct. 1846, 31 Dec. 1846, 30 June 1847, 30 Sept. 1849. N.A.G.
[3] M.C.P., 25 July 1845. McClintock's Report, 30 June 1845. N.A.G.
[4] M.C.P., 5 June 1846. McClintock's Report, 31 Dec. 1845. N.A.G.
[5] M.C.P., 6 Dec. 1849. McClintock's Report, 30 Sept. 1845. N.A.G.
[6] C.O. 116/4. J.T. to the Hon. J. L. Smith in *The Royal Gazette*, 12 Sept. 1843.
[7] C.O. 116/5. Editorial of *The Royal Gazette*, 2 Mar. 1844.

In 1843, though the Arawaks, 'these gentlemen' as McClintock called them, had the greatest aversion to performing labour connected with the manufacture of sugar, they were giving valuable service as jobbers. The Warraus, the most useful workers, now employed at the estates of Dumbarton Castle and Caledonia, were looked upon as the answer to the planters' prayers.[1] Yet in the hue and cry, and the scramble for cheap immigrant labour from the West Indies, Africa, India, and Madeira, it was scarcely realized that Indians were working satisfactorily on the Essequibo sugar estates,[2] possibly because their numbers never rose into the thousands. In 1844 100 were employed and in the following year 300.[3] Attorneys, Proprietors, and Managers of the estates of Windsor Castle, Anna Regina, Coffee Grove, Sparta, La Belle Alliance, Henrietta, Land of Plenty, Mainstay, Tapecooma Lock, and Richmond wrote certificates to the Combined Court testifying to the effective and beneficial labour performed by the Indians in cutting and weeding young canes, cleaning trenches, cutting wood, and serving as jobbers. All acknowledged that the services of these Indians were due to the instrumentality, influence, and efforts of McClintock.[4]

Governor Light expressed satisfaction that the Indians were so useful to the Essequibo planters and evincing habits of industry, and drew the attention of the Combined Court to the reports.[5] There was no response from the Court except to note that they were 'taken for notification'. The constant repetition of this phrase led McClintock to deduce correctly that it was a by-word for rejection.[6]

Not all the hearts of the members of the government were hardened to Indian welfare. In 1844, Mr. McCrae, Vice-President of the Financial Representatives, proposed to the Combined Court that a sum of $10,000 be placed on the estimate to establish an Indian village in the neighbourhood of the estates. To lure the Indians,

[1] M.C.P., 30 Oct. 1843. McClintock's Report, 30 Sept. 1843. N.A.G.
[2] Even today it is not widely known that the Indians did work on sugar estates. Small numbers also worked on the Berbice estates, but such evidence was unfortunately destroyed during World War II in Liverpool. An executive of one of the estates, interested in writing a history of the sugar estates, had requested all relevant material to be sent to England. This material went up in smoke.
[3] C.O. 111/124. Report of W. Carbery, Stipendiary Magistrate in Light to Stanley, 2 Aug. 1845, and M.C.P., 25 July 1845. McClintock's Report, 30 June 1845. N.A.G.
[4] Certificates of Managers, Attorneys, and Proprietors of Estates on the Arabian Coast, 25, 27, 28 Aug. 1845.
[5] C.O. 111/232. Address of Light to Combined Court, 16 Mar. 1846.
[6] M.C.P., 20 Oct. 1847. McClintock's Report, 30 Sept. 1847. N.A.G.

cottages were to be erected and acres of ground provided for gardens.[1] This projected experiment with its 'laudable object' of bringing 'the interesting aboriginal tribes . . . from the wilderness into civilized society; and thus while their own sphere of enjoyment is enlarged, to render them capable of assisting in the increase of the colonial resources',[2] won instant praise from the local press. But the Item for the Establishment of the Indian village, with its cost of $10,000, was painfully pushed through the Combined Court. To Mr. Arindell, it would be money thrown away 'upon a mere chimera'. 'Why', he demanded to know, 'merely upon a whim, or caprice, so large a sum, or any sum, should be placed at the disposal of God knows whom, merely for the purpose of erecting a Village, which is to be populated by savages from the interior . . . I cannot understand. And in the present state of the finances of the colony.'[3] Arindell spoke for most of the government to whom the Indian was, once and for always, a savage, and they had too much on their financial plate to throw away money on such beings. A hot debate followed, McCrae stoutly championing his 'novel experiment'. It was passed only by the governor's casting vote, and a committee was appointed for devising the best means of putting the experiment into effect.[4]

The site of the experiment was to be Leguan Island, but the Indian village never got beyond the writing on the Estimate. McClintock maintained that such a plan would die a-borning on account of 'insuperable obstacles':

firstly and principally, the incessant toil to which they [the Indians] would be compelled to undergo to enable them to support themselves and families, or, in other words, to abandon a life of ease and pleasure for that of constant labour . . . ; secondly, their food being so totally different to what they could procure on the coast, would of itself be quite sufficient to deter the Indians from residing constantly on the estates; thirdly, the swampy lands of the coast, compared with the salubrious hills of the interior, mosquitoes, scarcity of fuel wood, bad water, frequent and most unwelcome visits from other labourers, besides many other reasons . . .[5]

[1] M.C.C., 23 Mar. 1844. N.A.G. See also C.O. 111/121. Light to Stanley, 1 June 1844.
[2] C.O. 116/5. Editorial of *The Royal Gazette*, 4 Apr. 1844.
[3] Ibid., M.C.C., 27 Mar. 1844, in *The Royal Gazette*, 2 Apr. 1844.
[4] Ibid.
[5] B.G.B. *Appendix to The British Case*. VI. McClintock to H. E. Young, 3 July 1844, pp. 133–4.

No Indian would be persuaded to live on an island where there were no fishing and hunting grounds or land for planting cassava. McClintock knew the mentality of the Indians, and the Court must have clutched at his objections like a drowning man at a straw. The Indian Village experiment never became a reality.[1] Yet this fact did not stop McClintock from importuning the government for the Indian labourers who had, as far as he was concerned, a claim on the colony's bounty for their contribution of labour on the sugar estates. He insisted that if one-third of the money spent on the Negro were expended on the Indians who were 'more willing and active, civil and ingenious' over 15,000 to 20,000 would flock to the coast for employment.[2]

In 1850 the Rose Report, a brief for immigration, attested that the need for labour was desperate and 'a large and continuous stream of immigration . . . necessary to maintain British Guiana as a sugar-producing country, and save the invested capital in estates . . . from eventual annihilation'.[3] To Peter Rose, Chairman of the Commission of Enquiry into the Condition and Prospects of the Colony, immigration was the 'one all-important subject, as beside it, all others sink into complete insignificance'.[4] Rose and his committee expressed the sentiments of a planter-minded government. A look at the estimates in the mid-nineteenth century showed only too well that all other subjects—schools, hospitals, goals, police, the poor, public roads, bridges, ferries, public buildings, and expenses of justice—were indeed of complete insignificance in contrast to immigration. The Indian did not even feature as a separate item. The labour problems continued and the 20,000 creole labourers working on the sugar estates were always 'a source of much anxiety to the Executive Government',[5] but even so the Indians did not win

[1] By 1849 not one cent had been expended on the experiment. M.C.P., 6 Dec. 1849. McClintock's Report, 30 Sept. 1849. N.A.G. Previously when McClintock asked the Court of Policy for $2,000 for bringing Indians to settle nearer the coast to train them in agricultural pursuits, there was no comment from the Court. C.O. 116/7. M.C.P., 4 July 1847 in *The Royal Gazette*, 5 Aug. 1847.

[2] M.C.P., 24 Aug. 1850. McClintock's Report, 30 June 1850. N.A.G.

[3] Great Britain, Parliamentary Papers. *British Guiana. Miscellaneous Papers.* 1850-1, II. Report of the Commissioners . . . 28 Dec. 1850, pp. 256-7.

[4] Ibid. In the first decade of the nineteenth century, there had been over 450 producing estates in Demerara, Essequibo, and Berbice. By 1848 with the scarcity of labour, over 200 had been abandoned, including those of cotton and coffee. See C.O. 111/262. A. Currie to Grey, 4 Mar. 1848.

[5] C.O. 111/369. Hincks to Buckingham, 31 Aug. 1868.

favour because the planters felt they could not depend on them for continuous labour.[1]

The 1860s brought an increased demand for cotton. The Indians, especially the Arecunas, the Macusis, and the Akawois, natural cultivators of it, would have been ideal growers. McClintock, undaunted, submitted plans for the laying out of extensive cotton plantations, the erecting of buildings to store the cotton, and the engaging of agents to deal with the finances. Governor Hincks agreed that it would be a marvellous idea to induce the Indians to become more industrious by growing cotton commercially, but all such attempts 'were surrounded with difficulties as to money'.[2] And again, another scheme to further Indian civilization collapsed at the mention of money. Not even the unrest and riots on the sugar estates in 1872 and 1873 made the government reconsider their policy. The colony's fortunes rested myopically and unstably on a single industry, which Governor Scott called a 'suicidal policy'.[3]

In the 1870s the Indians of the Moruka and Pomeroon districts were still working in small groups on the estates, but unscrupulous gangs who hired the Indians and then deprived them of their wages, caused their numbers to decrease.[4] In the woodcutting grants along the rivers and creeks where the Indians had long been working, 'such service being congenial to their original habits and mode of life', the woodcutters, also, hoodwinked them by either neglecting to pay them their full wages or by paying them in rum. The postholders and Superintendents of Rivers and Creeks, whose duty it was to keep an eye on the woodcutters, were themselves the violators of rules and regulations. In 1839 in support of Articles VI, X, and XI of the No. 6 of 1838 Ordinance,[5] and as addenda to the regulations governing licensed grants of land, Section III of the Regulations of 28 May 1839 enjoined the woodcutters employing Indians to keep books of the rates paid to the Indians for their services and/or for any timber or materials purchased from them. It was again forbidden to pay the Indians in 'rum or other spiritous liquors'.[6] But neither this repeated

---

[1] B.G.B. *Appendix to the British Case*, VI. McClintock's Report, 30 December 1849, 177.　　　　[2] M.C.P., 14 July 1864. N.A.G.

[3] C.O. 111/399. Scott to Kimberley, 21 Oct. 1873.

[4] B.G.B. *Appendix to the British Case*. VI. McClintock's Report, 31 Dec. 1849, 177.

[5] Article VI forbade the payment of Indians in spirituous liquors; Article X and XI regulated the residing and cutting of wood on Crown lands.

[6] 'Regulations for the Information and guidance of all Persons desirous of obtaining

201

order nor the previous one in Article VI of No. 6 of 1838 stopped the woodcutters from paying the Indians in rum. Moreover, the proprietors of a woodcutting establishment in the Supenaam Creek, G. and W. Jeffrey, protested against the 1841 Rum Ordinance, declaring that it was absolutely necessary to supply the Indians with rum in order to get any work out of them.[1] Every missionary and traveller wrote of the wretched and demoralising effect of rum-drinking on the Indians and deplored such a system of payment. Woodcutters gave the Indians as much as seven drams of rum per day. 'Is there no remedy for such a crying evil?' demanded Superintendent Shanks.[2] 'Keep them from rum', pleaded the press, 'and there is no better class of workmen . . . In the squaring of wood they are unmatched.'[3]

Indeed the Indians were first class workers on the woodcutting grants in cutting and squaring timber, and splitting shingles. But they were often duped by both the licensed and unlicensed woodcutters, hucksters, and storekeepers who gave the Indians articles on trust in return for cut timber from the Crown lands. According to Articles X and XI of No. 6 of 1838, only Indians were allowed to cut timber on Crown lands; unlicensed woodcutters were strictly forbidden to do so on pain of seizure of the timber. Even the licensed woodcutters, always greedy for more profits, took advantage of the Indians' privileges. Robert King, Superintendent of Rivers and Creeks, Berbice, condemned the illegal timber traffic and suggested that, as a deterrent, the Indian privileges be restricted.[4] With the heavy loss of revenue to the colony, the Crown Surveyor, J. Hadfield, more ruthlessly advised the complete withdrawal of all such concessions and immunities to the Indians.[5]

The Indians had long been encouraged to bring their timber to the posts where the Superintendents were supposed to arrange for its sale. But the credulous Indians, bribed with various commodities and rum, found it more beneficial to trade with the woodcutters. On the grounds of more complaints the Indians were allowed to cut only

Grants of Land in British Guiana—addenda to these regulations established on 21st March, 1835, 28th May, 1839', *Government Notice*. N.A.G.

[1] Petition of G. and W. Jeffrey to the Governor and Court of Policy, 14 Aug. 1841. N.A.G.

[2] Report of J. Shanks, 30 June 1839. N.A.G.

[3] C.O. 116/12. Editorial of *The Royal Gazette*, 20 June 1855.

[4] Report of R. King, 20 Dec. 1843. N.A.G.

[5] Report of J. Hadfield, 1 Jan. 1844. N.A.G.

firewood for sale but not large timber.[1] Even the timber cut by the Indians for the Revd. J. H. Bernau's mission was seized by the Commissioner of the Penal Settlement. Though the Governor consequently ordered its release, the Indians considered such action an attempt at oppression. The press warned that such interference with the rights of the Indians would result in the loss of their services which the woodcutters could ill afford, 'as they are by far the most valuable class of labourers'.[2] The loss of revenue, a result of the illegal traffic in timber, led to the issue of regulations forbidding the Indians to cut timber without a licence, as no one would ever take out a licence if he could get Indians to cut his timber.[3]

A revised code of regulations for the disposal of Crown lands and the granting of woodcutting licences was drafted, stipulating that: 'No Indian being entitled to cut timber on ungranted Crown Land except for his own use, any person receiving timber from any Indian so cut, whether for payment or not will be liable to have his license withdrawn.'[4] The Attorney General, J. Lucie Smith, questioned the proposed draft which prohibited the Indians from cutting wood for barter. He felt that it would be more satisfactory to restrict rather than prohibit, so as not to curtail any disposition of the Indians for honest employment.[5] He also admitted the perennial dilemma which faced the government, the upholding and safe-guarding of the Indians' rights and the financial welfare of the colony. He concluded: 'No doubt the rights and interests of the Indians ought to be regarded, but on the other hand the Revenue must be protected, and it is necessary to guard against dishonest traders carrying on an illicit traffic under color of the aboriginal owners of the soil.'[6] But he did suggest that matters should be left *in statu quo* and the rights of the Indians protected. The final draft of the Ordinance, No. 14 of 1861, thus provided: 'that nothing in this Ordinance contained shall be construed to prejudice, alter or affect any right or privilege heretofore legally possessed, exercised, or enjoyed by any Aboriginal Indian of this colony'.[7]

[1] W. B. Wolseley, Government Secretary to McClintock, 20 Jan. 1854. L.B.
[2] C.O. 116/15. Editorial in *The Colonist*, 5 Sept. 1853.
[3] Wolseley to McClintock, 18 Feb. 1854. L.B.
[4] C.O. 111/319. Walker to Stanley, 7 Apr. 1858.
[5] C.O. 111/331. J. L. Smith to Walker, 5 Aug. 1861.
[6] Ibid.
[7] No. 14 of 1861. *An Ordinance to make better Provision for the Care and Superintendence of the Rivers, Creeks, Crown Lands and Forests of the Colony*. Section 40. N.A.G.

The government, never quite certain how to treat the Indians, took away with one hand and returned with the other. Unfortunately the woodcutters continued to take advantage of the immunity of the Indians for cutting wood without licences, and the timber traffic expanded. About 7,000 feet of timber were supplied by the Indians, but they rarely received just remuneration for their services.[1]

Mr. J. G. Wright, Revenue Officer, imprudently impounded 7,000 feet of greenheart cut by the Indians on the grounds that they had exceeded their rights by cutting timber on ungranted Crown lands. The Indians complained against his action, and requested a lawyer, Mr. E. Spencer Carbery, to plead their case with the governor. Carbery reminded the governor that the rights of the aboriginals to wood on such lands were 'recognised and affirmed by Section 10 or 11 of Ordinance No. 6 of 1838 and Section 40 of Ordinance No. 14 of 1861', and 'no private instructions by any one member of the Government could override, control or alter public Ordinances . . .'[2] Kanimapoo, the chief of the Akawoi tribe, petitioned Mr. J. Jenkins, lawyer and representative of the Anti-Slavery and Aborigines Protection Society, to plead before the society against the illegal seizure of their wood.[3] They had been told there was no ordinance in existence prohibiting their cutting timber of a certain size, except the instructions of the late magistrate, G. W. Des Vœux. Kanimapoo claimed that the Indians derived 'no benefit *whatever from the British Government*, and the little timber cut . . . ought to be granted to us ungrudgingly by the Government . . .'[4] Furthermore, they cut wood at the foot of the Great Falls in the Demerara river, far removed from woodcutting grants, and saw no difference between cutting large trees and small trees.

This petition was forwarded to F. W. Chesson, Secretary of the Aborigines Protection Society, through Edward Jenkins, a Liberal M.P., who wrote to Chesson that if the society did not take up the case, he would have to do so himself.[5] There is no actual evidence to prove that pressure was brought to bear on the local government by either the Aborigines Protection Society or the home government,

---

[1] M.C.P., 3 Aug. 1870. Report of P. Grant, Superintendent of Essequibo, 30 June 1870. N.A.G.

[2] *Anti-Slavery Papers*. MSS. British Empire, S22 G38, E. S. Carbery to J. M. Grant, Government Secretary, 19 July 1870. Rhodes Library.

[3] Ibid. Petition of Kanimapoo to J. Jenkins, Barrister, 29 Aug. 1870.

[4] Ibid.

[5] Ibid. S18 C139/71. E. Jenkins to F. W. Chesson, 1 Nov. 1870.

but in early 1872 the Government Secretary circularized the Superintendents of Rivers and Creeks that Crown Surveyors were 'not to make any surveys of Crown Lands for Wood-cutting licences or Grants of Occupancy which may interfere with Indians . . .'.[1] Privileges regarding woodcutting and the granting of land were also limited to pure Indians only.[2] In June 1873 in his last report as Superintendent of Rivers and Creeks, McClintock wrote that the Arawaks were industriously supplying persons on the Essequibo coast with small size timber for building cottages, while the Akawoi preferred to cut troolie leaves, and the Caribs to remain habitually idle.[3]

The privileges of the Indians in cutting wood were bound up with their rights to the land. In 1831 Governor D'Urban claimed that the government had not dispossessed the Indians of their territory, which they occupied as freely and uninterruptedly as they had before the arrival of the British.[4] But this claim was purely theoretical. Legally speaking, the land was alienated from the Indians as Crown land, and as governor he could grant it away. President Wray of the Criminal Court of Justice, in his argument that political jurisdiction over the Indians presupposed legal jurisdiction, affirmed that the Indians were 'a conquered nation',[5] and a conquered nation loses its rights to land. Governor Light stated in the Court of Policy that the government were 'possessors *de facto*, of the soil . . .'.[6] Also, Indians had to apply for a grant of Crown lands to counteract the possibility of others being given grants to lands on which their homes were already built.[7] The government had agreed, on the condition that the Indians did not sublet the land, but refused to waive the payment of fees despite 'their acknowledged right of settlement on lands the Property of the Crown'.[8] In such instances the government chose to close its eyes to the rights of the Indians. And there was no comparable *Recopilación de Leyes* constantly to remind government officials and others of the rights of the Indians. Maybe it was hoped that once the Indian lost his land, he would be obliged to labour for

[1] Circular to Superintendents of Rivers and Creeks, 12 Mar. 1872. L.B.
[2] J. M. Grant, Government Secretary, to C. W. F. Hancock, Superintendent of Berbice, 21 June 1872. L.B.
[3] M.C.P., 8 Aug. 1873. McClintock's Report, 30 June 1873. N.A.G.
[4] D'Urban to Goderich, 26 Nov. 1831. N.A.G.
[5] Extract of Notes of C. Wray, 8th Criminal Session, 28 Feb. 1831. N.A.G.
[6] M.C.P., 11 Dec. 1838. N.A.G.
[7] Report of W. Crichton, 5 Sept. 1838. N.A.G.   [8] Ibid.

his livelihood, and thus plantations and wood grants would be assured of a labour force.

The Indians were not unaware of their rights to their own land and were suspicious of any encroachments or regulations regarding the land.[1] As early as 1815 the Indians had expressed 'alarming dissatisfaction' that their land was being surveyed and parcelled out to woodcutters.[2] In 1839 an Indian, Tauinari, complained to the Superintendent against another Indian, Pero Manoel, who had forcibly dispossessed his family of its cassava grounds, and Manoel was ordered to move on and make a new settlement for himself.[3] This underlined the fact that once the Indian settled and planted on a portion of land, even though he might afterwards leave it for years, on his return he still could rightfully claim that land. If deprived of their land the Indians were deprived of their livelihood. On the rivers and creeks they hunted and fished; on the land they planted their cassava. This was their life. In the 1850s and 1860s with the expansion of the timber industry and the beginnings of the gold which caused the white man to move further into the interior, there were violations of the Indians' rights. The characteristic response of the Indian was, 'The land is wide, we need not meet the white man everywhere'.[4] It was a vast territory indeed, and the Indian could disappear into remote areas far up the rivers and creeks out of the white man's reach. The Revd. W. H. Brett sadly commented that 'the land of their fathers is now that of our Queen—sold and granted away to settlers from under their feet'.[5]

More and more as the forest resources became a lucrative source of revenue, the government issued regulations to safeguard the land. Ordinance 9 of 1873 established a Crown Lands Department. Section 53 of the Ordinance again assured the aboriginals that their rights would be preserved, subject however, to any regulations made by the governor.[6] Nothing more positive was done for the Indians until the first decade of the twentieth century when the Aboriginal Protection Ordinance No. 28 of 1910 was promulgated. According to

[1] Report of W. Crichton, 5 Sept. 1838. N.A.G.
[2] C.O. 111/20. Codd to Bathurst, 4 Sept. 1815.
[3] B.G.B. *Appendix to the British Case*, VI. Crichton's Journal, Jan.–Apr. 1839, p. 71.
[4] C.O. 116/15. Editorial in *The Colonist*, 5 Sept. 1853.
[5] E10. Missionary Reports. Brett to Bullock, 3 Feb. 1862. U.S.P.G.A.
[6] No. 9. 1873. British Guiana. *An Ordinance to Make Provision for the Establishment of a Crown Lands Department, and for the Care and Superintendence of the Crown Lands, Forests, Rivers and Creeks, of the Colony.* N.A.G.

Vincent Roth, 'That Government, even in 1910, did not consider the protection of the aboriginal inhabitants of the Colony a matter of prime importance, was evidenced by the fact that the office of Chief Protector was not a whole-time one . . .'.[1]

In the early decades of the nineteenth century, Dr. Hancock had written that the only available land for settling free colonists was that occupied by the Arawaks and the Akawois and could not be taken 'without exterminating the Indians'.[2] Such an act of cruelty and injustice he was sure the British government would never commit, but they could '. . . in return for the occupation of their lands' give them 'the benefits of civilization'.[3] Such benefits were always seen in the guise of the blessings of Christianity, as an inestimable and advantageous exchange for the Indians. Whether 'the only rightful possessors of the soil' saw it in that light never entered the heads of members of the Church or State.

Schomburgk indefatigably pressed home his almost axiomatic formula to the home and local governments: 'This [Christian instruction] is the only recompense which England can tender to them for the loss of their lands, and for the miseries which Europeans have inflicted upon them.'[4] Indeed, that was the only recompense that the local government would have considered. Financial recompense was out of the question. To make the uncivilized Indians members of a civilized society, according to the golden rule of McClintock, industry had to be combined with civilization, and civilization would be the major by-product of Christianization. For such a mammoth undertaking the missionaries, 'the best of civilizers',[5] were the kingpins.

[1] Roth, 'Amerindians and the State', p. 13.
[2] Hancock, pp. 47–8.
[3] Ibid.
[4] Second Report of R. Schomburgk, Demerara, August 1841 enc. in *Further Documents Relating to the Question of Boundary between British Guiana and Venezuela* (London, 1896), p. 20.
[5] M.C.P., 26 Nov. 1852. McClintock's Report, 30 Sept. 1852.

VIII

THE ROLE OF THE MISSIONARIES IN THE PROTECTION, CIVILIZATION, AND CHRISTIANIZATION OF THE INDIANS

THE need for missionaries to effect a metamorphosis in the lives of the Indians coincided happily with the religious revival among the Protestant and Catholic churches in the nineteenth century. Dynamic changes had taken place at the political and economic levels and influenced the religious. The zest of the explorers and the thrust of the industrial revolution had brought new lands within the grasp and the knowledge of the West. As the churches looked upon these lands gained either by treaty or conquest, they saw fields white, or more correctly, black and brown, for the harvest.

And for the reaping of this harvest new phenomena were born, the inter-denominational or undenominational missionary societies under whose auspices the labourers would venture out. The nineteenth century in England is mostly remembered as the Age of Reform, but above all, it was 'the great age of societies'.[1] Humanitarian societies abounded, and so too, the missionary societies—the London Missionary Society, the Church Missionary Society, the Society for the Propagation of the Gospel in Foreign Parts, and a host of others. These societies gave impetus to the work in the so-called heathen lands, and missionaries offered themselves to go to all parts of the world, willing and eager to take up the Christian burden, because they felt it was 'the duty of all Christians to employ every means in their power to spread the knowledge of the Gospel both at home and abroad'.[2]

In general, missionary enterprise during the nineteenth century was an export of the cultural and social patterns of the West. Here

---

[1] Stephen Neill, *A History of Christian Missions* (London, 1964), VI, 252.
[2] Richard Lovett, *The History of the London Missionary Society, 1795–1895* (London 1899), I, 12.

lay a pitfall. The nineteenth-century missionaries, however, did not view their work as a cultural export. To them it was a glorious 'opus Dei', illuminating the darkness of the primitive and savage minds with the light of the Gospel. This desire became their magnificent obsession, enabling them to bear the almost unendurable hardships and frustrations, disappointments, and discouragement in the midst of inhospitable terrains and unkind climates. The Revd. W. H. Brett would write after twenty-two years of service up the rivers and creeks of the Pomeroon, Moruka, and Essequibo: 'The life of a solitary labourer in this vast wilderness has little the world counts pleasant . . . the heat and the damp of these rivers is most trying, not one man in a hundred can stand it long.'[1] Yet Brett became that 'one man in a hundred' who did stand it for over forty years, incontestably earning the title of 'Apostle of the Indians'.

But the saga of missionary endeavour among the Amerindians in British Guiana did not begin with Brett. This distinction rests with the Moravian missionaries, who during the Dutch period visited the Indians on the Berbice river in 1738, gained their confidence, but made little progress in introducing the gospel because of their ignorance of the Indian language. Not until nine years later did they make their first convert, an Arawak woman crippled with age. Her baptism inaugurated a series of other baptisms, and by the end of 1756 367 Indians had been Christianized. But this success was shattered by disease and famine, and destroyed by the 1763 Berbice Slave Rebellion which forced the missionaries to leave the area. The Corentyne Indian settlement begun in 1757 also collapsed as a result of the rebellion, but it was recommenced higher up the river at Hope in the following year. Besides bringing the gospel the white missionaries brought disease, and as epidemics swept the settlements the Indians reverted to their roving life. The situation improved under the enterprising missionary, J. J. Fisher, but in 1796 the war between Great Britain and Holland again endangered the slow progress of the missions. More disasters followed—famine, inter-tribal warfare, small-pox, and fire further reduced the mission at Hope. In the face of such overwhelming calamities the missionaries left the colony in 1817 and removed to Nickerie in Surinam to preach to the Negroes on the neighbouring plantations. Yet their greatest obstacle had been that in the Indians 'that awakening of

[1] E10. Missionary Reports. W. H. Brett to the Revd. W. J. Bullock, 3 Feb. 1862. U.S.P.G.A.

true Conversion of the Heart was still wanting'.[1] Nevertheless, the Moravians left with the knowledge that 855 Indians had been baptized on the Berbice and Corentyne Rivers.

The British missionary enterprise among the Indians dated from 1831 when the Revd. John Armstrong of the Church Missionary Society asked the permission of the Governor, Sir Benjamin D'Urban, to establish a mission at Bartica Point at the junctions of the Mazaruni and Essequibo Rivers.[2] A grant of Crown land was given for this purpose to the Revd. Leonard Strong,[3] Rector of St. Matthew's Parish, on behalf of the Church Missionary Society. If the missionaries arrived with any preconceived programme, this was due to the general mission policy of their society, for at this point neither the British government nor the local government had a clue as to what was needed among that benighted section of the population. The Fiscal, George Bagot, had suggested to him that if the British Government intended to send out missionaries among the Amerindians, it would be preferable to send those of the same society (the Moravians) who already had some knowledge of their language.[4] As early as 1812 a member of the Court of Policy, agreeing that 'missionaries were the best propagators of the Christian Faith', had opted for the Roman Catholic missionaries; to him a Jesuit was worth a thousand of the others.[5] The Colonial Office showed a philanthropic concern over the civilizing and Christianizing of the Indians, but felt that this duty rested with the local legislature. In 1829 Sir George Murray forwarded a communication from the Revd. J. H. Pinder to D'Urban in which he suggested measures for the education of Indians under clergymen.[6] The Governor praised Pinder's motives, but felt that because of the roving habits of the Indians, the proposals were impractical and unrealistic.[7] In July 1831 Lord Goderich wrote to D'Urban: 'I have not heard of any

[1] Bagot to D'Urban, 17 Oct. 1831. N.A.G.

[2] C.O. 111/117. John Armstrong to D'Urban, 14 Feb. 1831.

[3] CW/o8c/2. 'Grant of Land to Church Missionary Society . . . for the purpose of establishing a mission to the free coloured and Indians of that District.' Also C.O. 111/117. Official Grant of Land, 10 Aug. 1831.

[4] Bagot to D'Urban, 17 Oct. 1831. N.A.G.

[5] C.O. 111/13. Extract of a letter from Demerary, 26 Dec. 1812; presumably written by a member of the Court of Policy.

[6] C.O. 112/7. Sir George Murray to D'Urban, 18 Aug. 1829.

[7] D'Urban to Murray, 6 Feb. 1830. C.O. 111/69. In C.O. 111/68. See letter of Revd. John H. Pinder to the Lord Bishop of Barbados and the Leeward Islands, outlining missionary programme.

effort to convert the Indians of British Guiana to Christianity, or to impart to them the arts of social life . . .'[1] but with a characteristic volte-face, Governor J. Carmichael Smyth was informed two years later that 'during the progress of the Abolition of Slavery it will be hardly possible for His Majesty's Government to devote their attention to the civilization of the Indians'.[2]

Schomburgk had stirred up interest in 'the rightful owners of the soil' whose conversion to Christianity had been much neglected.[3] To T. Foxwell Buxton, President of the Aborigines Protection Society, he emphasized that 'the establishment of missions to the Indians of British Guiana is of the greatest importance'.[4] Yet missionaries had not rushed to Guiana in great numbers since little or no encouragement had been given them by the Governor or Court of Policy. The first decade of British occupation had been concerned with the consolidation of power and with a slave uprising in 1823 which culminated in the government's distrust of all missionaries.[5] The Court of Policy were caught up in the political and economic tangles of the day, including administrative organization of the three counties, Demerara, Essequibo, and Berbice into one British Guiana in 1831. As a prelude to Emancipation the British government freed the Winkel or shop slaves in Berbice amidst the angry uproar of the planters, and against the advice of the Governor. The Consolidated Slave Ordinance, promulgated by Order in Council, granting civil rights to the slaves, only added fuel to the fire.[6] With such a prelude, the resolutions of the Emancipation Act, 1833, were carried out in an atmosphere tense with bitterness and open hostility. Amid such political storms, it would be difficult to condemn any Governor for not attending to that section of the population which was out of sight and out of the context of the political scene.

But the Indians were not completely out of sight or utterly neglected, for the missionaries, though a paltry few, were already at

---

[1] Great Britain. Parliamentary Papers. *Aborigines*, II. Goderich to D'Urban, 21 July 1831, 182.

[2] C.O. 112/18. Stanley to Carmichael Smyth, 20 Aug. 1833.

[3] C.O. 111/150. Schomburgk's account of Indians in Smyth to Glenelg, 30 Aug. 1837.

[4] Great Britain. Parliamentary Papers. *British Guiana*. Miscellaneous Papers, 1812–49. I. Schomburgk to Buxton, 25 Aug. 1838, in Light to Glenelg, 17 Dec. 1838.

[5] The Revd. John Smith of the London Missionary Society was tried by court-martial for not notifying the government of the planned Negro revolt at Pln. La Resouvenir. He was found guilty and sentenced to death. However, Smith died in prison before receiving word of His Majesty's pardon and was henceforth known in Guiana as 'The Demerara Martyr'.   [6] Webber, pp. 162–3.

work. In 1828 the Revd. J. Tucker, while travelling up the Esse-quibo for a 'change of air' had come in contact with the Indians, and the postholder had suggested to him the establishment of schools as the method most likely to communicate Christian in-struction to the natives.[1] Tucker recommended to the Secretaries of the Church Missionary Society to send a 'pious and zealous man' in the capacity of a catechist or schoolmaster. He outlined the following qualifications for a missionary: 'He must ... be a man entirely devoted to the work. He must *love* it. He must be prudent in his conduct and prepared to meet with difficulties, and content to be spent in the service of his Saviour, otherwise he will not be qualified to reside 60 miles in the interior of this country.'[2] What supermen these missionaries were expected to be, and undoubtedly many were, but they were also men of flesh and blood and as such fell prey to all the failings of their human nature. Under a flickering candle and badly-smelling oil lamp the missionaries would write lengthy and detailed letters and reports to their superiors, providing a looking-glass into their activities and into the lives of their children of the forest. It must be remembered that the pictures would tend to be distorted as the missionary, from the height of his religious, cultural superiority, looked down on the inferior Indian whom he felt obliged to uplift, Christianize, and civilize.

It is no easy task to establish a mission among native peoples anywhere on earth, and Armstrong's venture at Bartica—'red earth' —was no exception. He faced the suspicion of the Indians, the ignorance of the language, the lack of supplies, the dampness of the climate, but most of all, a lack of co-operation from the local com-mittee of the Church Missionary Society. The arrival of Thomas Youd in 1833 as his assistant only highlighted the differences be-tween Armstrong and the Corresponding Committee. A deputation of the Committee had descended on Armstrong at Bartica Point, disapproved the site chosen for his mission house as one with 'an eye for beauty and not for souls', and deplored 'a lack of spiritual power and feeling at the station, in the midst of secular cares and worldly prospects'.[3] Armstrong had built a carpenter's shop and

[1] CW/o1oc/3e & 3b. Extract of Letter from the Revd. J. Tucker enclosed in Letter of U. H. Havergal to Secretaries of the Church Missionary Society, 2 Oct. 1828. C.M.S.A. All CW documents are in the C.M.S.A.

[2] Ibid.

[3] CW/o8c/4 and CW/o8c/1. Report of Deputation to Bartica Mission signed by Leonard Strong, William Roberts, and B. Williams (n.d.). C.M.S.A.

a blacksmith's forge and had planted a kitchen garden; such were the secular cares decried by the Committee. Yet Armstrong was carrying out minutely the injunctions of the Committee of the Church Missionary Society to its missionaries: '. . . instruct the natives in husbandry, in the erection of houses, and in the useful arts of life, and instead of waiting to civilize them before you instruct them in the truths of the Gospel, or to convert them before you aim at the improvement of their temporal condition, let the two objects be pursued simultaneously'.[1]

This problem of which should come first, Christianization or civilization, plagued all missionary enterprise, not only among the Indians of Guiana, but among all other natives. These two aspects were merged in the school: teaching became preaching and vice versa. In his minor classic, *The Spiritual Conquest of Mexico*, Robert Ricard gets to the heart of the matter in one sentence: 'Nothing is more evident in the stablization of the Church, than the importance of the school.'[2] Fanon's observations on the African can be applied equally to the Amerindian society. Native society is not simply a society lacking in values [Western]. 'The native is declared insensible to ethics, he represents not only the absence of values, but also the negation of values.'[3] Christian values had then to be poured into him, and these through the school. The Mission Station with its Chapel-School combination became the *doctrina* of British Guiana; the missioners, the *doctrineros*.

In the early stages of the Bartica Mission a Chapel had been erected which also served as a school. Always hampered by a lack of funds, the Committee was caught in the decisions of building a new chapel at Bartica Point or at the Grove, repairing the old building, and erecting a special school room.[4] Armstrong realized that, in order to wean the Indians to the settlement to be Christianized and civilized, they must be supplied with provisions. His request for 110 guilders for planting the land with cassava was turned down by the Committee who asserted that it was not the design of the C.M.S. to supply Indians with provisions.[5] Since neither the

---

[1] Great Britain. Parliamentary Papers. *Aborigines*, II. Instructions of the Committee of the Church Missionary Society to the Revd. and Mrs. W. Watson on their mission to N.S.W. and the Aborigines of New Holland, 7 Oct. 1831.
[2] Robert Ricard, *La 'conquête spirituele' du Mexique* (Paris, 1933), p. 249.
[3] Fritz Fanon, *The Wretched of the Earth* (London, 1965), pp. 33–4.
[4] CW/08c/1 and CW/08c/4. Report of Deputation to Bartica Mission.
[5] CW/016/3. Meeting of the Corresponding Committee, 17 Dec. 1835.

Corresponding Committee nor Armstrong could agree on policy, the Committee members resigned, later resuming their duties. Armstrong severed his connections with the C.M.S. and left for Barbados.[1]

In June 1835 the Revd. J. H. Bernau arrived in the colony, and prior to taking up his mission in Berbice had visited the Bartica Station with Youd. He very quickly summed up the situation and remarked that there 'was something very interesting in this station, and if Mr. Armstrong and Mr. Youd carry on the work in *unity and love*, much good may result from their labour to the poor Indians'.[2] This was Bernau's first introduction to the Indians among whom he would labour for eighteen years. The situation at Bartica went from bad to worse, and in 1837, at the request of the Corresponding Committee, Bernau was sent there to assess the state of the mission. Consequently Bernau was transferred to Bartica to perform, it was hoped, a miracle of change.[3] In his early years on the missions Bernau had gained an insight into the 'religious' mind of the Indian on his trips up the Corentyne river where the Moravians had laboured eighty years before. He had observed that not only were their dwellings surrounded by bush, but their minds 'so overgrown with superstition and indolence, that it would appear that every vestige of consciousness of the existence of a supreme good Being were completely closed'.[4] A similar overgrowth of superstition and indolence among the Indians around the vicinity of Bartica faced Bernau and his sole aim was to cut down and weed out all such evil practices and bad habits.

The Indians were gradually locating themselves at the Grove where the missionary's house was moved to near the school. At the same time a recently married Mr. Youd returned from Barbados, but in a few months was off to visit the Macusi tribes. Youd had always felt drawn to these distant tribes.[5] Bernau obviously approved this expedition, while the Corresponding Committee looked

[1] CW/016/4a & 4b. Corresponding Committee to C.M.S., 15 Jan. 1836 and CW/016/6. Meeting of the Corresponding Committee, 30 Sept. 1836.

[2] CW/018/2a. Bernau to D. Coates, Secretary of the C.M.S., 11 Aug. 1835.

[3] CW/018/11f. Bernau to Coates, 12 Jan. 1837. Bernau was placed at head of missions with salary of £300 p.a.

[4] CW/018/11c. Bernau to Coates, 22 Dec. 1836.

[5] Youd had undertaken one compilation of vocabularies of English, Creole, Dutch, Carib, and Akawoi, and now planned to add the Macusi language for which he was granted an interpreter. CW/016/7. Meeting of the Corresponding Committee, 19 Jan. 1837.

on it as exploratory regarding the location, language, number, and disposition of the Indians to receive instruction and the advisability of a new station.[1] Nothing could restrain Youd's zeal, not even his young wife's illness. The Committee tried unsuccessfully to cool his over-sanguine expectations without damping his zeal, reminding him that 'Bartica Mission Station should be first consolidated so as at once to give hope of its stability and permanency and of its *forming a stay and support for stations further in the interior'*.[2]

While Youd went blithely off on his Macusi expedition, Bernau was striving for miracles in Bartica. With typical Victorian fervour he tried to induce the Indians 'to leave their despicable huts and exchange their miserable mode of living for a better one'.[3] The means to this end was one advocated by all missionaries—educate the children and raise up a new generation of civilized Christians. In Bernau's words: 'It is my intention to establish a normal School taking from each of the different tribes two or three children and thus prepare them for teaching, because I believe that by these means we shall succeed best in bringing all acquainted with the Gospel.'[4]

At the end of the following year he could report that there were already thirty-nine children attending school while an evening adult school numbered twenty-eight. The C.M.S. had helped towards the building of a residence for the children attending school and a boarding-school-cum-orphanage was launched.[5] Despite the success with the children, Bernau was disillusioned with the adult Indians 'who seemed not much concerned to hear about God'.[6] He met with a similar lack of interest among the Caribs at Cartabo. The Caribs were difficult to convert or to accustom to civilized living, and even when Hannah, the first Carib, asked for baptism, Bernau wondered whether she would persevere in the faith.[7]

The Indians were certainly not happy to leave their children at the Mission Station. They were not unique in this as African parents reacted similarly.[8] Nevertheless the English minister concluded that the Indian children were hopelessly pampered and spoiled.[9] Still,

[1] CW/o16/8. Meeting of the Corresponding Committee, 14 Mar. 1838.
[2] Ibid.
[3] CW/o18/13a. Bernau to Coates, 4 Dec. 1837.   [4] Ibid.
[5] CW/o16/9. Meeting of the Corresponding Committee, 10 Oct. 1838.
[6] CW/o18/16b. Bernau to Coates, 9 Dec. 1838.
[7] CW/o18/18b. Bernau to Coates, 28 June 1839.
[8] David Welsh, *The Roots of Segregation. Native Policy in Natal, 1845–1910* (Cape Town, 1971), p. 48.
[9] CW/o18/18a. Bernau to Coates, 28 June 1839.

there were some Indians who were induced to leave their children at the mission school where they were instructed in sacred music (psalmody), Church history, English history, Writing, Arithmetic, and Composition. Manual labour, such as cleaning, weeding, planting, and carpentry were also part of the curriculum.[1] At their own expense the Society maintained between eight to ten boarders of Akawois, Warraus, and Arawaks. Discipline was the key-note of the schools and 'decency in dress and behaviour' were stressed.[2]

Mr. Bernau's ambition was to establish a Normal School. To further this project he petitioned the Governor and the Court of Policy in 1840 for £500, outlining the progress of the work at the Grove. There were already two native teachers as well as Mr. Edmund Christian who had recently arrived, very eager to work among the 'degraded' Indians.[3] Bernau's view of a Normal School 'in this age of intellectual industry' was 'to arrange Plans of Popular Education, as to combine the teaching of the scholars and the training of some of them to become teachers themselves. Thus in the Art of Education nothing is suffered to go to waste.'[4]

The school for orphan children became a reality in 1841.[5] At the beginning of the year there were twenty-three boarders, but the parents had gradually taken away their children and the number dwindled to fourteen, all of whom were orphans with the exception of one. Bernau had no choice but to prefer orphans. Even though suffering from illness and famine, the Akawois on the opposite side of the river refused to leave their children; they had heard that Bartica Grove was a place from which people never returned.[6] Bernau proceeded to make little English men and women of the orphans, and wrote to the Society that so fluently did they speak English that it was 'difficult to distinguish them from English born children were it not for their complexion'.[7] Teaching English to the Indians was both imperative and practical. There were neither text books nor Bibles available in the various dialects, and years of

[1] CW/018/15b. Bernau to Coates, 21 July 1838.
[2] Ibid.
[3] CW/024/2. Christian to Coates, 10 Feb. 1840.
[4] M.C.P., 12 Feb. 1840. 'Petition of Rev. J. H. Bernau and Mr. Edmund Christian for grant of £500 in aid of C.M.S. to enable them to erect a chapel and school at Bartica Point.'
[5] CW/018/23. Bernau to Coates, 30 June 1841.
[6] CW/018/24. Bernau to Coates, 1 Dec. 1841.
[7] CW/018/22. Bernau to Coates, 24 Oct. 1840.

experience proved that English was the only medium through which the Indians could be civilized and Christianized.

Meanwhile the Normal School progressed slowly. Mr. Christian complained that only two of his best pupils out of the eleven had 'got as far as compound multiplication and besides Scriptures . . . got through Sherman's Geography'.[1] Bernau worried about the poor health of his teachers, Mr. Christian and a Miss Elkins, both of whom had to be replaced later.[2]

While Bernau was struggling to put his school on a strong foundation, Mr. Youd was still in Macusi country. At Pirara he became involved with the Brazilians who were in the area enslaving the Indians. This set off a chain reaction as the British government rushed troops to the border with the primary aim of protecting the Indians. With such an explosive frontier situation, Youd gave up hopes of settling at Pirara and chose a spot, Urwa, supposedly within the British territory but which Bernau felt was 'yet too near to the boundary of lawless people'[3] (Brazilians). Bernau suggested the more northerly Waraputa as the most desirable location because of its fertility, its previous settlement of Indians, its remoteness from the contended boundary, and its nearness to Bartica which would provide an asylum for the Indians. The present location at Urwa necessitated more travelling which was both expensive and time-consuming.[4] On the whole, Bernau never favoured an interior mission and deplored Youd's involvement with the boundary question—'a question altogether of a political nature rather hindering than furthering the missionary's object'.[5] He looked on Youd as being too over-ambitious and warned: 'A Missionary ought to lay his plans not on too large a scale as rather deep and broad tho' in his days he should not see the fruit of his labor. Neither must he be desirous of grasping too much, lest he should lose that which he already occupies.'[6]

Despite misgivings, the Waraputa Mission was established and Mr. J. Dayce left the Caribs at Cartabo in the Mazaruni to teach in the day school there. But sickness and epidemics swept the Indians from Waraputa 'like a broom'.[7] Dayce later dissociated himself

[1] CW/024/4. Christian to Coates, 20 Jan. 1841.
[2] CW/018/24. Bernau to Coates, 1 Dec. 1841 and CW/018/25. Bernau to Coates, 16 July 1842.
[3] CW/018/19b. Bernau to the Revd. W. Jawett, 10 Sept. 1839.   [4] Ibid.
[5] CW/018/25. Bernau to Coates, 16 July 1842.   [6] Ibid.
[7] CW/034/2. J. Dayce to the Corresponding and Parent Committees of C.M.S., 31 Aug. 1841. There were now less than 100 Indians there, including children.

from the C.M.S. and the situation became acute at the infant settlement. Moreover, it was rumoured that the Roman Catholics were planning to send priests to Pirara, and it was feared that this would prevent the Indians from settling at Waraputa. Here was an example of the unhealthy competition between denominations for the souls of the Indians. The Indians near the Brazilian border were Catholics, and the Roman Catholic Church felt that the C.M.S. missionaries were overstepping their bounds. This feeling was mutual; the C.M.S. missionaries had arrived first in the area. The rumour of an R.C. settlement caused such consternation among the members of the Corresponding Committee that *they sprang* into action. They decided to reoccupy Pirara, gained the Governor's assurance that the land would be granted as soon as the territorial débâcle was settled, sanctioned Youd's permanent residence at Pirara, and appealed to the C.M.S. to send another missionary to Waraputa.[1]

At this period the Parent Committee of the C.M.S. was still floundering in a sea of financial difficulties. Hoping to receive help through a Parliamentary grant for education, it sent S.O.S. signals to the Colonial Office which regretfully turned down the appeal and referred the matter to 'the sympathy and support' of the Combined Court in Guiana.[2] The Combined Court were slow in giving either sympathy or support. Finally Bernau, pledging the impoverished Society to a similar amount, cajoled £500 from the Court by his faith in their 'earnest desire . . . to raise this degraded race in the scale of human beings and make them more useful to society than heretofore.'[3] Schomburgk, who visited Waraputa and gave a glowing description of Youd's work there, added his plea for a zealous missionary.[4] The Revd. James Pollitt was sent by the Society in anticipation of the government's financial support, and Governor Henry Light promised a grant of land.[5]

In less than a month a despondent Pollitt requested a change of mission. Bernau dispassionately concluded that he was not the stuff of which missionaries were made. Since the government had granted the £500 he hastened to assure the Society that it would be foolish to

[1] CW/o16/10. Meeting of the Corresponding Committee, 17 Dec. 1841.
[2] C.O. 111/197. Stanley to Coates, 21 June 1842.
[3] M.C.C. 27 July 1843. 'Petition of Rev. J. Bernau and James Pollitt for and on behalf of the Church of England Missionary Society.' N.A.G.
[4] C.O. 111/198. Schomburgk to Light, 24 July 1842.
[5] M.C.C. 27 July 1843. N.A.G.

withdraw on account of the failure of the expectations and health of an individual missionary.[1]

One calamity followed another for the C.M.S. missions. The Waraputa Mission was ministerless, so too was the Pirara. Youd's wife had been poisoned by a Macusi, and Youd himself had died of slow-poisoning on the voyage home—Indian revenge on the Youds for dissuading the Macusi's two sons from attending their festival dances.[2] Youd had fallen victim to the missionary's disease—impatience and a lack of understanding of the Indian mind. The few remaining Indian converts at the Waraputa station were transported to Bartica Grove.

In the meantime, what was the state of the Bartica mission? In early 1843 the mission was visited by the Governor, the Bishop of Guiana, W. P. Austin, the Archdeacon, and the Inspector of Schools for the consecration of the new chapel of St. John the Baptist.[3] The reports were encouraging: both the population and the schools were progressing, and the children were considered 'the flower of our Mission'.[4] There were also the inevitable problems, pastoral and personal. Funds were vitally needed to promote the industry and civilization of the Indians, and there was always the language barrier. Bernau experienced personal sorrow on the death of his wife in June 1845. Grieved but resigned, he went to Europe leaving the mission in care of the Revd. G. Woodman and Mr. Butler. He returned to find it weakened by the misunderstandings between the missionaries and an epidemic of whooping cough. Seventy-eight out of a population of 260 had died, and one-third were suffering from fever. Medicines were immediately requested of the Society.[5] But neither medicine nor medical missionaries could so easily solve a geographical problem. Bartica Point, though high and picturesque, had a swampy water-side and Bartica Grove, where the missionary dwellings had been relocated, was low and constantly required drainage.

[1] CW/018/27b. Bernau to Coates, 30 Aug. 1843.
[2] CW/018/29. Bernau to Coates, 4 Jan. 1844, also CW/018/33b. Bernau to Coates, 23 Dec. 1845. At the back of Bernau's letter was written this observation: 'I feared that poor Bernau himself had had a dose also just before the illness which obliged him to leave for Barbados—the paralysis of his limbs appeared a very extraordinary symptom' (Signed. W.B.P. 19/3/45).
[3] CW/018/26. Bernau to Coates, 2 Jan. 1843.
[4] CW/018/29. Bernau to Coates, 4 Jan. 1844.
[5] CW/018/34. Bernau to the Revd. H. Penn, 26 Aug. 1847.

By mid-century Bartica was no longer the quiet mission settlement frequented by gentle Indians. Its peaceful life had been shattered by the onrush of strangers and discharged convicts from Her Majesty's Penal Settlement directly opposite on the bank of the Cuyuni river. Together with bands of sailors, these questionable characters pillaged the Indians' huts, burnt their fields, and raped their women. The timber trade flourished, and the woodcutters who employed the Indians from the missions completed their demoralization with a lavish distribution of rum. Bernau dejectedly wrote: 'Bartica Grove will henceforth not realize the expectations of your Committee in becoming the Centre of our labours.'[1]

The greatest problem was still the inability of the missionaries to hold the Indians permanently at the Station. The Indians were by temperament, rovers, but in this situation, necessity as well as habit propelled them away from the mission. The soil at Bartica had become exhausted, and for his mere existence the Indian had to wander in search of fields and food. In the dry season he went to the falls to fish and to hunt and thus for months would be away from the mission. This concern with his temporal affairs was seen as 'a sad draw back to his spiritual concerns'.[2] This would always be the fly in the ointment of missionary policy. The Indian was concerned with his body and averse to settling in one place; the missionary was concerned with the Indian's soul and insisted that he settle for his own good. Neither compromised. Even after vast sums had been expended on the mission the results were far from promising. After his visit to Bartica Grove in 1846, a disenchanted Governor Light wrote to Gladstone:

> It is difficult to reclaim an adult Indian; his attendance at chapel requires decent clothing, but he is too happy to throw it off. I question whether any permanent benefit to the agriculture or commerce of the colony will result from this mission, yet it is highly creditable to the C.M.S. by which it was instituted and continues to be maintained, and I shall be glad if my ideas are mistaken.[3]

Discouraging, also, was the drifting away of the many who had

[1] CW/018/35. Bernau to Penn, 12 Dec. 1847.
[2] CW/018/43b. Bernau to Penn, 22 Oct. 1850. This was a far cry from the bright prospects of Bartica ten years before when there were eighteen cottages built by the Indians, each with its acre of land planted in provisions, and there were over 100 Indians living in 'a comparatively civilized condition'. M.C.P., 12 Feb. 1840. N.A.G.
[3] Light to the Rt. Hon. W. E. Gladstone, 31 Mar. 1846. N.A.G. Also see C.O. 111/232.

benefited from the education at the mission school. With dogged determination the missionaries held on, for 'after all, it is the education of the young which promises most, for it cannot be expected that a savage Indian however deeply impressed shall live in all respects to God's glory and worthy of the Christian's name, unless he be christianized and civilized at the same time'.[1]

With the constant influx of coloured people Bartica Grove became more of a parish than a mission. Even the experienced missioner Bernau was at a loss to decide on the best policy for the settlement. On one hand he regretted that the mission had not been established in the interior, and on the other he considered the Indians in the interior too inaccessible.[2] If the Bishop of Guiana were prepared to take over the mission, the time had come for the C.M.S. to relinquish it, 'there being neither men nor means' for its efficient running.[3] In the interior the boundary problem had halted the advance of missionary work. It was imperative to gain a foothold among the Macusi before accomplishing any thing worth while in that region, and as long as the boundary was still *in statu quo* the C.M.S. rightly and prudently refrained from extending its work. Nevertheless, the Macusi seemed anxious to have a teacher, and built a house and prepared a field for Mr. Lohrer who had promised to visit them. But he died in 1853, and the Macusi refused to move from their savannahs to the woody regions. Bernau frankly admitted: '. . . we do not know how to act'.[4]

In 1853 Bernau, broken in health, returned to Europe. With the station ministerless, many Indians left and settled along the Mazaruni, Cuyuni, and Essequibo rivers. The boarders were dismissed and the schools decreased in number.[5] The Revd. Hillis arrived on the scene, hoping his presence would bring about the revival of the mission. However, during 1856 and 1857 epidemics of measles and cholera swept through the mission, and the terrified Indians fled with their children.[6] After the wave of the epidemics the schools gradually recovered, but Bartica Grove never revived. There was no one to fill Bernau's shoes; it was even difficult to obtain any clergyman for the post. At this crucial period the C.M.S. withdrew

[1] CW/018/43b. Bernau to Penn, 22 Oct. 1850.
[2] CW/018/47a. Bernau to Major Hector Smith, 29 Sept. 1852.
[3] CW/018/48b. Bernau to Penn, 10 Oct. 1852.
[4] CW/018/48a. Bernau to Penn, 10 Nov. 1852.
[5] CW/04/3/2. Wm. Hackett Bracey to the Revd. J. Chapman, 6 Dec. 1855.
[6] CW/049/3 and CW/049/4. Hillis to Penn, 10 June 1856 and 26 June 1857.

its aid, and this resulted in the total collapse of the mission. No support could be expected from the government as the Clergy Bill would not be on their agenda until 1859.[1] The mission dwellings fell into decay; the Boys' School was later taken over by the government for a hospital and a dispensary. One of the missionaries, Augustus Tanner, wrote its epilogue: 'After all the money and labour that have been expended by the C.M.S., it is very distressing to see this once flourishing station reduced to the last extremity.'[2]

For over twenty-one years the roster of frustrations at Bartica was crushing enough to discourage the most zealous of missionaries. Yet their attitude could be summed up: 'As to the hardships of Missionary labour there is much to be endured, but in all our tribulations we have these things to sweeten the bitter cup—a desire to save perishing souls . . .'[3]

The bitter cup had been drained, but to what purpose? The Indians were still reluctant to leave their children with the missionaries; adults and children were not fond of learning and preferred their life of hunting, fishing, eating, and relaxing in their hammocks to a disciplined, civilized life. The squatters on the mission, and the woodcutters along the rivers either drove the timid Indian away or demoralized him with rum.[4] The missionaries were baffled at the Indians' unconcern with the spiritual. Bernau had been aghast at the absence of the word 'sin' in all the different languages. It does seem ironic that the missionaries laboured to 'convince them [the Indians] of their being sinners in the sight of God'.[5] The seed had indeed been sown among the 'children of the forest', but the harvest was yet far off.

Bartica Grove declined as a mission, but in the 1860s became the busy centre of a burgeoning gold industry and a later rendezvous of the famous 'pork-knockers'.[6] The missionary activity in that area

[1] CW/049/5. Hillis to Lord Bishop of Guiana, 24 Feb. 1858.
[2] E14. Missionary Report 2967/1864. Tanner to Hawkins, Secretary of S.P.G., 23 Jan. 1864.   [3] CW/049/1. Hillis to Penn, 4 Apr. 1856.
[4] CW/018/19d. Bernau to Jawett, 10 Sept. 1839. Also Thomas Farrar, *Notes on the History of the Church in Guiana* (British Guiana & London, 1892), p. 25.
[5] CW/018/18b. Bernau to Coates, 28 June 1839.
[6] In 1863 gold nuggets were found in the Cuyuni River and a Gold Mining Company was formed under a Government Ordinance. Bartica had a superb position at the junction of the three rivers, the Cuyuni, the Mazaruni, and the Essequibo. The word 'pork-knocker', used to describe the free-lance Negro prospectors, has given rise to much conjecture as to its etymology. Webber suggested that originally it might have been 'pork barrel knocker', 'meaning a potential, if not actual, broacher of barrels of pork . . .'

was revived in 1870 in the three Indian mission stations along the Mazaruni, Cuyuni, and Essequibo rivers—St. Edward, the Martyr (Mesopotamia) on the right bank of the Mazaruni five miles from the Penal Settlement, Holy Name (Macedonia) on the Essequibo in the opposite direction, and St. Mary (Thessalonica) thirteen miles beyond Bartica Grove. These missions were established by the Revd. Thomas Farrar who also paid visits to the defunct Bartica mission. Supported by the Society for the Propagation of the Gospel and the Guiana Diocesan Church Society established in 1852 with the prime object of supporting missions to the Indians, day schools and Sabbath schools were founded. The Warden of the Indian Missions, J. S. Wallbridge, reported that the spiritual health of the missions was good while the Indians appreciated 'the advantage of having catechetical instruction, which as the tutorial system of the Church, is so admirably adapted to promote the inward disgestion and easy assimilation of the verities of the Christian religion'.[1] What Mr. Wallbridge did not venture to say was how far the Indians digested and assimilated these verities.

These three missions which had provided for the famine-struck Akawois from the Pomeroon region, showed an increase of population in the 1870s; and gradually the Indians were taught habits of industry as they helped to support the missions by their labour. In this more hopeful state, let us leave this central mission area and look at the Catholic mission of Santa Rosa in the north-west region of the colony.

Santa Rosa Mission

The background history of the Catholic Mission at Santa Rosa is unique and romantic. In 1817 when revolution shook the Spanish colony, today the Republic of Venezuela, the Capuchin missions fell in a holocaust of brutal massacres. The Spanish Arawaks, obeying the injunctions of their missionary fathers not to have any part in rebellion, fled from the revolutionaries across the Orinoco into

and also offered a previous suggestion of one 'who knocks from port to port' (pp. 323–4). Swan gave a less adventurous explanation as those who 'knocked the pork', meaning those who ate the government rations of rice and pork-tails (p. 184). Whatever its meaning, the word stands unique in the vocabulary of the gold-mining industry of Guiana.

[1] Report of the Warden, H.M.P.S., 28 Oct. 1869. G.D.C.S.

British territory seeking asylum.[1] Governor-General Murray of Demerara and Essequibo by no means welcomed these 500 semi-civilized Indians with open arms. On the contrary, for security reasons he contained them within limits of the Moruka river, hoping that when the tumult and the shouting died down in Venezuela they would return there. Over 100 were transported to Puerto Rico; some eventually returned to the Orinoco; but the majority settled down on the banks of the Moruka.[2] The Spanish refugees wisely chose the elevated land suitable for growing crops of cocoa, coffee, tobacco, and other provisions. The Moruka river flowing into the Atlantic, as well as linking up with other rivers leading to the Orinoco, provided an ideal highway for trade.[3] Here the Spanish Arawaks settled and were soon recognized as an industrious, courteous, and civilized people—a credit to the training of the Spanish Capuchins. Hilhouse, who for years championed the Indian cause in general and this mission in particular, affirmed that they had 'a certain degree of intelligence, and a refinement of feeling, which marked . . . the early impress of civilization and religion',[4] and again: 'These Indians are very industrious and expert in the use of fire-arms; their cultivation is very extensive, and their houses of a much superior description to those of the Coast Tribes.'[5]

Cut off from their country, their homes, and their faith, these refugees yearned for the security which their religion had given them. In 1829 they requested the Revd. John Hynes, the R.C. Vicar-General, to visit their settlement at Mariaba as the mission was first called. On 24 June 1830 Hynes was given a wildly demonstrative welcome by the Indians. During his three-day visit he baptized seventy-eight of their children and married two couples. On his return to Georgetown, he reported to Governor D'Urban on the condition of these people and on the vital need for a resident Catholic priest. D'Urban gave every 'encouragement and assistance' and promised to use his influence in the Court of Policy to procure a

[1] Acta, 1835. Holy See, Sacred Roman Congregation 'de Propaganda Fide', Vol. 198, pp. 347 ff. 'Report of Fr. John P. Hynes, O.P. on the West Indies.' Father John Hynes was an Irish priest, and Vicar General in British Guiana.

[2] Early account of the Santa Rosa Mission. Santa Rosa Archives, Guyana.

[3] McLintock's Report, 30 June 1869, with a brief history on the Santa Rosa Mission, N.A.G.

[4] Letter of William Hilhouse, n.d. J.D.A.G.

[5] Reconnaissance of the Port of Pomeroon, with the adjacent Indian settlements in the Morocco Creek, and its vicinity, by William Hilhouse, Quartermaster-General of the Indians, Nov. 1823. N.A.G.

maintenance for a permanent Indian Missionary.[1] A Spanish priest, J. Espinal, was sent out for the Moruka settlement, but his ministry was extremely short-lived. He declared he had no intention of risking his life among savages and took the next boat back to Trinidad.[2] In May 1833 D'Urban, who had shown such interest in the cause of this mission, was transferred to the governorship of the Cape of Good Hope. Sir James Carmichael Smyth, succeeding him in a crucial moment of the colony's history, did not as enthusiastically espouse the missionary cause to the chagrin of the Revd. J. T. Hynes. An appeal from Hynes for the establishment of a Catholic Mission at Mariaba and for a small grant-in-aid to the priest to serve the Indian refugees, was shelved with vague officialese that the Governor could not 'immediately say what may be proper to do, but the interests of humanity evidently require that the people . . . should not be allowed to relapse into barbarism'.[3]

Hilhouse swamped the press with letters advocating the establishment of this mission, and for his pains as well as his caustic remarks on government policy in this regard, earned the irritable dislike of J. C. Smyth. Other letters poured into the local newspapers, the majority objecting to the extensive grant of land required for the mission.[4] On the recommendation of a specific area by Captain Tonge, a tract of land was made out to the Protector and postholder of the Pomeroon and Moruka rivers by the Governor without consulting the Court of Policy's Committee of Indian Affairs.[5] Hence it was not considered valid. Not until July 1840 was the tract of land —the site of the settlement of Mariaba—surveyed by William Hilhouse, officially granted to the Roman Catholic Church 'to occupy, cultivate, and improve' with the proviso: '. . . that the occupant of the said land, or any of them, or any person or persons employed by them, shall not use any violence or outrage upon the persons, or commit any depredation on the property of the Indians'.[6]

Although Hynes labelled Governor J. C. Smyth a bigoted Methodist who placed obstacles in the way of the Catholic mission, the

[1] C.O. 111/125. John Thomas Hynes to Goderich, 23 Aug. 1832.
[2] Acta, 1835, and C.O. 111/120. D'Urban to Howich, 7 Apr. 1832.
[3] J. C. Smyth to J. T. Hynes, 27 Oct. 1833. L.B.
[4] J. R. F. Hutson, *The Royal Gazette*, 13 Feb. 1834. J.D.A.G. and C.O. 116/1. *The Guiana Chronicle*, 5 Jan. 1835.
[5] C.O. 116/1. Ibid.
[6] Grant of Land to Roman Catholic Mission by Governor Light, 20 July 1840. J.D.A.G. See Appendix XII.

Governor petitioned Bishop MacDonnell for a permanent priest for the Spanish Indians. In his letter which read like a 'want ad' in a modern newspaper, J. C. Smyth offered a stipend of 700 Spanish dollars to 'a zealous and intelligent spiritual instructor of conciliating manners and good moral character',[1] and strongly recommended to the Court of Policy 'the policy and propriety' of affording such assistance to the Moruka Indians.[2] Smyth, however, had no intention of following the advice of Hilhouse who urged a Spanish mission system in which the ecclesiastical and magisterial functions would be united. No Spanish type church and state relationship for the Governor who made it quite clear that he would tolerate 'no independent Catholic Clergyman exercising Civil and Religious Control over his flock; no imperium in imperio'.[3]

In July 1837 the Revd. Apollinaire Hermant arrived from Trinidad as the R.C. Pastor of the Moruka Mission. A month after his arrival at the mission Hermant wrote the 'Enlightened Governor' of the 'eager inclination of the Indians . . . for their Religious and Social improvement'.[4] His days were full—baptisms, marriages, assembling the Indians to vote for a new Captain, and a visit from the Warraus asking to settle near the mission. His was a made-to-order mission, but the material needs were present. The church, previously erected by the Indians themselves, was in need of repair. Hermant held services in the logie[5] which served as his dwelling at night. He asked for 1,500 guilders for the erection of a chapel and for liturgical requirements, but received only 1,200 guilders for the repair of the logie.[6]

Early in his missionary career Hermant was accused of selling rum to the Indians and running a huckster's shop, but these accusations stemmed from the jealousy of the woodcutters, as Hermant was cutting wood and selling for the Indians, making no personal profit.[7] He was championed by the Indian chiefs who came in a deputation

[1] J. C. Smyth to the Rt. Revd. Dr. MacDonnell, Bishop of Olympus, 1836. L.B.
[2] M.C.P., 13 Feb. 1837. N.A.G.
[3] C.O. 111/133. Extract of a Minute to Government Secretary by J. C. Smyth, 29 Mar. 1834.
[4] Hermant to J. C. Smyth, 28 Sept. 1837. N.A.G.
[5] A simple one-roomed hut with thatched roof of troolie palm leaves. The troolie palm (*Manicaria saccifera*) has very large leaves which are excellent for roofing these huts.
[6] Petition of Morocco Indians . . . submitted by Pastor A. Hermant to the Governor, 29 June 1838. N.A.G. Also, Crichton's Report No. 6, 1838, N.A.G.
[7] C.O. 116/3. M.C.C., 20 Mar. 1839, in *The Guiana Chronicle*, 22 Mar. 1839.

to the Governor certifying that 'he was a kind and good missionary, and had done much good among them'.[1] This was substantiated by Bishop Clancy who visited the mission early in 1839 and had no complaints against Hermant. The Combined Court, assured of Hermant's good behaviour, voted 3,000 guilders for the mission.[2]

When in the midst of groundless charges, Hermant offered to resign, the Superintendent Crichton regretted such a move, not only from a religious point of view—the mission was in a flourishing condition—but from a political, 'as the situation of these settlements placed as they are on the line of internal communication between the inhabited parts of this Colony and the Republican Province of Venezuela on the Orinoco renders it necessary . . . to keep a watchful eye over the place'.[3] The missionary at Santa Rosa was both spiritual guide and unofficial, political watch-dog.

The first episcopal visitation among the Indians was made in 1839 by the Revd. Dr. William Clancy, gazetted as the Parish Priest of Georgetown for the R.C. community earlier in the year.[4] His report of the mission was a glowing one. He administered the sacraments among a 'civilised, well-clothed, industrious and sober people, growing coffee, annotto, cassada [cassava], and some corn, living in perfect independence of the luxuries of refined society, but apparently contented',[5] and viewed his visit as morally productive and tremendously successful.

In the 1830s Santa Rosa was the mission in the news. There were continuous letters of Hilhouse to the press on behalf of the mission. Although an Anglican, he gave great credit to the work being done among the Spanish Indians by the Roman Catholic Church, claiming that 'everything that has been done in favour of the Aborigines of this continent and colony, has been done by the Roman Catholics, from Las Casas to Dr. Clancy . . .'[6]—a statement more complimentary than truthful. Mr. Hilhouse seemed to have ignored or was ignorant of the work of the C.M.S. at Bartica, Pirara, and Waraputa.

Santa Rosa gained a new missionary in 1840 and Fr. Hermant returned to Martinique. The Revd. John Cullen would earn the distinction of being the only priest to reside at that mission for thirteen years. These years were filled with visits to all the Catholic Indians

---

[1] Ibid. [2] Ibid. [3] Crichton's Report, No. 6, 1838. N.A.G.
[4] C.O. 111/162. Light to Glenelg, 10 Jan. 1839.
[5] C.O. 116/3. *The Guiana Chronicle*, 27 Mar. 1839.
[6] C.O. 116/3. Hilhouse to the Editor, *The Guiana Chronicle*, 17 Apr. 1839.

even as far as the Orinoco, and Cullen was everywhere respected and loved.[1] Every missioner is by necessity a builder, and Cullen's first venture was the building of a church and a presbytery. In 1841 the Feast of St. John the Baptist was solemnly observed in the logie which did not hinder the children from singing the Gregorian Mass very ably. Other festivities were held afterwards as the missioner knew how to combine the sacred and the secular. *The Royal Gazette* could not praise the religious and educational progress of the mission enough. In a rather over-emotional report on the 'Catholic Church' it directed the attention of the local government to the:

serious consideration to the spiritual wants of and to the incalculable benefits that will accrue to the neglected tribes, as well as to the community at large, by imparting liberally and extensively to all the Indian tribes the blessings of religious and moral instruction, to which they are equally entitled with any other class of human beings, as they are the children of the same common father of all . . .[2]

The Court of Policy granted $900 for the erection of a chapel, and in 1843, $500 for its completion.[3] The mission progressed and the Indians were 'honourably distinguished for their superior enlightenment and civilization'—a tribute attributed to the zeal of the R.C. priesthood.[4] On 27 October 1844 the new church, spacious and well-built, was solemnly dedicated by the Rt. Revd. Dr. Hynes, and together with the mission, placed under the patronage of St. Rose of Lima, a saint revered by the Christian Indians of Spanish America.[5] The mission is still called the Santa Rosa Mission. The missionary and his flock showed their spiritual calibre, when in 1847 during the potato famine in Ireland, the Spanish Indians of Santa Rosa contributed $44.88 to the Irish and Scotch Relief Society—'the verge of civilization . . . sending its mite of assistance and comfort to what is generally supposed to be its centre'.[6]

After this 'model Priest and devoted Missioner' left Santa Rosa in 1853, the mission was periodically visited by Fr. Francis Hayden and Fr. Joseph Fitzgerald, O.P.[7] In 1857 the mission passed into the

[1] 'British Guiana. Mission of Santa Rosa', *Letters and Notices*, Vol. VIII (Sept. 1872), 227. J.A.L.
[2] C.O. 115/5. 'The Catholic Church', *The Gazette and General Advertiser*, 8 July 1841.   [3] M.C.P., 20 Apr. 1842, and M.C.C., 24 July 1843. N.A.G.
[4] C.O. 116/5. Editorial of *The Royal Gazette*, 7 Nov. 1844.
[5] Fr. J. Cullen's Diary. J.D.A.G.
[6] C.O. 116/7. *The Royal Gazette*, 4 May 1847.
[7] Fr. de Betham, 'British Guiana. Stray Notes of Fr. de Betham', *Letters and Notices* II (1864), 146. J.A.L.

hands of the Jesuits. From a materialistic point of view it was no flourishing mission which the Jesuits inherited. Since the departure of Cullen the mission had fallen into decay; but although the buildings were in ruins, the faith of the Indians remained strong.[1] The first Jesuit missioner, Fr. Benedict Schembri, arrived at this almost inaccessible outpost in December 1857, and in less than a month had returned to Georgetown to negotiate for a house and repairs on the Church. Whether the challenge was too overwhelming, or the need for a priest among the ever-increasing Portuguese in the city greater, Fr. Schembri remained in the city.[2]

Despite the fact that the Jesuits did realise its worth, Santa Rosa became the Cinderella of missions. Fr. de Betham declared: '. . . nothing is required but the constant attendance of a priest, and the frequent visitation of the people dispersed over those rivers and creeks, to ensure a really flourishing mission.'[3] But there was neither constant attendance nor frequent visitation. Visiting missionaries de Betham, Woolett, and Negri made temporary and periodic visits concentrating their efforts among the Catholic population of 1,800 on the plantations on the West Coast Demerara and the Essequibo instead of among the 350 Indians on the Moruka river. Not only did the Portuguese on the coast outnumber the Spanish Indians eight to one, but with their 'mere external manifestations of religion', they were more in need of spiritual guidance than the staunchly religious Catholic Indians.[4] For such a vast mission field the Jesuits had neither the men nor the means.

From the writings of Fr. de Betham on his trips up the various rivers and creeks, we get intimate and humourous glimpses of the Indian and of mission life that are entirely missing in the rather statistical and biblical accounts of other missionaries. The rough and tedious corial trips, the hunt for food, the type of food—a dish of monkey considered more palatable than roast crocodile—are vividly described. There was even evidence of the independence of women—an early women's liberation attitude among the Maiongcong tribe whose women objected strongly to marriage for fear of becoming slaves of their husbands. de Betham assured them that Christian women were not slaves! Among the other tribes,

[1] Fr. James Etheridge to the Revd. Fr. Provincial, 25 Aug. 1857. J.A.L.
[2] Bishop Etheridge's Diary. J.A.L.
[3] Fr. de Betham, *Letters and Notices*, II (Apr. 1864), 84. J.A.L.
[4] de Betham, 'Stray Notes', *Letters and Notices*, II (1864), 147. J.A.L.

polygamy, 'the great impediment to Christianity amongst the Indians', was in vogue. The celebrated Warrau chieftain, Mai-ce-wari, had fifteen wives—the first wife, however, ruled the harem, and surprisingly there was no jealousy among the wives—each wife knowing and keeping her place in the marriage scale.[1] The piai-man was another obstacle and was found even among the Catholic Indians at Santa Rosa. The irony of this paradoxical situation of Catholic medicine men was summed up by de Betham: 'I preached on witchcraft, to the great discomfiture of some old rascals, who get medicines from me, and then pretend to cure people with the rattle of their matracca, and fumigations of tobacco.'[2]

During the visits of Fr. Woolett and de Betham, Santa Rosa was rebuilt, but it soon fell a prey to wood ants. In 1865 Fr. Casano was heart-broken to find a fallen church and house infested with rats, bats, and all manner of vermin.[3] The first episcopal visit of Bishop Etheridge to the mission in March 1865 almost ended in tragedy when the old church collapsed, nearly causing the deaths of the Bishop and two priests.[4] With the chronic shortage of priests Santa Rosa was attached to the Essequibo mission from which Frs. Negri, Casano, Swift, and Messini paid annual visits to the Moruka, spending two or three weeks there. Despite the fact that these visits were so seldom the Indians remained faithful.

In 1869 rumours that Moruka was no longer under British rule upset these Indians to whom the British had pledged protection since 1824. The Superintendent of the Rivers and Creeks in the Pomeroon, Mr. McClintock, reported to Governor Scott and the Court of Policy that these most industrious and well-behaved of all the colony's Indians were being subjected to many abuses by Spanish and Portuguese interlopers since the withdrawal of British

[1] de Betham, op. cit., 'Narrative', p. 81.
[2] Ibid., 'Report of a Missionary Voyage up the Moruca and Wayini', p. 199. de Betham obviously means 'maracca' and not 'matracca'. This 'magic' instrument was a hollow calabash, containing seeds and held by a long handle passing through the middle, and topped by a plume of variegated feathers. The piai-man or medicine man fumigates the house of the sick person while singing his charms, and rattling his 'maracca'. Superstition mixed with Catholicism is noted by de Betham: '. . . one of the Catholic *piai-men* tried to persuade the people, that Almighty God lived on the top of an immense tobacco tree—guarded at the bottom by a large dog; that he himself had been up three times to heaven, and conversed with God.' See de Betham, op. cit., 'Stray Notes', pp. 151–2.
[3] Fr. Nicholas Casano, *Letters and Notices*, III (1866), 354. J.A.L.
[4] Bishop Etheridge's Diary, J.A.L.

protection from that area,[1] but received no reply regarding this complaint. de Betham stoutly maintained that the Venezuelan claim 'is denied by the whole of the Indians, who accept captaincies from the Queen, and look up to her for protection against those republicans'.[2]

Apart from the insecurity of the frontier situation resulting in periodic depredations by the Spaniards, the difficulties experienced at this mission differed somewhat from the missions of the other denominations. There had been no painful sowing of the seed and no constant frustration stemming from little or no harvest. The Catholic missionaries were involved in keeping the faith alive—that faith which had been so deeply planted in the Spanish Indians and bequeathed to each generation. The priests always found them 'disposed to work for God's sake', willing to rebuild their ruined church, industriously planting their crops.[3] The two main fears were, first, that these Catholic Indians might be influenced by the pagan customs and example of the Warraus, and secondly, that the Caribs might be lured away to the Protestant missions. These fears were well-founded, for during the long absences of the priest from Santa Rosa and its vicinity, the Indians were enticed to the Waramuri mission.[4]

The missioners struggled with the usual language barrier and faced the inevitable climatic and financial difficulties. The lack of continuous surveillance was the biggest drawback in the Santa Rosa Mission, and it speaks highly for the Indians that their faith has survived even to the present time. Not until 1878 was the present 'white chapel on the hill' permanently erected.[5]

The Pomeroon and Moruka Missions of the S.P.G.

The 1840s witnessed a tremendous missionary movement particularly on the Pomeroon river, to the right of and parallel to the Moruka river. Since 1835 the Revd. J. H. Duke, Rector of Holy Trinity, Essequibo, had worked among the aboriginals in that area.[6]

---

[1] McClintock's Report, 30 June 1869. N.A.G.
[2] de Betham, op. cit., 'Stray Notes', p. 153.
[3] Casano, op. cit., pp. 354–8. J.A.L.
[4] de Betham, op. cit., p. 84. J.A.L.
[5] Notes on Santa Rosa Mission. J.D.A.G. See also 'Name Poem' of Guyanese poet, Arthur J. Seymour.
[6] B.G. 1, 1834–58. The Revd. J. H. Duke to Sir J. C. Smyth, 2 June 1834. U.S.P.G.A.

Financed by the Society for the Propagation of the Gospel in Foreign Parts, W. H. Brett arrived at Pompiaco in the Pomeroon to assist Duke. This was the beginning of a forty-year saga of missionary achievement unsurpassed by any other missioner in British Guiana. In an estimated population of 400–500 Arawaks and Caribs in the Pomeroon and its tributaries, the work began slowly. The Sunday congregation did not exceed five or six Indians, but progress was soon assured with the conversion of the Arawak Captain, Cornelius. In a year Brett reported thirty-four students in the day school, including ten to fifteen adults, apparently enjoying the scholastic training.[1]

Pompiaco was considered unhealthy for a mission[2] and in 1840 a new mission at Cabacaburi on the Pomeroon was under way. By 1845 another mission was established with the support of Superintendent McClintock and the voluntary help of 347 Indians. This mission was very appropriately called by the Indians 'Waramuri'— species of black ants—for in the future these ants would constantly devastate the buildings. In 1845 missionary statistics showed that there was a population of 1,000 at both the Pomeroon and Waramuri missions under W. H. Brett and J. H. Nowers respectively. They reported that the population was increasing, and so too were Christianity and industry among the Indians.[3]

The S.P.G. supported Brett and Nowers, but with numerous demands for its financial help elsewhere, it was finding it difficult to upkeep the Pomeroon and Moruka missions permanently. For this reason Brett petitioned and received from the government $933 for the annual salary of a clergyman in order to continue Waramuri— 'the flourishing and increasing Mission Station'.[4] Disaster struck both missions with the illness of Brett and Nowers. Bereft of their missionaries the Indians abandoned the missions, and the houses were overrun by the wood ants. Both the Governor[5] and Superintendent McClintock were concerned over their decline—so too were the Indians. McClintock attested that: 'the Indians generally, but more

[1] C.O. 111/181. Brett to Archdeacon Austin, 4 Dec. 1841.

[2] Ibid. Pompiaco was an ideal mission centre with direct links with the upper and lower Pomeroon River, so that the Arawaks from Tapacooma Lake and the Caribs from Issororo had easy access to it, but it was unhealthy and was later replaced by the Cabacaburi mission.

[3] Mission Statistics. B.G. I, 1834–58. U.S.P.G.A. See Appendix XIII.

[4] M.C.C., Brett to the Governor and Combined Court, 6 Apr. 1846. N.A.G.

[5] William Walker, Govt. Secretary to the Revd. A. J. Borlinder, Registrar of the Diocese, 16 Oct. 1847. L.B.

especially those who reside in the vicinity of Waramury Hill are most sorely disappointed at the manner in which their indefatigable exertions in clearing upwards of 100 acres of dense forest and erecting a village thereon, have been treated . . . and are sadly grieved at it.'[1]

In 1850 both the Waramuri and Cabacaburi missions were re-established.[2] Cabacaburi catered mostly to the Arawaks. The Caribs had withdrawn, and McClintock, with his experienced knowledge of the Indian, pointed out to Brett 'the impolicy of trying to bring up . . . under the same roof two tribes whose habits of language differed so materially from each other'.[3] Years later McClintock concluded that it was jealousy born of reasonable fear that accounted for the reluctance of the Caribs to mix with other tribes. If their children were instructed with those of other nations, when they reached the age of puberty the females 'might feel disposed, when not in sight of their natural Protectors to form alliances in a Tribe from whom the Parents would prefer being separated'.[4] Hence the Caribs always begged for a teacher to live and work among them.

It was becoming increasingly difficult to staff the missions. W. P. Austin, the Bishop of the Missions, who during his forty-two years episcopate travelled the length and breadth of the colony visiting his beloved 'children of the forest', spearheaded a Guiana Diocesan Church Society in 1852. Its primary and most important object was to support the missions to the Indian tribes.[5] The subscriptions that were solicited for this work kept the missions alive throughout the nineteenth century. To this Society the missionaries wrote their begging letters outlining the needs of the missions and detailing the hardships.

And it was not 'roses, roses, all the way'. Among the Caribs the results were disappointing. Only the chief of the Caribs, Commodore, and his son, Peter, remained faithful. Among the 250 Arawaks in the Upper Pomeroon there was a falling off in church attendance, not merely on account of employment on the estates, and sickness, but because of their distrust in the mission's stability

[1] M.C.P., 10 Jan. 1849. McClintock's Report, 30 Sept. 1848. N.A.G.
[2] M.C.P., 26 Feb. 1849, and 24 Aug. 1850. N.A.G.
[3] M.C.P., 24 Aug. 1850. McClintock's Report, 30 June 1850. N.A.G.
[4] M.C.P., 28 July 1868. McClintock's Report, 30 June 1868. N.A.G.
[5] C.O. 116/9. *The Royal Gazette*, 8 May 1852.

after its abandonment for two years.[1] Yet this depressing state of affairs brightened. Attendance picked up, while other tribes, the Warraus and the Akawois, brought their children for instruction.[2] The Waramuri mission was still without a clergyman, and McClintock again pressed for the re-establishment of the mission as he was convinced that there was 'nothing so likely to create a change for the better in the minds of the untutored Indians, and so effectually to keep him from harm's way . . . as religious instruction'.[3] The S.P.G. heeded these pleas and granted £100 per annum for the revival of the mission while the Bishop engaged the Revd. J. W. Wadie to take charge of it.[4]

In the eleven years since its establishment in January 1852, the G.D.C.S. had raised $6,710.14 from the Governor's Contingency Fund, Proprietors of Estates, friends in England, local committees in the colony, and Anniversary Receipts for the Indian missions,[5] but that sum dwindled considerably when shared out among the various missions. Nevertheless, if it were not for the supporting funds of the G.D.C.S. the Indian missions throughout the colony would surely have collapsed. There were other discouragements besides the usual crises of mission life, which Brett asserted, rose from three causes:

First,—The frequent abandonment of the Mission in former years, unavoidable indeed, but most unfortunate. Secondly,—The fact that the Waraus, the great mass of the surrounding population, are, of all, the Indians, the most superstitious, degraded, and filthy. Thirdly,—There are two classes of people continually passing to and fro among them, whose demoralizing influence is excessive . . .[6]

Brett faced similar problems to those of Bernau in Bartica when his settlement was invaded by the traders and gold-diggers who soon began 'to ruin our stations and destroy our simple people, body and soul'.[7] This mixed population interfered disastrously with the primary work among the Indians, and placed heavier burdens on the already overburdened missionaries.[8]

In November 1860 Brett again collapsed, completely exhausted

[1] C.O. 116/10. Ibid., 11 Jan. 1853. First Annual Meeting of the G.D.C.S.
[2] Ibid., 14 Apr. 1853.
[3] G.D.C.S., McClintock's Report, 26 Dec. 1853, in *The Royal Gazette*, 12 Jan. 1854.
[4] Wolseley, Government Secretary to McClintock, 20 Feb. 1854. L.B.
[5] Report of the G.D.C.S., 1863. *The Royal Gazette*, 1864.
[6] E10. *Missionary Reports*. Brett to Bullock, 3 Feb. 1862. U.S.P.G.A.
[7] E14. Ibid. Brett to Bullock 3 Feb. 1862. U.S.P.G.A.
[8] E14. Ibid. 1863. No. 2969/1864. Brett to Bullock, 5 Jan. 1863. U.S.P.G.A.

and debilitated by the climate, but he still kept going despite the pains and the pangs. During his twenty-one years of missionary service he had seen the extension of Christianity among the Guaicas or Waikas, a branch of the formidable Akawoi nation. Many had been baptized and their children were progressing in school, particularly in the study of English.[1] Next arrived the infamous Akawois whose evil reputation as 'kanaima' or night murderers seemed incongruous with their desire for baptism. Their conversion was little short of miraculous and resulted in a spread of the interest in Christianity into the interior, bringing the distant Maiongcongs asking for baptism. So unexpected and spectacular were these two episodes that Brett feared to be over-sanguine and hopeful lest disappointment loomed around the corner.[2]

The missionaries hoped that the Akawois, 'the pedlars and news carriers of the whole eastern coast', would, in turn, become the bearers of God's word in the inaccessible territories. The Akawois did eventually bring with them in their woodskin corials the tall, tattooed, and ornamented Arecunas from the Cuyuni and Caroni rivers in the Pakaraima region. They, too, the missionaries felt, would spread 'the knowledge at least of the Saviour's name, in regions untrodden as yet by civilized man'.[3]

In 1865 Bishop Austin, and in 1866 Governor Francis Hincks, visited the Cabacaburi and Waramuri missions, both never-to-be-forgotten events by the Indians. Over a thousand Arawaks, Caribs, Warraus, Akawois, and Maiongcongs gathered together for the occasion, although Brett realistically observed that most of them had turned out for the excitement and the presents brought by the Governor. On his visit the Bishop opened the new chapel at Waramuri and was encouraged and heartened at the state of the mission. The Governor was no less impressed with the *feu de joie* which was fired as he, in his full military regalia, landed on the mission.[4]

[1] E8. Ibid. No. 2378/61. Brett to Bullock, 21 Dec. 1860. U.S.P.G.A. Later at their request Bishop Austin, the Revd. W. H. Brett, the Revd. F. J. Wyatt, and Philip, a Christian Indian, visited the Waikas at the Great Falls on the Demerara river. A settler, Mr. George Couchman, became their teacher. See the Revd. H. P. Thompson, *Into All Lands. A History of the S.P.G. in Foreign Parts, 1701–1950* (London, 1951), p. 246.

[2] M.C.C., 18 May 1864. McClintock's Report, 31 Dec. 1863. N.A.G., and Brett's Report, 18 Aug. 1864, in *The Colonist*, 19 Nov. 1869.

[3] Brett's Report, 24 Nov. 1865. Ibid.

[4] D. 28. 6820/1866. Governor's Visit to the Shell Mound at Waramuri, Feb. 1866. U.S.P.G.A.

The G.D.C.S. continued to finance the missionary work, and the glowing reports from Brett of the ever-increasing Christianization and civilization along the Pomeroon and Moruka rivers assured them that the funds were being well utilized. But the S.P.G. in 1866, after a quarter of a century of support, felt that the colony should contribute more adequately to the missions. Bishop Austin appealed to the Governor, reminding him that 'ever since the establishment of the missions the population has markedly increased'.[1] The Revd. J. H. Wadie at Waramuri had sanguinely reported of 1857–8 that 'the schools upon which we mainly place our hopes for the future are daily increasing.[2]'

While the missionaries built up the spiritual life of the Indians, the wood ants undermined the buildings which had to be constantly repaired or replaced. At Waramuri—the hill of the ants—a third chapel was devoured: nothing was left 'but the bully-tree frame of the nave'. There were the sorrows and losses which the missions could ill afford. In 1868 their first Arawak convert, Cornelius, for twenty-eight years a faithful and exemplary Christian, died; in 1871 Mr. Duncan Campbell, the teacher at Waramuri, and in the following year Miss Reed, who had worked so zealously among the girls and women.[3] But the greater problems came from the Portuguese and mixed races who debauched the Indians with rum, stole or burnt their firewood, and even their villages under the very noses of the missionary teachers. Brett's reports of 1870 and 1871 complained that the last straw was the opening of a grog shop on the left bank of the Moruka river to 'the great impoverishment and demoralization of the Indians'.[4]

Despite these obstacles there was a numerical increase of converts. The work was enhanced and lightened by the catechism in the four Indian tongues, printed by the Society for the Propagation of Christian Knowledge.[5] The thirty-three-year period of missionary enterprise in the Pomeroon and Moruka areas can be summed up no better than in the words of Brett himself, the man who was mainly responsible for the solid establishment of those missions: 'It is a matter of comfort to me to be able to report the steady

---

[1] C.O. 111/365. Bishop of Guiana to Governor Hincks, 20 Oct. 1866.

[2] B.G. I. 1834–58. 10193/57 and 7722/57. J. Wadie to Bullock, 30 Sept. and 30 June 1857. U.S.P.G.A.

[3] Brett's Report of the Indian Missions of Cabacaburi and Waramuri for the years 1870, 1871, 1872. *Report of the G.D.C.S.* (Demerara), pp. 7 and 12.

[4] Ibid. (1870), p. 7, and (1871), p. 13.   [5] Ibid.

coming in of the various heathen tribes on every side. The Waraus, who dwell on our swampy shores . . . are making a considerable advancement in Christian knowledge.'[1]

The Demerara River Missions

Forming a link between the Essequibo and the Berbice rivers were the Demerara missions of Malali, Muritaro, and the Great Falls, under the zealous guidance of C. D. Dance. Malali, at the foot of the First Falls, 100 miles from Georgetown, replaced the Arampa mission in 1861 because of a population shift. Its early history was one of stagnation, but by 1873 it was a busy mission centre with its day and Sunday schools. In 1868 the Indian chief Kanaimapo, with about 380 of his tribe had been baptized during the Bishop's visit and this mass conversion set the mission on its feet.[2] Eighty miles from Georgetown was Muritaro, an offshoot of Malali which had grown rapidly after the Macusi Indians arrived from Bartica requesting a teacher. They remained and built a substantial, though primitive, school and chapel.[3] At this mission, which had grown up more or less spontaneously, were also Akawois, Arecunas, and Paramonas (Patamonas) from as far as the neighbourhood of Mount Roraima on the borders of Brazil and Venezuela.[4] By mid-century the timber trade was booming, and the Indians were more and more engaged as woodcutters along the Demerara river. Muritaro became the focal centre for the migrating Macusi and other tribes from the interior. To the Great Falls 150 miles up the river, came the Akawois from the interior, appealing for Christian instruction. The G.D.C.S. employed an old settler, Mr. Couchman, whose influence among the Indians was well known, as he was married to an Indian woman and spoke several dialects. By 1872 this settlement had grown to 300 industrious Indians who were also progressing in Christian knowledge with the help of Brett's catechetical works in Akawoi. As in all other missions, sickness and death were ever present. It was normal for the superstitious Indians to regard their troubles 'as a punishment for their renouncing the superstitions of their fathers',[5] and leave the missions in times of death. These

[1] Brett's Report of 1873, p. 14.
[2] Farrar, p. 49.
[3] Brett's Report, 1873. *Report of the G.D.C.S.*, p. 14.
[4] Memorial of C. Dance to the Board of Education on behalf of the Great Falls and Muritaro Indian Missions, 21 May 1872. Ibid., p. 14.
[5] C. D. Dance to the Revd. J. H. May, 1 Dec. 1873. *Report of the G.D.C.S.*, p. 17.

missions on the Demerara river, however, represented a penetration to the interior tribes and 'thus, on the Demerara as well as on the Essequibo, an intercourse of the most interesting character opened with races who dwell not only on, but beyond, the South Western frontier of our own Colony'.[1]

Another interesting mission was located on the Mahaicony river or creek at Kiblerie. While the Revd. Brett launched out on his pioneer work on the Pomeroon in 1840, the Revd. J. B. Bourne began his labour among the Arawaks and Warraus on this creek.[2] Kiblerie got off to a discouraging start. It took eleven years to arrive at some modicum of success, and by this time Brett's influence had reached these Indians in his Arawak translations of the Introductions to the Gospels of St. Matthew and St. John. The native missioner, Louis de Ryck, finally induced the Indian Captain Caetano to give up two of his wives, but of course his surplus spouses still posed an impediment to his baptism.[3] It was not surprising that Indian women were not among the ardent converts on this mission; for which woman of any race, primitive or modern, likes to be put away as an impediment and that at the command of an outsider?

In 1858 Bishop Austin visited the mission and held a convocation with the Indian chiefs concerning the religious advancement of the mission. The chiefs, asserting their authority over their irate wives, asked for their catechist to be replaced.[4] By 1864 there were over eighteen houses on the mission, but the population of 135 fluctuated because of illness and the eagerness of the Indians to join the balata-bleeders at a nearby establishment.[5] This isolated mission, 100 miles from civilized society, fell a constant prey to illness. Without a steady supply of medicines and proper nourishment the health of the Taylers, the new catechists, collapsed. Somehow the mission rallied. The Taylers' labours were not in vain, and the Stipendiary Magistrate of the District, Mr. Benson Maxwell, testified that the conduct of the people manifested the religious and educational training given by the catechists.[6] By 1873, because of increasing financial pressure, the G.D.C.S. regretfully withdrew its aid from this mission.[7]

---

[1] Brett's Report, 1873. Ibid., p. 15. [2] Thompson, p. 246.
[3] B.G. I. 1834–58. Missionary Report of Louis de Ryck, 1853. U.S.P.G.A.
[4] B.G. I. 1834–58. 3981/58. The Revd. H. May to the S.P.G., 1858. U.S.P.G.A.
[5] Tayler's Report, 1864. *Report of the G.D.C.S.*, p. 17, and ibid., 1866, p. 8.
[6] *Report of the G.D.C.S.*, 1873, p. 5.
[7] Ibid. Funds were given to the Ituribisci Mission for the first time, obviously in preference to the Kiblerie Mission.

The Berbice and Corentyne Missions

On the Upper Berbice river were Hittia and Cumaka, mission settlements among the Arawaks. Cumaka formed the link with the Essequibo and Corentyne mission of Orealla. Here was the usual Chapel-School building, erected at all settlements. The mission had once been reduced by a smallpox epidemic, but by 1869 life was back to normal. The numbers were increasing and the Bishop advised an enlargement of the chapel to accommodate the increase.[1] Later both a Church and Mission-house were built.[2]

As previously noted, the Moravian missionaries had begun the work among the Indians on the Corentyne as far back as 1757, and had gallantly struggled through a politically chaotic period before leaving for Surinam. With their departure the Indians had relapsed into 'Manichean Pagans, without worship, without altars, without temples'.[3] Proposals to re-establish this mission had been discussed in 1828 and again in 1839, but had evaporated. Under the determined efforts of the Curate of St. Margaret's, Skeldon, the Revd. W. T. Veness, the mission had been revived at Orealla with a government grant of ten acres of land and the help of generous subscribers in England to whom Veness had made impassioned pleas for the 'simple-minded and neglected and grievously wronged Aborigines of this river...'[4] The Bishop procured a salary from the Board of Education for a teacher, J. L. White, who tried to gather the three nations—the Arawaks, anxious for evangelization, and the Warraus and Caribs, indifferent and decidedly averse to a metamorphosis in their lives. The Warrau Captain Christmas was a piai-man and used his influence among his people to turn them away from the missionaries. Gradually Orealla, 'the last link in our chain of river posts across the Colony' forged by Veness, showed signs of progress. A large 60-by-30-foot chapel was built by the Indians. With the baptism of the grandson of Christmas, the Warraus were won over and a large body came from the Cabouri creek to live at Orealla. Veness concluded that Christmas must either have lost his influence, changed his tactics, or been touched by the Spirit of God.[5] In the history of missions it was always vital

[1] Dance, 30 Nov. 1869. *Report of the G.D.C.S.*, p. 12.
[2] Farrar, p. 53.
[3] C. B. Seiferth, Superintendent of the Orealla Mission, to the Revd. H. J. May, 1 Feb. 1876. *Report of the G.D.C.S.*, p. 24.
[4] Veness to May, 15 Nov. 1871. Ibid., p. 19 and C.O. 111/365.
[5] Veness, 'Early History of the Orealla Mission', Nov. 1869, p. 14.

to win over the chief. Once this was accomplished the people followed his lead; what was good for the chief was right and fitting for them, also.

At Orealla, there were the usual baptisms, confirmations, marriages. There was the inevitable blend of progress and regression. The squatters from Surinam lured away the susceptible Indians with rum, and there was much illness and death.[1] Veness accepted these tribulations with calm faith, realizing that 'These seasons of discouragement have marked the history of all our Indian Missions.'[2] From the Pomeroon to the Corentyne the missionaries looked to the future with hope.

Missions of the London Missionary Society

As early as 1815 the missionaries of the London Missionary Society had come into contact with the Indians on the Berbice river. The London Missionary Society, 'child of the evangelical revival in England',[3] was founded in 1795 for the purpose of 'sending Missionaries to the heathen and unenlightened countries'.[4] In less than a quarter of a century its missionary field stretched from the South Seas to the West Indies. In the British West Indies, however, its primary mission was to uplift the Negro slaves with the proviso that they should in no way raise the hopes of these slaves for earthly freedom. In such a work, John Wray and John Smith, were outstanding. But early in his career Wray, who had established a mission among the Negroes on an estate in the Berbice river in 1813, became interested in the other heathen, the Indians, through a little Indian boy's attachment to his wife.[5] In 1815 he visited an Indian village of Warraus and Arawaks along the Berbice river where he spoke of the blessings of Christianity to a few assembled Indians. This visit was memorable for his encounter with the piai-men, making their instruments of incantation, the peti-cabba, which they refused to give the curious missionary.[6] He also met an old Indian Christian, a convert of the Moravian missions in the Corentyne river, who begged Wray to come and instruct them as

[1] Veness, 15 Nov. 1871. *Report of the G.D.C.S.*, p. 19.   [2] Ibid.
[3] Lovett, I, 3.   [4] Ibid., p. 25.
[5] John Wray, 'Fragments of History', Berbice Box 1: 1813–24. L.M.S.A. The Berbice Mission was begun at the request of and under the patronage of the Commissioners of Crown Estates who had about 1,100 slaves under their care.
[6] Ibid., fol. 1818–20. L.M.S.A. Wray describes the 'peti-cabba' in a similar way to de Betham's description of the 'maracca' used by the piai-men in the Pomeroon and Moruka rivers. They were definitely the same instrument and used by all piai-men.

'it would make them happier and prevent them from killing one another and that it would be a blessing to their children'.[1]

This request gave a fillip to Wray's hopes of bringing the Indians to an understanding of the Gospel, as well as making them industrious workers. In this desire he was not encouraged by the planters who considered the Christianizing of the Indians an utter waste of time.[2] But the unconcern of the planters did not deter Wray who became more convinced that 'something might be done for these poor people'.[3] In November 1815 he realized a long cherished dream to visit the old Moravian mission station on the Corentyne River—a hazardous trip as the entrance to the Corentyne was shallow and dotted with dangerous sandbanks. Along the Equevi creek, forty miles from the mouth of the river, was a Warrau settlement. The Warraus were too caught-up with drinking and their implicit belief in their piai-man to pay any attention to Wray's counsels. But the visit was not wholly fruitless; in 1823 a Warrau attended the meeting of the Berbice Auxiliary Society and begged for the establishment of a school among his people on the Corentyne. Supported by Mr. Ross, the Protector of Indians, Wray jumped at the possibility. The estimated number of Arawaks, Warraus, and Caribs was between 600 and 700—a fertile ground. At Maria Henrietta an Indian station was established, financed by the Berbice Auxiliary Missionary Society and the L.M.S.[4] The Revd. J. McArthur, a native of Demerara, was appointed to the mission in 1858. The station soon boasted a chapel and showed every sign of progress through the sustained interest of the Indians.[5]

While Wray was reconnoitring for missionary establishments on the Berbice and Corentyne rivers, the Revd. R. Eliot was assessing the possibilities of working among the Indians on the Demerara river at the request of Governor Murray. The Protector of Indians on the Demerara river had been urging Murray to encourage Indian missions and Murray finally agreed to any action that was 'best calculated for their religious instruction, civilization, and training in habits of industry'.[6] This early suggested policy of the

[1] Ibid.   [2] Ibid.

[3] John Wray to David Langton, 21 Nov. 1815. L.M.S.A.

[4] Wray to William Hankey, Treasurer of the L.M.S. B.G. Berbice, 1813–24; f. 1821–2. L.M.S.A.

[5] *Missionary Magazine* (October 1861), XXIV, 293, L.M.S.A.

[6] Eliot to the Revd. George Burder, 20 Mar. 1816. 2 B.G. Demerara. 1815–22. f. 1. Jacket C. L.M.S.A.

Governor would be unceasingly reiterated by W. McClintock, who in the mid-century and beyond advocated an education-cum-industry plan for the Indians.

On the banks of the Demerara the Revd. R. Eliot found the Indians quiet, harmless, and kind people, not altogether set against religious education *per se*, but in general they preferred to remain as they were, fearing that it was a plan of the government to enslave their children. Eliot believed that an incumbent minister among them would help to dispel both prejudice and fear. Hence the L.M.S. should heed the calls of those 'benighted and degraded people'.[1] Despite Eliot's sanguine hopes, neither the Governor nor the L.M.S. heeded the calls. In 1830 public opinion criticized the apathy of the government and the Directors of the L.M.S. to the needs of the Indians. Mrs. Davies, the wife of the missionary, wrote to the Revd. T. Arundel in England expressing the hope that the L.M.S. would approach the colonial government for assistance for the enlightenment of 'this barbarous people'.[2]

While the activity of L.M.S. on the Demerara river remained virtually static, a zealous coloured young catechist, Marcus Peter, had established a station at Fort Island on the Essequibo without the aid of either the L.M.S. or the government. This mission found support from the congregation of the church of the Revd. Joseph Ketley of the L.M.S. On 10 February 1830 Union Chapel at Fort Island was officially opened by Ketley on a grant of land made by the Governor.[3] The congregation of Indians grew so rapidly that a year later the chapel had to be enlarged. Peter was an unusual man, a layman in the category of a Brett and a Bernau. Indefatigably he worked for years among the Indians opening mission after mission. In 1832 he opened a station at Caria-Caria on the west bank of the Essequibo, and before the year was out a chapel was erected there and the site renamed Castricome. Another station at Tiger Island was soon added. Peter visited over fourteen other creeks in the area, holding services and teaching the Indians to pray in a deeply pentecostal manner. The work among the Arawaks and Caribs seemed singularly blessed, and this was undoubtedly due to the kindness and devotion of Peter to these people. A succinct account

[1] Eliott to the Revd. George Burder, 20 Mar. 1816, 2 B.G. Demerara. 1815–22. f. 1. Jacket C. L.M.S.A.

[2] Mrs. Sarah Davies to the Revd. T. Arundel, 8 Oct. 1830. 4. B.G. Demerara. 1830–5. f. 1. B. L.M.S.A.

[3] *Missionary Sketches* (July 1835), LXX. n.p. L.M.S.A.

in the missionary magazine of the L.M.S. gives a mere glimpse of the missionary labours of Peter:

The labours of this devoted teacher, Mr. Peter, have been greatly extended among the Indian tribes in the creeks of the Essequibo; and according to his report for 1834, he was endeavouring, under encouraging circumstances, to instruct the Indians at the following places, viz.: Arawary or Castricome, Schonhoven, Caperwary Creek, Arawa Creek, Tocapeyo Creek, Ocho Creek, Arawagua Creek, Apacury Creek, Barbara Creek, Pirana Creek, Tiger Creek, Great Creek, and Cuyurucurma Creek.[1]

The work involved in these visitations staggers the imagination!

Ketley adopted Peter as his protegé and without much reference to the L.M.S. took over the personal overseeing of the missions at Fort Island, Castricome, Tiger Creek, and the others. He regularly visited them, examining and receiving converts, administering the sacrament, and even expelling members for immorality for the edification of all concerned.[2] He seemed particularly proud of the chapel at Castricome which was rebuilt in 1837. Peter, whose labours were very much divided among his flocks at Fort Island, Castricome, and Tiger Creek, opened yet another station on the Supinaam river in 1838.[3]

Ketley became so involved with these missionary ventures that he joined Caria-Caria (Castricome) station to his Providence New Chapel, on the grounds that the land on which the chapel and other buildings had been erected had been purchased by his congregation. This was severely criticized and questioned by the Revd. James Scott who informed the L.M.S. that the land had been given by an estate proprietor, Mr. Faber, for the use of, and in the name of, the L.M.S. He only conceded that the houses were built on land purchased by the people.[4] As a result of this controversy the Western Committee of the L.M.S. concluded that Fort Island could not be separated from Caria-Caria, and the best solution was to drop them from the list of the L.M.S. stations.[5] Ketley was accused of trying to override the authority of the L.M.S., setting himself

[1] Ibid. Also Ketley to Ellis, 11 Oct. 1834. 4. B.G. Demerara. 1830–5. f. 4. D. L.M.S.A.
[2] Ketley to Foreign Secretary of the L.M.S., 11 June 1837. 5. B.G. Demerara. 1836–8. f. 3. C. L.M.S.A.
[3] Ketley to Ellis, 27 Feb. 1838. Ibid., f. 4. A. L.M.S.A.
[4] James Scott to Ellis, 22 May 1838. Ibid. L.M.S.A.
[5] Meeting of the Western Committee, 25 May 1838. 1 Committee Minutes, West Indies, Book 2. Jan. 1838–Feb. 1840. L.M.S.A.

up as the spiritual leader and sole financier of the Essequibo missions.[1] Subsequently Ketley severed his connection with the L.M.S. and vested the church property in the hands of thirteen trustees in Georgetown.[2] Here the documentary history of these missions comes to an abrupt end. Yet they were obviously continued by Ketley, as in January 1870 there is an account of £100 given to Ketley by the G.D.C.S. in aid of the Mission Station and Relief of the Indians at Caria-Caria.[3]

The Role of Education in Missionary Enterprise

In the midst of all conflicts and controversies the missionaries never swerved from their goal of educating the Indian. They were primarily teachers, and the traditional pattern of the Chapel-School combination with its Day and Sabbath schools was followed in every well-established mission. One of the major difficulties was obtaining salaries for their catechists. There were constant appeals to the Governor and the legislature, but in most cases the appeals went unheard. The attitude of the Governors to the cause of educating the Indian was ambivalent; that of the majority of the Combined Court mostly unconcerned. Governor D'Urban in 1830 had few illusions, less patience, and not very much hope in educating and civilizing the Indian. The habits of the Indian were 'altogether erratic, capricious and uncertain'.[4] Several inhabitants of Guiana who were familiar with the Indians concurred in the Governor's view. The only solution to effect the education and religious instruction of the Indians, according to D'Urban, would be through 'well-chosen, persevering, conciliatory and judicious missionaries'.[5] D'Urban's view regarding the value of missionaries was quite Hispanic.

His successor, Sir James Carmichael Smyth, saw the need for Christianizing, but not civilizing, the Indians. Their love of independence and freedom from control would make any attempt to educate them unavailing and injudicious.[6] In his first fervour Governor Henry Light evinced great hopes of bringing the blessings of civilisation to the 'unfortunate wanderers'. In a lengthy Minute

---

[1] Scott to Ellis, 9 Jan. 1839. 6. B.G. Demerara. 1839–45. f. 1. A. L.M.S.A.
[2] Committee Minutes, 1838. L.M.S.A.
[3] C.O. 111/389. 'Return of Civil List Contingencies for the year 1870.' Enclosed in Governor John Scott to Kimberley, 22 Feb. 1872.
[4] D'Urban to Murray, 6 Feb. 1830. N.A.G. [5] Ibid.
[6] J. C. Smyth to Stanley, 5 Oct. 1833. N.A.G.

to the Court of Policy on the subject of the Aborigines on 13 December 1838 he questioned the government on what was being done for 'the poor remnants of those who once ranged over it (the soil of the colony) in full supremacy'.[1] In Light's words can be detected the overtones of the criticisms levelled against the government of British Guiana by the Parliamentary Report of 1837 that the 'tribes had been almost wholly neglected, are retrograding and are without provision for their moral or civil advancement'.[2] Light saw a good omen in the desire of the Indians to obtain grants of land for cultivation, for 'Instead of precarious livelihood obtained by hunting and fishing, habits of industry will be strengthened which will induce new wants; these once raised, the progressive advancement in society is secured.'[3]

The Combined Court had no such sentiments about 'the noble savage'. Any philanthropic ideas they might have held were thrown to the winds after Emancipation. The Court was adamant against investing in any venture that would yield no dividends. The education of the Amerindian was such a venture. Light had already taken the measure of his legislature, and dolefully concluded to Lord Glenelg:

> I have no great hopes of any immediate success attending my minute in favour of the Indians here, for the Members of the Court of Policy as well as the Financial Representatives take a gloomy view of the prospects of the Colony, and I fear will be unwilling to give money for the prospective good, but it will give publicity to the subject, discussion will ensue; I shall renew it and I trust in the end to accomplish what humanity and sound policy dictate and require.[4]

And renew the subject he did on the 19 December 1838 when in the Court of Policy he moved the following resolution: 'That this Court will take into its favourable consideration the expediency of adopting measures as it may deem Practicable for promoting the civilization of the Indian Tribes in the remote parts of the Colony.'[5] The sum of six thousand guilders was reluctantly voted for promoting the civilization of the Indians, but later thrown out by the Combined Court. Not only Light, but every Governor of British Guiana in the nineteenth century, found himself in the straitjacket of the legal and constitutional structure of the government of

---

[1] M.C.P., 13 Dec. 1838. N.A.G.   [2] Parliamentary Papers. *Aborigines*. II. 9.
[3] Light, M.C.P., 13 Dec. 1838. N.A.G.
[4] Light to Lord Glenelg, 17 Dec. 1838. N.A.G.
[5] M.C.P., 19 Dec. 1838. N.A.G.

British Guiana. He could only persuade, advise, suggest, recommend, or remind the Court of their responsibility, but his policies were hampered and his hands tied as the Combined Court held the financial reins. It seemed that the Colonial Office, despite its lip-service to humanitarian ideals, gave the plantocracy—strongly represented in the Combined Court—*carte blanche* in legislation to appease them for the lack of full compensation for their loss of labour. Yet this freedom in managing the government did not stop them from groaning throughout the century 'of the great agricultural and commercial distresses they suffered since Emancipation'.[1]

In 1840 Light visited a few Indian reservations and was more than ever convinced that 'the only chance . . . of making the rising generation of the Aborigines permanently useful to the Colony, is by religious and moral instruction'.[2] In his address to the Court he asked for £200 per annum for salaries for resident clergymen on the three main rivers. The Bishop of the Diocese would match this amount out of the Church's funds if the Court agreed.[3] Reluctantly the Court provided for the instruction of the Indians. In an enclosure from Archdeacon Austin regarding the Estimate of 1841 for the Education of Indians, the sum is noted as $2,000 shared out equally among the Missions on the Pomeroon, Essequibo, Demerara, Corentyne, and Berbice. In his letter to the Court asking for the continuation of the amount on the 1842 Estimate, as his ministers were planning to erect schools and hire schoolmasters, the Archdeacon pointedly added: 'It seems unnecessary to enlarge upon the advantage of extending the benefits of Christian instruction among a class hitherto so neglected as our Indian brethren have been.'[4]

In April 1842 the Revd. Joseph Austin directed a frantic plea to the Governor and the Court of Policy on hearing that the Court had decided to strike off the Estimate the $2,000 for Indian instruction. He had begun teaching among the Indians at Wickie in compliance with the wishes of the Lord Bishop of the Diocese and in the faith of the grant made last year by the Governor and the Court in aid of the Indian missions. Because of the scattered settlements it had been impracticable to have the children as day scholars and the expense of boarding them had been considerable—involving a teacher and costing $700. There was no other source for this need

[1] M.C.P., 1 Mar. 1847. N.A.G.
[2] C.O. 111/170. Light to Court of Policy, 28 Feb. 1840.   [3] Ibid.
[4] M.C.P., 2 Dec. 1841. Letter from Archdeacon Austin. N.A.G.

except the Court. The Court did order that the sum be placed on the Estimate and a detailed account of its distribution be given by the Archdeacon, but held out no hopes for the future continuance of funds for Indian missions.[1]

The Colonial Office, despite its sense of divine mission, was always caught between humanitarian impulses on the one hand, and the crude facts and cold logic of economics on the other. In 1844 Lord Stanley severely rapped Light on the knuckles for proposing to appropriate £100 from the Civil List Contingent Fund towards the payment of two schoolmasters for the Indians.[2] Again in 1845 in a cold note to Light: 'I am not aware that it is in my power to give effect to the wish you have expressed for the extension to the Indians of the means of Religious education. I should wish you to point out in what manner you consider so desirable an object could be practically accomplished.'[3] Three years later, at the end of his administration, a disillusioned Light doubted the feasibility of civilizing the Indians, 'despaired of Indian Missions and regretted the sums expended to so little purpose'.[4]

Because of the ill-defined, indeterminate, and vague policy of the Combined Court, and the shifting of the responsibility for the Christianization and civilization of the Indians by the Colonial Office on to the local legislature, the churches and their missionary societies had to bear the burden as best they could. With funds always at a low ebb and never very certain, the missions never progressed as they might have under favourable circumstances. No one more than W. C. McClintock, continuously and persistently advocated a more definite system for the advancement of the Indians—that of combining industry with education. He showed that out of a total of 3,500–4,000 Warraus in his area, not more than 200 derived any benefit from the missions. 'This fact loudly calls for the immediate adoption of some active steps to try and improve the condition of these unfortunate children of the woods—something to stimulate them to more constant habits of industry . . .

[1] M.C.P., 8 Apr. 1842. N.A.G.
[2] C.O. 112/26. Stanley to Light, 18 Apr. 1844.
[3] Ibid., Stanley to Light, 23 Mar. 1845.
[4] C.O. 111/253. Light's Memorandum, 9 Oct. 1848. A scribbled comment of Henry Taylor described this memorandum of Light's as 'a very interesting and also lively and entertaining account of the missions in the remote settlements in Br. Guiana' but, 'As to the founding of Missions it is a business which Governments do not seem competent to undertake . . . and can only be done successfully by Religious Bodies' (H.T., 11 Oct. 1848).

in other words *to combine industry with education*.'[1] If this were not done then very little hope remained of lifting the Indians from their present deplorable state of barbarism. McClintock voiced his surprise that 'although the system of combining one with the other is universally acknowledged to be the only one at all likely to civilize the Indians, still nothing ever has been adopted to put so praiseworthy a plan into execution'.[2]

His extensive visits to, and knowledge of, the Indians, especially the Warraus, Caribs, and Arawaks, convinced McClintock that the present hit-or-miss system of education was 'utterly inefficient, not to say preposterous'.[3] What was this system so roundly condemned? In McClintock's words:

An Indian by frequent visits of the missionary to his settlement is induced through persuasion of said Missionary to attend a school at which there is taught reading, writing, and arithmetic—to these branches of education the Indian is kept until a knowledge of such (no matter how trifling—as it generally is) be acquired; after this the Indian is discharged —the missionary considering that he is either too big to continue longer among Children—then composing the school or that he has picked up enough learning to enable him to work out an honest livelihood for himself.[4]

The government ignored McClintock's industry-with-education theme, but he never ceased to harp on the theme.[5] In 1855 McClintock was again stressing the need for this type of education. He saw himself as 'an advocate for extending education . . . such an education as would render them (the Indians) not only moral and religious but industrious, frugal and provident'.[6] At the end of the year he asked the Court's permission to move from Pomeroon to Moruka where he might be in a better position to promote his desire of civilizing the Indians through education and industry.[7] But the Court of Policy never seemed too impressed with McClintock's opinions on, and arguments for, the education-cum-industry scheme. His reports were merely acknowledged and laid on the table.

Yet the missionaries did try to make the Indian an industrious Christian. The Bishop acquainted Governor Walker with the satis-

---

[1] M.C.P., 23 Oct. 1846. McClintock's Report, 2 Oct. 1846. N.A.G.
[2] Ibid.
[3] M.C.P., 6 Dec. 1849. McClintock's Report, 30 Sept. 1849. N.A.G.
[4] Ibid.   [5] McClintock's Report, 31 Dec. 1849. N.A.G.
[6] M.C.C., 27 May 1856. McClintock's Report, 30 June 1855. N.A.G.
[7] Ibid., 31 Dec. 1855. N.A.G.

248

factory state of the missions on the Mahaicony and Moruka rivers; the missionaries in charge imparted both mechanical and religious instruction so that 'the Indians under their supervision are likely to improve in industrial habits, as well as in the ordinary branches of scholastic training'.[1]

In the evangelization and education of the Indian, women played a large and vital role. They were as zealous, if not more so, than the men in this service, coping with births and epidemics and deaths, and feeding and clothing the orphans. They proved excellent schoolmistresses and in this field their name is legion: the wives of the missionaries Youd, Bernau, White, Tayler, and many others. The Catholic religious Sisters were by no means the first single women to dedicate their lives to the missions. There were many 'misses' in missionary work: Miss Davson of Bartica, Miss Richardson of Thessalonica, Miss Reed of Waramuri, the Misses Austin of the Essequibo. Most outstanding of these missionary ladies was Miss Anna Austin, daughter of the 'Old Dean', William Austin of St. John's Parish, Essequibo. The school at Dufferyn Arawak Mission, begun in the Rectory grounds in 1841, was removed to Anna's home in Dufferyn in 1866. Of the fifty children on the school books in 1873, sixteen were orphans.[2] Anna taught the girls needlework and the boys industry. This mission won the praise of the Revd. T. Farrar as 'one of the most interesting, and certainly one of the most really successful, in this colony'.[3] Miss Austin was the voluntary superintendent of the mission, with her hands full in caring for the bodies and souls of her orphans. With the constant sickness of the children and the need for more nourishment her expenses were always high, and in 1875 the G.D.C.S. placed the mission on its list[4] as a mark of gratitude for her services. The ladies found their consolation amid their frustrations in the assurance that they were involved in the great 'civilising mission'.

This great 'civilising mission' was barely supported by the government. The special grants in aid of the Indian schools which had been previously voted remained static. In 1856 the figures on the Estimate of Expenditure of the Colony were as follows:

Bartica	$400
Cabacaburi	$320

[1] C.O. 111/260. Walker to Grey, 13 Dec. 1848.
[2] Ituribisci Indian Mission Report, *Report of the G.D.C.S.*, 1873, p. 13.
[3] Farrar, p. 39.   [4] *Report of the G.D.C.S.*, 1873, p. 5.

and the Presbyterian school established in 1841

Indiana $400.[1]

To these were added in 1860 Good Hope and Kiblerie with the aid of $320 each.[2] This expenditure for Indian education totalled $1,760 and could well be compared with the expenditure for immigration in the same year: $244,530.44![3] There was no mistaking where the Court's interest lay.

In such a maze of complexities, in such a sea of struggles to reach the goal of Indian Christianisation and civilization, it is no mean task to draw up the balance sheet of missionary endeavour in British Guiana and outline a coherent analysis. Undoubtedly the missionaries rose to heroic heights. Despite the exotic aura of missionary lands, the missionary's life was no romance. His house was 'sans comfort, sans money, sans everything'.[4] There were the long days of depression and the even longer nights of suffocating darkness. They bore the pangs and faced the problems of life in the wilderness while they tried to avoid the pitfalls and precipices of their work, convinced that 'The Indians are worth all that is being done, and all that can be done for them. Much has been accomplished, but very much more remains to be done.'[5] Richard Schomburgk, a layman, was the first of many who witnessed and praised the unselfish and heroic work of the missionaries: 'I have never again got to know men like Youd, or women like his wife who, practically without any help at all, have gone into the interior of Guiana, where supported and fortified by high and beautiful ideals they have been willing to suffer all the troubles, hardships and privations of which the modern missionary cannot have an inkling.'[6] With very few exceptions this eulogy could be written of the missionary stalwarts of the nineteenth century who truly 'bore the burden of the day and the heat' in laying the foundation of missionary enterprise. But these valiant men were also products of their age. Just as the British political, economic, and legal institutions had been exported to her colonies, so too had her religious ones. This imposition of a culture riddled all institutions, and was a source of pride, as Gladstone's words attested: 'We feel proud

---

[1] M.C.C., 2 June 1856. Estimate of Educational Purposes for 1856. N.A.G.
[2] C.O. 111/330. B.G. Receipts and Expenditure of the Year, 1860.   [3] Ibid.
[4] Farrar, p. 9.   [5] Walter Heard to H. J. May, 31 Dec. 1876. U.S.P.G.A.
[6] Richard Schomburgk, II, 322.

when we trace upon the map how large a portion of the surface of the earth owns the benignant sway of the British Crown and we are pleased with the idea that the country which we love should so rapidly produce its own image.'[1]

From the thrust of the educational policy it seemed that the missionaries sought to make their savage brethren into the image of the English Christian gentleman. In many cases the missionaries regarded the Indians as souls with ears.[2] With such an attitude they insulated the Indian from his environment so that his ears might be better attuned to hear only the pure Word of God. The result was cultural shock because the mission environment was alien to the Indians' simple way of life. Taken from his forest home, the Indian was placed in Day Schools and Sunday Schools—the time-table of both based on that followed in the towns of nineteenth-century England among the middle class. Denomination vied with denomination and competition was high. The Jesuits called their rivals in the Moruka 'gentlemanly heretics' while the 'heretics' in turn accused them of preaching Popish error and heresy.[3] The missionary work was marred by the personality clashes among missioners within the same denomination and between the missioners and their respective societies regarding mission policy. Sometimes the disagreements assumed such bitter proportions that they considerably weakened the impact of the Christian message and halted the progress of the churches. These minor 'religious wars' increased the confusion in the already confused minds of the Indians who probably wondered whose God was the right one.

With the exception of the few missions they financially supported, the colonial legislature evinced no special interest in the Christianization and civilization of the Indians. Whenever the Court of Policy discussed the Indian it was usually from the point of view of economic expediency. Even Governor Light with his sanguine hopes for the moral advancement of the Indian stated in his 1848 memorandum that the Christianized Indians at Bartica had benefited neither commerce nor industry,[4] and that advocate of the education-cum-industry scheme, McClintock, looked on the civilized Indian

[1] Memo on Colonies, n.d. Gladstone Papers, British Museum, Add. MSS. 44738.
[2] J. G. Davies, *Dialogue with the World* (London, 1967), p. 50.
[3] de Betham, 'Stray Notes', *Letters and Notices* (1864), II, 149 and 'Indian Missions in Guiana', *The Church Missionary Intelligencer* (Jan. 1852), III, 11–18.
[4] C.O, 111/253. Light's Memorandum, 9 Oct. 1848.

as one who would, above all, boost the agricultural economy of the colony.[1]

What temporal benefits did the Indians gain from Christianity? From our Western vantage point they were decently clothed, housed, and trained in habits of industry. Wives were liberated, and polygamy and other un-Christian and superstitious practices warred against, although almost every missionary admitted his failure to reform the drunkards. To the Indians the missionary offered the new lamps of virtue for the old of vice—spiritual benefits in compensation for their miserable, degraded lives. On the other hand, in his alien environment the Indian encountered trials and tribulations previously unknown to him. No doubt he asked himself: was it worth it? Did clothes and Christian morality compensate the bewildered, baffled, and bemused 'denizens of the forest' for the sense of loss, disinheritance, and sense of inferiority? Did the future reward of heaven held out to them suffice for the loss of their earth—the Gospel for their 'green mansions'? Yes, the missionaries were sincere in wanting to transport the Indian from his primitive life into the 'Divine Milieu'—to plunge him into God—the Christian God. But this God was a far-removed God. Instead of bringing the God-Man to men, they laboured to raise men to God. The missionaries who raged against the mumbo-jumbo of the piai-men tried to perform their own brand of magic—the reincarnation of an alien God for an earthly people. They failed to have the third dimension; they believed in this God, sincerely believed theirs was the duty and obligation to instil this belief in the Indians, but it is questionable whether they led the Indian to touch and find Him in their daily lives. Though the missionaries were versed in the theology of their day, they were neither anthropologists, psychologists, nor sociologists. And this dimension of nineteenth-century missionary endeavour must not be forgotten.

But surely there were some strengths, some successes for almost a half-century of missionary endeavour? In the realm of the spiritual it is difficult, if not impossible, to assess results. On paper, missionary statistics showed the desire of the Indians for Christian instruction and baptism. They undertook long, arduous journeys from the interior to the missions, and many did remain faithful, as can be seen on the missions to the present day. Although the reports of the missionaries and the Superintendents were mostly written

[1] M.C.P., 26 Nov. 1852. McClintock's Report, 30 Sept. 1852. N.A.G.

in support of a cause, they cannot be wholly dismissed as fantasy or gross exaggerations. The seed of the faith was planted by these early missionaries. Watered and cultivated by their successors, it gradually took root. Yet the call of the wild was always strong, and deep-rooted customs died hard among the Indians. Missionary enterprise was sincere, but superficial and still very much unfinished among the Guiana Indians.

IX

THE BALANCE SHEET OF BRITISH POLICY

It has been observed that 'Indian Policy in Brazil, as in many countries, was a confused mixture of religion, humanitarianism and greed'.[1] In British Guiana, Brazil's neighbour, the mixture was a similarly confused one, with the exception that expediency must be substituted for greed, and the ingredients reversed. For expediency and pragmatism were the prominent features of both the Dutch and British policies and these two features continued to mark British policy throughout the nineteenth century.

At the beginning of the century in 1803 the British inherited from the Dutch a territory and a policy which was to bind the Indians to them by presents and annual subsidies. These presents assured the administration of Indian support against the runaway and rebellious Negroes. With emancipation the usefulness of the Indian ceased, the presents and subsidies were abolished, and the welfare of the Indian submerged by the scramble for immigrant labour. In turbulent Venezuela the Indians had become so much grist for the revolutionary mill. In that country, as in the other Spanish colonies in rebellion against Spain, the New Laws of Charles V promulgated in 1542 'to take especial care of' and 'for the preservation, good government and treatment of the said Indians'[2] was a dead letter.

What were the hall-marks of British policy towards the Indians in British Guiana? There is no simple definition of such a policy because of the complexities involving people and situations. In

[1] Mathias Kiemen, 'Status of the Indian in Brazil after 1820,' *The Americas*, XXI (1965), 263.
[2] Spain. Laws and Statutes. *The New Laws for the Government of the Indies and the Preservation of the Indians*, 1542–3. A Facsimile Reprint of the Original Spanish Edition together with a Literal Translation into the English Language to which is prefixed an Historical Introduction by the late Henry Stevens and Fred W. Lucas. Reprint of the Facsimile edition London, 1893 (Amsterdam, 1968).

general, it was a conglomerate of the policy of liberal and conservative, pro- and anti-humanitarian members of the Colonial Office, of sugar-minded and money-grubbing members of the Combined Court, of strong- and weak-willed Governors, of interested and uninterested officials, and of zealous missionaries. Only one thing was certain: there was no consistent policy. It has always been British policy to shy away from written constitutions or written policies, preferring to govern by rule of thumb. This fact was borne out in their attitude towards the indigenous people in their South American colony.

First, Indian policy, if it can be so called, was a blend of humanitarian idealism and economic realism. Secondly, the policy of the Combined Court was to have no policy towards the Indians, for they were outside the body politic and economic and were of negative value, good for nothing. The only policy that absorbed the local legislature was connected with cheap labour and the monomania for saving the estates, positive factors in the welfare of the colony. Thirdly, the policy of the governors ranged from the obsession of Bentinck to procure the friendship of the Indians, to the outraged reaction of Carmichael to their demands, to the optimistic *naïveté* of Light, and to the consequent disillusionment and scepticism in both him and later governors. By the end of the century the governors had, more or less, washed their hands of the Indians, but still wanted to save face by showing some slight interest in this minority group in their population. In 1863 Governor Hincks transmitted six documents in one dispatch to the Colonial Office, five of which were missionary reports. He remarked that they were of no statistical value, 'but . . . will at least prove that the Aborigines are not wholly lost sight of'.[1] The fact that they were missionary reports showed that only the missionaries had not lost sight of the Indians.

A minority of officials such as McClintock, and missionaries such as Youd, Bernau, and Brett, looked towards the future of the Indians and had definite, clear-cut ideas of what should be done for them. Though their motives and their zeal were unquestionably sincere, their vision was limited to what *they* expected the Indians to become. Youd claimed that it was necessary 'to revolutionize the whole state of feelings and habits of the life of the Indians, before they could be brought to the practice of the Christian religion'.[2]

[1] C.O. 111/342. Hincks to Newcastle, 21 Dec. 1863. [2] Veness, pp. 23–4.

255

This, in short, was the credo, the blueprint of all missionaries. Bernau's idea was to immerse the Indian so completely in his new Christian environment that he would forget his primitive way of life, customs, and beliefs.[1] McClintock, who heartily supported the whole missionary venture, advised caution in this respect, as there was 'nothing likely to cause discontent and eventually a removal' as too early and too drastic an interference with, and curtailment of, the Indians' customs.[2] McClintock's policy, which was written so often that it should have burnt itself into the minds of the Combined Court, was 'to combine industry with education', an education imparted by the missionaries. Schomburgk had advocated a very similar idea when he wrote, '. . . we know that with religion, civilization and industrious habits go hand in hand . . .'.[3] The missionaries and McClintock had confidence and faith in the educability of the Indians, which though weakened, never wavered.[4]

Thus British policy towards the Indians in Guiana meant many things to many men. To several ministers and senior officials in the Colonial Office like Goderich, Grey, Stanley, Russell, and Stephen influenced by humanitarian principles, the Indians were to be protected. This protection was viewed as a divine mandate, 'the manifest destiny' of the British people 'to take up the white man's burden'. This outlook brought many a headlong collision with the penny-pinching Treasury in London, and the planter-dominated Combined Court in Guiana. And in such collisions, as in many others, the colonists usually won the day.[5] No wonder that to James Stephen '. . . a colony [was] as turtle soup to an alderman—daily fare and hardly palatable'.[6] The Combined Court resented any interference by the home government in their domestic affairs, and the Colonial Office, in most cases, quite prudently kept their finger out of the pie. Hence, when the colony appealed to the Colonial Office for raising loans for immigration, they referred to the apprehension of the Treasury at the rising expenditure, and caustically replied that they could not be 'answerable for the pecuniary results

[1] CW/018/13a. Bernau to Coates, 4 Dec. 1837. C.M.S.A.
[2] M.C.P., 5 Jan. 1846. McClintock's Report, 30 Dec. 1845. N.A.G.
[3] Schomburgk, *A Description of British Guiana*, p. 145.
[4] M.C.P., 6 Dec. 1849. McClintock's Report, 30 Sept. 1849. N.A.G.
[5] D. B. Swinfen, *Imperial Control of Colonial Legislation, 1813–1865. A Study of British Policy towards Colonial Legislative Powers* (Oxford, 1970), p. 140.
[6] Paul Knaplund, *James Stephen and the Colonial Office, 1813–1846* (Madison, 1953), p. 74.

of distant Colonial enterprises, in which they have little voice and on which any intervention of their Government is apt to be resented'.[1] Thus the Colonial Office, possibly owing to its resentment of the *lèse majesté* attitude of the colonial legislature, and needing a convenient scapegoat for its wish to frustrate that unhelpful body in an area that hurt, used the Treasury for this purpose.[2]

The Parliamentary Committee on Aboriginal Tribes reported a series of injustices committed against native peoples in all British colonies, and strongly urged that they be protected from the vices of the white man. But they, too, had a double standard, admitting that the Indians had a right to their own lands, but as the land had become the *de facto* possession of the British settlers who had introduced many evils, it was the duty of the British government 'to give them compensation for those evils, by imparting the truths of Christianity and the arts of civilised life'.[3] Again it was the eternal compromise. The Committee pointed the way to a policy to be adopted by the British government: 'The protection of the Aborigines should be considered as a duty belonging and appropriate to the Executive Government, as administered in this country or by the Governors of the respective Colonies.'[4] With few exceptions involving interference, and those only taking the form of advice, the home government considered the duty of aboriginal protection as belonging to the governors.

The governors of British Guiana saw the Indian in various guises during their respective administrations. Before emancipation, they were allies to be gratified and propitiated with presents; after emancipation, simple people to be protected against the aggressions of the Brazilians and the Spaniards, 'naked denizens of the forest' to be brought, willy-nilly, into the pale of civilization. But by the 1860s gold metal had become more interesting and lucrative than

[1] M.C.C., 2 Dec. 1856. Extract of Despatch from Labouchere to Wodehouse, 16 Jan. 1856, read in the Court.

[2] Ann M. Burton in her article on the Treasury, demythologized the image of a tight-fisted Treasury and felt it was used as a whipping-boy by other departments. In this way, the Treasury gained an unwarranted name and reputation of a Scrooge which had 'the indirect influence' as a potential check—often a convenient one—on excessive Colonial demands and the prevalent popularity in Parliament of an economic policy which strengthened the efficacy of the Treasury's 'moral suasion'. See Burton, 'Treasury Control and Colonial Policy in the Late Nineteenth Century', *Public Administration*, XLIV (1966), 192.

[3] Klauss E. Knorr, *British Colonial Theories, 1570–1850* (London 1963), p. 386.

[4] Great Britain. Parliamentary Papers. *Report from the Select Committee. Aborigines*, II. 77.

brown people. However, the governors of British Guiana cannot be too harshly condemned. Generally, colonial governors were merely expected to preserve the peace and balance the budget during their administrations. The governors of British Guiana had an even worse task: to balance the budget, to maintain peace among a growing cosmopolitan and restless population, and above all, to keep the peace and work with the Combined Court, that rather recalcitrant body of men who seemed constantly out to get the blood of the executive. The governors then had to steer a course fraught with dangers, between the Scylla of the Colonial Office and the Treasury and the Charybdis of the less easily-placated Combined Court. Governor 'Mr. Greatheart' Light began his career gallantly but naïvely. His predecessor, Carmichael Smyth, had not survived his proclamation to the Apprenticed Labourers more than a month. After his death in March 1838 Light succeeded him to a heavy burden indeed. By the end of 1838, the now completely freed apprenticed labourers removed themselves as far away as possible from the estates and their ex-owners, and the labour shortage became acute.

In this political and economic climate Light strove to create, initiate, and establish some definite post-emancipation policy towards the Indians. On 11 December 1838, in a pro-Indian address, he reminded the Court of Policy that the country was indebted to those people, and legislation should be henceforth broadened to provide for their welfare.[1] A few days later, considerably moved by a dispatch of Schomburgk regarding the aggressions of the Brazilians against the Indian tribes on the Brazilian frontier with Guiana, he recommended: 'That this Court will take into its favourable consideration the expediency of adopting such measures as it may deem practicable for promoting the civilization of the Indian tribes in the remote parts of the Colony.'[2] The resolution was supported only by the Honourable Colonel M. M'Turk who spoke highly of the honesty of the Indians, and regretted their neglect by the government. It ran the gauntlet of the Court while Light pleaded, '. . . let us do something towards showing the interest which we take in the advancement of these people and the prosperity of the Colony'.[3]

---

[1] M.C.P., 11 Dec. 1838. N.A.G.
[2] M.C.P., 19 Dec. 1838. N.A.G.
[3] Ibid. See also C.O. 115/4. *The Royal Gazette*, 22 Dec. 1838, in which the debate is reported.

The latter was but a sop to the Court which would have none of it, especially when that something was to the tune of 6,000 guilders recommended for the civilization of the Indians. The argument raged between the conflicting opinions of whether the Indians were savages or not; if they were not, 'why offer to civilize them?'[1] If they wanted to be civilized, that is, 'if they want churches and religion, let them come here to us'—an objection to financing missionary establishments in the interior. The upshot of the debate on Indian policy was the resolution accepted only with the amendment 'as far as consistent with the financial resources of the Colony'.[2] With the financial resources of the colony daily diminishing, as far as the plantocracy was concerned, Indian welfare became not only inconsistent, but as remote as the Tierra del Fuego.

From this reaction Light realized that he could hardly expect any success as the Combined Court had such 'a gloomy view of the prospects of the Colony', but proposed to reopen the issue.[3] Two years later he complained to the Colonial Office of the lack of liberality in the colonists who viewed the task of civilizing the Indians as hopeless.[4] Whenever money talked, humanity was silent.

By the end of his administration in 1848, Light had reached a similar conclusion to that of his Court. His memorandum on the state of the population was in sad contrast to his optimistic views of 1838. In the meantime Light had moved around the country; not only was he devoured by mosquitoes on his Indian safaris, but he was torn by disillusionment. He observed that contact with the white man had demoralized the Indians who were decreasing in numbers, 'The nearer the Indian is located to civilisation the more degraded he is found . . .'.[5] He summed up the Indian's life: '. . . a squalid infancy—a youth without instruction—a manhood of sloth and sexual gratification—an old age of misery and abandonment',[6] all worsened by his addiction to rum and piwari 'that filthy liquor'.

The nomadic habits of the Indian had militated against the success of the Indian missions and though there had been some signs of progress in the past, now Light despondently noted: 'there were no symptoms of further desire for civilised life'.[7] These doom-like

[1] Ibid. The six thousand guilders grant was later struck off the Estimate by the Financial Representatives. See C.O. 111/165. Light to Normanby, 6 Aug. 1839.
[2] Ibid.   [3] C.O. 111/156. Light to Glenelg, 17 Dec. 1838.
[4] C.O. 111/180. Light to Russell, 20 Aug. 1841.
[5] C.O. 111/253. Light's Memorandum, 9 Oct. 1848.   [6] Ibid.   [7] Ibid.

predictions were a far cry from the early breezy hopes of Light who had seen in the donning of petticoats for women, 'a step towards civilization'.[1] The distribution of Bibles and church attendance were other signs, although one of the Superintendents, J. Shanks, had criticized the Bible distribution as 'a farce—Cant as well as Humbug',[2] and claimed that the Indians used the Bibles either 'as wadding for their guns' or as 'an object of Obeah'.[3]

Indeed, the Indians had not always fared too well at the hands of the whites. Even the Superintendents and their predecessors, the Protectors and postholders appointed for their protection, had violated their trust, purchased them as slaves, paid them in rum, and exploited them in various ways. Rules and regulations governing the duties of these officials strove to curb these extreme evils. Conscientious officials like McClintock were few and far between, and even the overzealousness and the importunity of McClintock bored and irritated the Members of the Combined Court, most likely because it disturbed their consciences.

So the Indians, cherished during the days of slavery, were now outcasts, for 'The men at the head of Colonial Affairs in the Colony will do nothing for them and affirm that as they are of no use to agriculture—the Colonists are not bound to support them in any way'.[4] The Colonial Office had long told Governor Light that it was the responsibility of the local legislature to fend for the Indians, and not that of Her Majesty's Government.[5] But nothing was of any interest to this body except estates and immigration.

The Chief Justice, ironically called the 'Learned Judge' who had 'a great contempt for estates, and a proportionate respect for the gentlemen of the woods',[6] rightly attested that the planters harped constantly on estates as if they were the only things to be considered.[7] Uncertainty and the impossibility of Indian labour stemming from the Indians' dislike of agricultural labour as slave labour, had not endeared them to the plantocracy. Only McClintock and

---

[1] C.O. 111/170. Light to Russell, 22 Jan. 1840, and C.O. 111/212. Light to Stanley, 28 Aug. 1844.

[2] C.O. 111/203. Supplement to the Memorial of J. Shanks, 15 Sept. 1843.

[3] Ibid. It was not surprising that, after such an indictment of Light's policy, Shanks was not reappointed to the post of Superintendent of Rivers and Creeks.

[4] C.O. 111/253. Light's Memorandum, 9 Oct. 1848.

[5] C.O. 111/197. Stanley to Coates, 21 June 1842.

[6] C.O. 115/4. *The Royal Gazette*, 22 Dec. 1838.

[7] Ibid.

the minority of managers on the Essequibo coast had experienced and reaped on a small scale the results of Indian labour.

To the Combined Court, the Indians were financial millstones around its neck; to the Courts of Justice they were legal albatrosses. The Courts of Justice, representative of British law, insisted that Indians committing murder be brought to trial, but neither the judges nor the jury were ever certain what punishment they deserved. The Select Committee had declared that 'To require from the ignorant hordes of savages . . . the observance of our laws would be absurd, and to punish their non-observance of them by severe penalties would be palpably unjust . . .'.[1] But this declaration never solved the dilemma for the Courts. Should they insist on law without justice, or should they allow the Indians to carry out their own justice? The latter was unthinkable as it would be a denial of the rights of British law, as well as its superiority. In the cases of Indian murder, the Courts invariably took the *via media*: and no Indian, throughout the century and to the present day, was ever convicted of murder. Through the years they tried, by this half-way method of applying the law, gradually to accustom the Indian mind to the ways of British justice. Michael Swan, observing this system in the twentieth century, remarked, 'Amerindians are thus taught the idea of British justice, though what they make of it is a different matter.'[2]

The missionaries were in no less of a quandary: on one hand, all signs seemed favourable and conducive to the civilization and the Christianization of the Indians, who were showing themselves anxious for articles of clothing, and for religious and moral instruction;[3] on the other, they were still addicted to rum, and were suffering the consequences of various epidemics: in 1843 smallpox, and in 1856–7 measles and cholera, decimated the Indians at the mission settlements. It was admitted that the Indian children were better fed in the bush with their parents, and not at the mission

[1] Report of the Select Committee, p. 84. Among the 'General Suggestions', VII, the Committee advised that when British law was violated, 'the utmost indulgence compatible with a due regard for the lives and properties of others, should be shown for their [Aboriginal] ignorance and prejudices'. p. 80.

[2] Swan, pp. 166–7. Swan recounted that in a 1955 murder case an Indian boy was acquitted because the jury decided that he had acted according to the tribal laws of self-defence in killing an old man who had threatened to wipe out his family by a tribal curse.

[3] C.O. 111/165. Light to Normanby, 6 Aug. 1839 also, C.O. 111/260. Walker to Grey, 13 Dec. 1848.

stations where fever was attributed 'to the want of a sufficient quantity of fresh animal food'.[1] The Revd. J. H. Bernau had despaired of the Indian ever settling down at the mission stations; even children, who had been weaned from their primitive surroundings at an early age, had returned without a backward glance. The Indians were also confused in their minds with the various religious groups. Bagot once wrote that 'a very intelligent native, who had been observant of the different sects of Missionaries' said 'that he could not embrace Christianity nor form a good opinion of it, since the Teachers, and Ministers of it were not agreed among themselves'.[2] Although these remarks referred more to forms of worship than to doctrine, the want of uniformity among religions made some impression on the Indians. It was difficult for them to understand why missioners fought missioners for the love of God.

Missionary policy was concerned and obsessed with numbers as all their reports show, as if the statistics of baptisms, communions, confirmations, marriages, and average attendance at church and school were conclusive evidence that the Indians had miraculously, after less than fifty years of missionary enterprise, become firmly rooted and grounded in the Christian faith. But lack of funds constantly bogged down missionary work, and the deterioration of churches and schools probably drove the missionaries to tot up numbers of converts in order to show their societies and the local government some tangible results of their work. The Church and State never completely formed an alliance for the progress of the Indians because the Church was uncertain of the means and results of progress, and the State unwilling to part with money for such a questionable venture, the myth of Indian civilization. Money was forever at the root of, and an obstacle to, Indian policy.

Garcilaso de la Vega in his *Royal Commentaries of the Incas*, recounted the anecdote of an Inca princess, daughter of Huaina Capac, who was asked whether she wanted to marry a Spanish captain, Diego Hernandez. She replied in the Quechua language, 'Ichch munani, ichach mana munani', which meant 'maybe I will, maybe I won't'.[3] This anecdote could be used to illustrate the attitude of the Amerindian to civilization and Christianization: may-

[1] C.O. 116/12. Report of the Anniversary Meeting of the Guiana Diocesan Church Society. 'Letter of W. Austin to Archdeacon Jones', 28 Nov. 1854.
[2] C.O. 111/123. Bagot to D'Urban, 4 Sept. in D'Urban to Goderich, 3 Nov. 1832.
[3] Garcilaso de la Vega, *Royal Commentaries of the Incas*, II, Book VI (Texas, 1966), 1229-30.

be he did want it, maybe he didn't. His temperament and philosophy of life could not be so easily and radically changed after centuries of living in his own, carefree way. One finds it impossible to disagree with Postlethwaite's agent, Patrick Horan, who, after his observation of the Indians, concluded: 'There are few of them, who do not prefer the solitude of the forest, to the tranquility and blessings of civilised life.'[1] Governor Walker, also, pointed out this attitude of the Indian to Earl Grey in one of his dispatches on the state of the population. He considered it a truth, that despite 'whatever pains may have been taken with children of this race to accustom them to the arts, conveniences, and associations of civilized life', it was a rare occasion when they did not 'prefer to return to their nomadic habits and simple employments in the forest, if the opportunity presents itself'.[2]

Yet the government were often reminded that they were occupying the lands of the Indians, and even though they were 'now comparatively insignificant in numbers and in importance'[3] they should be acknowledged in some way as repayment of a debt. As Dr. Hancock had suggested earlier in the century, the Indians should have been treated as men, but they were constantly treated as children because of their docility, and advantage taken of them.[4] Recompense was always seen in the blessings and knowledge of the gospel. The aim was to convert, to reform, and to remould the Indian. Rafael Squirru of Argentina, in one of his lectures, 'The Intellectual Responsibility of Specialists on Latin America', delivered at the Library of Congress in Washington, D.C., on 16 May 1963, stressed the point that 'change must not be change for its own sake. It must spring from a wise vision of what men are about, where they want to go, and where they have come from'.[5] This remark of Squirru, although geared to the new man of Latin America, can well be applied to the Amerindian in the Guiana of 1873 and even now. His environment, his attitudes, customs, beliefs, and values should have been considered.

By 1873, to the Church and State both at home and abroad, the Indian had become stereotyped. He had deteriorated from 'the

[1] 'A Narrative of Patrick Horan . . .' N.A.G.
[2] C.O. 111/256. Walker to Grey, 17 Aug. 1848.
[3] C.O. 111/322. Bishop of Guiana to the Under Secretary of State, 26 Nov. 1858. Also Schomburgk, *A Description of British Guiana*, p. 145.
[4] Hancock, pp. 38–9.
[5] Rafael Squirru, *The Challenge of the New Man* (Washington, D.C., 1964), p. 19.

noble savage' to a museum piece who was patronized, proselytized, protected, and paralysed within his own environment. After emancipation, 'The liability for the protection and civilization of the Indians',[1] recognized and accepted by both the home and local governments as an inheritance from the Dutch, was shifted to the missionaries. The missionaries undoubtedly did their duty, but expected of the Indians too much, too soon.

Who was really qualified, and who still is qualified to decide what is sound policy for the Indians? Was it the Church or the State? In either case, a happy medium would not have been reached. The Indian would be considered either under-Christianized or over-Christianized, under-protected or over-protected. A *laissez-aller* policy might have been the best solution, somewhat on the style of the Brazilian Decree of 11 December 1911, which for the first time legally established '. . . respect for the indigenous tribes as people who had the right to be themselves, to profess their beliefs, to live in the only way they knew how, [practising] what they had learned from their ancestors'.[2]

In 1873 it would have been utopian to expect Church and State to hold such an opinion. It is even less possible today. Maybe what the Indians of British Guiana of 1873 wanted but could not articulate was expressed by the American Indians at a nationwide convention in 1961: 'What we ask (of America) is not charity, not paternalism . . . The Indians ask for assistance, technical and financial, for the time needed, however long that maybe, to regain . . . some measure of the adjustment they enjoyed as the original possessors of their native land.'[3]

[1] C.O. 884/4. *British jurisdiction over all Natives east of the Orinoco* (The British Case and Claim . . . Mr. C. A. Harris's Memorandum on the Hague MSS., Sept. 1888), pp. 6–7.

[2] As quoted in Kiemen, p. 271.   [3] *Time*, 19 Mar. 1973.

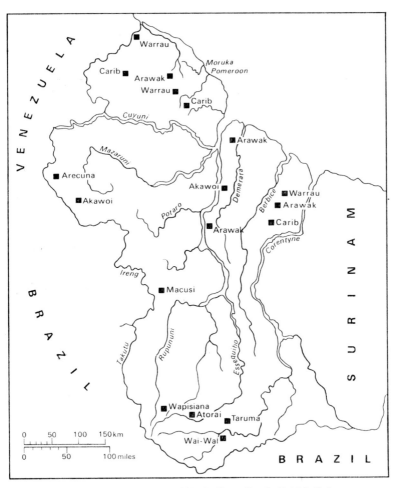

Map showing the location of the Indian tribes in British Guiana

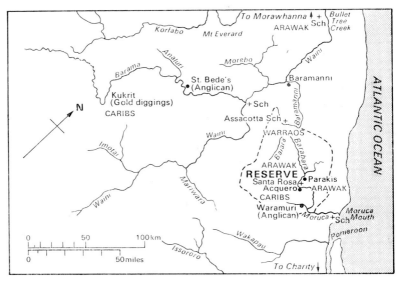

Map of the Mission of Santa Rosa

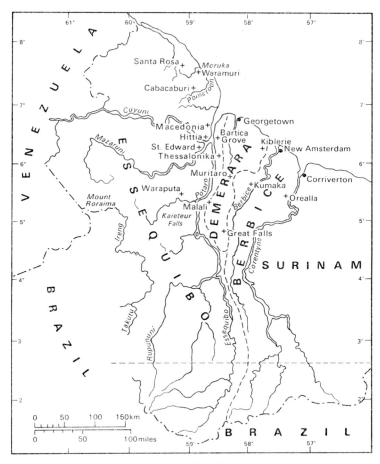

Map showing the Principal Mission Stations 1817–73

APPENDICES

CONTENTS

		Page
I.	Amerindian Population	271
II.	Hilhouse's Proposed Expenditure for an Indian Military Establishment compared with Present Expenditure	275
III.	Returns of Indian Population, Essequibo and Demerara, 1830	276
IV.	Quarterly Return for Indian Post, Three Friends, Mahaicony, from July 1st 1831 to September 30th 1831	277
V.	Instructions by which the Postholder of Canje shall Regulate Himself, 18th July, 1756	278
VI.	Postholders' Instructions, 14th May, 1803	279
VII.	Duties of the Postholders, 1824 and 1826	282
VIII.	Instructions to the Postholders of the Indians in Demerary and Essequibo	283
IX.	Instructions for the Protectors of Indians	284
X.	Commission Form for Indian Captains	286
XI.	Employment of Indians on Plantations, 1842, and Return of Indians working on Plantations in District H	287
XII.	Grant of Land to Roman Catholic Mission, July 20, 1840	289
XIII.	Mission Statistics for Pomeroon and Waramuri, 1845	290
XIV.	List of Secretaries of State, etc.	292

269

APPENDIX I

AMERINDIAN POPULATION

DURING the pre-Emancipation decades of the nineteenth century the local government of British Guiana were concerned with the numerical strength of the aboriginal population only in so far as they needed an estimated number of all able-bodied men, willing to assist in the bush expeditions against the runaway Negroes. For this service, as was noted in Chapter II, presents were distributed to the loyal natives. When this gift-giving increased expenditure, the government required the Protectors and postholders to assess as accurately as possible the numbers of Indians in order to calculate the equivalent cost of presents. The number of men who served in bush expeditions was specially noted in the returns.[1] In 1821 the numbers of Indians in Demerara and Essequibo were estimated at 5,502;[2] in 1830 at 5,096.[3]

Not until 1831 was Berbice united with the other colonies, Demerara and Essequibo, to form one united British Guiana, hence the Berbice returns were sent in separately. In 1825 the Commandant of Indians, J. V. Mittelholzer, transmitted returns of his area, the Berbice river, estimating the number of Indians there to be 709.[4]

After emancipation, when the Indians were no longer required to police the forests for runaway slaves, the distribution of presents ceased, and the Indians began to retreat further into the interior. It became even more impossible to gauge the numbers of the scattered Indians. However, in the 1840s and 1850s, W. C. F. McClintock, Superintendent of Rivers and Creeks in the Pomeroon district, encouraged the utilization of Indian labour on the estates on the Arabian or Essequibo coast. Thus the need for some knowledge of the Indian population in that area arose. It was McClintock himself who suggested the taking of a census, while others felt that on account of their 'erratick habits' a census would most likely

---

[1] Lists of Indian Chiefs in the various districts with the number of Men, capable of bearing Arms, their Women and Children, specifying their Nation, general place of Residence, and distance from the Post. N.A.G.

[2] Return of Indian Presents and Number of Indians at each District, 20 Mar. 1821. N.A.G.

[3] C.O. 111/117. Average total of the Indian Population in Demerary and Essequibo, 1830, enclosed in D'Urban to Goderich, 26 Nov. 1831.

[4] J. V. Mittelholzer to the Honourable Council of Government, Berbice, 29 July 1825, N.A.G.

prove an impossible undertaking. In 1848 Governor Light reported to the Colonial Office that the Indian population had dropped from 15,000 in the early decades of the century to 5,000. He blamed this considerable decrease on the vices, particularly the drinking of rum, and the diseases brought among the Indians by civilized man.[1] McClintock was more sanguine than Governor Light regarding the Indian population. An official notice read:

The aboriginal inhabitants were estimated in 1851 at about 7,000; but the best authority in the Colony, Mr. McClintock, Superintendent of Rivers and Creeks, Pomeroon District, carries the number now as high as 20,000 or 21,000. He is of the opinion, that the return of 1851 was greatly underestimated, and that the disturbances in Venezuela have caused large accessions to the numbers of the tribes within the British territories.[2]

But even though McClintock was 'the best authority' on the subject, he could not have possibly given a definitive number of Amerindians who roamed the forests, rivers, and creeks, over an area of approximately 70,000 square miles. When, later in the century, Everard im Thurn suggested that '20,000 [was] probably, slightly but not much below the real number',[3] and Charles Barrington Brown of the Geological Survey pushed the number to 50,000, they were nothing more than educated guesses.[4]

Since 1831 a decennial census was taken in British Guiana, but not until 1881 were the Amerindians officially included in the census, and then only an estimated number was recorded. The 1861 and 1871 censuses estimate the number of Amerindians at about 7,000.[5] It seemed very unlikely that the Superintendents, sometimes given the census regulations at short notice, would have been able to muster the Indians on one particular day at their settlements so widely scattered along the rivers and creeks. It was even more incredible that the Indians would consent to take part in a census which produced 'no commensurate results' for them, as it had done in the past. The 1871 census assumed that the Indian population had not decreased during the past ten years.[6] The 1881 census was grossly inaccurate.[7] In 1891 the census included the Amerindians on the estates, farms, and villages, as well as those on the settlements along

[1] C.O. 111/253. Light's Memorandum, 9 Oct. 1848.
[2] P.R.O. *The Colonial List for 1873* (London, 1875), p. 21.
[3] im Thurn, p. 157.   [4] Veness, p. 9.
[5] Results of the Census of the Population of the Colony of British Guiana as taken on 3 Apr. 1871. N.A.G.
[6] Ibid.
[7] Results of the Decennial Census of the Population of British Guiana taken on 3 Apr. 1881. N.A.G. The total number of aboriginals in the preface reads 7,656 and in no way corresponds to the 7,708 in the section on Aboriginal Indians.

the rivers and creeks. Of the total of 7,463, the number of 134 in George-town was explained by the fact that at the time the census was taken a large group of aborigines was 'visiting the city to sell wares and curiosities'. The percentage of the aboriginal population was given at 2·681 per cent of the total population of the country, 278,328.[1]

In the 1880s the missionaries had reported deaths, particularly among the Arawaks, resulting from the failure of the cassava crops, partly due to a severe drought, and partly due to the ants which were always very destructive during the dry season. Not only had the numbers of the Arawaks been reduced through death, but they had removed to other places. Previously the periodic epidemics of smallpox in 1841 and 1854, the cholera in 1857, and the constantly recurrent measles caused a fluctuation in the numbers obtained. Many of the stricken Indians went into the unaccessible parts of the forest to die. The missionaries blamed 'the fiery rum' for lowering the resistance of the Indians to disease, while others blamed the good missionaries for insisting that the Indian wear clothes.[2] As Rodway pointed out, 'in a climate like Guiana, where sudden showers fall almost without warning, the naked man will always be less liable to chills and fever' and 'after all, health is more important than conventionality'.[3]

The migratory habits of the Indians, the constant epidemics, and the results of rum on their health all militated against an accurate assessment of the Indian population. But to the local government the real reason was always the monetary one. The taking of the census attempted in the last decade of the nineteenth century proved too difficult, but above all, too expensive an undertaking and one 'productive of results of little economic value'.[4] Thus at the beginning of the twentieth century (no census was taken in 1901), careful estimates of the Amerindian population were com-piled from previous returns.

Would the Amerindians become extinct? Any intimation of such a possibility was to im Thurn, 'as a red rag to a bull'.[5] He insisted that: 'despite the general opinion, these people need not die out, and should not be allowed to die out, and that if they are dying out, it is not because no efforts have been made on their behalf, but because wrong efforts have been made.'[6] With the initiation of various health schemes the Indian did not die out. On the contrary, the Amerindian population rose to 30,000 in

[1] Results of the Decennial Census of the Population of British Guiana, 1891. N.A.G.
[2] Swan, p. 165. See also Rodway, *Guiana: British, Dutch, and French* (London, 1912), pp. 184–5 and 224.
[3] Rodway, p. 185.
[4] Results of the Census of the Population of British Guiana, 1931. 'Estimate Abori-ginal Indians.' N.A.G.
[5] im Thurn, 'Measles and a Moral', *The West Indian Quarterly* (1887–8), p. 267.
[6] Ibid.

1965. According to the Knapp Report of 25 February 1965, the figures were as follows:

	Amerindians
1. In the coastal area where 90% of the population lives	6,500
2. In the North West including the Moruka Indian reservation	12,000
3. In the Rupununi—the largest district	10,000
4. In the Upper Mazaruni	2,500
	31,000[1]

In the last census taken on 7 April 1970, in the total population of 740,196, the Amerindians numbered 32,794.[2] The Amerindian in Guyana is still very much around.

[1] S. C. Knapp. *Report of the Amerindians of British Guiana and Suggested Development Programmes* (Georgetown, 25 Feb. 1965). Known as the Knapp Report.

[2] *The West Indies and Caribbean Year Book*, 1974, p. 193.

HILHOUSE'S PROPOSED EXPENDITURE FOR AN INDIAN MILITARY ESTABLISHMENT COMPARED WITH PRESENT EXPENDITURE

Present Expenditure (1828)

Allowances and Rations to Indians	f18,722
6 Postholders @ f2,200 each	f13,200
3 Assistants @ f1,100 each	f3,300
⅓ of Triennial Presents	f12,000
Total Annual disbursement =	f47,222 or £3,500 sterling

Proposed Expenditure

Commandant	f3,300
Schoolmaster	f2,200
2 Lieutenants—schoolmasters	f4,400
150 Men (half on duty) at f1 per diem	f27,375
6 non-commissioned officers or Indian captains at f2	f4,280
Total Annual disbursement =	f41,555 or £3,000 sterling

(C.O. 111/68. William Hilhouse to Sir George Murray, Colonial Secretary of State, 23 Apr. 1829.)

APPENDIX III

RETURNS OF INDIAN POPULATION ESSEQUIBO AND DEMERARA, 1830

Demerary,
November 24th, 1831

Sir,

In obedience to Your Excellency's Commands I have the honour to submit the following Report on the Indian Population of Demerary and Essequibo, shewing the average strength of the respective Posts or Districts, and enclosing also for Your Excellency's further Information Documents explanatory of the System under which the Indian Establishments of the Colony is conducted:

	POSTS	Men	Women	Children	Total
Essequibo	Essequibo River	490	440	520	1450
	Pomeroon do.	750	650	900	2300
	Demerary do.	290	210	340	840
Demerary	Mahaicony Creek	105	95	135	336*
	Mahaica do.	28	20	36	84
	Borasirie do.	28	20	36	84
		1691	1435	1967	5096*

The above Number of 5096 was the average Total of the Indian Population composed of the four Nations or Tribes viz. Caribs, Arrowaks, Warrows, and Accoways at the last distribution of Triennial Presents in 1830 . . .

I have the Honor to be
Sir
Your Excellency's Most Obedient
and most Humble Servant
James Hackett
Civil Commissary

His Excellency
Major General Sir Benjamin D'Urban
K.C.B. . . .
Governor of British Guiana

* The total of 336 is an error in addition and should read 335. The final total of 5096 is also in error and does not correspond with the horizontal addition of the final totals. It should read = 5093 and *not* 5096. [M.N.M.]

(C.O. 111/117. Enclosed in D'Urban to Goderich, 26 Nov. 1831.)

QUARTERLY RETURN FOR INDIAN POST, THREE FRIENDS, MAHAICONY FROM JULY 1ST 1831 TO SEPTEMBER 30TH 1831

Observations

JULY	Served out to the Indians Plantains, fish, Sugar, Molasses & Rum. Much Thunder & heavy rains at the Post . . .
AUGUST	Served out to the Indians Plantains, fish, Sugar, Molasses & Rum. The Water in the bush has again increased. The Indians about the Post & its vicinities much annoyed with fever.
SEPTEMBER	Served out to the Indians, Plantains, fish, Sugar, Molasses, Salt, Rum and Flints. The Water has fallen in the bush considerably . . .

(C.O. 111/117. Enclosed in D'Urban to Viscount Goderich, 26 Nov. 1831.)

INSTRUCTIONS BY WHICH THE POSTHOLDER OF CANJE SHALL REGULATE HIMSELF

18th July, 1756

Article 1. He shall not oppress nor molest the Indians but rather encourage them in a friendly manner to serve the Colony . . .

Article 2. He shall employ Indians to plant . . . and to make canoes and corials for the Service of the Fort.

Article 3. He shall prevent Indians from selling or bartering to free persons any crafts or fowls.

Article 4. —forbids free persons from selling or bartering guns, other firearms, powder and shot to the Indians.

Article 5. —close surveillance of the River Canje to ascertain that no one fells timber on colonial lands or fishes in creeks.

Article 6. —persuade Indians to send 2 men every 5 months with parties releasing sentries.

Article 7. Indians must be at Fort Nassau two days before the Reliefs.

Article 8. —take particular notice of what concerned Canje fishery. Time for fishing to be fixed; Indians to help 'stop' off Creeks.

Article 9. The Postholders to receive a remuneration for every Canoe—five guilders and for a Corial—two Guilders and ten stivers.

(Translated from the Dutch by D. Haufman)

(C.O. 111/111. Fort Nassau, 17 July 1756. ff. 123–5. Dutch copy—ff. 274–6.)

APPENDIX VI

POSTHOLDERS' INSTRUCTIONS

As Enacted by the Honourable Court of Policy on the 14th of May 1803

Article 1

The Post Holder shall keep an Accurate Journal of his proceedings; and of all the occurrences at the Post.

Article 2

He shall transmit (quarterly) a copy of his Journal to the protector of his district.

Article 3

In case of any extraordinary occurrence; at or near the Post, he shall immediately acquaint therewith the Protector.

Article 4

He shall take care to keep the Post in good order; and he shall use his utmost exertions to attach to the Post, the Indians who call upon him, or who live in his vicinity.

Article 5

He shall endeavour on all occasions to prevent misunderstandings or quarrels between the several Indian Tribes; and where any such exist, he shall exert himself to restore peace.

Article 6

When required by the Protector, he shall be obliged to repair to him without loss of time, and to execute promptly any orders he may receive from the Protector.

Article 7

He shall not permit any Persons, whether Whites, free coloured, or Negroes, to pass the Post unless they show him a pass, from the Governor, or from one of the Protectors of the Indians; the latter being empowered to grant such passes, which must always specify the reason why the Persons therein named are to go beyond the Post.

Article 8

If any Person not provided with such a Pass should attempt to pass the Post—the Post Holder should be authorised, and is even obliged to detain such person or persons, and bring them to town before the Governor: at the same time giving notice to the Protectors.

Article 9

But to persons having a proper Pass he shall give every assistance in his power towards forwarding the business they are upon.

Article 10

He shall not be allowed to carry on any traffic, nor shall he compel the Indians to sell to him the Articles they bring down, but he shall suffer them to proceed without any molestation whatever in their Trade.—Any Articles bought from them he will cause to be duly paid for.

Article 11

He is on no account to compel the Indians to do any job, or work of whatever nature for him.

Article 12

He shall not take nor appropriate to himself the property of the Indians, much less their Wives or Children, on pretence of their being indebted to him, even in case of an Indian having had goods from him on credit and refusing to pay for the same.—The loss arising therefrom to be for the Post Holder.

Article 13

Should any Indian apply to him with complaints of ill treatment against other persons, he shall repair with such Indian to the protector, who will then examine and enquire into the complaint and give redress if the case requires it.—All exclusive of the Action which the Fiscal might think proper to bring against the offender, or offenders.

Article 14

Any White or free Coloured person about the Post, who might be desirous to have an Indian woman to live with them, shall acquaint therewith the Post Holder, who is then to wait on the protector with such Woman, and her parents or nearest relations in order that the protector may be enabled to enquire and ascertain whether such cohabitation takes place with the free consent of the parties, and whether the Woman be not engaged to some Indian—and the protector is then either to sanction or refuse such cohabitation as he may think right.

Article 15

Should the Post Holder be desirous of employing any Indians for clearing wood, or for fishing, or paddling his Boat, he shall be at liberty to hire them for that purpose, with the consent of the Protector, who shall previously enquire whether such engagement has been entered into voluntarily and who will at the same time inform the Indians that if they are not fully paid as agreed upon, they may complain to him.

Article 16

He shall be present at the Annual distribution of presents to the Indians.

Article 17

He shall apply from time to time to the Protector for the rum he may want for the purpose of giving a dram to the Indians who call upon him.

Article 18

In case of any Indians passing the Post to go down the River, the Post Holder shall recommend to them to wait on the Protector.

(C.O. 111/60. Instructions of Post Holders forwarded in D'Urban to Wilmot Horton, 16 May 1827.)

APPENDIX VII

DUTIES OF THE POSTHOLDERS, 1824

'The duties of the Indian Postholders, (and their assistants) consists [*sic*] in superintending and keeping order amongst the different tribes within their respective districts . . . To receive and distribute Provisions, Presents, etc. and to report all Extraordinaries (through their Protectors) to the Lieutenant Governor.'

(C.O. 116/193. Blue Books.)

DUTIES OF THE POSTHOLDERS, 1826

'The Duties of the Postholders are to keep the Posts in good order—to use every exertion to attach the Indians who may visit them (or who may live in their vicinity) To the Several Posts—to endeavour on all occasions to prevent misunderstandings and quarrels between the several Indian Tribes, and to preserve peace and good order among them—to prevent persons, whether Whites, free colored, or slaves from passing the different posts without a pass from the Lieutenant Governor or one of the Protectors of Indians—to give in quarterly Returns of their Proceedings (through their respective Protectors) and are restricted from trafficing with the Indians.'

(C.O. 116/194. Blue Books.)

APPENDIX VIII

INSTRUCTIONS TO THE POSTHOLDERS OF THE INDIANS IN DEMERARY AND ESSEQUIBO

Demerary
September 15th 1813

CIRCULAR

Sir,

I have the honor to request that you will by the first opportunity transmit to me for the information of His Majesty's Ministers, answers to the following questions, and the Return sent herewith is to be transmitted henceforward every three Months, beginning with the first of next October.

Question 1. How far do the Indians under you contribute to their own support by cultivating the Ground, raising Stock, hunting or fishing?

Question 2. What kind of Rations or Allowances are given to the Indians at your Post, and what expences may the establishment of your Post, annually cost the Government?

Question 3. What employments are the Indians under you generally engaged in, and could not their labour in some manner be directed to objects useful to themselves and the Country, so as to lessen the annual expence of supporting them?

Question 4. What is your opinion of the practicability of inducing the Indians to raise Cattle, Goats, Pigs, Stock, etc. for their own benefit, or could they learn any useful Trade?

Question 5. By what means in your opinion could the Indians be made more useful to the Colony, without being so great an expence as at present?

I have the honor to be
Sir
your most obedient
humble servant
signed Edward Codd
Acting Governor

To
Mr ——
Postholder
(*Letter Book*, p. 30. N.A.G.)

INSTRUCTIONS FOR THE PROTECTORS
OF INDIANS

1. The Protectors of Indians will to the utmost of their power give effect to, and enforce among their respective PostHolders a strict and diligent observance of the Instructions originally issued on the 18th of May 1803, and subsequently reprinted and issued afresh by authority on the 2nd May 1815.—And in case of any Post Holder abusing his trust, or being negligent or remiss in the Discharge of his Duties as prescribed by the above Instructions, the Protector of the District will make a special and immediate report to the Lieut. Governor (or Comd. in Chief for the time being) in order that if necessary the said Post Holder may be removed from his Office, and replaced by another person.

2. —When the Protectors shall have received from their respective Post Holders, the regulated Quarterly Journals and shall have affixed to them their signatures of approval, they will, on the 1st day of January—April—July—and October of each year transmit the same to the Lieut. Governor (or Comd. in Chief for the time being) together with the Post Holders Requisitions, also bearing their (the Protectors) Signatures of approval for the order of supplies wanted for the ensuing Quarter stating the quantity of each article, as well as for any extraordinary assistance which may require the sanction of the Executive or of the Court of Policy.

3. —The Protectors will accompany the Quarterly Returns by a confidential Report to the Lt. Governor (or Comd. in Chief for the time being) stating, as nearly as can be ascertained the numbers of Indians in their respective Districts, their Tribes, Captains, Increase or Decrease since last Return, and the probable cause of either,—their general Health and condition—Disposition, whether apparently satisfied or dissatisfied with us, and if the latter what is the probable cause.

The Age, capacity, and conduct of their Post Holders, whether they have fulfilled their Duties in strict conformity to the Instructions already cited, and whether they are liked and well thought of by the Indians of the respective Posts.

In every July Report the Protectors will mention such Indians, Captains, or others as from any particular instance of good conduct or ability they may think deserving of any special mark of distinction or favour in the ensuing distribution of Presents.

To these distinct heads of report they will be so good as to add any remarks or suggestions which they may think expedient for the Lt. Governor's information and consideration.

Memorandum

Each Protector is requested to prepare and transmit for the immediate information of the Lt. Governor, such a Report as is prescribed by the 3rd Head of these Instructions, as soon as possible after he shall have received them.

Signed   B. D'Urban

(C.O. 111/60. Enclosed in Governor B. D'Urban to Wilmot Horton, 16 May 1827.)

APPENDIX X

COMMISSION FORM FOR INDIAN CAPTAINS

By His Excellency, William Walker . . .

'To Damon—Chief of the Warrow Indians in the District of Pomeroon and Haimuracabara Creek—.

In pursuance of the practice hitherto observed of conferring on the Chiefs of the different Indian Tribes residing within the boundary of British Guiana the office of Captain and Constable, and in consequence of the recommendation in your favour of the Superintendent of Rivers and Creeks in the Pomeroon District I do hereby constitute and appoint you Damon—to the office of Captain and Constable for the Warrow Indians in the Haimuracabura Creek directing and enjoining you to perform the duties of the said Office in the manner most conducive to the welfare and well-being of the Indians thus placed under your protection.'

Given under my Hand . . .

(Wolseley, Government Secretary to McClintock, 18 September 1848. Letter Book. N.A.G.)

APPENDIX XI

EMPLOYMENT OF INDIANS ON PLANTATIONS, 1842

Copy

Sheriff's Office—Essequibo
22nd June 1842

Sir

I have the honor to forward a Return of the Indians at present working on the Estates in District H. I have great satisfaction in stating for the information of His Excellency the Governor that I am informed they are performing their work most satisfactorily. The wages given are the same as to the other labourers and the work equally well done especially that of cutting canes.

I have the honor to be
Sir
Your most obedient humble Servant
signed M. L. Fowler

The Honorable H. E. F. Young
Government Secretary

P.S. I cannot learn that there are any Indians similarly employed in any other part of the County although I have made every enquiry.

M. L. Fowler

(C.O. 111/191. M. L. Fowler, Stipendiary Magistrate to H. E. F. Young, Government Secretary, 22 June 1842.)

Return of Indians working on Plantations in District H—County of Essequibo—this 22nd June 1842

Location	Total Number			At Work			Mortality in the last Month			General State of their Health	Remarks as to Wages, Lodgings, &c.
	Men	Women	Children	Men	Women	Children	Men	Women	Children		
Anna Regina	15	—	—	15	—	—	—	—	—	Good	Provided with houses, Medical attendance and land to cultivate; have been employed 13 months in the general work of the Estate at the same rate of wages as the other people.
Coffee Grove	12	—	—	12	—	—	—	—	—	do.	do. do.
Sparta	10	5	12	10	5	12	—	—	—	do.	Have been at work six weeks. Cutting Canes at One Guilder per Cord; cutting down bush and taking in abandonned [sic] Cane Fields at Seventy Seven Guilders for 5 Acres; receive 8 Pints of Rice; ,, 3 lbs of salt ,, fish ,, Molasses ,, 2 bunches of Plantains when there is no Rice.
Hampton Court	6	—	—	6	—	—	—	—	—	do.	Doing general work at the usual Wages.

288

Signed M. L. Fowler S.M.   A true Copy W. B. Wolseley
Assist. Govt. Sec. B. Guiana

GRANT OF LAND TO ROMAN CATHOLIC MISSION, JULY 20, 1840

By his Excellency Henry Light, Esquire, Governor and Commander-in-chief in and over the colony of British Guiana, Vice-Admiral, and Ordinary of the Same, etc. etc.

Whereas an application has been presented to me by the Right Rev. William Clancy, Bishop of Oriense and Vicar Apostolic of British Guiana, praying for a grant of a tract of land situate, lying and being, on the left bank of the Morocco Creek, on the west coast of the county of Essequibo, commencing at the upper boundary of the Settlement of the Indian Captain Punsha, and extending upwards or westwards there from 32 roods in facade, and northwards 50 roods in depth, and containing 7 Acres, the said tract having been the site of an Indian Settlement known by the name of Mariaba, as described in the chart of diagram of the same made by the Sworn Land Surveyor, William Hilhouse, dated April 1840, hereunto annexed; and whereas the sum of 7l has been paid into the hands of the Receiver General of this Colony, as *consideration Money* being at the rate of 1l. per acre, for and in behalf of Her Majesty's Treasury of this Colony, as consideration money or quit rent for the Said land.

Now I therefore, in the name and on behalf of Her Most Gracious Majesty, do hereby grant unto the said Right Rev. William Clancy, as aforesaid, and his successors in office, for the use of the Roman Catholic Church in Guiana, this my licence and permission to occupy, cultivate, and improve the herein before described tract of land, with all its appurtenances, during Her Majesty's pleasure, Subject to the following condition and restriction, viz:

That the said tract of land shall be subject to the Laws of Regulations respecting Roads and Bridges now in force in the Colony, or yet to be enacted.

And that the occupant of the said land, or any of them, or any person or persons employed by them, shall not use any violence or outrage upon the persons, or commit any depredations on the property of the Indians.

Given under my hand and seal of office at the Guiana Public Buildings, this 20th day of July, 1840, and in the fourth year of Her Majesty's reign.

Registered July 20, 1840
(Signed)
J. Hadfield. C.S.

(Jesuit Diocesan Archives, Georgetown, Guyana.)

MISSION STATISTICS FOR POMEROON AND WARAMURI, 1845

DIOCESE OF GUIANA

Station	Clergyman	Mission Established	Present Clergyman Estab.	Parsonage	Gross Population	Number of Congregation	Number of Comm.	Chief Occupations & Means of Support of Inhabitants whether settled or migratory	If increasing in population, wealth & General industry	Nearest Market town
Pomeroon, Essequibo	Brett, W. H.	1840	1840	yes	1,000	300	90	Cultivation of cassava root and hunting and fishing; they migrate frequently to the Plantations on the coast for labour	Yes, with Christianity industry is increasing	Georgetown—80 miles distant
Warramurie, Essequibo	Nowers, J. H.	1845	1845	yes	1,000	300	—	„	„	Georgetown—120 miles distant

Station	No. of Churches in Mission and Services at each	By what means?	If the duty of supporting clergyman is urged	Amount contributed by Congregation for support of clergy	Contributions within mission for General Church Purposes	Temporal discouragements of Clergyman	Schools				Means by which schools were erected	Maintenance of the Masters or Mistresses
							Sunday	Attendance at	Daily	Attendance at		
Pomeroon, Essequibo	1 chapel } 2 services weekly; 1 Logie (tent) } at each	by late Rev. J. H. Duke	Yes	Indians are too poor to contribute much at present	The Offertory is established and has brought in during last 3 years $450	None, but ill-health at present	2	60	2	60	1 with land purchased by S.P.G. The other is lent	One Master is an Indian paid $100 by the Dem. & Essq. District of the S.P.G.; the other is paid $416 by the Colony. Education is offered gratuitously
Warramurie, Essequibo	A thatched Church is in course of erection—a regular and catechetical service. Church & residence built by District S.P.G. Indians cheerfully contributing their labour		Yes	„	—	Ill-health for some time past	1	50	1	50	no house	The clergyman teaches gratuitously

(B.G. I, 1834–1858. U.S.P.G.A.)

APPENDIX XIV

SECRETARIES OF STATE FOR THE COLONIAL AND WAR DEPARTMENTS, FROM 1804 TO 1854

1804   Earl, late Marquess Camden
1805   Viscount Castlereagh, late Marquess of Londonderry
1806   Rt. Hon. W. Windham
1807   Viscount Castlereagh
1809   Earl of Liverpool
1812   Earl Bathurst
1827   Viscount Goderich/Rt. Hon. W. Huskisson
1828   Sir George Murray
1830   Viscount Goderich, late Earl of Ripon
1833   Rt. Hon. E. G. Stanley, Earl of Derby
1834   Rt. Hon. Thomas Spring Rice, late Lord Monteagle Earl of Aberdeen
1835   Rt. Hon. Charles Grant, later Lord Glenelg
1839   Marquess of Normanby
       Lord John Russell, now Earl Russell
1841   Lord Stanley, Earl of Derby
1845   Rt. Hon. W. Ewart Gladstone
1846   Earl Grey
1852   Rt. Hon. Sir John S. Pakington, Bart.
       Duke of Newcastle

SECRETARIES OF STATE FOR THE COLONIES, 1854–1873

1854, 10th June	Rt. Hon. Sir G. Grey
1855, February	Rt. Hon. Sidney Herbert, afterwards Lord Herbert of Lea
1855, 15th May	Earl John Russell, G.C.M.G.
21st July	Rt. Hon. Sir W. Molesworth, Bart.
17th November	Rt. Hon. Henry Labouchere, afterwards Lord Taunton
1858, 26th February	Lord Stanley, now Earl of Derby
31st May	Rt. Hon. Sir Edward Bulwer Lytton, Bart., now Lord Lytton, G.C.M.G.
1859, 18th June	Duke of Newcastle

1864, 4th April	Rt. Hon. Edward Cardwell
1866, 6th July	Earl of Carnarvon
1867, 8th March	The Duke of Buckingham and Chandos
1868, 10th December	Earl Granville
1870, 6th July	Earl of Kimberley

UNDER-SECRETARIES OF STATE FOR THE COLONIES

1833	John Shaw Lefevre
1835, April	Sir John Grey, Bart.
	James Stephen (Permanent)
1839, February	Rt. Hon. Henry Labouchere
August	Rt. Hon. Robert Vernon Smith
1841, September	George W. Hope
1845, January	Lord Lyttleton, K.C.M.G.
1846, July	Benjamin Hawes
1847, November	Herman Merivale (Permanent Secretary in place of Sir James Stephen)
1849, May	Sir T. F. Elliot, K.C.M.G. (Asst. Under-Secretary)
1851, November	Rt. Hon. Sir Frederick Peel, K.C.M.G.
1852, February	Earl Desart
December	Rt. Hon. Sir F. Peel
1855, April	John Ball
1857, May	Rt. Hon. Chichester S. Fortescue, M.P.
1858, February	Earl of Carnarvon
1859, June	Rt. Hon. Chichester S. Fortescue, M.P.
1860, May	Sir F. Rogers, Bart. K.C.M.G. (Permanent in place of H. Merivale, Esq.)
1865, November	Rt. Hon. W. E. Forster, M.P.
1866, July	Rt. Hon. Sir C. B. Adderley, K.C.M.G., M.P.
1868, December	Sir F. R. Sandford (Assistant in place of Sir F. T. Elliot)
	Rt. Hon. W. Monsell, M.P.
1870, February	R. G. W. Herbert (in place of Sir F. Sandford)
31st March	H. T. Holland
1871, 14th January	E. H. Knatchbull-Hugessen, M.P.
21st May	R. G. W. Herbert (in place of Lord Blachford)

(*The Colonial Office List for 1873* (London, 1873), pp. 8–9.)

LIEUTENANT-GOVERNORS OF ESSEQUIBO AND DEMERARA UNDER THE BRITISH

| 1803, October | Lieutenant Colonel Robert Nicholson |
| 1804, August | Dr. Antony Beaujon |

1805, October	Brigadier-General James Montgomery
1807, September	Lieutenant-Colonel Robert Nicholson
1808, June	Lieutenant-Colonel Rose
1809, April	Henry William Bentinck
1812, September	Major-General Hugh Lyle Carmichael
1813, May	Brigadier-General John Murray
1824, April	Major-General Sir Benjamin D'Urban

LIEUTENANT-GOVERNORS OF BERBICE

1804, June	Abraham J. V. T. Van Batenburg
1806, December	Lieutenant-Colonel Robert Nicholson
1807, September	Major-General James Montgomery
1809, March	William Woodley
1810, January	Major-General Samuel Dalrymple
1810, December	Robert Gordon
1812, June	Major-General John Murray
1813, February	Robert Gordon
1814, June	Henry William Bentinck
1820, November	Major Thistlewayte
1821, January	Lieutenant-Colonel Sir John Cameron
1821, March	Henry Beard
1825, March	Major-General Sir Benjamin D'Urban
1826, July	Henry Beard

GOVERNORS OF BRITISH GUIANA, 1831–1873

1831, July	Major-General Sir Benjamin D'Urban
1833, May 7	Lieutenant-Colonel C. Chalmers
1833, May 17	Colonel Sir C. F. Smith
1833, May 26	Major-General Sir James Carmichael Smyth
1835, May	Sir Lionel Smith
1835, June	Sir James Carmichael Smyth
1838, March	Major W. U. Orange
1838, May	Colonel Thomas Bunbury
1838, June	Sir Henry Light
1848, May	William Walker
1849, February	Sir Henry Barkly
1853, May	William Walker
1854, March	Philip E. Wodehouse
1857, July	William Walker
1858, May	Philip E. Wodehouse
1861, May	William Walker
1862, January	Sir Francis Hincks

1866, May	Major Robert M. Mundy
1869, January	John Scott
1873, June	Edward Everard Rushworth

LIST OF PROTECTORS AND POSTHOLDERS OF THE INDIANS

1825

Protectors of Indians	Posts	Postholders
J. C. Brandes	Demerara River	W. Bremner
D. S. van's Gravesande	Mahaica Creek	D. S. van's Gravesande
R. Watson	Mahaicony and Abary Creeks	M. Mauville
John Newton	Boeraserie Creek	J. Spencer
George Bagot	Essequibo River	H. C. Wahl
G. Timmerman	Pomeroon River	A. F. Stoll

(*The Demerara Vade-Mecum containing Laws and Regulations of the United Colony* (Georgetown, 1825).)

1833

Protectors of Indians	Posts	Postholders	Assistant Postholders
J. D. Patterson	Demerara	John Spencer	D. Simon
(vacant)	Boeraserie	J. Mottet	—
George Bagot	Essequibo	T. Richardson	W. Playter
J. Croal (Actg)	Pomeroon	B. Tonge	W. Trotman
R. Watson	Mahaicony	J. H. Watson	—
D. S. V. Gravesande	Mahaica	J. D. S. V. Gravesande	—

(C.O. 116/202. *Blue Book*. District of Demerara and Essequibo, 1833.)

J. V. Mittleholzer	Berbice	J. V. Mittleholzer	—
(Capt. Commandant of Indians)			
	Corentyne	N. J. de Wolff	—
	Canje	H. E. Hockin	—

(C.O. 116/180. *Blue Book*. District of Berbice, 1833.)

1838

Superintendents of Rivers and Creeks	Posts	Date of Appointment
1. William Crichton	Essequibo	9th June 1838
2. Robert King	Demerara	9th June 1838
3. James Shanks	Berbice	9th June 1838

Postholders	Posts
1. James Spencer	Seba
2. L. A. Gravesande	Mahaica
3. J. H. Watson	Mahaicony
4. Dr. Gilbert	Pomeroon
5. D. Falant	Fort Island
6. J. C. Schmidt (died 7th January)	Boeraserie
D. J. C. Barkey	,,
7. G. Hawker	Berbice
8. N. J. De Wolff	Corentyne
9. W. C. F. McClintock	Canje
10. D. J. C. Barkey	Ampa

All Appointments made by the Governor. Salaries paid from the Colony Chest.

(C.O. 116/207. *Blue Book*. Colony of British Guiana, 1838.)

LIST OF POSTHOLDERS AND COMMISSARIES OF TAXATION UNDER THE NEW SYSTEM

1843   *Demerary*

Richard Hancock   Abary, Maiconi (Mahaicony) and Mahaica Creeks, and Parish of St. Mary as far as Mahaica Village.

Thomas Fennell   Demerary River from Sand Hills and Hyde Park and Creeks (displaced Superintendent).

Essequibo

A. F. Baird   From Fort Island upwards, both Banks.

W. C. F. McClintock Pomeroon and Creeks, and Settlement downwards.

Berbice

Robert King   Upper District of Berbice River and Upper District of Canje, from Plantation New Forest upwards, both banks.

N. de Wolff   Corentyne and Coast as far down as No. 68 Creek.

LIST OF POSTHOLDERS WHO HAVE LOST THEIR SITUATIONS SINCE THE NEW SYSTEM

R. Darley   unworthy
George Hawker   left the Colony in June, having been refused leave.
(C.O. 111/203. Enclosed in Light to Stanley, 15 November, 1843.)

SUPERINTENDENTS OF RIVERS AND CREEKS, ACTING ALSO AS COMMISSARIES OF TAXATION

1853

R. Hancock	Demerara River
R. King	Berbice River
A. F. Baird	Essequibo River
W. C. F. McClintock	Pomeroon River

(C.O. 116/222. *Blue Book*, 1853.)

1863

The Stipendiary Magistrate of the Upper Demerara District	Demerara River
E. Croker	Berbice River
F. E. Dampier	Essequibo River
W. C. F. McClintock	Pomeroon River

(C.O. 116/232. *Blue Book*, 1863.)

1873

Superintendents of Rivers and Creeks (a)

Stipendiary Magistrate of the Upper Demerara District	Demerara River
P. A. J. Grant	Essequibo River (b)
C. W. F. Hancock	Berbice River (c)
W. C. F. McClintock	Pomeroon River (b)

(a) On the 30th June, these Offices were abolished and Special Magistrates for the Essequibo and Pomeroon Rivers appointed.

(b) On abolition of Office, Mr. Grant and Mr. McClintock were appointed Special Magistrates.

(c) Mr. Hancock died on 19th January and Mr. Gallagher acted on the 30th June, when the Office was abolished.

(C.O. 116/242. *Blue Book*. British Guiana, 1873.)

BIBLIOGRAPHY

I. BIBLIOGRAPHIES AND GUIDES

ASPINALL, Sir Algernon. *Pocket Guide to the West Indies and British Guiana, et cetera.* 10th edn. revised by J. Sydney Dash. Methuen, London, 1954.

BAYITCH, S. A. *Latin America and the Caribbean. A Bibliographical Guide to the Works in English.* University of Miami Press, Florida, 1967.

BLACK, Clinton V. *Report on the Archives of British Guiana.* The Daily Chronicle, Georgetown, 1955.

BROWN, Ann Duncan. *British Possessions in the Caribbean Area.* Library of Congress, Washington, D.C., 1943.

COMITAS, Lambros. *Caribbeana, 1900–1965.* Ch. XIII. 'Population Segments: Amerindians.' University of Washington Press, Seattle, 1968.

CUNDALL, Frank. *Bibliography of the West Indies (excluding Jamaica).* Institute of Jamaica, Kingston, 1909: reprint edn. Johnson Reprint Corporation, New York, 1971.

FORD, P. and G. *A Guide to Parliamentary Papers—what they are, how to find them, how to use them.* New edn. Basil Blackwell, Oxford, 1956.

GIUSEPPI, M. S. *Guide to the Contents of the Public Record Office.* II. Revised to 1960. H.M.S.O., London, 1963.

GRIFFIN, Charles C. (ed.). *Latin America. A Guide to the Historical Literature.* University of Texas Press, Austin, 1971.

GROPP, Arthur E. *Guide to the Libraries and Archives in Central America and the West Indies, Panama, Bermuda, and British Guiana.* University of Louisiana, New Orleans, 1941.

Handbook of Latin American Studies. University of Florida Press, Gainesville, 1963–71.

HEWITT, A. R. *Guide to the Resources for Commonwealth Studies in London, Oxford, and Cambridge.* With bibliographical and other information. University of London. Institute of Commonwealth Studies, London, 1957.

HISS, Philip Hanson. *A Selective Guide to the English Literature on the Netherlands West Indies. With a Supplement on British Guiana.* Booklets of the Netherlands Information Bureau, New York, 1943.

HUMPHREYS, R. A. *Latin American History. A Guide to the Literature in English.* Oxford University Press, London, 1966.

Latin America and the Caribbean. Analytical Survey of Literature. U.S. Government Printing Office, Washington, D.C., 1969.

List of Colonial Office Confidential Print to 1916. P.R.O. Handbook No. 8. H.M.S.O., London, 1965.

O'LEARY, Timothy J. *Ethnographic Bibliography of South America.* Human Relations Area Files, New Haven, 1963.

PUGH, R. B. *The Records of the Colonial and Dominions Offices.* P.R.O. Handbook No. 3. H.M.S.O., London, 1964.

STEWARD, Julian H. (ed.). *Handbook of South American Indians.* III. Smithsonian Institution. Bureau of American Ethnology. U.S. Government Printing Office, Washington, D.C., 1948.

VÉLIZ, Claudio. *Latin America and the Caribbean: A Handbook.* Anthony Blond, London, 1968.

WALNE, Peter (ed.). *A Guide to Manuscript Sources for the History of Latin America and the Caribbean in the British Isles.* Oxford University Press, London, 1973.

West Indies and Caribbean Year Book, 1974, The. Thomas Skinner Directories, Croydon, 1974.

II. PRIMARY SOURCES

A. Manuscript

i. *Public Record Office*

Colonial Office Records

C.O. 111/1–401	*Original Correspondence.* British Guiana (1781–1873) Governors' Despatches to the Secretaries of State, Miscellaneous Letters, etc.
C.O. 112/1–42	Letters from the Secretaries of State to the Governors of British Guiana (1837–72).
C.O. 113/1–5	Acts (1837–73).
C.O. 114/1–26	Sessional Papers (1806–75).
C.O. 116/138–9	Fiscals' Reports (1819–23).
C.O. 116/170–89	*Berbice.* Blue Books (1821–42).
C.O. 116/190–242	*Demerara and Essequibo.* Blue Books (1821–73).
C.O. 502/1 Ind. 13064	Correspondence, Register of Out-Letters (1872–7).
C.O. 537/2–4 & 95	Supplementary, Original Correspondence. Despatches, Offices and Individuals (1759–1813) and (1872–96).
P.R.O. 30	Governor Carmichael Smyth's Papers:
35/18	Vol. 1 Despatch Book. Demerara (1833–5).
35/19	Vol. 2(a) „ „ „ (1835).
35/20	Vol. 3 „ „ „ (1836).

P.R.O. 474/195   Despatch of the Director of the Zeeland Chamber of the West India Company, 21 February, 1768.

ii. *National Archives, Guyana*

1. Letter Books of British Guiana (1803–80).
2. Minutes of the Combined Court (1803–80).
3. Minutes of the Court of Policy (1803–80).
4. Memoranda of the Governors of British Guiana.
5. Journals and Reports of the Postholders, Protectors of Indians, and Superintendents of Rivers and Creeks (1803–86).
6. Returns of the Indians and Lists of Presents (1803–30).
7. Schomburgk's Reports, 1838–44.
8. Miscellaneous Documents on Amerindians:
   a. 'Reconnaissance of the Post of Pomeroon, with adjacent Indian settlements in the Morocco Creek, and its vicinity,' by William Hilhouse, Quarter-Master General of the Indians, November, 1823.
   b. 'Narrative of Patrick Horan, as Agent of William Postlethwaite, to the Orinoco (Angostura) . . .' 17th July, 1832.
   c. Managers' Certificates, 1845.

iii. *Law Courts, Guyana*

Indictment Registers and Records of Sentences (1829–32).

iv. *University of Guyana Library, Guyana*

EHRENREICH, Dr. Paul. *The Myths and Legends of the South American Aborigines and their relation to those of North America and the Old World*. Berlin, 1905. MS. translated by W. E. Roth.

HARTSINCK, Jan Jacob. *The Discovery of Guiana and Description of the various European Possessions there*. Translated by W. E. Roth from *Beschrijving van Guiana*. 2 vols. Amsterdam, 1770.

—— '*The Story of the Slave Rebellion in Berbice 1762*. [!] Translated by W. E. Roth from *Beschrijving van Guiana*.

Journal of W. J. van Hooghenheim. Kept since the Revolution of the Negro slaves in Rio Berbice begun 28 February 1763. Transcribed and translated by Barbara L. Blair (Mrs. J. D. Bangs) and read in comparison with the original Dutch by Jeremy Dupertius Bangs, 1973.

v. *Missionary Societies*

Church Missionary Society Archives, London

01–   Committee Minutes
    (b) British Guiana Corresponding Committee:
       1–8. Minutes, 1835–7.
         9. Letter to Committee, 1839.
       10. Minute re Pirara mission, 1841.

02(c)	Bishop of Guiana:	
	1–6. Letters, 1823, 1844, 1852, 1855.	
04/3	Reports. British Guiana:	
	1–2. Bartica Grove: Reports of School, 1848, 1855.	
08(c)	1–5. British Guiana.	
010(c)	1 and 6. British Guiana.	
CW/014.	14–37.	Letters of the Revd. J. Armstrong.
CW/018.	11–48.	Letters of the Revd. J. H. Bernau.
CW/021.	1–3.	Letters of D. Butler.
CW/024.	1–9.	Letters of E. Christian.
CW/034.	1–3.	Letters of the Revd. J. Dayce, including his journal of an excursion to the Pomeroon, Moruka, and different creeks.
CW/049.	1–7.	Letters of the Revd. T. Hillis.
CW/055.	1–9.	Letters of the Revd. J. Lohrer.
CW/081.	39–40.	Letters of the Revd. L. Strong.
CW/100.	1–52.	Letters of the Revd. T. Youd.
	30–49.	Youd's Journal, 1833–41.
	51.	Specimen of Indian school boys' writing.
	52.	Macusi phrase book.

Jesuit Archives, Farm St., London

Letters of Jesuit Superiors in British Guiana to the Father Provincial in London, 1857–1901.
Bishop Etheridge's Diary, 1865.
Maps of the Santa Rosa and Hosororo Missions.
Mission Reports printed in *Letters and Notices*. See Printed Documents.

Jesuit Diocesan Archives, Guyana

Letters of William Hilhouse.
Grant of Land to the R.C. Mission of Santa Rosa by Governor H. Light, 20th July, 1840.
Fr. Cullen's Diary.
Notes on Santa Rosa Mission.

London Missionary Society Archives, London (at CCWM)

The Revd. John Wray's Journal and 'Fragments of History' (1811–15).
Committee Minutes. *West Indies*. Book 2: 3rd January, 1838–4th February, 1840.
British Guiana. *Berbice*. Box 1: 1813–24.
             Demerara. Box 2: 1815–22.
                  ,,   Box 4: 1830–5.
                  ,,   Box 5: 1835–8.
                  ,,   Box 6: 1839–45.

Santa Rosa Archives, Guyana

Missionary Statistics.

Journal of the Mission.

Early Account of the Santa Rosa Mission; its establishment from the arrival of the Spanish Arawaks in 1817.

United Society for the Propagation of the Gospel Archives, London.

British Guiana 1: 1834–8. Letters of the S.P.G. missionaries to the Secretary of the S.P.G.

Reports of W. H. Brett and other missionaries:

E8.   Missionary Reports, 1861.
E10.   ,,   ,,   1862.
E11.   ,,   ,,   1862, 1863.
E14.   ,,   ,,   1864.
D28.   Letters and Papers, 1860–7.

vi. *Other Libraries*

British Library.

Gladstone Papers. Additional MSS. 44738.
Sloane MSS. 3662. 'General Byam's Journal'.
Additional MSS. 34205. Schomburgk's Journal, 1843.
          ,,   ,,   37057. 'Account of British Guiana', by William Hilhouse (*c.* 1830–5) with 2 maps together with a journal of an expedition up the River Cuyuni, 1830.
          ,,   ,,   35444; 38364, 38377; 38379; 38380 & 38746.
          ,,   ,,   16936, *Drawings and Sketches*, by E. A. Goodall, 16939. illustrating the scenery of the interior of B.G., and manners of the native inhabitants, made on occasion of his accompanying, as draughtsman, the expedition of Sir R. Schomburgk to the sources of the Takutu, etc., in 1842, 1843. In four volumes. Large Folios.

Rhodes Library, Oxford

Anti-Slavery Papers:

Miss. *British Empire*. S18 G139/71. Letters from Government Officers.
          ,,   ,,   S22 G36.   Apprenticeship system.
          ,,   ,,   S22 G37.   British Guiana: 1836–50.
          ,,   ,,   S22 G38.   British Guiana: 1850–70.

Other

Holy See, Sacred Roman Congregation 'de Propaganda Fide', *Acta, 1835*. Vol. 198, p. 347 ff. 'Report of Fr. John Hynes, O.P. on the West Indies'.

B. Printed Documents

i. Collections of Documents

BELL, K. N. and MORRELL, W. P. (eds.) *Select Documents on British Colonial Policy, 1830–1860*. Clarendon Press, Oxford, 1928.

KEITH, A. B. *Selected Speeches and Documents on British Colonial Policy, 1763–1917*. (Oxford, 1961).

Spain. Laws and Statutes. *The New Laws for the Government of the Indies and the Preservation of the Indians, 1542–1543*. A Facsimile Reprint of the Original Spanish Edition together with a Literal Translation into the English Language to which is prefixed an Historical Introduction by the late Henry Stevens and Fred W. Lucas. Reprint of the Facsimile edition, London, 1893. Amsterdam, 1968.

The Laws of British Guiana. Waterlow & Sons Ltd., London, 1923 and 1954.

ii. Parliamentary Papers

Great Britain. British Guiana Boundary Arbitration with the United States of Venezuela:

The Case on Behalf of the Government of Her Britannic Majesty. London, 1898.

The Counter-Case on Behalf of the Government of Her Britannic Majesty. London, 1898.

The Argument on Behalf of the Government of Her Britannic Majesty. London, 1898.

Appendix to the Case on Behalf of the Government of Her Britannic Majesty. Vols. 1–6. London, 1898.

Atlas to accompany Case presented on the part of Her Britannic Majesty. London, 1898.

Documents and Correspondence Relating to the Question of Boundary between British Guiana and Venezuela. No. 1. London, 1896.

British and Foreign State Papers, 1899–1900. London, 1903.

British Guiana. Miscellaneous Papers, I, 1812–49.

British Guiana. Miscellaneous Papers, II, 1850–1.

Report from the Select Committee on Aborigines (British Settlements) with the Minutes of Evidence, Appendix, and Index, 1837. Vols. I & II.

Venezuela. Venezuela–British Guiana Boundary Arbitration:

The Case on Behalf of the United States of Venezuela before the Tribunal of Arbitration. New York, 1898.

The Printed Argument on Behalf of the United States of Venezuela before the Tribunal of Arbitration. 2 vols. New York, 1898.

The Guyana Boundary Dispute. *Official Report of the Condition of Affairs in the Disputed Territory.* Mar. 1890.

Further Documents relating to the Question of Boundary between British Guiana and Venezuela. Nos. 4 & 5. London, 1896.

Great Britain. *West India Royal Commission, 1938–39.* Statement of Action taken on the Recommendations, June 1945. H.M.S.O., London, 1945.

Great Britain. *West India Royal Commission Report.* H.M.S.O., London, 1945.

iii. Almanacs and Newspapers

British Guiana. *Almanack and Local Guide of British Guiana containing the Laws, Ordinances and Regulations of the Colony, the Civil and Military Lists with a List of Estates from Corentyne to Pomeroon Rivers:* Demerary: The Royal Gazette Office, 1832.

The Demerara and Essequibo Vade-Mecum. Georgetown, 1825.

Local Guide of British Guiana containing Historical Sketch, Statistical Tables and the entire Statute Law of the Colony in force, January 1, 1843. Demerary: The Royal Gazette Office, 1843.

British Guiana. *The Official Gazette.*
The Guiana Chronicle (on microfilm).
The Royal Gazette (on microfilm).

Great Britain. Public Record Office, London:
C.O. 115/1–3. *The Berbice Gazette* (1841–9).
4–20. *The Royal Gazette* (1838–51).
21–43. *The Official Gazette* (1851–3).
C.O. 116/1–3. *The Guiana Chronicle* (1835–40).
4–12. *The Royal Gazette* (1843–56).
13–16. *The Colonist* (1848–56).

iv. Miscellaneous:

Printed Reports. Public Record Office, London.

C.O. 884/4. *British Guiana Boundary. Précis of Documents from the Hague Archives by J. A. Sweetenham.* With Memorandum thereon and Maps.

F.O. 420/27B. *Translation of Spanish Documents Relating to the Boundary Dispute Between British Guiana and Venezuela: 1597 to 1875.* Printed for use of F.O., June 1896.

The Colonial List for 1873. London, 1875.

National Archives, Guyana.
Ordinances, 1840–80.
Results of the Decennial Census of the Population of British Guiana, 1881, 1891, 1931.

Church Missionary Society Archives.
Missionary Register, 1813–55.
Church Missionary Intelligencer, 1850–1906.
Church Missionary Review, 1850–1927.

Jesuit Archives, London.
  Letters and Notices.

Other:

Reports of the Guiana Diocesan Church Society. Demerara: The Royal
  Gazette Office, 1863–5 (Anglican Church Archives, Guyana).
The Governor's Visit to the Shell Mound at Waramuri. Demerara, 1866 (in
  Rev. W. H. Brett's 'Letters and Papers', D28, U.S.P.G.A.).
Roth, Vincent. 'Observations upon the operation of the aboriginal pro-
  tection laws of British Guiana and cognate matters' (Typescript, 27
  Nov. 1941).
——, *Report of the Amerindian Policy Comments Committee, 17th June,
  1949.*
Report of a Survey of Amerindian Affairs in the Remote Interior (with
  additional notes on coastland population groups of Amerindian
  origin). *The Peberdy Report,* 14 Jan. 1948.
*Report of the Amerindians of British Guiana and Suggested Development
  Programmes. The Knapp Report,* 25 Feb. 1965.
The Royal Commission in British Guiana 1939. The Daily Chronicle,
  Georgetown, 1939.
Report of the British Guiana Independence Conference 1965. H.M.S.O.,
  London, 1965.
Report by the Amerindian Lands Commission. Georgetown, Aug. 1969.
LADOC Documentation:

 III, 23a. 'Our Proselytizing and the Indians' Own Religion', A Talk by
     Monsignor Samuel Ruiz, Bishop of San Cristóbal, Mexico,
     9 Nov. 1971.
 III, 23b. 'The Church and the Racial Problem in Latin America', A
     Document issued by the Latin American Movement for
     Evangelical Unity, Paraguay, Mar. 1972.
 III, 23c. 'New Horizons for the Christian Indian', A report in the
     Boletín de Informaciones, Asunción, 30 July 1972.

III. SECONDARY SOURCES

Contemporary Accounts (nineteenth century)

ALEXANDER, Captain J. E. *Transatlantic Sketches.* 2 vols. Richard Bentley,
  London, 1832.
BERNAU, the Revd. J. H. *Missionary Labours in British Guiana with Re-
  marks on the Manners, Customs, and Superstitious Rites of the Aborigines.*
  J. F. Shaw, London, 1847.
BOLINGBROKE, Henry. *A Voyage to Demerary, containing a Statistical
  Account of the Settlements there and those of the Essequibo, the Berbice,
  and other Contiguous Rivers of Guiana.* R. Phillips, London, 1808.

305

BRETT, the Revd. W. H. *Indian Missions in Guiana*. George Bell, London, 1851.

—— *Guiana Legends*. S.P.C.K., London, 1931.

—— *The Indian Tribes of Guiana: Their Condition and Habits*. Bell and Daldy, London, 1868.

BRONKHURST, H. V. P. *The Origin of the Guyanian Indians ascertained; or the Aborigines of America (especially of the Guyanas), and the East Indian Coolie Immigrants compared*. The Colonist Office, Georgetown, 1881.

CASTELL, W. *A Short Discoverie of the Coasts and Continent of America*. Printed in London in the yeer [*sic*], 1644.

DE PONS, François. *A Voyage to the Eastern Part of Terra Firma on the Spanish Main in South America, during the Years, 1801, 1802, 1803 and 1804*. 3 vols. Richard Phillips, London, 1806.

DUFF, the Revd. Robert. *Notes on British Guiana*. Georgetown, 1865; T. Murray & Son, Glasgow, 1866.

FARRAR, Thomas. *Notes on the History of the Church in Guiana*. W. McDonald, Berbice, 1892.

HANCOCK, Dr. John. *Observations on the Climate, Soil, and Production of British Guiana, and on the Advantages of Emigration to and Colonizing the Interior of That Country*. 2nd edn. C. Richards, London, 1840.

HARLOW, V. T. (ed.) *Colonising Expeditions to the West Indies and Guiana, 1623–1667*. Second Series. Hakluyt Society, London, 1924.

HILHOUSE, William. *Indian Notices, or Sketches of the Habits, Characters, Languages, Superstitions, Soil and Climate of the Several Nations; with Remarks on their capacity for colonization, present government, and suggestion for Future Improvement and Civilization, also, the Icthyology of the Fresh Waters of the Interior*. Published by the Author. Demerara, 1825.

HOWITT, William. *Colonization and Christianity: A Popular History of the Treatment of the Natives by the Europeans in all their Colonies*. London, 1838: reprint edn. Negro University Press, New York, 1969.

IM THURN, Sir Everard F. *Among the Indians of Guiana*. Kegan Paul, Trench & Co. London, 1883; reprint Dover edn., New York, 1967.

—— *On the Animism of the Indians of British Guiana*. Harrison and Sons, London, 1882.

IRELAND, Alleyne. *Demerariana. Essays: Historical, Critical, and Descriptive*. Baldwin, Demerara, 1897.

—— *Tropical Colonization. An Introduction to the Study of the Subject*. Macmillan and Co. Ltd. London, 1899.

KIRKE, Henry, *Twenty-Five Years in British Guiana*. Sampson Low, Marston & Co., London, 1898: reprint the Guiana Edition No. 12, The Daily Chronicle, Georgetown, 1948.

NETSCHER, P. M. *History of the Colonies Essequebo, Demerary & Berbice. From the Dutch Establishment to the Present Day.* Translated by W. E. Roth. 'S Gravenhage Martinus Nijhoff, 1888: reprint The Daily Chronicle, Georgetown, 1929.

PINCKARD, George. *Notes on the West Indies . . . including observations on the island of Barbadoes, and the settlements captured by the British troops, upon the coast of Guiana. . . .* 3 vols. Longman, Hurst, Rees and Orme, London, 1806: reprint the Guiana Edition No. 5, The Daily Chronicle, Georgetown, 1942.

RAIN, the Revd. Thomas. *Life and Labours of John Wray, the Pioneer Missionary in British Guiana.* J. Snow & Co., London, 1892.

SCHOMBURGK, Richard. *Travels in British Guiana, 1840–1844.* 2 vols. Translated and edited by W. E. Roth. J. J. Weber, Leipzig, 1847, 1848: The Daily Chronicle, Georgetown, 1922.

SCHOMBURGK, Sir Robert H. *A Description of British Guiana.* Simpkin, Marshall & Co., London, 1840; reprint edn. Frank Cass & Co., London, 1970.

—— *On the Natives of Guiana.* Paper read before the Royal Geographical Society, 27 November 1844.

—— (ed.). *Discovery of the Large, Rich and Beautiful Empire of Guiana.* Hakluyt Society, London, 1848.

STEDMAN, Captain J. G. *Narrative of A Five Years' Expedition against the Revolted Negroes of Surinam in Guiana, or the Wild Coast of South America, from the year 1772 to 1777,* 2 vols. J. J. Johnson and J. Edwards, London, 1796; reprint edn. Edited by R. A. J. van Lier, University of Massachusetts Press, Massachusetts, 1972.

STRICKLAND, the Revd. Joseph, S. J. *Documents and Maps on the Boundary Question between Venezuela and British Guiana.* From the Capuchin Archives in Rome. Unione cooperative editrice, Rome, 1896.

VAN BERKEL, Adrian. *Travels in South America between the Berbice and Essequibo Rivers and in Surinam, 1670–1689.* Translated by W. E. Roth. The Guiana Edition, No. 2. The Daily Chronicle, Georgetown, 1948.

VAN'S GRAVESANDE, Laurens Storm. *The Rise of British Guiana.* Compiled from his despatches by C. A. Harris and J. A. J. Villiers. 2 vols. Hakluyt Society, London, 1911.

VENESS, the Revd. W. T. *El Dorado or British Guiana as a Field for Colonisation.* London, 1866.

—— *Ten Years of Mission Life in British Guiana, being a Memoir of the Rev. Thomas Youd.* S.P.C.K., London, 1875.

WATERTON, Charles. *Wanderings in South America.* Macmillan & Co. Ltd., London, 1879.

WHITFIELD, Richard H. *The Present Position and Future Prospects of*

British Guiana Further Considered. 2nd edn. The British and Colonial Publishing Co., London, 1872.

WINTER, A. *Indian Pictured Rocks of Guiana (with a short Account of the Potaro Indian Mission).* Judd and Co., London, 1883.

Books

BENNETT, George W. *An Illustrated History of British Guiana.* The Colonist Office, Demerara, 1866.

BONILLA, Victor Daniel. *Servants of God or Masters of Men?* Penguin Books, London, 1972.

BRICEÑO, Marcos Falcon. *La Cuestion de limites entre Venezuela y Guayana Britanica.* Publicaciones del Ministerio de Relaciones Exteriores, Caracas, 1962.

BUTT, Audrey. 'Systems of Belief in Relation to Social Structure and Organisation with reference to the Carib-Speaking Tribes of the Guianas.' Typescript.

CELL, John W. *British Colonial Administration in the Mid-Nineteenth Century: The Policy-Making Process.* Yale University Press, New Haven, 1970.

CLEMENTI, Sir Cecil. *A Constitutional History of British Guiana.* Macmillan & Co. Ltd., London, 1937.

CLEVELAND, Grover. *The Venezuelan Boundary Controversy.* Princeton University Press, Princeton, 1913.

COOK, Sherburne F. and SIMPSON, Lesley Byrd. *The Population of Central Mexico in the Sixteenth Century.* University of California Press, Berkeley, 1948.

DAVIES, J. G. *Dialogue with the World.* SCM Press Ltd., London, 1967.

DOSTAL, Dr. W. *The Situation of the Indians in South America.* World Council of Churches, Geneva, 1972.

EVANS, E. W. *The British Yoke. Reflections on the Colonial Empire.* William Hodge & Co., London, 1949.

FANON, Fritz. *The Wretched of the Earth.* Penguin Books, London, 1967.

FARABEE, William Curtis. *The Central Arawaks.* Anthropological Publications, Oosterhout N. B., The Netherlands, 1967.

—— *The Central Caribs.* Anthropological Publications, Oosterhout N. B., The Netherlands, 1967.

FISHER, L. E. *The Intendant System in Spanish America.* University of California Press, Berkeley, 1929.

FRANCO, Jean. *The Modern Culture of Latin America.* Penguin Books, London, 1970.

GALBRAITH, John S. *Reluctant Empire. British Policy on the South African Frontier, 1834–1854.* University of California Press, Berkeley, 1963.

GIBSON, Charles. *The Aztecs under Spanish Rule.* Stanford University Press, Stanford, 1964.

GORDON, Donald C. *The Moment of Power. Britain's Imperial Epoch.* Prentice-Hall, New Jersey, 1970.

GOUVEIA, Elsa. *A Study of the Historiography of the British West Indies to the End of the Nineteenth Century.* Instituto Panamericano de geografía & historia, Mexico, 1956.

GREY, Henry George (Earl). *The Colonial Policy of Lord John Russell's Administration.* 2nd edn. 2 vols. Richard Bentley, London, 1853, reprinted Krauss Reprint Co., New York, 1972.

Handbook of British Guiana. The Argosy Co. Ltd., Demerara, 1909.

HANKE, Lewis. *Aristotle and the American Indians. A Study of Race Prejudice in the Modern World.* Indiana University Press, Bloomington, 1959.

—— *The Spanish Struggle for Justice in the Conquest of America.* University of Pennsylvania Press, Philadelphia, 1949.

HENFREY, Colin. *The Gentle People. A Journey Among the Indian Tribes of Guiana.* Hutchinson & Co. Ltd., London, 1964.

HUMPHREYS, R. A. *Tradition and Revolt in Latin America.* Weidenfeld and Nicolson, London, 1969.

IRELAND, Gordon. *Boundaries, Possessions and Conflicts in South America.* Harvard University Press, Massachusetts, 1938.

KENSWIL, F. W. *Children of the Silence. An Account of the Aboriginal Indians of Upper Mazaruni River.* Interior Development Committee, Georgetown, 1946.

KNAPLUND, Paul. *James Stephen and the Colonial Office, 1813–1846.* University of Wisconsin Press, Madison, 1953.

KNORR, Klaus E. *British Colonial Theories, 1570–1850.* Frank Cass & Co. Ltd., London, 1963.

LEE, Robert Warden. *An Introduction to Roman–Dutch Law.* 5th edn. Clarendon Press, Oxford, 1953.

LOVETT, Richard. *The History of the London Missionary Society, 1795–1895.* 2 vols. Henry Frowde, London, 1899.

MACMILLAN, Mona. *Sir Henry Barkly. Mediator and Moderator, 1815–1898.* A. A. Balkema, Capetown, 1970.

MAC NUTT, Francis Augustine. *Bartholomew de las Casas. His Life, His Apostolate, and His Writings.* G. P. Putnam's Sons, New York, 1909.

MAIR, Lucy. *Private Government.* Penguin Books, London, 1970.

MALINOWSKI, Bronislaw. *Sex and Repression in Savage Society.* Routledge & Kegan Paul, London, 1961.

MAUSS, Marcel. *The Gift. Forms and Functions of Exchange in Archaic Societies.* Translated by Ian Cunnison. Routledge, London, 1970.

MERIVALE, Herman. *Lectures on Colonization and Colonies.* Longman, Green, Longman, and Roberts, London, 1861: reprint edn. Frank Cass & Co. Ltd., London, 1967.

MORÓN, Guillermo. *A History of Venezuela*. Edited and translated by John Street. Allen & Unwin, London, 1964.

MORRELL, W. P. *British Colonial Policy in the Mid-Victorian Age*. Clarendon Press, Oxford, 1969.

NATH, Dwarka. *A History of Indians in Guyana*. 2nd edn. Published by the Author, London, 1970.

NEILL, Stephen. *A History of Christian Missions*. Vol. VI. Penguin Books, London, 1964.

NUÑEZ, Enrique Bernardo. *Tres Momentos en la Controversia de Limites de Guayana*. 2nd edn. Ministerio de Relaciones Exteriores, Caracas, 1962.

OJER, Pablo. *Robert H. Schomburgk. Explorador de Guyana y Sus Lineas de Frontera*. Universidad Central de Venezuela, Caracas, 1969.

PASCOE, C. F. *Two Hundred Years of the S.P.G.: An Historical Account of the Society for the Propagation of the Gospel in Foreign Parts, 1701–1900*. London, 1901.

RICARD, Robert. *La 'conquête spirituelle' du Mexique*. XX Travaux et Mémoires de l'Institut d'Ethnologie, University of Paris, 1933. Translated L. B. Simpson, University of California Press, Berkeley, 1966.

RIDGWELL, W. M. *The Forgotten Tribes of Guyana*. Tom Stacey, London, 1972.

RODWAY, James. *Guiana: British, Dutch and French*. T. Fisher Unwin, London, 1912.

—— *History of British Guiana*. 3 vols. J. Thomson, Georgetown, 1891.

ROJAS, Rafael A. *Los limites de Venezuela con la Guyana Britanica*. Ministerio de Relaciones Exteriores, Caracas, 1962.

ROTH, Walter Edmund. *An Inquiry into the Animism and Folk Lore of the Guiana Indians*. Smithsonian Institution, Bureau of Ethnology, Government Printing Office, Washington, D.C., 1915.

—— *An Introductory Study of the Arts, Crafts and Customs of the Guiana Indians*. Smithsonian Institution, Bureau of Ethnology, Government Printing Office, Washington, D.C., 1924.

—— *Additional Studies of the Arts, Crafts and Customs of the Guiana Indians*. With special reference to those of southern British Guiana. Smithsonian Institution, Bureau of Ethnology, Government Printing Office, Washington, D.C., 1929.

SCOLES, the Revd. Ignatius, S.J. *Sketches of African and Indian Life in British Guiana*. The Argosy Press, Demerara, 1885.

SHAHABUDDEEN, M. *The Legal System of Guyana*. Guyana Printers Ltd., Georgetown, 1973.

SIMMONS, Jack (ed.) *From Empire to Commonwealth. Principles of British Imperial Government*. Odhams Press, London, 1949.

SIMPSON, Lesley Byrd. *The Encomienda in New Spain*. 3rd edn. University of California Press, Berkeley, 1950.

SMITH, J. C. and HOGAN, Brian. *Criminal Law*. 2nd edn. Butterworth, London, 1969.

SQUIRRU, Rafael. *The Challenge of the New Man*. Pan American Union, Washington, D.C., 1964.

STECK, Francis Borgia, O.F.M. *Motolinia's History of the Indians of New Spain*, Academy of American Franciscan History, Washington, D.C., 1951.

SWAN, Michael. *British Guiana. The Land of Six Peoples*. Her Majesty's Stationery Office, London, 1957.

SWINFEN, D. B. *Imperial Control of Colonial Legislation, 1813–1865. A Study of British Policy towards Colonial Legislative Powers*. Clarendon Press, Oxford, 1970.

THOMPSON, the Revd. H. P. *Into All Lands. The History of the S.P.G. in Foreign Parts, 1701–1950*. S.P.C.K., London, 1951.

TODD, Alpheus. *Parliamentary Government in the British Colonies*. Longmans, Green & Co., London, 1894.

VEGA, Garcilaso de la. *The Royal Commentaries of the Incas and the General History of Peru*. 2 vols. University of Texas Press, Austin, 1966.

WALTON, C. S. *The Civil Law in Spain and Spanish America*. W. H. Lowdermilk & Co., Washington, 1900.

WEBBER, A. R. F. *Centenary History and Handbook of British Guiana*. The Argosy Co. Ltd., Georgetown, 1931.

WELSH, David. *The Roots of Segregation: Native Policy in Natal, 1845–1910*. Oxford University Press, Capetown, 1971.

WILLIAMSON, James A. *The English Colonies in Guiana and on the Amazon, 1604–1688*. Clarendon Press, Oxford, 1923.

WORTLEY, B. A. *Jurisprudence*. Manchester University Press, Manchester, 1967.

WYNDHAM, The Hon. H. A. *The Atlantic and Emancipation*. Problems of Imperial Trusteeship Series. Oxford University Press, London, 1937.

YDE, Dr. Jens. *Material Culture of the Wai-Wai*. National Museum of Copenhagen, Copenhagen, 1965.

Articles and Periodicals

BLAKE, Nelson M. 'Background of Cleveland's Venezuelan Policy', *The American Historical Review*, XLVII (Jan. 1942), 259–77.

BOLTON, John. 'The Facts about the Venezuela Boundary', *The Nineteenth Century* (London), XXXIX (Feb. 1896), 185–8.

BROWN, C. G. 'Indian Picture Writing in British Guiana', *Journal of the Anthropological Institute of Great Britain and Ireland*, II (1872), 255–6.

BURR, G. L. 'The Search for the Venezuela–Guiana Boundary', *The American Historical Review*, IV (Apr. 1899), 470–7.

—— 'The Guiana Boundary', ibid. VI (Oct. 1900), 49–64.

BURTON, Ann M. 'Treasury Control and Colonial Policy in the Late Nineteenth Century', *Public Administration*, XLIV (1966), 169–92.

CARNEGIE, Andrew. 'The Venezuelan Question', *The North American Review*, CLXII (Feb. 1896), 129–44.

DAVIS, N. Darnell. 'A British Colonist upon the Venezuela Boundary Question', *The Nation*, LXII (23 Jan. 1896), 72–4.

—— 'Pope Alexander VI's Bull and the Treaty of Munster', ibid. (12 Mar. 1896), 213–14.

EDMUNDSON, the Revd. G. C. 'Relations of Great Britain with Guiana', *Royal Historical Society*, VI (1923), 1–21.

FOSSUM, Paul R. 'The Anglo-Venezuelan Boundary Controversy', *Hispanic American Historical Review*, VIII (Aug. 1928), 229–329.

GILLIN, John. 'Crime and Punishment among the Barama River Caribs of British Guiana', *American Anthropologist*. New Series. XXXVI (1934), 331–44.

—— 'Social Life of the Barama River Caribs of British Guiana', *The Scientific Monthly*, XL (Mar. 1935), 227–36.

HARLOW, V. T. 'British Guiana and British Colonial Policy', *United Empire*, XLII (1951), 305–9.

HARPER, W. 'Tribes of British Guiana', *Anthropological Institute*, II (1873), 254–7.

HILHOUSE, William. 'Memoir in the Warrow Land of British Guiana', *Journal of the Royal Geographical Society*, IV (1834), 321–33.

—— 'Notices of the Indians settled in the Interior of British Guiana', ibid., II (1832), 227.

HOWARD, Colin. 'What Colour is the "Reasonable Man"?', *Criminal Law Review* (1961), 41–8.

'Indian Missions in Guiana', *The Church Missionary Intelligencer*, III (Jan. 1852), 11–18.

IM THURN, Sir Everard. 'Measles and a Moral', *The West Indian Quarterly* (1887–8), 267.

KIEMEN, Mathias. 'Status of the Indian in Brazil after 1820', *The Americas*, XXI (1965), 263–73.

KIRCHWEY, George W. 'Criminal Law', *Encyclopedia of Social Sciences*, IV, 569–78.

LA FEBER, Walter. 'The Background of Cleveland's Venezuelan Policy: A Reinterpretation', *The American Historical Review*, LXVI (July 1961), 947–67.

MALINOWSKI, Bronislaw. 'Culture', *Encyclopedia of Social Sciences*, IV, 621–45.

Missionary Magazine, VIII (Aug. 1844), 126; XXV (Oct. 1861), 293. 'Historical Sketch of the West Indian Missions—Berbice.' L.M.S.A.

Missionary Sketches, I (Aug. 1820), XIV (July 1821), LXX (July 1835). L.M.S.A.

MURDOCK, Richard K. 'Indian Presents: To Give or not to give . . .', *Florida Historical Quarterly*, XXXV (1956–7), 326–46.

PENSON, L. M. 'Making of a Crown Colony', *Royal Historical Society*, IX (1926), 107–34.

RADCLIFFE-BROWN, A. R. 'Primitive Law', *Encyclopedia of Social Sciences*, IX, 202–6.

SAPIR, Edward. 'Custom', ibid. IV, 658–62.

SCHOENRICH, OTTO. 'The Venezuela–British Guiana Boundary Dispute', *The American Journal of International Law*, XLIII (July 1949), 523–30.

SEGGAR, W. H. 'The Changing Amerindian', *Journal of the British Guiana Museum and Zoo of the Royal Agricultural and Commercial Society*, XL (Jan.–June, 1965).

THURSTON, the Revd. Herbert. 'The Venezuela Boundary Question', *The Month*, LXXXVII (June 1896), 153–75.

—— 'The Dutch Claims in Guiana', ibid. (July 1896), 396–415.

—— 'The Venezuela Boundary and the Treaty of Munster', ibid. (Aug. 1896), 525–45.

WILLIAMS, the Revd. James. 'The Aborigines of British Guiana and Their Land', Revue International d'Ethnologie et de linguistique, *Anthropos*, XXXI (1936).

—— 'The Warrau Indians of Guiana and Vocabulary of Their Language', Extrait du *Journal de la Société des Américanistes de Paris*, 1929.

Articles on the Amerindians and relevant material from *Timehri*—The Journal of the Royal Agricultural and Commercial Society of British Guiana, 1882–1967:

ANTHON, Michael. 'The Kanaima', Fifth Series. XXXVI (Oct. 1957).

BUTT, Audrey. 'The Burning Fountain from whence it came', Fifth Series. XXXIII (Oct. 1954).

——. 'Birth of a Religion', Fifth Series. XXXVIII (Sept. 1959).

'Couvade', No. 2a, II (Dec. 1883).

'Couvade', No. 3a, III (Dec. 1884).

DAVIS, N. Darnell. 'Beginnings of British Guiana', New Series. No. 12, VII (June 1893).

—— 'Capitulation to the French in 1762', N.S., No. 11, VI (June 1892).

—— Records of British Guiana', N.S., No. 7, II (June 1888).

DE LA BORDE, Pere. 'History of the Caribs', Translated by G. J. A. Boschreitz, No. 5a, V (Dec. 1886).

HARTSINCK, Jan Jacob. 'Indians of Guiana', Translated from the Dutch. N.S. No. 12, VII (June 1893).

IM THURN, Sir Everard F. 'Animism', No. 3a, III (Dec. 1884).

—— 'Essequibo, Demerara and Berbice under the Dutch', No. 2a, II (Dec. 1883) and No. 3a, III (Dec. 1884).

—— 'Indian Privileges', No. 1, I (June 1882).

IM THURN, Sir Everard F. 'Primitive Games', N.S., No. 8, III (June 1889).
—— 'The Schomburgk Brothers', No. 3, III (June 1884).
—— 'Tame Animals Among the Red Men of America', No. 1, I (Dec. 1882).
—— 'Red Men; some of their Thoughts', No. 5, V (June 1886).
LEIGH, Captain Charles. 'First English Colony in Guiana', N.S., No. 14, IX (June 1895).
LICKERT, the Revd. S. J. 'Moruca', Third Series, No. 19, II (July 1912).
McCLINTOCK, W. C. H. F. 'Census of Indians of Pomeroon', No. 3a, III (Dec. 1884).
—— 'Colonial Jottings', No. 5a, V (Dec. 1886).
—— 'Spanish Arawaks of Morooka', No. 3, III (Dec. 1884).
—— 'An Accawoi Peiaiman', ibid.
MYERS, Iris. 'The Makushi of British Guiana. A Study in Culture Contact', Parts I & II. Fifth Series. XXVI (Nov. 1944), and XXVII (July 1946).
PATERSON, John D. 'Crown Lands of British Guiana', No. 13a, VIII (Dec. 1894).
POONAI, N. O. 'Extinct Tribes and Threatened Species of the South Savannahs', XLIII (Jan.–Dec. 1967).
QUELCH, J. J. 'Materials of Urali Poison', N.S., No. 14, IX (June 1895).
RODWAY, James. 'Constitution of British Guiana', N.S., No. 10a, V (Dec. 1891).
—— 'Indian Policy of the Dutch', N.S., No. 15, X (June 1896).
—— 'Life History of an Indian', N.S., No. 13, VIII (June 1894).
—— 'The Old Boundary of Essequibo', N.S., No. 14a, IX (Dec. 1895).
—— 'The Schomburgks in Guiana', N.S., No. 8, III (June 1889).
—— 'Schomburgkiana', N.S., No. 15, X (June 1896).
—— 'Scraps of Indian Folk-lore', N.S., No. 12, VII (June 1893).
—— 'Timehri, or Pictured Rocks', Third Series. No. 23, VI (Sept. 1919).
ROTH, Vincent. 'Amerindian and the State', Fifth Series. No. 31 (Nov. 1952).
—— 'Hilhouse's "Book of Reconnaissances and Indian Miscellany"', Fourth Series, No. 25 (Dec. 1934).
ROWLAND, Dr. E. D. 'Census of British Guiana', New Series. No. 11, VI (June 1892).
WILLIAMS, the Revd. James. 'Americans of the Interior of British Guiana', Third Series. No. 19, II (July 1912).
—— 'Indian Languages', Third Series. No. 21, IV (June 1917).
WOOD, B. R. 'Curare', Fifth Series. No. 26 (Nov. 1944).
YDE, Dr. Jens. 'Agricultural Level of the Wai-Wai Indians', Fifth Series. No. 36 (Oct. 1957).

INDEX

Aberdeen line (1844), 170–2
Aberdeen, Lord, 6
Aborigines Protection Society:
    and Indians, 204, 211
    and planters, 12
    establishment of, 13
Acarabisi River, 170
actus rea, 150
adultery, 128, 130, 150
Africa, 15, 152, 177
Aguilar, Captain Juan of Arawaks, 25
Akawois:
    allies of Dutch, 46
    Chief of, 204
    Christianization of, 234–5, 237
    feuds of, 171
    Hallelujah religion of, 37–8
    missions among, 171, 223
    monogamy among, 33
    occupations, 201
    settlements and characteristics of, 24
Alexander, Captain J. E., 82–3, 105
Amacura River, 22, 168–70 n., 178
Amerindians:
    accept British jurisdiction, 178
    and slave rebellion, 47–8
    and slave traffic, 184–9
    as Captains and Constables, 118, 144–5, 178
    as museum pieces, 29
    as woodcutters, 201–2
    attitude to labour, 29–30, 116, 190–2, 199, 201
    attitude to land, 41, 201–2, 205–7
    attitude to nature and disease, 32–3
    attitude to Negroes, 31–2
    attitude towards Europeans, 19, 191
    birth among, 34
    blood feuds, 129, 132, 134–5, 142, 149, 166, 171
    census, 119, 127, 271–4
    characteristics and temperament, 29–31, 40–1, 103, 184
    commissions to, 144–5
    complaints to governor, 172, 206
    dances of, 38–9
    dislike of Venezuelans, 178
    dissatisfaction with 1838 Bill, 105
    Dutch names of, 42
    epidemics among, *see* epidemics
    hunt runaways, 58–61, 67, 71, 190
    ill-treatment of, 147–8, 156, 161, 165, 168, 176
    legal protection of, 147, 149, 157, 261, *see also* Ch. V
    lex talionis, 129–31
    marriage customs, 33, 229–30
    missionaries among, Ch. VIII
    murder cases, 130–9, 140–5, 150–1, *see also* murder cases
    names and tribal divisions of, 19–21
    oaths, 136–8
    occupations, 206, 222
    on estates, 196, 260
    population, 19–23, 122, *see also* Appendices I, III, IV
    receive British presents, Ch. II
    receive Dutch presents, 48–9
    relations with Dutch, 41–2
    religion of, 34–9
    rum supplied to, *see* rum
    timber rights of, 202–5
    view of Christianity, 262
Angostura, 167–8, 174 n., 193
animism, 36–7
anotto (annatto, arnatto), 2–4, 227
Anti-Slavery Society, 12
apprenticeship, 8
Arawaks:
    allies of Dutch, 46–7
    and labour, 198
    arrival in Guiana, 24, 157
    Captain of, 25
    characteristics of, 24–5
    Christianization of, 233, 235–6, 238–42
    Dutch use of, 24
    enslaving other tribes, 184–5, 187, 189
    monogamy, 33
    murders, 130, 132, 145
    'the people', 18
    population in Pomeroon, 232

Arawaks (*cont.*):
  postholders' reports on, 80
  protest enslavement, 168
  Santa Anna Efeerocoona, Chief of, 83
  Spanish, 157, 223–4
Arecunas:
  characteristics of, 27
  Christianization of, 235, 237
  description of, 26
  occupations, 201
Armstrong, Revd. John, 32, 157, 210, 212–14
Articles of Capitulation (1803), 6, 8, 49, 74, 181, 184
Atorai, 27, 160, 166
Attorney-General, decisions of, 141, 186–9, 203
Austin, Revd. Joseph, 246–7
Austin, W. P. (Bishop of Guiana), 219, 221, 233, 235, 238–9, 246, 248–9
Australia and native policy, 16–17, 136–7, 140 n., 152

Bagot, George, 84, 88, 99–100, 132, 134, 147, 192, 194–5, 210, 262
Baird, A. F., 122
Baird, Henry, 80
Barama River, 178
Barima River, 7, 22–3, 44, 136, 146–7, 156, 167–9, 171, 178
Barkly, Sir Henry:
  and boundaries, 172
  and Colonial Office, 172
  and Combined Court, 11
  and immigration, 11
  and Indians, 70
  and legal jurisdiction, 146
  and Taylor, 172 n.
  Civil List, 121, 171
  protection of Indians, 165
  reduction of officials, 122
  succeeds Light, 11
Barrington Brown, Charles, 28, 272
Bartica Grove, 213, 216, 219–23
Bartica Point, 210, 212–14, 219
Beaujon, Governor Antony, 5, 7–8
Bentinck, Governor H. W., and Indian policy, 53–5, 63, 181, 255
Berbice River:
  British conquest of, 5, 49
  Dutch plantations on, 156
  early colonization of, 3, 155
  English attack (1665), 3

missionaries on, 209–10, 239–41
murders on, 142, 145
slave rebellion on, 47
trade along, 3
van Pere of, 3
Berbice Association, 8
Berbice Auxiliary Society, 241
Berbice Slave Revolt, 47, 156, 209
Bernau, Revd. J. H., 157, 162, 203, 255–6, 262
  and Youd, 217
  at Bartica, 214–22, 219 n.
blood feuds, 129, 132, 134–5, 142, 149, 166, 171
boundaries:
  and gold discovery, 172–3, 176
  and protection of Indians, 154, 157–9, 161–8, 170, 174
  and Youd, 217
Brazil:
  boundary survey, 160, 164
  Convention of Three Articles, 163–4
  enslavement and ill-treatment of Indians, 157–8, 161, 165–6, 217, 258
  Foreign Minister, 160–1, 163, 166
  relations with Great Britain, 157, 162–3, 166
Brenner, H., 78
Brett, Revd. W. H., 18
  and Arawaks, 25
  and Hinck's visit to Waramuri, 68, 235
  and legal jurisdiction, 146–7
  and protection of Indians, 177
  catechetical works, 237–8
  in Pomeroon and Waramuri, 232–8
  on mission life, 209, 236–7
British Guiana:
  area of, 19
  Crown colony, 5
  Indian policy in, 254–64
  problems of governors of, 245–6, 258
  unification, 211, 271
  value of, 6
British Guiana Gold Company, 176–7
Bronkhurst, H. V. P., 21, 37
'bucks', 61
  Dutch derivation of term, 18
  presents to, 50
burgher officers, 5
Bury, F. M., 28
bush expeditions, *see* expeditions
bush Negroes, 50–5, 61, 156, 181

bush settlements, 51–3
Buxton, Thomas Fowell, 13, 211

captains, Indian, 48, 118–19, 144–5, 148, 166, 168, 178
Capuchin missions, 224–5
Caribs:
  allies of Dutch, 45, 47–8, 156
  and bush Negroes, 156
  'Carinya', 18
  characteristics of, 23–4
  Chief of, 23
  Christianization of, 233–5, 239, 241–2
  feuds of, 171
  polygamy, 33
  population and location, 22–3, 232
Carmichael, Maj.-Gen. Hugh Lyle:
  abolishes College of Kiezers, 8
  and British law, 152
  and Indian labour, 196
  and Indian presents, 23, 55–7, 181, 255
Carmichael Smyth, Sir James:
  and Indian expenditure, 65
  and Indian labour, 195–6
  and Indian policy, 66, 211
  and legal jurisdiction, 134–5
  and mission policy, 225–6, 244
  and 1838 Ordinance, 104–5
  proclamations re apprentices, 8–9, 258
Caroni River, 26, 171, 193, 235
cassava, 39, 206, 213, 227
cassiri, 38
Cathrey, Thomas, 98, 100
census, 119, 127, 272–4
Chief Justices, views of, 133–5, 141–2, 260
Christianization, Ch. VIII:
  missionaries and, 13–14, 213, 215, 217, 221
  of aborigines, 160, 247, 259, 264
  of Negroes, 240
  Postlethwaite project, 192–4
  role of women in, 249
  Spanish view of, 45
Christianization and civilization, 13, 45, 213, 215, 217, 219, 221, 247, 259, 261, 264, see also Ch. VIII
Church Missionary Society, 157, 162, 164, 208, 210, 212–15, 218, 221–2
Ciudad Bolívar, 174 n-5, see also Angostura
Civil List:
  controversy over, 10, 111, 121, 171

Rodway on, 9
Peter Rose and, 11
Clancy, Revd. Dr. William, 227, 289
Codd, Colonel Edward,
  and Edmonstone, 100
  and Indian labour, 196
  and Indian policy, 58
  complaints v. postholders, 77–8, 80, 91
College of Kiezers, 5, 8
Colonial Financial Department, 5
Colonial Office:
  and Aboriginal Oath Ordinance, 137–8
  and Barkly, 172
  and boundaries (Brazil), 160, 163
  and Boundaries (Venezuela), 167–9, 175–6, 178
  and Indian labour, 196–7
  and Indian policy, 69, 125
  and legal jurisdiction, 133, 138, 143, 146
  and Light, 167, 169, 259–60
  and missionaries, 218, 247
  and presents, 56–7
  and Scott, 177
  and Taylor, 175
  and Treasury, 165
  objection to rum distribution, 64
  protection of Indians, 164, 166, 189
  relations with local government, 111–12, 138, 256–7
Colonist, The, see newspapers
Colony Chest, 8 n.
Combined Court:
  and Civil List, 121, 171, 190
  and Creek Bill, 105–8
  and home government, 256
  and immigration, 190
  and Indian labour, 128
  and Indian policy, 189–90, 245, 247, 255, 259
  and missionaries, 218, 244, 247
  and Superintendents of Rivers and Creeks, 110–14, 260
  Barkly and, 11
  control of finance, 69–70, 114
  establishment of, 5, 8
  governors' objections to, 10–11
  Members of, 16
  money for Indian presents, 54, 57, 65
  money for Indian village, 71, 198–200
  objection to postholdership, 86–90
  Peter Rose and, 11
  powers of, 10–11, 70 n.

Combined Court (*cont.*):
  reduction of salaries, 121–2
  sensitivity of, 100–1
Commissaries of Taxation, 90, 112–13, 115, 117, 126, 296–7
commissions to Indians, 129, 144–5, 286
Commission of Enquiry (1849), 200
Commissioners of Enquiry (1870), 147
Commissioners of Legal Inquiry (1824), 183
Committee of Indian Affairs, 66, 225
Committee, West Africa and colonization, 14
constables, Indian, 144
Contingency Fund, 68 n.–9, 120, 234, 247
Convention of London (1814), 49
Convention of Three Articles, 163–4
Corentyne River, 22, 155–6, 210, 214, 239–41
corials, 25, 35 n.
Council of Justice, 5
Council of Policy, 5
Council of Ten, Amsterdam, 46
courida trees, 2
Courts of Justice, 130–1, 133–6, 139–40, 147, 152, 183, 261
Court of Policy:
  and Indian policy, 245, 251, 258–9
  and legal jurisdiction, 132, 134–6, 138
  and Light, 258
  and McClintock's schemes, 248
  and missionaries, 210–11, 216
  and money for bush expeditions, 53–4, 58–9
  and reports of postholders, 81–2
  D'Urban and, 65
  establishment of, 5
  Indian Chief and, 23
  instructions to postholders, 75, 81–2
  objections to Indian expenditure, 63–4
  powers of 769–70 n.
  proclamations of Carmichael Smyth and, 8–9
couvade, 34
Creek Bill, *see under* Ordinances
Crichton, William, 25, 110, 167, 186–8
Crown Lands, 90–1, 102, 120–1, 123–4, 149, 157, 185, 202–5
Crown Lands, Department of, 126, 206
Crown Law Officers, 10
Crown Surveyor, 149, 202, 205
Cullen, Dr. Edward, 120
Cullen, Revd. John, 227–9

curare, 27 n.
currency, 50 n.
Cuyuni River, 4, 23, 26, 52, 169, 172, 176, 178, 193, 220–3, 235

Daily Chronicle, The, see newspapers
Daly, John, 181–2
Davson, Mary, 31
Dayce, Revd. J., 217–18
de Betham, Fr., 33, 35–6
Demerara River:
  British conquest of (1781), 5, 49
  Dutch on, 155
  English planters on, 4
  Gravesande's policy and, 4
  meaning of term, 4 n.
  missionaries on, 237–8, 242
  slave traffic on, 188
Depons, François, on Dutch policy, 45–6
de Ryck, Louis, 238
de Wolff, N. J., 114, 117, 148
Diguja, Don José, 155
doctrina, 179, 194, 213
Drios, 20, 28
Duke, Revd. J. H., 231–2
D'Urban, Sir Benjamin:
  and Indian labour, 191–4
  and Indian land rights, 205
  and Indian presents, 62–3
  and Indian slavery, 183
  and *lex talionis*, 131
  and missionaries, 210, 224–5, 244
  cancellation of Hilhouse's appointment, 101–2
  committee formed by, 62
  objection to Hilhouse's policy, 59–60
Dutch, the:
  early government in Guiana, 4–5, 155
  hatred of Spaniards, 2, 44
  in Brazil, 3
  jurisdiction over Indians, 178
  planting of sugar under, 3
  policy towards Indians, 45–9, 73–4, 118, 129, 156
  policy towards Spain, 3, 44
  relations with Indians, 41–2, 46, 155–6
  settlements under, 2, 44–5
  trade with Indians, 2, 44
  treaties with Indians, 41–2, 46, 155–6
  Wars, 3, 44, 155
Dutch West India Co.:
  appointment of Indian captains, 118, 129

appointment of postholders, 73
Charter of, 44–5
difficulties of, 3
establishment of, 2
foundation of new West India Co., 4,
  45
Gravesande and, 156
policy of, 2, 155
protection of Indians, 47–8, 128, 181
trade with Indians, 2–3

Edmonstone, Charles, 51, 54, 57, 100, 182
Elbers, F. C., 99
El Dorado, legend of, 1, 172
Eliot, Revd. R., 241–2
Emancipation Act (1833), *see* slave
  emancipation
encomenderos, 179–80
epidemics:
  cholera, 120 n., 261, 273
  measles, 120 n., 261
  smallpox, 120 n., 209, 239, 261, 273
  whooping-cough, 219
Essequibo, colony of:
  British conquest of, 5, 49
  British jurisdiction in, 178
  in English hands, 3
  meaning of term, 2 n., 44
Essequibo River:
  Dutch settlements on, 2, 44
  Dutch trade on, 3
  English planters on, 4
  missionaries on, 210, 223, 239, 242
  sugar estates on, 4, 156, 197
estates:
  cotton and coffee, 4, 9, 200 n.
  planters and, 260
  sugar, 196–201
Etheridge, Bishop, 230
expeditions:
  bush, 4, 50–9, 76, 271
  Edmonstone, 51
  Holmes and Campbell, 173
  Schomburgk, 158, 161, 166–7, 196

Falant, D., 91
Farrar, Revd. Thomas, 223
Fennell, T., 117, 122
Financial Representatives, 5, 8, 87, 199
Fiscals, 102 n., 132, 134, 147, 184, 192,
  210
Foreign Office, 160–1, 166–7, 169, 173–5,
  178

Fortique, Señor, 170–1
Fort Island, 91
Fraser, Mrs. S., 92, 185–9
Fraser *v.* Spencer case, 185–9

Glenelg, Lord, 13
Goderich, Lord, 8, 63, 131–3, 183, 192,
  256
gold, 172–3, 176, 206, 222, 234, 257–8
Gordon, S. W., 183–4
Grant, P. A. J., 118–19, 146
Great Britain:
  boundary disputes with Brazil, 154 ff.,
    163–76, 178
  boundary disputes with Venezuela,
    154 n., 166 ff.
Great Falls, 188, 203
Grey, Earl, 121, 138, 256, 263
Grey, Sir George, 14, 16
Guaicas (Waikas), 235 n.
Guiana Chronicle, The, see newspapers
Guiana Diocesan Church Society, 223,
  233–4, 236–8, 249

Hackett, James, 64
Hadfield, J., 66, 109, 186, 202
Hague Tribunal, 154, 170, 178
hammocks, 26
Hancock, Dr. John, 84, 105, 190, 207, 263
Hancock, Richard, 109, 117, 119, 122
Hartsinck, J. J., 26, 46
Herbert, Charles, 134
Hermant, Revd. Apollinaire, 226–7
Hilhouse, William:
  against 1838 Bill, 106, 108
  against postholders, 77, 81–3, 91–2, 185
  against Protectors, 101–4
  and expenditure, 275
  and Indian policy, 60–1
  and missionaries, 227
  and Spanish Arawaks, 224–6
  appointment as Quartermaster-
    General, 59
  appointment cancelled, 101–2
  division of tribes, 19
  D'Urban's objections to, 59–60
  evidence at Arawak trial, 130
  nominated for Superintendent of
    Rivers and Creeks, 106–7
  on Indian labour, 195–6
  surveyor, 225
  views of Warraus, 25
  Wilmot Horton and, 60

Hincks, Sir Francis:
  and gold discoveries, 176–7
  and Indian policy, 176, 255
  and Indian presents, 68
  visit to missions, 235
Hislop, Colonel, 49–50
Horan, Patrick, 193–4, 263
Horton, Wilmot, 60, 102
humanitarianism v. colonization, 14, 17
Hynes, Revd. John:
  and Moruka Indians, 25, 224–5, 228
  and Postlethwaite project, 192
  support of Indians, 65–6

Imawali, 36–8
Immigration:
  and Rose Report, 200
  Emigration Bill and, 10
  from Madeira, Africa, India, China, 123, 198
  from Malta, 195 n.
  from West Indies *et al.*, 190, 198
  1850 grant for, 121
  1840 ordinance for, 110, 138 n.
  Parliamentary loan for, 11
  Portuguese and East Indian, 10
  sole interest of planters, 12, 16–17, 200, 260
  supported by Barkly, 11
im Thurn, Sir Everard, 190, 272–3
Indian Affairs, Committee of, *see* Committee of Indian Affairs
ita (siroco), 26 n.

Jesuits in Santa Rosa, 228–31
jurisdiction, civil, 147–50
jurisdiction, criminal, 130–1, 133–6, 140–7, 151
jurisdiction, legal, Ch. V

kanaima, 36, 38, 129, 235
Kanaimapo, Chief, 142, 145, 237
Ketley, Revd. Joseph, 242–4
King, Robert, 92, 117–18, 122, 136, 141, 148, 185, 202
Kingston, Lt.-Col. Robert, 49, 74
King's Chest, 8 n., 98
Knapp Report, 274
Knollman, J., 95–6, 100–1
Kyk-over-al, Fort, 2, 3, 44

Labouchere, Rt. Hon. Henry, 173
labour, immigrant, 190, 196

labour, Indian:
  and Postlethwaite project, 191–6
  as jobbers, weeders, woodcutters, 198
  attitude of Indians to, 29–30, 190–2
  McClintock and, *see* McClintock and Indian labour
  on estates, 116, 196–8, 206, 271, 287–8
  planters' view of, 191, 201, 260
labour, Negro, 10–11, 64–5
land:
  and Christianity, 207
  European demand for, 15
  grant to mission, 289
  Indian rights to, 205–7
law:
  British v. native, 15, Ch. V
  Dutch, 152 n.
  Indian attitude to, 128 ff.
  Sir George Grey and native, 16
Leguan island, 199
lex talionis, 129–31, 138–9 n., 145, 150–1
licences, woodcutting, 202–5
Light, Sir Henry:
  and Aboriginal Oath Ordinance, 137
  and boundaries, 168–9
  and civilization of Indians, 220, 244–6, 251
  and Indian labour, 196–8
  and Indian policy, 109, 244–6, 251, 255, 258–60, 272
  and legal jurisdiction, 136
  and missionaries, 218, 247, 289
  and Spencer case, 185–8
  and Superintendents of Rivers and Creeks, 110–12, 115
  Civil List controversy, 10, 111
  Fraser case, 92
  Hilhouse and, 108
  Pirara expedition, 161–3
  protection of Indians, 159–60, 163–4, 167–8, 188, 258
  territorial rights, 205
Linau, H., 78, 84
logie, 226 n.
London, Convention of, *see* Convention of London
London Missionary Society, 208, 240–4
Lucie Smith, J., 123–4, 203
Luckoo, J. A., 139 n.

macquari dance, 38
Macusi:
  characteristics of, 27

claim British protection, 160
enslavement by Brazilians, 158, 164;
by other tribes, 185–9
missionaries among, 214–15, 217–19,
221, 237
occupations, 201
ourali poison and, 27
population and settlements of, 27
village at Pirara, 157
Youd and, 163
Madeira, 123, 190, 198
Magistrates:
Special, 126–7, 297
Stipendiary, 110, 117, 126, 147, 171,
297
Mahaica River, 75, 78, 81, 122
Mahaicony River, 75, 78, 122, 238
Mahanarva, Chief of Caribs, 23, 182
Mahu River, 163–4
Mai-ce-wari, Warrau Chief, 33, 230
Maiongkongs, 28, 158, 165, 229, 235
Makonaima, 36–7
Maopityans, 20, 28
Maoris, 14–15
maracca, 35, 230 n., 240
mari-mari dance, 38
Maroni River, 44
matapie, 39, 41
Mathison, Kenneth, 172, 174–5 n.
Mauvielle, M., 78
Mazaruni River, 4, 23, 84, 178, 210, 221,
223
McClintock, W. C. F.:
and boundaries, 171, 176–7
and census, 119, 120
and civilization of Indians, 207, 242,
247–8, 251–2
and Indian captains, 144–5
and Indian labour, 196–200, 205, 207,
261, 271
and Indian policy, 116–17, 127, 207,
242, 247–8, 251–2, 255–6
and Indian population, 23, 272
and Indian village, 199–200
and legal jurisdiction, 141, 145–6, 148–9
and Maiongkongs, 158, 165
and missions, 171, 230, 232, 234, 242,
247
as Special Magistrate, 115, 126
at Moruka, 177, 248
knowledge of Indians, 28–9, 31–2, 116–
17, 124–5, 248
marriage of, 115

objection to rum distribution, 70, 116
praise of Arawaks, 25
protection of Indians, 68, 70, 127, 164–
5, 176–7, 260
reports of, 116–17, 176, 197, 205, 230,
248
support of cotton industry, 201
McLeod, Sir Henry, 9, 10, 111, 190
mens rea, 150
missionaries:
and Chapel-Schools, 213
and Colonial Office, 164–5, 189
and education, 215–17, 221, 223, 236,
241, 244–51, 256, 262
and European settlers, 14
as civilizers, 207
evaluation of, 250–3, 262
grants to, 244, 246, 249–50
hardships and crises of, 209, 212–13,
219, 222, 229, 231–4, 237–8, 240,
250, 261–2
Moravian, 209–10, 214, 239–41
objection to Indian customs, 33
policy of, 209, 213, 250–3, 255–6
protection of, 13, 163, 189
qualifications of, 212
report of, Appendix XIII
role of women, 249–50
Roman Catholic, 210, 218, 223–31,
289
salaries, 244, 246
Missionary Societies, 13, 72, 157, 208,
240, *see also* Church Missionary
Society, London Missionary Society,
United Society for the Propagation of
the Gospel
Mission Stations:
Bartica Grove, 210–23, 227
Cabacaburi, 232–3
Caria-Caria (Castricome), 242–4
Dufferyn, 249
Fort Island, 242–3
Great Falls, 237
Hittia, 239
Holy Name, 223
Kiblerie, 238
Malali, 237
Muritaro, 237
Orealla, 239–40
Pirara, 158, 160–2, 164, 227
Pompiaco, 232 n.
Santa Rosa (Mariaba), 223–31
St. Edward the Martyr, 223

Mission Stations (*cont.*):
St. Mary, 223
Supinam, 243
Tiger Island, 242-3
Urwa, 217
Waramuri, 231-6
Waraputa, 162, 217-19, 227
Mittelholzer, Captain J. V., 61-2, 118, 271
Moruka (Morocco):
British jurisdiction in, 178
Catholic mission at, 177, 223-31
Dutch settlements on, 44
Indians of, 24-5, 82, 136, 157, 192, 224, 228-9
trade with Orinoco, 169, 224
Venezuelan interference with, 167
Mosaic Law, see *lex talionis*
M'Turk, Sir Michael, 67, 108, 126-7, 258
Munster, Treaty of, 44
murder cases of Indians:
Alfred, 139 n.
Anchabur Ray, 140
Arawaks on Berbice River, 145
Bagit, 152
Billy William, 130-1, 134
Frederick, 132-4
John Maul, 136
Maicarawari, 138-9, 143, 150-1
Mayaroo, 142-4, 151
Simon, 134-5
Murray, Maj.-Gen. John:
and Indian labour, 196
and Indian policy, 57
and missions, 241
and Spanish Arawaks, 157, 224
appointment of Hilhouse, 59

Negroes, *see* bush Negroes *and also* Negro Slavery
Netscher, P. M., 1, 3
New Laws, the, *see* Spain
newspapers:
The Colonist, 143
The Guiana Chronicle, 82, 108-9, 151, 159, 185-7
The Royal Gazette, 72, 107, 114, 123, 139, 142-3, 186, 197, 228
The Daily Chronicle, 139 n., 153 n.
New Zealand:
Association, 14
native policy in, 16-17

representative government, 15
Sir George Grey and, 14
Taranaki and Waikato Wars in, 15
Normal School, 215-17
North American Indians, 13
North West District, 22, 170
Nova Zeelandia, 3
Nowers, Revd. J. H., 232

oaths, 136-8
obeah, 260
O'Leary, Daniel, 168-9
Ordinances:
Aboriginal Oath, 137-8
Aboriginal Protection (1910), 206
Census (1861), 119
Consolidated Slave, 211
Immigration, 110, 138 n.
Rum (1841), 202
1636 Slave, 184
1793 Slave, 181
1807 Slave, 182 n.
Tax, 111
No. 6 of 1838, 16, 64, 67-8, 71, 88, 104-10, 115, 120, 123, 201-2, 204
No. 14 of 1857, 123
No. 14 of 1861, 123-4, 203-4
No. 1 of 1869, 125
No. 12 of 1871, 125
No. 9 of 1873, 126
Orinoco River, 1, 22, 45, 52, 155, 168-9, 192-3, 223
Owen, Professor Richard, 38

Pakaraima Mts., 37
Paramona (Patamona) tribes, 84, 134-5, 237
Paterson, John, 92, 186-7 n.
Penal Settlement, 203, 220, 223
Peter, Marcus, 242-3
peti-cabba, 240 n.
piai-man, 35-7, 138, 147, 150, 230 n., 240 n., 252
Pianghottos, 20, 28
Pinckard, George, 52
Pirara, 157-8, 160-2, 164-6, 176, 178, 217-19, 227
piwari, 38, 39, 259
Plan of Redress (1789), 5
planters:
and Colonial Office, 246
and Indian labour, 191, 198, 260
and missionaries, 241

desire for immigrants and profits, 10, 260

financial control, 246

in Combined Court, 8, 256

objection to manumission Bill, 8–9

police:
  Indians as interior, 58, 61, 67, 71
  establishment of colonial force, 67, 171

Pollitt, Revd. James, 218

Pomeroon River, 3, 22–3, 44, 122, 136, 155, 167, 169, 178, 231

pork-knockers, 222–3 n.

Portuguese, the, 229

posts:
  at Corentyne and Canje, 62
  at Arinda, Cuyuni, Mahaicony, and Moruka, 73
  at Mahaica and Boeraserie, 75, 99
  at Mahaica, Masseroeni, and Pomeroon, 98–9
  committee on, 86
  establishment of, 4, 73
  Indians at, 54
  purpose of, 73

postholders:
  absence from posts, 85
  abuses of, 84–6, 91–3, 201
  and civil jurisdiction, 148
  Assistants, 75, 95
  character of, 76
  coloured, 96
  critique of, 82–3
  difficulties of, 84, 90–1
  drunkenness among, 83
  duties of and instructions to, 73–128, see also Appendices V, VI, VII, VIII
  dwellings of, 73, 75
  government questions system of, 87
  Hilhouse's denunciations of, 77, 81–3, 91–2
  little knowledge of Indians, 28
  reason for, 4, 73–4
  reduction of, 89
  relations with Protector, 75
  reports of, 53, 77–81, 90
  salary of, 86, 89–90, 91–3, 201
  under Superintendents of Rivers and Creeks, 88
  uniform of, 84

Postlethwaite, William, 191–6, 263

Postlethwaite project, see Postlethwaite, W.

presents to Indians, Ch. II:
  attraction of, 71
  cost of, 63–5
  discontinuance of, 65–7
  Indians' objection to discontinuance, 65–7, 254
  numbers of Indians receiving, 61
  requisition for, 97
  to Chief Kanaimapo, 145

Protectors of Indians, Ch. III:
  abolished, 88
  character of, 28
  duties of, 93, 95–9, 128
  established, 93–4
  instructions to, 129, Appendix IX
  number and appointment of, 94
  reports of, 53
  qualifications, 28

provocation, legal aspects of, 139–40

Puerto Rico, 224

quipu, 37

Raleigh, Sir Walter, 1, 25, 44

Recopilación de Leyes, 179, 180 n., 205

revenue, 123–5, 127, 203

Rio Branco, 22, 158, 160

Rivers of British Guiana:
  Acarabisi, 170
  Amacura, 22, 168–70 n., 178
  Barama, 178
  Barima, 7, 22–3, 44, 136, 146–7, 156, 167–9, 171, 178
  Berbice, see Berbice River
  Caroni, 26, 171, 193, 235
  Corentyne, 22, 155–6, 210, 214, 239–41
  Cuyuni, 4, 23, 26, 52, 169, 172, 176, 178, 193, 220–3, 235
  Demerara, see Demerara River
  Essequibo, see Essequibo River
  Mahaica, 75, 78, 81, 122
  Mahaicony, 75, 78, 122, 238
  Mahu, 163–4
  Maroni, 44
  Mazaruni, 4, 23, 84, 178, 210, 221, 223
  Moruka, see Moruka
  Pomeroon, 3, 22–3, 44, 122, 136, 155, 167, 169, 178, 231
  Rupununi, 20, 27
  Takutu, 163–4
  Waini (Wyana), 7, 22, 52, 147, 167–9, 171, 178

323

Rodway, James, 2, 22, 46, 100, 273
Rose, Hon. Peter:
  and legal jurisdiction, 135
  denunciation of home government, 11
  opposition to postholders, 89
  Rose Report and immigration, 200
Roth, Hon. Vincent, 29, 72, 207
Royal Gazette, The, see newspapers
Royal Geographical Society, 166
rum:
  objections of Light to, 71, 188; of
    McClintock, 70
  Ordinances forbid distribution of, 124,
    201–2
  supplied to Indians, 39–40, 64, 84, 149,
    201, 220, 222, 240, 260, 273, 277
Rupununi River, 20, 27
Russell, Lord John, 111–12, 136–7, 138 n.,
  187–8, 256

salempore, 54, 61–2
Santa Anna Efeerocoona, 83
Santo Thomé de la Guyana, 155, 174 n.
Schomburgk, Sir Robert:
  and boundaries, 158–60, 163–4, 177,
    258
  and Christianization, 207, 211, 256
  and civilization of Indians, 29
  and Maiongkongs, 28
  and missionaries, 218
  and native law, 129, 138
  and postholders, 76
  and Timehri, 37
  and Wai-Wais, 27–8
  appointment to survey boundaries,
    160–1, 167
  description of Tarumas, 28
  expeditions, 158, 161, 166–7, 196
  impressions of Guiana, 6
  Indians as labour force and, 179
  names and estimates of tribes, 19, 21
  protection of Indians, 158–60, 163–4,
    177, 258
  reports of, 158, 160, 164, 166, 168, 177,
    258
Schomburgk line, 170, 179
Scoles, Revd. Ignatius, 26
Scott, Governor John:
  and Indian policy, 125, 177, 230
  and Indian presents, 69
  and sugar industry, 201
  criticism of system of government, 12
Scott, Major John, 3, 22, 25

Scruggs, William, 167
Select Committee on Aborigines (1837):
  censure of postholders and Protectors,
    93, 104 n., 137 n.
  policy of, 257, 261
  Report of, 14
  terms of reference of, 13
settlements, *see* bush settlements
Seymour, A. J., 36
Shanks, J., 109, 114–15, 260
slave emancipation, 59, 85, 211
slavery, cases of Indian:
  Bentinck's Indians, 182
  Crown *v.* Spencer, 185–9
  Joesinsky, 182–4
  Lubyn and Peyto, 183–4
  slaves of Mrs. Higgs, 185
  Sophia, 184
slavery, Indian:
  and Bentinck, 181–2
  and Carmichael, 182
  by Brazilians, 157–8, 161, 166
  by Dutch settlers, 181
  by Venezuelans, 167–8, 172, 176
  Light and regulations against, 92–3
  objections of Indians to, 3, 190
  postholders and, 109, 148, 260
  see also slavery, cases of Indian
slavery, Negro:
  compensation for slaves, 85
  early introduction to Guiana, 3
  missionaries and, 240
  runaways, 4, 6, 254, 271
  1823 revolt, 8, 59
  see also Berbice Slave Revolt
Smith, Revd. John, 211 n., 240
Smith, Sir Lionel, 9
Solano, Don José, 156
South Africa and native policy, 15
South American Indians, 30, 152
Spain:
  against Dutch, 156
  and missionary policy, 226
  and native labour, 179–80
  in Guiana, 44, 155
  invasion of (1808), 156
  New Laws of, 254
Spencer, John, 92, 185–9
Stanley, Lord, 112–13, 115, 137, 138 n.,
  162–4, 170, 194, 247, 256
States-General, Orders and Regulations
  of, 3, 8, 44, 184
staves of office, 118, 168, 178

Stedman, Captain J. G., 21
Stephen, James, 13, 133 n., 137, 143, 150,
    159–60, 169, 256
Strong, Revd. Leonard, 210
sugar industry, 3, 4, 9
Superintendents of Rivers and Creeks,
    Ch. IV:
    abolition of post of, 126
    abuses of, 109
    and legal jurisdiction, 128, 145, 148
    appointment of, 67–8, 88, 106–7
    appointment of Dutch, 114
    attitude of Combined Court to, 110–14
    duties of, 108–9, 117 f., 128
    Hilhouse for post, 106–7
    Hilhouse's objections to, 108
    number of, 107, 113, 117, 121–3
    recommendation of Indian captains,
        144
    reports of, 109, 117, 125, 147
    salaries of, 110–11, 113–24
Surinam, 156, 239–40

Takutu River, 163–4
Taranaki War, 15
Tarumas, 20, 28, 160
Taylor, Sir Henry:
    and Barkly, 172 n.
    and boundaries, 163–5, 172–3, 176, 178
    and gold mining, 176–7
    and Hincks, 176
    and Indian policy, 69
    and Indian slavery, 187–9
    and legal jurisdiction, 135–6, 143, 146
    and Postlethwaite project, 195
    and United States, 175
    protection of Indians, 163–5, 172–3,
        176, 178
    supportive of Crown colony govern-
        ment, 12
tibisiri, 26 n., 39
timber trade, 123, 125, 149
Timehri, 37
Timmerman, G., 58, 98–9, 103
Tordesillas, Treaty of, 44
trade:
    Dutch and Amerindians, 2, 3, 4
    in anotto, 2, 3, 4
    in fish, 169
    in hides, letterwood, tobacco, 2, 3, 4
    in provisions, 169
    in timber, 4, 123, 125, 149, 202–4, 206,
        220

Treaties:
    of London, see Convention of
    of Munster, 44, 155
    of Tordesillas, 44
    of Waitangi, 14 n.
    with Indians, 46, 130, 132, 154–5
Treasury, the, 178, 183, 256–8, 257 n.
Tribes and sub-tribes, see under Akawois,
    Arawaks, Arecunas, Atorai, Caribs,
    Drios, Macusi, Maiongkong, Maopit-
    yans, Paramona (Patamona), Pianghot-
    tos, Tarumas, Wai-Wai, Wapisiana,
    Warrau
trusteeship, nineteenth-century view of,
    12

United Nations General Assembly, 154
United Society for the Propagation of the
    Gospel, 208, 223, 232, 234, 236
United States, 173, 175

van Batenburg, Governor Abraham, 7
van's Gravesande, Laurens Storm, 4
    and Caribs, 23
    and Cuyuni expedition, 162
    and establishment of College of
        Kiezers, 5
    on runaway slaves, 52
    on policy for Demerara, 4, 47
    on policy towards Indians, Negroes,
        and Spaniards, 4, 47
    territorial claims of, 156
van Hoogenheim, W. J., 47
van Pere, Abraham, 3
Vaughan, T., 117
Veness, Revd. W. T., 239
Venezuela:
    and Foreign Office, 174
    and Scruggs, 167
    boundary concession to, 170
    independence of, 156
    internal upheavals in, 170, 172, 174–5,
        194, 223, 254
    rejection of Indian rights, 173
    see also Great Britain, boundary dis-
        putes with
villages, Indian, 71, 198, 200
von Humboldt, Alexander, 22

Wadie, Revd. J. W., 234, 136
Wahl, H. C., 80, 96
Waihahi (piai-man), 138, 151
Waikas, see Guaicas

Waini River, 7, 22, 52, 147, 167–9, 171, 178
Waitangi, Treaty of, 14 n.
Wai-Wais (Woyavais), 20, 27
  claim British protection, 160
  knotted cords of, 37
  occupations of, 28
  settlements of, 27
Walker, Lt.-Gov. William, 11, 140–3, 173, 248, 263
Wapisianas:
  claim British protection, 160
  enslavement by Brazilians, 158
  occupations of, 27
Waramuri, 197
Waraputa, 162, 217–19
Warraus:
  allies of Dutch, 46
  characteristics of, 25–6
  Christianization of, 234–5, 237–41, 247
  claim British protection, 168
  enslavement of, 189
  location of, 25
  Mai-ce-wari, Chief of, 33

missions for, 171
murder of, 141
names of, 20
on estates, 198
polygamy, 33
postholder's report on, 80–1
Warren, George, 106–7
Watson, John, 80–1
White, Governor Enrique, 56
Wild Coast, 19 n.
William, Billy, 130–1
Williams, Revd. James, 20, 26, 39
Winkels, 211
Wodehouse, Governor Philip E., 145–6, 166, 173–4
woodcutters, 108, 120, 124–5, 147, 149, 190 n., 201–5, 220, 222, 226
Wray, Revd. John, 240–1
Wray, Hon. Charles, 130, 205

Youd, Revd. Thomas, 157–60, 162–3, 212, 255
  among Macusi, 214–15, 217–19
  and boundaries, 217